Workshop Technology
for Mechanical Engineering Technicians
BOOK 2

The two volumes of *Workshop Technology* have been specially written
for students taking examinations in Workshop Processes
and Practice and Workshop Technology in the Mechanical
Engineering Technicians Course, of the City &
Guilds of London Institute. Book 1 is for Part I of the course,
and Book 2 for Part II. They should also be of interest to
students on related courses and to those studying for the
Ordinary National Certificate or Diploma in Engineering.

Every attempt has been made to present the subject-matter clearly,
vividly and concisely, and the numerous diagrams are a
particularly attractive part of the work.

The author has had many years' experience of teaching the subject
to students at Luton College of Technology.

D1093457

Workshop Technology

for Mechanical Engineering Technicians

BOOK 2

C. R. SHOTBOLT

C.Eng., F.I.Prod.E., M.I.Mech.E.,
M.I.Q.A., A.M.A.S.Q.C.

*Senior Lecturer in Production Engineering,
Luton College of Technology*

CASSELL · LONDON

CASSELL & CO. LTD
35 Red Lion Square, London WC1R 4SG
Sydney, Auckland
Toronto, Johannesburg
an affiliate of Macmillan Publishing Co. Inc., New York

First published 1972
Second impression July 1974
Third impression April 1975
Fourth impression 1976
Fifth impression January 1978

I.S.B.N. 0 304 93724 X

Printed in Great Britain by
The Camelot Press Ltd, Southampton

Preface

This book has been written to provide additional background reading in the subject of Workshop Technology to supplement the classroom and laboratory studies of students taking the Mechanical Engineering Technicians' course (no. 255), Part II, to the syllabus published by the City & Guilds of London Institute. Although the book is written primarily for students of the subject of Workshop Technology, it also covers the subject, where applicable, in the Special Technologies of course no. 255, Part II. Much of the syllabus of Plastics Mould-making Technology is covered, as is that for the subject of Materials and Processes in the Mechanical Engineering Drawing course. The author trusts that the book may also be of use to students and lecturers involved with the subject in other courses such as O.N.C. and O.N.D.

The modern mechanical engineering technician must have most of the practical capabilities of the craftsman plus the academic knowledge to enable him to translate the thoughts and ideas of the technologist so that the craftsman can convert them into hardware. He must be able to diagnose faults and may go on to be a planning engineer, a quality control engineer, a work study engineer, a foreman or a production superintendent. In all these occupations his knowledge of manufacturing methods and equipment will be the foundation on which his performance is based. This book attempts to present the information which, added to his college studies and his industrial experience, will enable the student technician to develop this foundation and also to bring together the subjects of science and mathematics to show where these can be applied.

At the time of writing the United Kingdom is changing over to the metric system of weights and measures. At the same time engineers and scientists are adopting the International System of Units (SI) and the technician must become familiar with these units. In this book SI units have been used throughout. The basic unit of mass is the kilogramme (kg) and the unit of force the newton (N), with the appropriate prefixes to indicate multiples or sub-multiples: thus MN and kN represent meganewton ($N \times 10^6$) and kilonewton ($N \times 10^3$) respectively. Similarly the basic unit of length used is the metre (m) with its submultiples the millimetre (mm) and micrometre (μm), the latter representing a length of 0·000 001 m or 0·001 mm. The author has used the unit N/m^2, with appropriate multiples, as the unit for pressure rather than the units pascal (1 N/m^2) or bar (100 kN/m^2).

The author gratefully acknowledges the assistance given him so generously by various organisations. Individual acknowledgements are made in the text to those which have supplied diagrams and photographs, but, apart from these, mention must be made of Production Tool Alloys Ltd, whose help with the section on powder metallurgy was greatly appreciated. Thanks are also due to colleagues at Luton College of Technology, particularly to Mr W. Vann, C.Eng., M.I.Mech.E., M.I.Prod.E., M.I.Q.A., who so carefully read the proofs, to Mr J. F. W. Galyer, C.Eng., F.I.Prod.E., who allowed me to use a considerable amount of work from our previous book *Metrology for Engineers*, to Mr D. C. Rochester for his help with the chapter on non-destructive testing, and to Mr E. M. Walsh of Geo. Kent Ltd for advice and information about nitriding.

Finally thanks are due to the ladies who prepared the typescript from the author's manuscript and last but by no means least to my wife, who gave encouragement when it was needed and uncomplainingly accepted living with the author while he was writing, drawing or just lost in thought.

Luton, 1971   C. R. S.

Contents

Interchangeable Manufacture
Limits and Fits; Selective Assembly; Limit Gauges

Just over 200 years ago an engineer, Richard Reynolds, made an entry in his diary to the effect that he 'Began this day to scour the bore of a great cylinder . . . of a bore 28 inches across, and in length 9 feet.' The cylinder had been cast in brass and to finish the bore Reynolds had the ends partially blocked off, a segmental shaped piece of lead being cast in the bore. Two iron bars were fixed to the lead and ropes tied to the bars. The cylinder was smeared with oil and emery, and the block of lead drawn back and forth 'by six sturdy and nimble men harnessed to each rope'. When that arc of the cylinder was smooth the cylinder was turned and the process repeated, *'until with exquisite pains and much labour the whole circumference was scoured to such a degree of roundness as to make the longest way across less than the thickness of my little finger greater than the shortest way; which was a matter of much pleasure to me, as being the best that we so far had any knowledge of'.*

In that 200 years we have progressed to a situation where we can manufacture, and measure under certain conditions, pieces of steel whose length is to within ±0·000 05 mm of the stated size. Notice, however, that man cannot as yet make anything *exactly* to size, and if by chance he succeeded in so doing he could not measure the size accurately enough to prove his success. Thus the engineer is presented with a problem. It is necessary to make a great many assemblies all basically the same, all of which must function correctly. In the simplest and commonest case, these consist of holes and shafts which must fit together in a particular way. Ideally all of the holes would be of one size, and all of the shafts of another size so that any shaft would fit any hole given the correct condition of assembly. We have said that this is not possible and the engineer is left with two practical methods of achieving the required result, which is the correct functioning of an assembly.

SYSTEMS OF LIMITS AND FITS

If a given fit is required between a hole and a shaft, the engineer can choose the nominal or basic size to suit the working conditions such as strength or stiffness and, if a running fit is necessary, decide upon the minimum clearance, or allowance, required between the two to give an ideal running fit. Knowing that the sizes of individual parts will vary he can decide on the direction and magnitude of the allowable variation to ensure that any hole will assemble with any shaft and that the two will function correctly for the design life of the assembly. It is not left to the individual engineer to decide on the limits and tolerances[1] for the required fit: they have been worked out for all sizes and all classes of fit and are set out in tabular form, so that the limits for the hole and the shaft can be selected without the necessity of individual calculations for each assembly.

A number of tables of limits and fits are available, all having certain things in common.

1. If the system is hole-based it will cover a variety of types of hole to cater for different methods of manufacture, e.g., drilling, reaming, grinding etc.

---

[1] It is assumed that the reader is familiar with the terms and definitions used. They are set out in Book 1 of this series on page 102.

2. A variety of types of fit is arranged by having a variety of sizes of shaft to give approximately the required amount of clearance or interference.

3. Regardless of the type of hole or shaft, as the size increases so does the tolerance.

In Book 1, two systems of limits and fits were examined briefly and it was shown in both cases that the above statements held good. It is now proposed to examine the structure of one system in detail.

BS 4500: 1969—LIMITS AND FITS FOR ENGINEERING

This is a comprehensive system based on that devised by the International Standards Organisation (I.S.O.), and is suitable for all types of work from fine gauges and instruments to heavy engineering. The system takes into account size of work and type of work, and provides for hole-basis systems or shaft-basis systems as required.

It must be emphasised that no organisation is expected to use the complete system but that each organisation should extract a sub-system for its own use, and we shall see how such a system can be extracted. Tables are provided showing 28 types of shaft designated **a, b, c, d** etc., 28 types of hole designated **A, B, C, D** etc., and to each type of shaft or hole may be applied one of 18 grades of tolerance designated **01, 0, 1, 2, 3, 4 . . . 16.**

The letter indicates the position of the tolerance relative to the nominal size, or the *fundamental deviation*, and the number indicates the magnitude of the tolerance, or the *fundamental tolerance*. A shaft is completely defined by its nominal size, letter, and number, e.g., 40 mm **f7.** Similarly a hole is completely defined by 40 mm **H8,** and the corresponding fit by 40 mm **H8/f7.** Thus the assembly consists of a hole of nominal diameter 40 mm of type **H** and with tolerance grade **8,** mating with a shaft of nominal diameter 40 mm, of type **f** and with tolerance grade **7,** and the tables give the limits for this hole and shaft.

Fig. 1.1 Table of fundamental tolerances. (This extract from BS 4500: 1969 is reproduced by permission of the British Standards Institution, 2 Park Street, London W1A 2BS, from whom copies of the complete standard may be obtained.)

FUNDAMENTAL TOLERANCE

Any hole and shaft of a given size and a given tolerance grade have the same tolerance. Thus an **H7** hole has the same tolerance as a **b7** shaft and a **K12** hole has the same tolerance as an **h12** shaft, as long as the nominal size is the same. BS 4500 publishes these tolerances separately for all sizes in the table of Fundamental Tolerances shown in fig. 1.1. These fundamental tolerances are designated IT01 to IT16 and are based on a fundamental tolerance unit 'i' where

$$i = 0 \cdot 45 \sqrt[3]{D} + 0 \cdot 001 D \text{ micrometres}$$

in which D is the geometric mean of the size step involved, in millimetres.

Thus if $D_1 = $ low limit of size step
and $D_2 = $ high limit of size step
then $D = \sqrt{(D_1 \times D_2)}$.

The values of IT01 to IT5 are arranged in an arbitrary but regularly increasing manner. IT6 is $10i$ and thereafter the fundamental tolerances increase in a series based on a five-series of *preferred numbers*.

A series of preferred numbers is a geometric progression arranged so that after n terms the next term is ten times the first. Thus in a five-series of preferred numbers the numbers are arranged in groups of five, the first term of the second group being 10 times the first term in the first group; the second term of the second group is 10 times the second term in the first group and so on. If we consider a geometric progression whose first term is a and whose common ratio is r

TABLE 1. STANDARD TOLERANCES

Tolerance unit 0·001 mm

Nominal sizes Over (mm)	Up to and including (mm)	IT01	IT0	IT1	IT2	IT3	IT4	IT5	IT6†	IT7	IT8	IT9	IT10	IT11	IT12	IT13	IT14*	IT15*	IT16*
—	3	0·3	0·5	0·8	1·2	2	3	4	6	10	14	25	40	60	100	140	250	400	600
3	6	0·4	0·6	1	1·5	2·5	4	5	8	12	18	30	48	75	120	180	300	480	750
6	10	0·4	0·6	1	1·5	2·5	4	6	9	15	22	36	58	90	150	220	360	580	900
10	18	0·5	0·8	1·2	2	3	5	8	11	18	27	43	70	110	180	270	430	700	1 100
18	30	0·6	1	1·5	2·5	4	6	9	13	21	33	52	84	130	210	330	520	840	1 300
30	50	0·6	1	1·5	2·5	4	7	11	16	25	39	62	100	160	250	390	620	1 000	1 600
50	80	0·8	1·2	2	3	5	8	13	19	30	46	74	120	190	300	460	740	1 200	1 900
80	120	1	1·5	2·5	4	6	10	15	22	35	54	87	140	220	350	540	870	1 400	2 200
120	180	1·2	2	3·5	5	8	12	18	25	40	63	100	160	250	400	630	1 000	1 600	2 500
180	250	2	3	4·5	7	10	14	20	29	46	72	115	185	290	460	720	1 150	1 850	2 900
250	315	2·5	4	6	8	12	16	23	32	52	81	130	210	320	520	810	1 300	2 100	3 200
315	400	3	5	7	9	13	18	25	36	57	89	140	230	360	570	890	1 400	2 300	3 600
400	500	4	6	8	10	15	20	27	40	63	97	155	250	400	630	970	1 550	2 500	4 000
500	630	—	—	—	—	—	—	—	44	70	110	175	280	440	700	1 100	1 750	2 800	4 400
630	800	—	—	—	—	—	—	—	50	80	125	200	320	500	800	1 250	2 000	3 200	5 000
800	1 000	—	—	—	—	—	—	—	56	90	140	230	360	560	900	1 400	2 300	3 600	5 600
1 000	1 250	—	—	—	—	—	—	—	66	105	165	260	420	660	1 050	1 650	2 600	4 200	6 600
1 250	1 600	—	—	—	—	—	—	—	78	125	195	310	500	780	1 250	1 950	3 100	5 000	7 800
1 600	2 000	—	—	—	—	—	—	—	92	150	230	370	600	920	1 500	2 300	3 700	6 000	9 200
2 000	2 500	—	—	—	—	—	—	—	110	175	280	440	700	1 100	1 750	2 800	4 400	7 000	11 000
2 500	3 150	—	—	—	—	—	—	—	135	210	330	540	860	1 350	2 100	3 300	5 400	8 600	13 500

*Not applicable to sizes below 1 mm †Not recommended for fits in sizes above 500 mm.

3

arranged in such groups we have

$$
\begin{array}{llll}
a & ar^5 & ar^{10} & \text{and so on.} \\
ar & ar^6 & ar^{11} & \\
ar^2 & ar^7 & ar^{12} & \\
ar^3 & ar^8 & ar^{13} & \\
ar^4 & ar^9 & ar^{14} &
\end{array}
$$

Since the first term in the second group is 10 times the first term in the first group,

$$
\begin{aligned}
10a &= ar^5 \\
r^5 &= 10 \\
r &= \sqrt[5]{10} \\
r &= 1\cdot585
\end{aligned}
$$

Thus each number grade should be $1\cdot585$ times its predecessor, but in practice this is rounded off. IT6 is $10i$ and it follows that:

$$
\begin{aligned}
\text{IT6} &= 10i \\
\text{IT7} &= 15\cdot85i \text{ or } 16i \text{ when rounded} \\
\text{IT8} &= 25\cdot1i \text{ or } 25i \text{ when rounded} \\
\text{IT9} &= 39\cdot8i \text{ or } 40i \text{ when rounded} \\
\text{IT10} &= 63\cdot1i \text{ or } 64i \text{ when rounded} \\
\text{IT11} &= 100i, \text{ that is, } 10 \times \text{IT6}
\end{aligned}
$$

From the first group of five preferred numbers the next group can be found by multiplying each fundamental tolerance in the first group by 10. Thus the complete series is as follows:

$$
\begin{array}{lll}
\text{IT6} = 10i & \text{IT11} = 100i & \text{IT16} = 1\,000i \\
\text{IT7} = 16i & \text{IT12} = 160i & \\
\text{IT8} = 25i & \text{IT13} = 250i & \\
\text{IT9} = 40i & \text{IT14} = 400i & \\
\text{IT10} = 64i & \text{IT15} = 640i &
\end{array}
$$

Consider now the size-step 30 mm to 50 mm.

$$
\begin{aligned}
\text{Geometric} \\
\text{mean } D &= \sqrt{(30 \times 50)} \text{ mm} \\
&= \sqrt{1\,500} \text{ mm} \\
D &= 38\cdot8 \text{ mm} \\
i &= 0\cdot45\sqrt[3]{D} + (0\cdot001D) \ \mu\text{m} \\
&= 0\cdot45\sqrt[3]{38\cdot8} + (0\cdot001 \times 38\cdot8) \\
&= 1\cdot52 + 0\cdot038\,8 \\
i &= 1\cdot5588 \ \mu\text{m}
\end{aligned}
$$

Starting from $\text{IT6} = 10i$, we can write the fundamental tolerances for this size-step (30 mm to 50 mm) as follows:

Tolerance grade	Multiple of i	Tolerance (μm)	Rounded tolerance (μm)
IT6	$10i$	$15\cdot588$	16
IT7	$16i$	$24\cdot9$	25
IT8	$25i$	$38\cdot9$	39
IT9	$40i$	$62\cdot3$	62
IT10	$64i$	$99\cdot5$	100
IT11	$100i$	$155\cdot88$	160
IT12	$160i$	249	250
IT13	$250i$	389	390
IT14	$400i$	623	620
IT15	$640i$	995	1 000
IT16	$1\,000i$	$1\,558\cdot8$	1 600

Note that the rounding-off is not necessarily to the nearest round figure, e.g., 623 is rounded to 620 rather than to 625. This is due to a preferred number series being used for rounding.

Compare the values in the final column with those given in fig. 1.1 for the size-step 30 mm to 50 mm, and calculate the tolerances for another size-step for comparison.

Applications of the complete range of fundamental tolerances are as follows:

IT01 to IT5	Gauges
IT6 to IT11	Fits
IT12 to IT16	Large tolerances, not to be used for fits.

FUNDAMENTAL DEVIATION Having found the fundamental tolerance, we now have to fix the position of this tolerance zone relative to the nominal size. The distance from the nearest tolerance boundary to the nominal size is called the *fundamental deviation*, and in general these deviations are disposed as follows.

Above nominal size	Bilateral	Below nominal size	
A B C CD D E EF F FG G H	JS J K	M N P R S T U V X Y Z ZA ZB ZC	HOLES
a b c cd d e ef f fg g h	js j k	m n p r s t u v x y z za zb zc	SHAFTS
Below nominal size	Bilateral	Above nominal size	

Specifically, the fundamental deviation is calculated from a formula given in BS 4500 for each class of hole and shaft. Thus in order to fix the limits for a hole or shaft it is necessary to calculate first the fundamental deviation and then apply the fundamental tolerance *away* from the nominal size.

Note: There is a special exception to this rule in the bilateral cases **J** and **j** where the tolerance is equally disposed about the nominal size.

The fundamental deviation for both **H** holes and **h** shafts is zero. The class **H** holes are particularly important since they form the basis of a unilateral hole-basis system of fits. The limits on all class **H** holes are $\pm {}^x_0$ where x is equal to the fundamental tolerance.

As an example, if we calculate the limits and extreme cases of the fit specified as 35mm **H8/f7,** then:

For Hole
Fundamental deviation, class **H**
$$= 0$$
Fundamental tolerance, IT8
$$= 0.039 \text{ mm (see p. 4)}$$
Limits of size for hole
$$= 35/35.039 \text{ mm dia.}$$
For Shaft
Fundamental deviation, class **f**
$$= -5.5 D^{0.41} \,\mu\text{m}$$
From calculation on page 4 geometric mean $D = 38.8$ mm
$\therefore$ Fundamental deviation, class **f**
$$= -5.5 \times 38.8^{0.41} \,\mu\text{m}$$
$$= -5.5 \times 4.47$$
$$= -24.6 \,\mu\text{m}$$
$$= -0.025 \text{ mm(rounded)}$$

Note that the minus sign indicates that this fundamental deviation is below the nominal size. Thus the high limit for the shaft is 35 mm $-$ 0.025 mm = **34.975 mm.**

Fundamental tolerance, IT7
$$= 25 \,\mu\text{m}$$
$\therefore$ Low limit of shaft
$$= 34.975 - 0.025 \text{ mm}$$
$$= 34.950 \text{ mm}$$
Thus, Limits of size for shaft
$$= 34.975/34.950 \text{ mm}$$
and Limits of size for hole
$$= 35.000/35.039 \text{ mm}$$

These values should be compared with those in BS 4500A[1] for this hole and shaft.

The extreme conditions of the fit can then be calculated by comparing the largest allowable shaft with the smallest allowable hole and vice-versa.

Thus,
Minimum clearance $= 35.000 - 34.975$ mm
$$= 0.025 \text{ mm}$$
Maximum clearance $= 35.039 - 34.950$ mm
$$= 0.089 \text{ mm.}$$

PRACTICAL APPLICATIONS A designer would not be expected to perform these calculations; the limits and tolerances are clearly set out in BS 4500. The only requirement in industry is to select from the Standard a system of fits suitable for application to the particular type of work involved. This can usually be accommodated on a sheet or card of A4 size or less. Let us consider a general manufacturing organisation setting up a unilateral hole-basis system of limits and fits. The reasoning would be as follows:

1. As the system is a unilateral hole-basis one, all holes will be of class **H.**

2. To cater for various degrees of precision it will be necessary to use various grades of

[1] See Appendix 1.

5

class **H** hole as follows:

H6 Precision grinding and honing
H8 Grinding and reaming
H11 Drilled holes, milled widths.

3. The range of fits required will be obtained by the association of different classes of shafts with the above three types of hole. Thus:

f6 Close running fits
j5 Keying fits   } with **H6** holes
n5 Light interference fits

f7 Medium running fits
n7 Tight keying fits   } with **H8** holes
v7 Heavy interference fits

c11 Coarse clearance fits with **H11** holes.

Thus we have a range of seven fits suitable for the work done in this organisation. These would be set out on a standard form showing the limits for various sizes of work as shown in fig. 1.2. Although this form would probably find its way into the works it is primarily for use in the drawing office. A designer would specify a light interference fit and the draughtsman, by referring to the form (fig. 1.2) would apply the limits for **H6/n5** to that particular dimension.

The relationships between the hole and shaft specifications are drawn to scale in fig. 1.3 for the size step 30 mm to 50 mm.

BS 4500 contains the limits and tolerances

Fig. 1.2 Table of limits and fits suitable for use by a general engineering firm. (The figures in this table are taken from BS 4500: 1969 by permission of the British Standards Institution, 2 Park Street, London W1A 2BS, from whom copies of the complete standard may be obtained.)

X.Y.Z. CO. LTD.   TABLE OF STANDARD LIMITS AND FITS   ALL LIMITS 0.001 mm UNITS

NOMINAL SIZE (mm) OVER	TO	HOLE LIMITS H6	CLOSE RUNNING f6	LIGHT KEYING j5	LIGHT INTERFERENCE n5	HOLE LIMITS H8	MEDIUM RUNNING f7	KEYING n7	HEAVY INTERFERENCE v7	HOLE LIMITS H11	COARSE CLEARANCE c11
		− +	− −	+ −	+ +	− +	− −	+ +	+ +	− +	− −
−	3	0 6	6 12	2 2	8 4	0 14	6 16	4 14	20 30	0 60	60 120
3	6	0 8	10 18	3 3	13 8	0 18	10 22	8 20	28 40	0 75	70 145
6	10	0 9	13 22	4 2	16 10	0 22	13 28	10 25	34 49	0 90	80 170
10	18	0 11	16 27	5 3	20 12	0 27	16 34	12 30	39 57	0 110	95 205
18	30	0 13	20 33	5 4	24 15	0 33	20 41	15 36	55 76	0 130	110 240
30	50	0 16	25 41	6 5	28 17	0 39	25 50	17 42	81 106	0 160	130 290
50	80	0 19	30 49	6 7	33 20	0 46	30 60	20 50	120 150	0 190	150 340
80	120	0 22	36 58	6 9	38 23	0 54	36 71	23 58	172 242	0 220	180 400
120	180	0 25	43 68	7 11	45 27	0 63	43 83	27 67	252 330	0 250	230 480
180	250	0 29	50 79	7 13	51 31	0 72	50 96	31 77	340 437	0 290	280 570
250	315	0 32	56 88	7 16	57 34	0 81	56 108	34 86	425 532	0 320	330 650
315	400	0 36	62 98	7 18	62 37	0 89	62 119	37 94	530 658	0 360	400 760
400	500	0 40	68 108	7 20	67 40	0 97	68 131	40 103	660 723	0 400	480 880

in tabular form, with an explanation of their derivation.

In the above, little mention has been made of the tolerance grades IT01 to IT5. These are reserved for very precise work such as gauges and are used only in exceptional cases for functioning assemblies. We have assumed in our extraction of a sub-system that our factory is making such assemblies, and only tolerances down to IT5 are to be used. Furthermore, these smaller grades are only used for sizes up to and including 500 mm.

SELECTIVE ASSEMBLY

In the introduction to this chapter it was stated that two methods are available to a production engineer to produce fits which consistently function correctly. Limits and fits have been discussed but may not be practicable if the available manufacturing process will not regularly produce parts to the high degree of precision required. Then, if a 'small' shaft is by chance assembled with a 'large'

hole, the fit will be too loose. Conversely, if a 'large' shaft is by chance assembled with a 'small' hole, the resulting fit will be too tight for correct functioning. This condition can be overcome by a system of selective assembly in which the parts are all measured and graded into groups of closer limits than the full range of limits which the machines are producing. We may have five grades[1] of shaft and five grades of hole, the grades being numbered. If a grade 5 shaft is assembled into a grade 5 hole the assembly will function correctly. If a colour code method is used, a green-code hole is always assembled with a green-code shaft, and so on.

It is worth examining this system rather more deeply. Why, when a machine is operating at a fixed setting, does it produce parts of different size? The size of a given part selected at random depends to some extent on a great many uncontrollable minor factors, no single one of which will produce a measur-

[1] The term 'grade' here should not be confused with the IT grades in BS 4500.

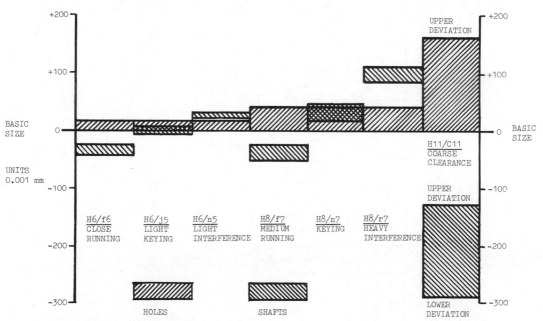

Fig. 1.3 Relationship between hole and shaft limits for a system of fits (to scale for size step 30–50 mm). See also fig. 1.2.

able change in the size of the part. Usually, some factors tend to produce an oversize part and some an undersize part; their effects cancel out and most parts are therefore close to the set size. Occasionally, more of these factors tend to oversize than undersize and an oversize part is produced, and vice-versa.

If then we take a batch of shafts from a machine whose work has a random variation of 0·025 mm and measure them to the nearest 0·005 mm, we should have five size groups, and most of the parts will be in the centre group, as shown in fig. 1.4. If we repeat this procedure with a batch of holes we see the same pattern emerging.

If we now arrange for grade I shafts to be mated with grade I holes, grade II shafts with grade II holes and so on, it can be seen from fig. 1.4 that there will be about the same numbers of each, provided the machine settings are controlled carefully.

This system of selective assembly is gener-ally used where two conditions prevail:

(*a*) The parts cannot be made economically to the required accuracy but can readily be measured and graded.

(*b*) The assembly is replaced as a complete unit when necessary, not repaired by replac-ing individual parts.

Typical applications of selective assembly are in ball and roller bearing manufacture and in cylinder bores and pistons, and pistons and gudgeon pins, in motor car engines.

LIMIT GAUGES

Adoption of a system of limits and fits logically leads to the use of limit gauges, with which no attempt is made to determine the size of a workpiece—they are simply used to find whether the component is within the specified limits of size or not. The simplest form of limit gauges are those used for inspecting holes and shafts.

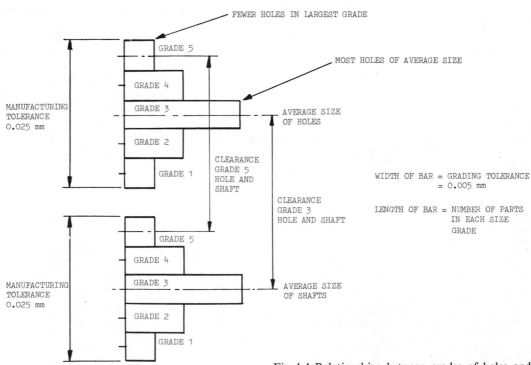

Fig. 1.4 Relationships between grades of holes and shafts in selective assembly.

Consider first a hole on which the limits on diameter are specified. It would appear that quite simply the 'GO' gauge is a cylinder whose diameter is equal to the minimum hole size, and that the 'NOT GO' gauge is a similar cylinder equal in diameter to the maximum hole size. Unfortunately it is not as simple as this, for the same reason that limits of size are required for the work; nothing can be made to an exact size and this includes gauges. Thus the gauge maker requires a tolerance to which he may work, and the positioning of this gauge tolerance relative to the nominal gauge size requires a policy decision. For instance, if the gauge tolerance increases the size of a 'GO' plug gauge, and decreases the sizes of the 'NOT GO' end, the gauge will tend to reject good work which is near the upper or lower size limits.

Similarly if the gauge tolerance increases the size of the 'NOT GO' plug gauge and decreases the size of the 'GO' end then the gauge will tend to accept work which is just outside the specified limits.

Obviously a firm which is quality conscious would use the system which rejects doubtful work but it must be realised that the gauge tolerance normally needs to be approximately 10% of the work tolerance. Therefore, using this system the production department is deprived of 20% of its allowed tolerance. This problem has been dealt with in BS 969 (1953), which lays down the following policy for the application of gauge tolerances.

The tolerance on the 'GO' gauge shall be *within* the work tolerance zone.
The tolerance on the 'NOT GO' gauge shall be *outside* the work tolerance zone.

This policy applies to all plain plug, gap and ring gauges.

In addition to the gauge maker's tolerance, allowance must be made for the initial wear which takes place on a new gauge. Thus a wear allowance of approximately 20% of the gauge tolerance is added to, or subtracted from, the nominal gauge size in opposition to the direction of wear. It should be noted that the wear allowance becomes too small to be useful when the work tolerance is less than 0·1 mm, and no allowance is made for components whose tolerance is less than this. Nor is the wear allowance applied to 'NOT GO' gauges as they should get little wear in use.

These principles may be summarised as follows and applied as shown on the diagrams in figs. 1.5 and 1.6.

Gauge tolerance = 10% of work tolerance to nearest 0·001 mm unit.
Wear allowance = 20% of gauge tolerance to nearest 0·001 mm unit.

In BS 969, tolerances on plug gauges are in some cases less than those for ring and gap gauges. This is due to the fact that plug gauges lend themselves more readily than do ring and gap gauges to measurements where the order of accuracy is less than 0·001 mm. Gauge Limits for Plain Plug, Gap and Ring gauges are set out in tabular form in BS 969. The disposition of the tolerances and the application of the wear allowance follow the rules set out above, but the gauge limits are not always strictly 10% of the work limits and the wear allowance may not be 20% of the gauge tolerance in all cases. These general percentage figures should only be used when BS 969 is not available for reference.

BS 969 sets out only the limits and tolerances for limit gauges. The actual design of gauges is set out in BS 1044: *Recommended Designs for Plug, Ring, and Gap Gauges.*

PLUG GAUGES The gauging members of plug gauges may be of plain carbon steel, hardened and stabilised, or of good quality case-hardening mild steel. There is little to choose between the materials and the one selected may depend upon availability and cost. The gauging members are usually fitted into hexagonal plastic handles so that the heating effects of handling are minimised.

Smaller gauges, up to 64 mm diameter, are of *taper-lock* design, that is, the gauging

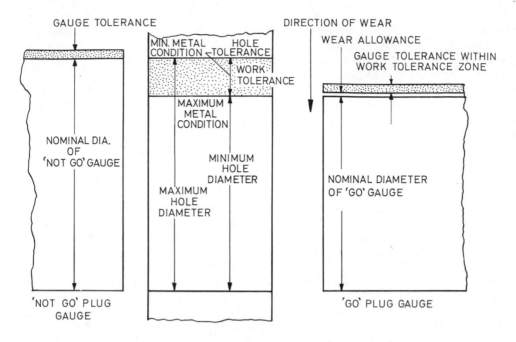

Fig. 1.5 Disposition of tolerances on general plug
gauges.

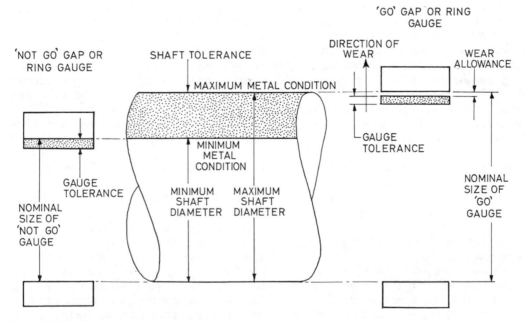

Fig. 1.6 Disposition of tolerances on general ring and
gap gauges.

10

member shank has a self-locking taper of 1 in 48 on diameter which fits into a matching taper in the handle.

Separate GO and NOT GO gauging units can be used in a double-ended gauge as shown in fig. 1.7(*a*), or a *single* progressive GO/NOT GO gauge can be used as shown in fig 1.7(*b*). The progressive type is more convenient to use but if one member wears or becomes damaged, both units need to be replaced.

Larger gauges of over 64 mm diameter are usually of the tri-lock design shown in fig. 1.8. A hexagonal plastic handle is again used but the gauging unit is held in place by a special screw and prevented from rotating by three locking prongs on the end of the handle which engage with grooves on the gauging member. The GO gauging members are reversible, to give a longer life. The initial wear on a gauge usually takes place at the nose of the gauge, where it enters the work, and when the wear becomes excessive the unit is reversed. Note that the lightening holes in larger gauges also provide venting for air which in blind holes would otherwise be trapped. Where smaller gauges are to be used in blind holes an air vent can be provided by drilling through the length of the gauge, the cross hole in the handle allowing the air to escape.

GAP GAUGES These gauges are used for checking shaft diameters and may be adjustable. The solid type may be made from flat plate or from a forging; either type can be obtained from gauge manufacturers, finished and ready for use, or in the soft state to be hardened, stabilised and finished to size by the user.

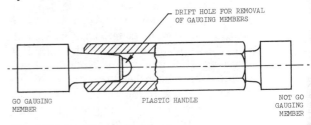

Fig. 1.7(*a*) Double-ended plain plug gauge.

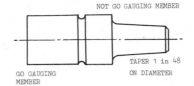

Fig. 1.7(*b*) Progressive plain plug gauge.

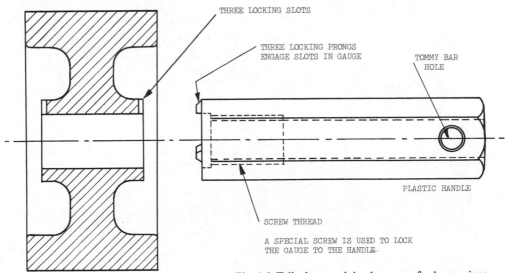

Fig. 1.8 Trilock-type plain plug gauge for larger rings.

Adjustable gap gauges have a forged frame in which adjustable anvils are fitted and can be set to reference discs. With care, the anvils can be set to within ±0·002 mm and thus allow full use to be made of the work tolerance, some of which may be taken up by the gauge tolerance in a solid gap gauge. The adjustment also allows wear to be taken up, while if the anvil faces become non-flat they can be reground and re-adjusted. The anvils normally have a screw adjustment but do not themselves rotate with the screw. A separate device is used to lock the anvil in the frame and, after locking, the gauge is again checked. Finally the adjustment is sealed by a lead or wax plug as shown in fig. 1.9. Note the plastic grip fitted to reduce heat transfer from the hand to the gauge frame.

One limitation of gap gauges is that they will not detect a particular form of non-roundness called *lobing*. The simplest lobed figure has three lobes and is based on an equilateral triangle, as shown in fig. 1.10. From each corner of the triangle is struck a large radius 'R' and a small radius 'r' so that the large radius blends with the small radius at the other two corners. This figure will always enter a pair of gauging anvils set at $(R+r)$ apart, but the smallest hole it will enter is much larger than $(R+r)$. This condition will not be detected by any measurement involving the use of parallel anvils such as those of a micrometer or comparator. It can be detected by rotating the lobed work under a dial gauge or comparator when the work is resting on a vee block as shown in fig. 1.11.

RING GAUGES   It can be seen from fig. 1.10 that a lobed figure will not enter a hole whose diameter is only the same as the gap between the anvil faces. If the machining process being used is likely to produce this form, e.g., with a capstan roller box or a centreless grinder incorrectly set, a GO ring

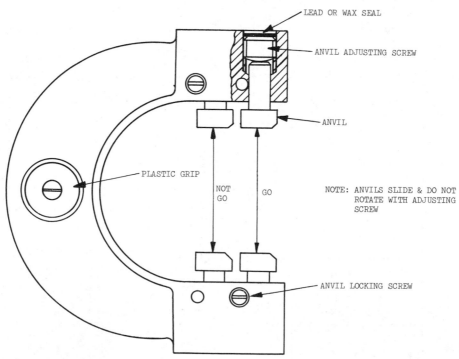

Fig. 1.9 Adjustable gap gauge.

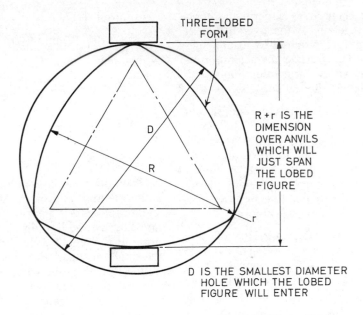

THREE-LOBED
FORM

D

R

r

R + r IS THE
DIMENSION
OVER ANVILS
WHICH WILL
JUST SPAN
THE LOBED
FIGURE

D IS THE SMALLEST DIAMETER
HOLE WHICH THE LOBED
FIGURE WILL ENTER

Fig. 1.10 Effect of lobing on cylindrical work.

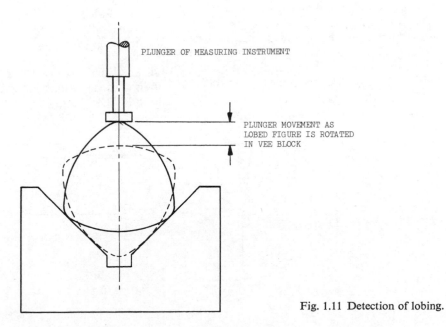

PLUNGER OF MEASURING INSTRUMENT

PLUNGER MOVEMENT AS
LOBED FIGURE IS ROTATED
IN VEE BLOCK

Fig. 1.11 Detection of lobing.

13

gauge should be used as a periodic check. BS 1044 gives details of the overall dimensions of ring gauges required to ensure sufficient rigidity. The outside diameter is normally finished to a fine or medium knurl with a generous chamfer on the corners.

GAUGE MARKINGS All gauges should be clearly marked with the size of the individual gauging members, the words GO or NOT GO, the type of gauge if necessary, e.g., General or Reference, and the manufacturer's name. For plug gauges with plastic handles, this information is engraved upon the handle and is more clearly visible.

THE GAUGING OF TAPERS Tapers can be checked by taper limit gauges. This seems an obvious statement but it must be emphasised that such gauges *do not* check the angle of taper. They are designed only to check the diameter at a particular position along the taper, usually at one end.

These gauges are usually *step*, or *thumbnail* gauges, the limits of diameter being defined at the top and bottom respectively of a step which is ground at the appropriate end of the gauge. Fig. 1.12 shows how a taper ring gauge is used to check the diameter of an external taper, while fig. 1.13 shows the geometric details of a taper plug gauge. The semi-angle of taper, $\theta/2$, can be determined by using sine bar centres while the diameter D of the small end is obtained by measurement over rollers (see Chapter 2).

From fig. 1.13,

$$\tan\left(\frac{\theta}{2}\right) = \frac{D\max - D}{2H}$$

$$D\max = \left[2H \times \tan\left(\frac{\theta}{2}\right)\right] + D$$

$$\text{and } D\min = \left[2(H - S) \times \tan\left(\frac{\theta}{2}\right)\right] + D$$

where S = step height.

It should be noted that a slight error in the angle of taper and/or the diameter makes a significant difference in the values of D max and D min, the limiting diameters, while an error in the length H has little effect, due to the angle of taper. For this reason it is suggested that the following method is adopted in making such gauges.

(*a*) Make the gauge overlength and to an angle as close as possible to that specified for the work.

(*b*) Remove the gauge from the machine and accurately measure the small diameter 'D' and the semi-angle $\theta/2$.

(*c*) Calculate the height 'H' and the step 'S' to give the required dimensions 'D max' and 'D min'.

(*d*) Grind the length to the calculated height 'H' and step 'S'.

HOLE DEPTH GAUGES These are also often made as thumbnail gauges as shown in fig. 1.14. The gauge is cylindrical and is made

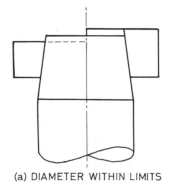

(a) DIAMETER WITHIN LIMITS

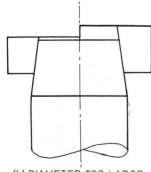

(b) DIAMETER TOO LARGE

Fig. 1.12 Method of using a taper ring gauge.

a close sliding fit in the sleeve which is used to check the step and also enables the gauge to be removed from the hole. The gauge is retained in the sleeve by a pin fitting in an elongated slot, which allows the gauge to be pressed to the bottom of the hole.

SUMMARY

Modern quantity production methods are usually based on systems of interchangeable manufacture. Where this is not possible, selective assembly is used. Interchangeable manufacture allows the work to be inspected by limit gauges, but it should be noted that such gauges tell little about the process used; merely that the part is right or wrong. In selective assembly it is necessary to measure the parts.

It is of interest to note that modern methods of process control by statistical methods are tending away from limit gauging because of the lack of information obtained, towards measuring samples of the work. Measurement gives more information but gauging is usually quicker and cheaper if a large number of components have to be sorted into good and bad.

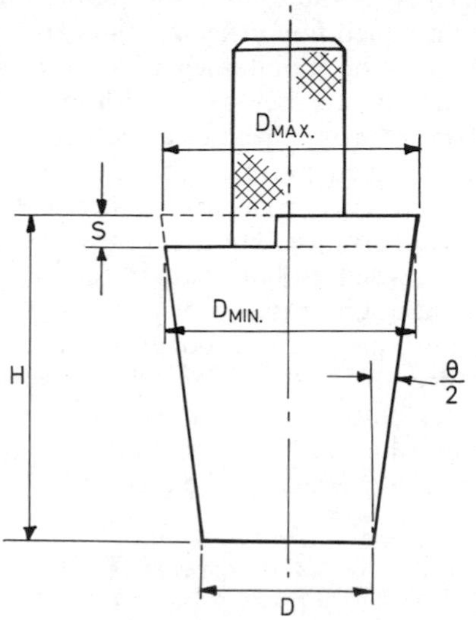

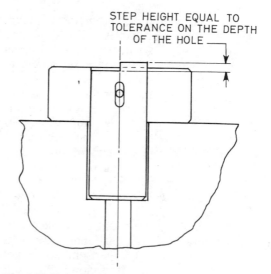

Fig. 1.13 Taper plug gauge.

Fig. 1.14 Hole depth gauge.

The technician studying this book should already be familiar with the basic forms of measurement encountered in the workshop. In this second volume we shall be considering the more sophisticated methods of measurement which have developed with the growth of modern technology.

Whatever method of measurement is used, there are certain principles which should be followed if errors are to be minimised. Even if every precaution is taken, no measurement is exact, and an estimate of the *accuracy of determination* of the measurement should always be made. For example, a gap gauge is measured by gauge blocks and its size is found to be 24·29 mm. This requires a combination of gauge blocks of 1·09 mm + 1·20 mm + 22·00 mm, each of whose individual errors may be negligible but in combination might be as much as ±0·000 5 mm. The sensitivity of feel or touch must also be considered, plus the fact that gauge blocks are manufactured only in 0·01 mm increments and thus, by direct comparison, we cannot subdivide this unit. It follows that our measurement cannot be confidently stated to closer than 0·01 mm and should be presented as follows:

Gap size = 24·29 mm to an accuracy of determination of ±0·01 mm

This may seem to be a longwinded way of putting it but at least everybody knows the true situation. The statement means, 'I have measured this gauge and find its size to be 24·29 mm but due to the possible existence of certain unavoidable errors it can be anything between 24·30 mm and 24·28 mm', which is longer still. (The gap size could be written '24·30 mm > Gap > 24·28 mm' but many people would not understand this.)

CAUSES OF ERROR IN FINE MEASUREMENT

1. TEMPERATURE The standard temperature at which measurements should technically be made is 20°C (68°F) and the room in which fine measurements are carried out should be maintained as nearly as possible at this temperature. Although this is important for the finest measurements, it is in all cases much more important that all the components in a measuring system are at the same temperature. Thus if a measurement is made on a length bar comparator (see p. 22) involving a comparison of two bars 400 mm long and all the components are at 18°C instead of 20°C, the error will not be significant. If, however, the measurement is made with one bar at 18°C and the other at 20°C the error incurred will be given by

$$\text{error} = l.a.t$$
$$= 400 \times 0 \cdot 000\ 011 \times 2$$
$$= 0 \cdot 008\ 8 \text{ mm}$$

in which
l = nominal length = 400 mm
a = coefficient of linear expansion
$\quad = 0 \cdot 000011/°C$
t = temperature difference = 2°C.

Thus the error due to different temperatures within the system is measurable and significant.

2. SINE AND COSINE ERRORS These errors are due to misalignment of the measuring instrument and the work. A simple case is a measurement made with a dial gauge which is not parallel to the required line of measurement.

In fig. 2.1,

$$\text{Dial gauge reading} = BC$$

$$\text{Actual measurement} = AB$$

$$\frac{AB}{BC} = \cos\theta$$

where θ = angle of misalignment.

3. PARALLAX ERRORS These are due to the observer's line of sight not being normal to the dial of the instrument being read. In fig. 2.2, point A is the correct reading and point B is the incorrect reading due to the eye viewing at parallax angle θ.

$$\frac{AB}{AP} = \tan\theta$$

$$AB = AP\tan\theta$$

where AP = distance from pointer to scale.

The parallax error AB will be reduced to zero if:

(*a*) The distance AP = 0. This can be arranged by putting the pointer in the plane of the scale.

(*b*) The angle θ is zero. This is done by ensuring that viewing is normal to the scale. Many instruments have a strip of mirror in the scale behind the pointer and the line of sight is at right angles to the scale when the pointer obscures its own image.

4. CALAMITOUS OR CATASTRO-PHIC ERRORS These are not usually errors of measurement but errors of arithmetic. The inspector fails to carry 1 in adding a slip pile and an error of 1 mm is produced; a micrometer is misread by 1·00 mm or 0·50 mm; the radius of a roller is used instead of its diameter when measuring a taper. There is a simple method of avoiding these errors; if the component is measured by a rule as a rough check the measurement will be within the order of ±0·25 mm. A greater difference than this between the final measurement and the rough check will generally be due to arithmetical error.

IMPROVED ACCURACY OF DETERMINATION

If a part is measured only once, the accuracy of determination is that of a single measurement. If a part is measured n times and the average measurement is then taken, the accuracy of determination of the average value is approximately $\pm x/\sqrt{n}$ where x is the accuracy of the single measurement. Thus if a measurement is made four times and the average of the four results is taken, the accuracy of determination of the average will be twice as good as that of the individual measurement.

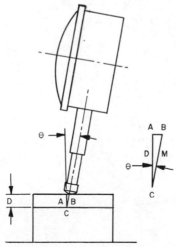

Fig. 2.1 Cosine error due to misalignment of measuring instrument.

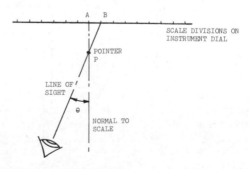

Fig. 2.2 Parallax error due to line of sight not being at right angles to scale of measuring instrument.

This is only true if the measurement is repeated completely *n* times, not just a part of it such as the final reading.

MEASUREMENT OF SIMPLE GAUGES

Simple gap and ring gauges can be measured by direct comparison with gauge blocks if the accuracy required is not greater than ±0·01 mm.

1. MEASUREMENT OF PLAIN GAP GAUGES

This type of measurement is made by building up gauge blocks until they 'just fit' the gap, i.e., until one size of gauge block combination will enter the gap and the next one will not. In practice this is done by a process of elimination. Consider a gap gauge measured with a rule and found to be between 24·97 mm and 25·03 mm. A 22·00 mm gauge block is taken and 1·07 and 1·90 mm blocks are wrung to it, the combination being offered to the gauge. It enters but a 25·00 mm gauge does not. Sizes over 25·00 mm are eliminated and the gauge is now known to be between 24·97 mm and 25·00 mm.

Now a gauge combination of 24·98 mm is offered and is accepted, so the 1·08 mm slip is replaced by a 1·09 mm one. If the 24·99 mm combination enters the gap but the 25·00 mm gauge does not, the gap is greater than 24·99 mm but less than 25·00 mm. The whole system should be left to stabilise so that any temperature differences can correct themselves and the gap gauge then rechecked with 24·99 mm and 25·00 mm gauge block combinations. If they check correctly the gap gauge is quoted as 24·995 mm to an accuracy of determination of ±0·01 mm.

This procedure has been given in some detail since it is the fundamental method to be used when working with gauge blocks. Other points to note are:

(*a*) Clean the equipment carefully and preferably wear chamois leather gloves to avoid

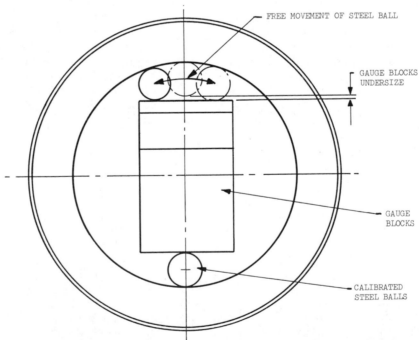

Fig. 2.3 Measurement of plain ring gauge using calibrated steel balls and gauge blocks.

corrosion from perspiration; some people are 'rusty fingered' and have corrosive sweat.

(b) Perform all such operations on a surface plate. Its mass acts as a heat sink and helps to equalise temperatures.

2. MEASUREMENT OF PLAIN RING GAUGES

A plain ring gauge can be measured by placing a pair of calibrated precision steel balls in the gauge and building up gauge blocks, by a similar process of elimination to that described for gap gauges, until a 'nice snug fit' is achieved. What constitutes a nice snug fit?

If the gauge blocks and gauge are lightly held down with three fingers of one hand, a steel knitting needle can be used to see whether any free movement of one of the balls is present, as shown in fig. 2.3. The gauge blocks are built up until any free movement is eliminated and the last combination of gauge blocks plus balls is taken as the correct size to an accuracy of determination of ±0·01 mm. The same procedure can be used with taper ring gauges.

The measurement should be carried out on a surface plate, not on a wooden bench, and excessive force must not be used. The use of the knitting needle enables false results from elastic deformation to be avoided. It must be remembered that the measurement involves four point-contacts, at all of which elastic deformation will occur under very light loads. The largest combination of gauge blocks which just allows movement incurs a minimum of such deformation.

3. MEASUREMENT OF PLAIN PLUG GAUGES

Cylindrical objects such as plug gauges are not measured by direct comparison with slip gauges. A measuring instrument suitable for making comparisons is used instead. Such an instrument is called a comparator and the various types of comparator will be considered later in this Chapter. Whichever type is used, the process is similar. A combination of gauge blocks is made up to the nominal size of the plug gauge and the instrument is adjusted to read zero on this combination. The plug gauge is then passed under the comparator and the reading noted, any movement from zero being the difference in size between the plug gauge and the gauge blocks. The gauge should be checked at each end and at the mid-point of its length to give evidence of non-straightness or taper, and this check should be repeated with the gauge turned through 90° to give evidence of ovality. It is suggested that the results be set out as shown in fig. 2.4, to show readily both non-parallelism and ovality.

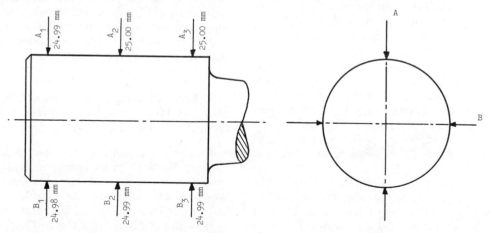

Fig. 2.4 A method of setting out results of measurement of a plain plug gauge.

For ease of handling, the gauging members of the plug gauge are normally removed from their plastic handles during testing.

COMPARATIVE MEASUREMENT OF GAUGE BLOCKS Gauge blocks for use as working standards of length are available in five grades, OO, Calibration, O, I and II. Grade II gauge blocks are intended for use in the workshop and must be checked for accuracy from time to time. This is done by direct comparison with one of the higher grades, usually grade O gauges, which have themselves been directly measured against the legal standard of length, which is the wavelength of a particular colour of light.

To compare a pair of gauge blocks and discern any difference in their lengths requires a comparator of very high magnification and an electrical comparator is frequently used (see p. 32). The two gauges are thoroughly cleaned and set up on the work stage of the instrument with the grade O gauge under the plunger. The instrument is adjusted to read zero on the grade O block at low magnification, then switched to high magnification (30 000 ×) and zeroed, using the fine adjustment. The whole system is left to 'soak', i.e., temperature variations are allowed to stabilise, the time required being a minimum of 20 minutes plus 1 minute per millimetre length of gauge block over 25 mm. When stability has been attained the comparator is adjusted to read any *known error in the grade O gauge*. The grade II gauge is now moved under the plunger and any error in it read directly, any error in the grade O gauge having been cancelled out by the pre-setting of the instrument.

This procedure is repeated a minimum of three times and the mean of the results is taken.

Such measurements should be carried out in a temperature-controlled room and a useful precaution is to have a perspex or wooden screen around the instrument with a hinged front for access. This prevents local temperature variations due to draughts and air movements. A thermometer can be lowered within the screen and the temperature noted and controlled at 20°C during the test.

INSTRUMENTS FOR COMPARATIVE MEASUREMENT
The direct use of gauge blocks enables measurements to be made in increments of 0·01 mm units, but the accuracy of determination is reduced by the 'feel' or 'touch' of the inspector. If we wish to improve the accuracy of determination an instrument is needed with scale divisions of 0·01 mm which are either subdivided into smaller fractions or can be further subdivided by estimation. Such instruments are called comparators and are made in various forms, all with certain common features.

1. An amplification system is needed to enable small movements of the measuring plunger to be shown by a larger movement of the pointer. The amplification may be by mechanical, optical, electrical or pneumatic means.

2. The range of measurements in such instruments is small and the higher the magnification the smaller is the range of measurement. Thus a comparator with a magnification of 500 × may have a range of ±0·15 mm while a similar instrument with a magnification of 3 000 × may have a range of only ±0·025 mm.

3. The measuring pressure should be constant, as far as possible, to prevent errors from elastic deformation.

4. The instrument should be robust to avoid deflections in its frame, and of fairly massive construction to act as a heat sink which absorbs small quantities of heat without undue local change of temperature.

It is interesting to note the cost aspects of certain measurements involving the use of comparators. If a plain ring gauge is to be measured by hand the equipment required is:

(*a*) Grade O gauge blocks £200
(*b*) Precision steel balls £120

Total £320[1]

This, as we have seen, will allow an accuracy of determination of the order of ±0·01 mm. If it is necessary to achieve an accuracy of ±0·002 5 mm or less, a comparator capable of internal measurement is required and the equipment costs are:

(*a*) Grade O gauge blocks £200
(*b*) Comparator £1 100

Total £1 300[1]

Thus, as tolerances decrease, not only does the cost of manufacture increase, but also the cost of measurement.

MECHANICAL COMPARATORS

1. THE MICROMETER AS A COMPARATOR The hand micrometer has an accuracy of determination over its complete range of approximately ±0·005 mm when used for direct measurement. Even if it is reading correctly at zero, we cannot be sure of a measured dimension to closer than 0·005 mm at other points on the scale because of variations in contact pressure, errors in subdivision of 0·01 mm units and pitch errors in the screw. This can be verified by calibrating a micrometer against gauge blocks over its whole range.

We can reduce these errors by systematically attacking their causes.

(*a*) *Feel and contact pressure* can be made constant by replacing the fixed anvil with an anvil attached to a gauge which gives a con-

stant reading at the same measuring pressure. Such a device is called a *fiducial indicator*.

(*b*) *Subdivision of 0·01 mm units* can be improved by making the thimble of the instrument much larger in diameter and thus making the 0·01 mm divisions large enough to be directly subdivided into 0·001 mm divisions. By then applying the vernier micrometer principle, the micrometer can be made to read to 0·000 2 mm.

(*c*) *Pitch errors in the screw* usually occur over the whole length of the screw. If we use less than one turn (0·5 mm) of the screw they are largely eliminated. This can be achieved by setting the micrometer to a standard setting-cylinder or gauge blocks until the pointer of the fiducial indicator is on its mark and noting the reading. The workpiece is then placed in the instrument and the reading on the workpiece noted. It follows that the difference in readings, added to the size of the setting standard with due regard to sign, is the size of the workpiece.

If a plain plug gauge of nominal size 30 mm is to be tested, a standard setting cylinder of 30 mm diameter is used to set the instrument.

Actual size of setting cylinder = 29·985 mm

Reading on setting cylinder = 15·813 mm
Reading on plug gauge = 15·810 mm
Difference = 0·003 mm

Note: (1) Because the instrument is used as a comparator, the reading of 15·813 mm bears no relationship to the cylinder diameter of 29·985 mm.

(2) The reading on the plug gauge is *smaller* than the reading on the setting cylinder and the difference must therefore be *subtracted* from the size of the setting cylinder.

Actual size of setting cylinder = 29·985 mm
Difference in readings = 0·003 mm
subtract 29·982 mm

[1] Values in 1966.

21

If we assume that this type of micrometer can give consistent repetition of readings to within 0·000 5 mm, we can say

Size of plug gauge = 29·982 mm ±0·000 5 mm

The instrument incorporating these features is called a *bench micrometer* and is illustrated in fig. 2.5. Note that the position of the fiducial indicator can be adjusted so that a micrometer head with a 25 mm range can be used for measurements from 0 mm to 50 mm. An adjustable work stage or stand is provided so that the work need not be held during measurement and temperature effects due to handling are thus minimised.

It is advisable to make the type of contact between the anvil and the workpiece as far as possible the same for the setting master as for the workpiece.

The bench micrometer principle is incorporated in other instruments such as the length-bar comparator, the taper-measuring machine, and the screw-diameter measuring machine.

2. THE LENGTH-BAR COMPARATOR

This is an enlarged version of the bench micrometer, consisting of a rigid bed carrying at one end a large drum-micrometer head and at the other a dial gauge reading to 0·002 mm. Between these units is a pair of vee supports to carry the work, both being adjustable vertically and one horizontally. All these units can be adjusted along the bed and the range of the instrument is from 150 mm to 1 metre, to an accuracy of determination of the order of 0·002 5 mm.

In this case the setting gauge consists of a combination of length bars rather than gauge blocks. The length bars are hardened steel

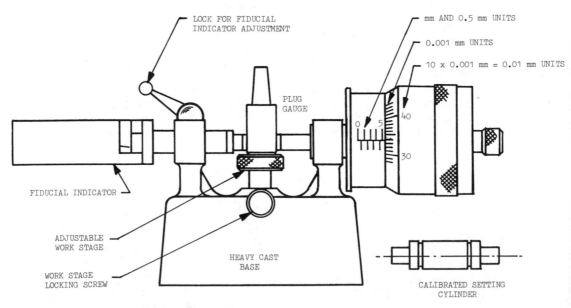

Fig. 2.5 Bench micrometer set to take readings on a plain plug gauge.

bars of 22 mm diameter whose end faces are lapped flat, parallel and to a wringing finish. The ends are drilled and tapped, loose-fitting studs being provided so that when the bars are assembled the faces take control rather than the screw, and misalignment is eliminated. The comparator and a length bar combination are shown in fig. 2.6.

To determine the length of a gauge a combination of length bars is made up as nearly as possible of the same length as the gauge. Any major difference can be overcome by wringing a gauge block onto one end of the length bar combination. The combination is now placed on the vee supports which are set centrally and at a distance of 0·577 L apart, where L is the overall length of the bars. This method of support ensures that the sag of the bar under its own weight is minimised and the slope at the ends is zero, thus making the end faces parallel.

The bar must be aligned accurately with the line of measurement between the two anvils, which is achieved by adjusting the vee supports. If the bar is initially out of line, the dial gauge reading reduces as it is brought into line. When the bar is taken out of line in the other direction the reading increases and at the reversal of the pointer movement the bar is correctly aligned.

The micrometer is now adjusted until the dial gauge reads zero, after which the length bar is replaced by the bar under test. The micrometer is again adjusted until the dial gauge has the same reading and the micrometer reading is noted. The difference in the two readings is the difference in length of the two bars.

3. BENCH-TYPE MECHANICAL COMPARATORS These are probably the commonest of the bench-type comparators and are extremely convenient in that they require no services such as electricity supplies or compressed air. They consist of a heavy base carrying the work stage and a column, up and down which the measuring head can be adjusted. Externally, the measuring head

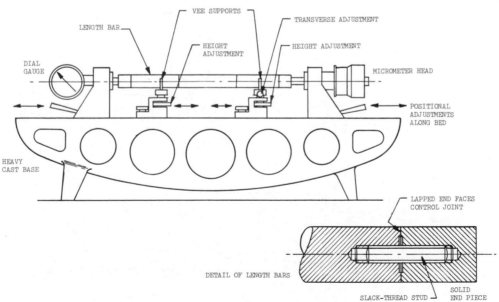

Fig. 2.6 Length bar comparator.

consists of the work contact plunger whose movement operates a pointer moving over a dial. Magnifications range from 500 × to 5 000 ×, a typical instrument being shown in fig. 2.7.

In use, a combination of gauge blocks is made up to the nominal size of the work to be measured. If the calibrated values of these blocks are known, the errors should also be totalled. Thus if the nominal size of the work is 51·57 mm we have:

Gauge block (mm)	Known error (μm)
1·07	+0·03
1·50	+0·02
9·00	+0·05
40·00	+0·05
Total = 51·57 mm	+0·15 μm

If the comparator is calibrated with the

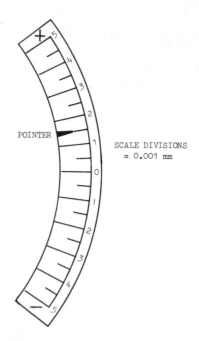

Fig. 2.8 High magnification comparator set to known error in gauge blocks.

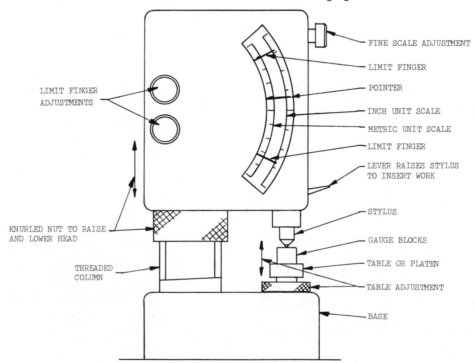

Fig. 2.7 Mechanical comparator showing operating adjustments.

smallest units of 0·000 1 mm it is now set at +1·5 of these units, as shown in fig. 2.8. The errors in the gauge blocks are thus cancelled by presetting the comparator and when the workpiece is inserted its error is read directly.

The Sigma Comparator is an example of a mechanical comparator whose amplification is obtained by means of a compound lever arrangement, a simplified form of which is shown in fig. 2.9(*a*). The overall magnification is the product of the two lever ratios, i.e.,

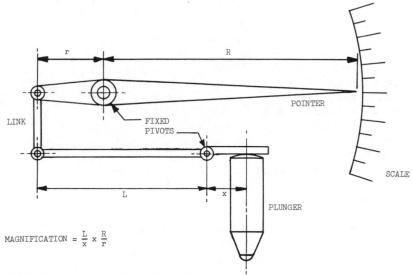

$$\text{MAGNIFICATION} = \frac{L}{x} \times \frac{R}{r}$$

Fig. 2.9(*a*) Essentials of compound lever type of comparator movement.

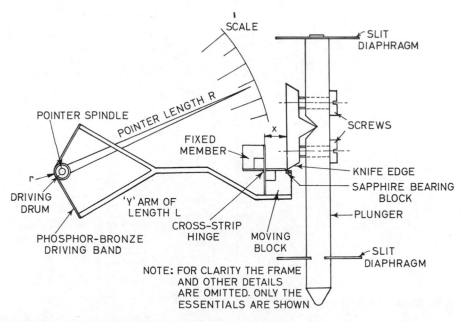

NOTE: FOR CLARITY THE FRAME AND OTHER DETAILS ARE OMITTED. ONLY THE ESSENTIALS ARE SHOWN

Fig. 2.9(*b*) Diagram of movement of Sigma mechanical comparator.

$$\text{Magnification} = \frac{L}{x} \times \frac{R}{r}$$

The actual movement is shown in diagrammatic form in fig. 2.9(b). As the plunger is raised, the moving block follows the knife edge and the Y-shaped arm moves about the cross-strip pivot. A phosphor-bronze driving band is carried from the ends of the Y-arm about a driving drum of radius r to which is attached a pointer of length R. Thus as the Y-arm moves it causes the drum to rotate, carrying the pointer with it.

The Johansson Comparator is a simple device based upon the same principle as that which operates the child's toy, in which a button is placed at the centre of a loop of twine, one end of which is hooked over each thumb. The button is now 'wound up' so that the twine is twisted in opposite directions on either side. If the thumbs are now alternately drawn apart and brought together the button spins rapidly with a satisfying buzz. A little

thought shows that a small linear movement of the thumbs produces a large angular movement of the button. Similarly, in a comparator, a small linear movement of the measuring stylus is required to produce a large angular movement of the pointer.

The Johansson Mikrokator shown in fig. 2.10 has the pointer mounted at the centre of a thin strip of metal permanently twisted in opposite directions on either side of the pointer. As the plunger is raised its movement is transmitted to the strip by the bell-crank lever arrangement, causing the strip to stretch and unwind, and the pointer to move across the scale.

OPTICAL COMPARATORS These are dealt with separately in the section on optical measuring instruments.

PNEUMATIC COMPARATORS
These instruments are sometimes known as proximity gauges. They operate on the

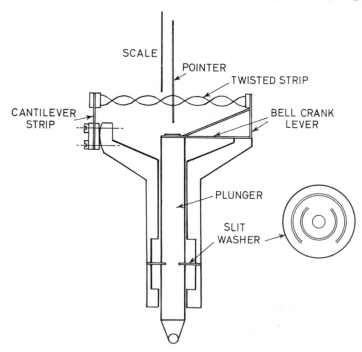

Fig. 2.10 Movement of Johansson Mikrokator.

principle that if an air jet is brought into close proximity with a surface the flow of air is restricted, and can change both the pressure in the system and the rate of flow of air through the system. Both these changes are used to indicate the distance between the jet and the work face.

BACK-PRESSURE AIR GAUGES Air gauges which indicate the change in a measured dimension by measuring a change in air pressure are called *back-pressure gauges*. They consist of two orifices, or jets, in series supplied with air at constant pressure, P_c. If the measuring jet is completely closed by the workpiece the air throughout the system remains at this pressure but if the measuring jet is gradually opened, by moving the workpiece, the back pressure between the jets, P_b, falls. Thus by measuring the pressure between the jets we have a measure of the distance L in fig. 2.11. The pressure gauge is calibrated not in kN/m² but in the units of length in which L is to be measured.

Magnification of the measurement increases as the input pressure is increased and as the control orifice area is reduced.

A practical application of this instrument is shown in fig. 2.12. This is the type made by

Solex Air Gauges Ltd, and shows an air plug gauge checking a bore.

The air from its normal source of supply, say the factory air line, is filtered and passes through a flow valve. Its pressure is then reduced and maintained at a constant value by a dip tube into a water chamber, the pressure value being determined by the head of the water displaced, with excess air escaping to atmosphere. The air at constant pressure then passes through the control orifice and escapes from the measuring orifice. The back pressure in the circuit is indicated by the head of water displaced in the manometer tube. The tube is graduated linearly to show changes of pressure resulting from changes in the measured dimension.

Another back-pressure air gauge is produced by Mercer Air Gauges Ltd, but this operates at the much higher pressure of 27·5 N/cm² gauge. The constant pressure input is produced from the line pressure by a diaphragm-type regulator and passed to the control orifice and thence to the measuring orifice.

Interesting features are:

(*a*) *Magnification adjustment*. This is achieved by means of a taper-needle valve in the control orifice and enables a single scale

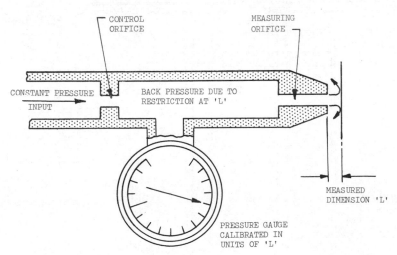

Fig. 2.11 Essentials of back-pressure type of air gauge.

to be used for all types of work by adjusting the magnification and zero settings.

(*b*) *Zero adjustment*. An air bleed, upstream of the measuring orifice and controlled by a taper-needle valve, provides a zero adjustment.

The pressure measuring device is a Bourdon tube type of pressure gauge, the dial being graduated in linear units, i.e., 0·01 mm, 0·001 mm or inch units.

As with all other comparators, initial setting is by means of reference gauges.

Air gauges of this type (and electrical gauging units) have a distinct advantage over mechanical and optical comparators in that a small measuring unit can be remote from the amplifying and indicating head, and can also be conveniently built into a multiple gauging unit as shown in fig. 2.13. The manometer tubes are set close together with coloured zones indicating the tolerance bands for the various dimensions and the operator can see at a glance whether all dimensions are within the limits or not.

A disadvantage of this type of comparator is that it does not have a linear response, i.e.,

a graph of measured gap against reading is not a straight line. Great care must be taken to ensure that the scale is correct over its whole length and not just at the zero and extreme values.

FLOW-VELOCITY AIR GAUGES In these air gauges, the measured gap between jet and workpiece is determined from the quantity of air passing through the system. Air enters the gauge at constant pressure into a tapered glass tube containing a 'float'. The float takes up that position in the tube where the upthrust of the air moving past it is equal to its own weight and will always take the same position at the same velocity of air flow. If the measured gap is large and a great quantity of air is flowing the float moves to the top of the tapered tube. If the gap is small, the quantity of air flowing is small and the float drops near to the bottom of the tube. The scale shown in fig. 2.14 is calibrated in 0·01 mm or 0·001 mm units, the magnification being altered by changing the tube to one of a different taper. Fine adjustments to the magnification are made by adjusting the

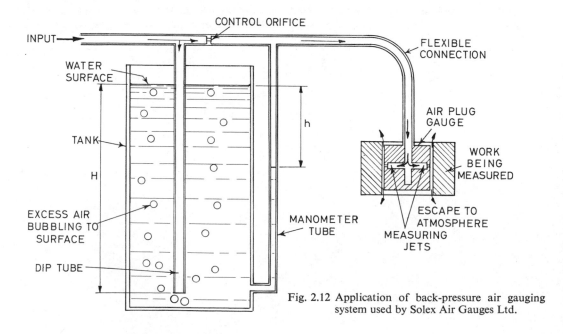

Fig. 2.12 Application of back-pressure air gauging system used by Solex Air Gauges Ltd.

supply pressure.

This type of air gauge lends itself to tool-room inspection work, a height-setting micrometer, shown in fig. 2.15, being used as a setting master. The measuring jet is attached to a height gauge for convenience and differences in height between the work and the setting micrometer are shown on the air gauge. The height gauge used should preferably be of the type with a screw adjustment at the base of the column and no readings are taken from its scale; it is simply a convenient mount for the measuring jet unit.

Types of Jet. The measuring jet may be a simple open jet, the air from which impinges directly upon the work. This has the advantage that it is self-cleansing, and the air will blow away small pieces of foreign matter and cutting fluid. Such jets are, however, prone to damage and the slightest burr on the jet

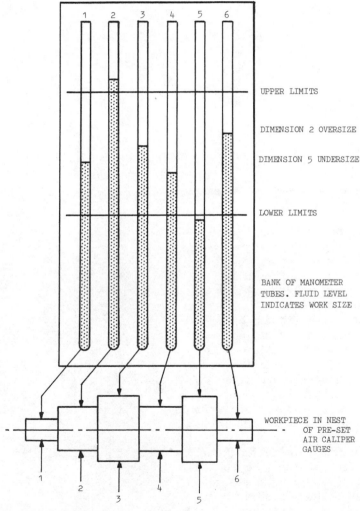

Fig. 2.13 Block diagram of multi-gauging set-up using air gauges.

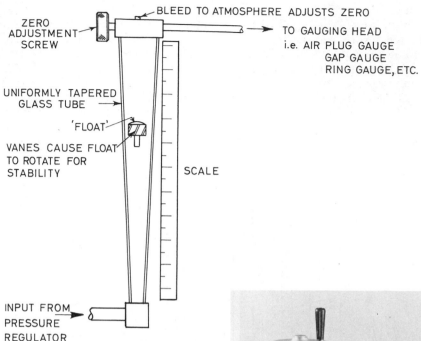

Fig. 2.14 Line diagram of flow-velocity-type pneumatic circuit.

edge will change the jet characteristics and cause incorrect readings. Open jets are normally used only where the nature of the gauge affords some degree of protection, as in the air plug gauge shown in fig. 2.12 or the air ring gauge in fig. 2.16.

For measurements where an open jet might be damaged, the gauge incorporates a plunger to contact the work. Movement of the plunger causes a taper needle to move in an orifice and thus open or close the jet. Such a measuring head is shown in fig. 2.17 and may be built into a stand to form a bench comparator or into portable gauges such as air gap gauges.

The dial gauge head shown in fig. 2.15(b) as part of the height gauge may be replaced by an air gauge measuring jet as shown in fig. 2.18. Pressure on the ball-ended measuring probe, or stylus, flexes the thin portion of the measuring head body, thus opening or

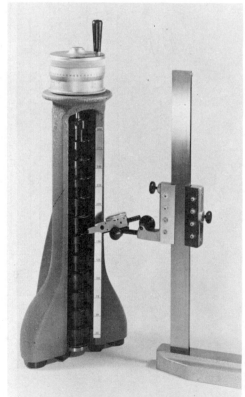

Fig. 2.15(a) Height Setting Micrometer.

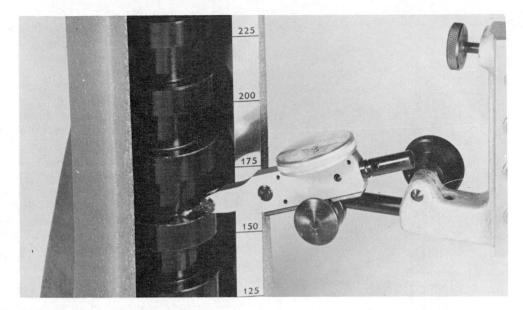

Fig. 2.15(b) Detail of indicator probe reading on micrometer step. (By courtesy of Verdict Gauge (Sales) Ltd.)
Note: Air gauges or electrical comparators may be used to replace test indicator if higher magnifications are required.

Fig. 2.16 Pneumatic ring gauge arranged to measure diameter and reveal lobing.

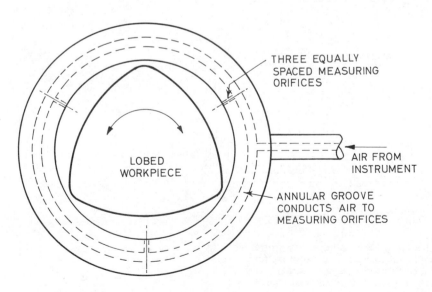

THREE EQUALLY SPACED MEASURING ORIFICES

LOBED WORKPIECE

AIR FROM INSTRUMENT

ANNULAR GROOVE CONDUCTS AIR TO MEASURING ORIFICES

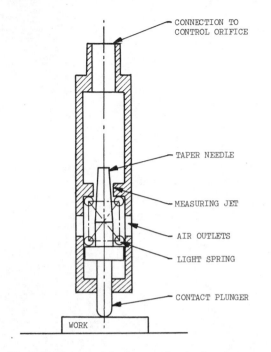

CONNECTION TO
CONTROL ORIFICE

TAPER NEEDLE

MEASURING JET

AIR OUTLETS

LIGHT SPRING

CONTACT PLUNGER

WORK

Fig. 2.17 Plunger type of measuring jet for air gauge.

closing the measuring jet.

As long as certain precautions are observed, air gauges are an extremely useful form of measuring device for repetitive inspection and precision toolroom work, and can be built into a machine for process control during manufacture. The supply pressure must be kept constant by the use of sensitive regulators, the air must be filtered to avoid particles of dirt blocking the jets, and great care must be taken to ensure that the jets are not damaged. The manometer-tube types lend themselves readily to selective assembly work, as the scale can be replaced by coloured zones corresponding to the size grades used. This method, in conjunction with an air plug gauge, is used to grade cylinder bores in motor car engines.

ELECTRICAL COMPARATORS

If an armature is moved and causes the air gaps to vary between itself and a pair of coils as shown in fig. 2.19, the impedance in the circuit is changed. This causes a variation in the current flow which can be amplified and

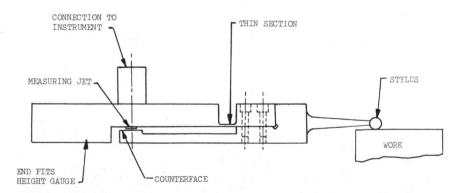

CONNECTION TO
INSTRUMENT

THIN SECTION

MEASURING JET

STYLUS

WORK

END FITS
HEIGHT GAUGE

COUNTERFACE

Fig. 2.18 Measuring jet suitable for use with height setting micrometer. The measuring force on the stylus causes the thin section to deflect and vary the distance between the jet and counterface.

32

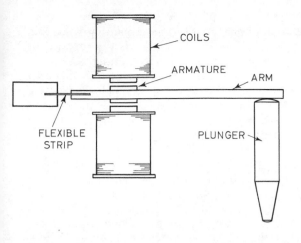

Fig. 2.19 Measuring head for electrical comparator.

measured on an electrical instrument calibrated to read in units of the plunger displacement.

These instruments have certain similar advantages to air gauges. The measuring head can be made extremely small and remote from the reading instrument, to which it is connected by flexible wires. It may thus be built into machinery and measuring fixtures. A further advantage is that the amplifier can be built to give different magnifications selected at will by turning a switch. A typical instrument made by the Sigma Instrument Company has magnifications of 10 000 ×, 20 000 × and 30 000 ×. At a maximum magnification the smallest scale divisions represent 0·05 μm, the instrument therefore being suitable for gauge block comparisons (see p. 20).

THE MEASUREMENT OF SCREW THREADS

INTRODUCTION Examination of BS 3643, dealing with the tolerances on commercial screw threads, shows that these tolerances are relatively large. Such threads are normally inspected by using limit gauges. However, certain threads must be held to much closer tolerances, and this is particularly true of the limit gauges used for screw

thread inspection. These threads must be measured, not gauged, to ensure that they are of a degree of accuracy sufficient to separate the good threads from the bad when used as tools of inspection.

Measurement, as distinct from gauging, of a screw thread can be extremely complex. There are a number of elements to be measured and, as will be shown, some are interrelated. A vee-form thread is composed basically of the following elements.

(a) Major or outside diameter.
(b) Minor or root diameter.
(c) Form, particularly flank angles. ⎫ Virtual
(d) Pitch.   ⎬ effective
(e) Simple effective diameter.   ⎭ diameter.

These elements are illustrated in fig. 2.20.

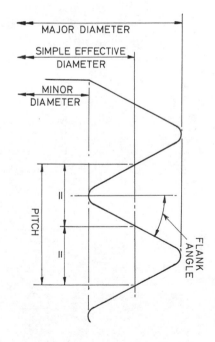

Fig. 2.20 Elements of a vee-form thread.
Note: Metric and Unified threads have flat crests and radiused roots.

The flank angle, pitch and simple effective diameter are grouped together above under the heading virtual effective diameter and it will be shown that errors in pitch and/or flank angle cause a change in effective diameter. Thus the virtual effective diameter of a thread is the simple effective diameter modified by corrections due to pitch errors and flank angle errors, and this virtual effective diameter is the most important single dimension of a screw-thread gauge.

MEASUREMENT OF THE MAJOR DIAMETER
The major diameter of a screw thread is defined as the diameter of an imaginary cylinder which contains all points on the crests of the thread.

It is most conveniently measured by means of a bench micrometer which has already been discussed in detail.

MEASUREMENT OF MINOR DIAMETER
The minor diameter may be defined as the diameter of an imaginary cylinder containing all points on the root of the thread.

It is measured by a comparative process, using a bench micrometer, but hardened and ground steel prisms are used to probe to the root of the thread as shown in fig. 2.22.

Due to the thread helix, a couple of $F \times p/2$ Nm is produced where F is the measuring pressure and p is the thread pitch. This couple would tend to rotate the thread through an angle depending on the pitch, and an erroneous reading would result.

The measurement is therefore carried out on a floating-carriage diameter measuring machine in which the thread is mounted between centres and a type of bench micrometer is constrained to move at right angles to the axis of the centres by an almost frictionless slide.

The instrument is shown in fig. 2.21 but is there fitted with measuring wires, not prisms, for measurement of simple effective diameter.

The readings are taken on the setting cylinder *with the prisms in position*, and then on the thread. If the prisms are considered as extensions to the micrometer anvils as in fig. 2.22 their size is unimportant and:

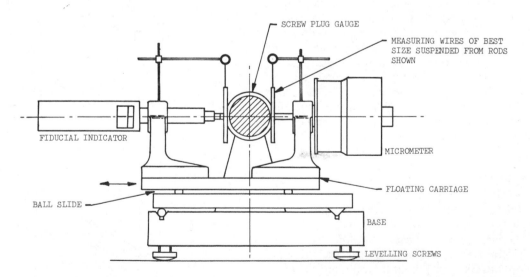

Fig. 2.21 Floating carriage micrometer for the measurement of screw diameters.

Note: The screw is supported between centres which are not shown for reasons of clarity.

Fig. 2.22 Use of prisms to measure minor diameter.

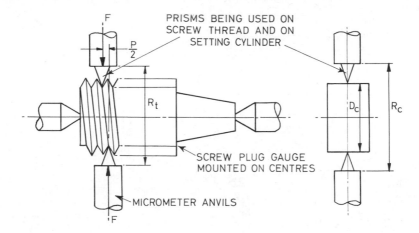

PRISMS BEING USED ON
SCREW THREAD AND ON
SETTING CYLINDER

F

$\frac{P}{2}$

R_t

D_c

R_c

SCREW PLUG GAUGE
MOUNTED ON CENTRES

MICROMETER ANVILS

F

$$\text{Minor dia.} = D_c + (R_t - R_c)$$

where D_c = diameter of setting cylinder
R_t = reading on thread
R_c = reading on cylinder

Readings should be taken at various positions on the thread to determine ovality and taper.

MEASUREMENT OF THREAD FORM The most important measurement of form to be made on a screw thread is the measurement of its flank angles. The flank angle is defined as the angle made between the straight portion of the thread flank and a line normal to the thread axis.

Flank angles on large threads may be measured by contact methods, but normally the only practical method of measurement is to use optical equipment. This can be done by projecting an enlarged profile of the thread and measuring the angle of the flank image on the screen, or by using a microscope with a goniometric head.

Screw Thread Projection. The simplest and probably the most effective projector for this class of work is known as the N.P.L. projector, since it was developed at the National Physical Laboratory.

It consists of a lamp-house whose optical outlet contains a condenser lens to give even illumination. The object to be projected is mounted on a stage between the condensers and the projection lens, which throws an enlarged image on the screen as shown in fig. 2.23.

The whole projector may be moved on rails normal to the screen to give the required degree of enlargement, and the work stage may be moved relative to the projection lens for focusing purposes. This focusing motion can be made from the screen by an ingenious arrangement of wires and pulleys. Thus an extremely sharp image can be produced at the screen without continual walking from screen to instrument.

An interesting point about the instrument is that to accommodate screw threads the work stage has centres and can be swung out of normal to the optical axis. This is to avoid interference due to the helix angle. If the thread is mounted with its axis normal to the optical axis the top of the thread, which is projected, is at an angle to the optical axis because of the thread helix.

By swinging the thread through its helix angle the thread helix is set parallel to the light rays. However, the flank angle is defined as being measured on a plane section parallel to the thread axis. This means that turning the

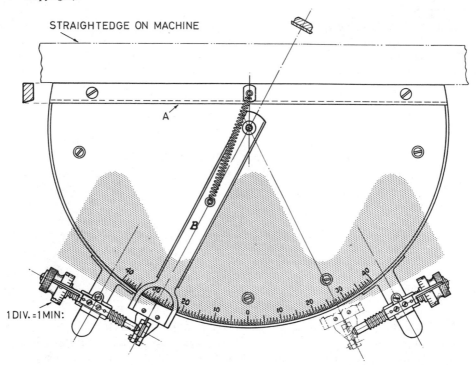

STRAIGHTEDGE ON MACHINE

1 DIV. = 1 MIN:

thread through the helix angle has a fore-shortening effect and induces a narrowing of the thread image as projected on the screen.

This problem can be overcome by swinging the lamp-house through the helix angle so that the light rays are not impeded as they pass through the thread to the objective lens.

Note that in this case the lens and screen are parallel to the thread axis and the fore-shortening effect, with its consequent distortion of the flank angles, is eliminated.

The actual measurement is made from a shadow protractor mounted on a ledge on the screen. The angle of the ledge can be adjusted until it is parallel to the image of the crests or roots of the thread. It is then assumed to be parallel to the thread axis and is used as a datum or base for the measurement.

The shadow protractor and image set up for measurement are shown in fig. 2.23.

Microscopic Flank Angle Measurement. Thread flank angles can be measured by a microscope with a goniometric head. This consists of a clear glass screen in the focal plane of the objective lens, carrying datum lines which can be rotated through 360°, the angle of rotation being measured direct to 1′ and by estimation to fractions of a minute.

The thread gauge is mounted on centres and illuminated from below. The microscope is mounted above the thread in such a way that it can be swivelled to be in line with the thread helix and avoid interference of the image. This is shown in fig. 2.24.

The centres are mounted on slideways which enable them to be moved through co-ordinate dimensions by micrometers reading to 0·002 mm, on a rotary table.

In operation, the microscope is focused with its axis vertical, on a focusing bar set so that the microscope is focused on a plane through the line of the centres, i.e., the axis of the thread to be measured. The thread is then set up in place of the focusing bar and the microscope swung through the helix angle of the thread to avoid interference.

The datum lines in the microscope head are set to zero and the table is rotated until the crests of the thread image coincide with the horizontal datum. The table is then locked and the datum lines in the microscope eyepiece rotated until they coincide with the thread flanks. The flank angles are then read off the eyepiece scale.

This equipment is normally among the attachments which can be set up on a tool-maker's microscope. The readings and settings can either be made through the microscope eyepiece or viewed on a screen as shown in fig. 2.25.

It should be noted that the optical axis is not normal to the thread axis and some distortion of the image still occurs. However, this technique is quite easy to set up and produces results of a reasonably high order of accuracy.

Whichever method is used, errors on both right and left flanks should be determined, as each can cause interference with the mating thread independently of the other, and both cause a change in effective diameter of the thread under test.

Effect of Flank Angle Errors. Consider a vee thread having flat crests and roots, of correct pitch but having an error on one flank only. The effect is to foul the mating thread above the pitch line if the error is positive and below the pitch line if the error is negative, as shown in fig. 2.26. In either case the effective diameter of the nut must be increased for an external thread if fouling is to be avoided, the diametral increase being δE_d.

It can be shown that for Whitworth threads,

$$\delta E_d = 0{\cdot}010\ 5p(\delta\theta_1 + \delta\theta_2)$$

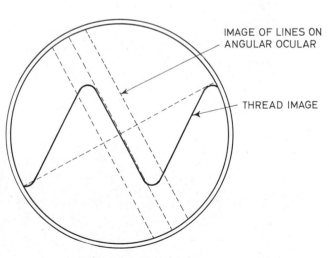

Fig. 2.24 Microscopic measurement of flank angles.

EYEPIECE

ANGULAR OCULAR IN FOCAL PLANE OF OBJECTIVE LENS

MICROSCOPE AXIS TILTED THROUGH HELIX ANGLE

PLANE OF IMAGE
PLANE OF TRUE PITCH

LIGHT SOURCE

IMAGE OF LINES ON ANGULAR OCULAR

THREAD IMAGE

Fig. 2.25 Screen viewer for microscopic measurement of flank angles.

and for B.A. threads ($47\frac{1}{2}°$),
$$\delta E_d = 0\cdot009\ 1p\ (\delta\theta_1 + \delta\theta_2)$$
and for Unified threads (60°),
$$\delta E_d = 0\cdot009\ 8p\ (\delta\theta_1 + \delta\theta_2)$$
and for Metric threads (60°),
$$\delta E_d = 0\cdot011\ 5p\ (\delta\theta_1 + \delta\theta_2)$$

where the values of $\delta\theta_1$ and $\delta\theta_2$ are the flank angle errors in *degrees*, regardless of sign, and p is the nominal pitch of the thread being measured.

PITCH ERRORS IN SCREW THREADS

If a screw thread is generated by a single-point cutting tool its pitch depends on

(a) the ratio of linear velocity of the tool and angular velocity of the work being correct

(b) this ratio being constant.

If these conditions are not satisfied, pitch errors will occur, the type of error being determined by which of the above conditions is not satisfied. Whatever type of error is present, the net result is to cause the total length of thread engaged to be too great or too small and this error in overall length of thread is called the *cumulative pitch error*. This, then, is the error which must be determined. It can be obtained either by

(a) measuring individual thread-to-thread errors and adding them algebraically, i.e., with due regard to sign

(b) measuring the total length of thread, from a datum, at each thread and subtracting from the nominal value.

TYPES OF PITCH ERROR

Progressive Pitch Error. This error occurs when the tool–work velocity ratio is constant but incorrect. It may be caused through using an incorrect gear train, or an approximate gear train between the work and the lead screw as when producing a metric thread from an inch-pitch lead screw with no translatory gear available. More commonly, it is caused by pitch errors in the lead screw of the lathe or other gener-

ating machine.

It the pitch error per thread is δp, the cumulative pitch error at any position along the thread is $n\delta p$ where n is the number of threads considered. A graph of cumulative pitch error against length of thread is therefore a straight line [fig. 2.27(a)].

Periodic Pitch Error. This type of error occurs when the tool–work velocity ratio is not constant. It may be caused by pitch errors in the gears connecting the work and the lead screw or by an axial movement of the lead screw due to worn thrust faces. Such a movement is superimposed on the normal tool motion reproduced on the work. It will be appreciated that errors due to these causes are cyclic, i.e., the pitch increases to a maximum, reduces through normal to a minimum and so on.

A graph of cumulative pitch error is thus of approximately sinusoidal form, as in fig. 2.27(b), and the maximum cumulative pitch error is the total error between the greatest positive and negative peaks within the length of thread engaged.

Thread Drunkenness. A drunken thread is a particular case of a periodic pitch error recurring at intervals of one pitch. This means that the pitch measured parallel to the thread axis is always correct and all that is in fact happening is that the thread is not cut to a true helix. A development of the thread helix is a curve and not a straight line. Such errors are extremely difficult to determine and except on large threads do not have any great effect.

MEASUREMENT OF PITCH ERROR

Apart from drunken threads, pitch errors can be determined by using a pitch measuring machine, the design of which originated at the National Physical Laboratory. A round-nosed stylus engages the thread approximately at the pitch line and operates a simple type of fiducial indicator. The thread is moved axially relative to the stylus, which can ride over the thread crests, by means of a micrometer whose readings are noted each

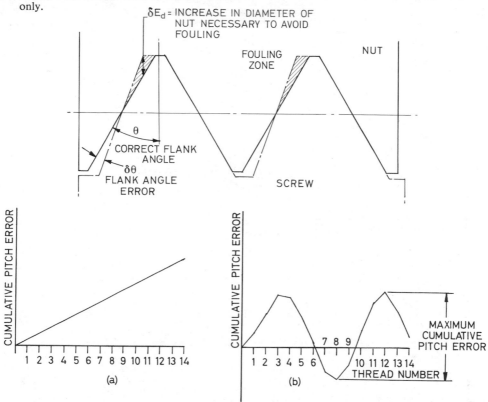

Fig. 2.26 Nut of perfect form mating with a screw having a flank angle error $\delta\theta$ on one flank only.

δE_d = INCREASE IN DIAMETER OF NUT NECESSARY TO AVOID FOULING

FOULING ZONE

NUT

θ

CORRECT FLANK ANGLE

$\delta\theta$

FLANK ANGLE ERROR

SCREW

CUMULATIVE PITCH ERROR

1 2 3 4 5 6 7 8 9 10 11 12 13 14

(a)

CUMULATIVE PITCH ERROR

1 2 3 4 5 6   7 8 9   10 11 12 13 14
THREAD NUMBER

MAXIMUM CUMULATIVE PITCH ERROR

(b)

Fig. 2.27 Progressive pitch error and periodic pitch error.

time the indicator pointer comes up to its fiducial mark.

The mechanism of the fiducial indicator is of interest and is shown in fig. 2.28.

The stylus is mounted in a block supported by a thin metal strip and a strut. It can thus move back and forth over the threads, the strut and strip giving a parallel-type motion. If the side pressures on the stylus, P and P_1, are unequal, the strip twists and the block pivots about the strut. The forked arm causes the crank to rotate and with it the pointer. Thus the pointer will only meet the fiducial mark when the pressures P and P_1 caused by the stylus bearing on the thread flanks are the same in each thread.

Errors in the micrometer are reduced by a cam-type correction bar and, with care, accuracies of greater than 0·002 mm can be consistently achieved.

If thread-to-thread pitches are required, each micrometer reading is subtracted from the next. More usually, cumulative pitch errors are required and can be obtained by simply noting the micrometer readings and subtracting them from the expected reading. The test should normally be repeated with the thread turned through 180°, in case the thread axis does not coincide with the axis of the centres on which the screw is mounted. The mean of the two readings, usually determined graphically, is then used as the pitch

39

Fig. 2.28 Fiducial indicator used on pitch-measuring machine.

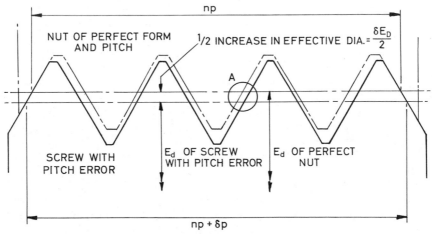

FIDUCIAL MARK

POINTER

FORK

CRANK

P

P₁

TRAVERSE ALONG THREAD

RADIAL MOTION ALLOWS STYLUS TO RIDE OVER THREAD

STRUT

FLEXIBLE STRIP

Fig. 2.29(*a*) Screw having cumulative pitch error δp in mesh with a nut of perfect form and pitch.

np

NUT OF PERFECT FORM AND PITCH

½ INCREASE IN EFFECTIVE DIA. $= \dfrac{\delta E_D}{2}$

A

SCREW WITH PITCH ERROR

E_d OF SCREW WITH PITCH ERROR

E_d OF PERFECT NUT

$np + \delta p$

error.

Effects of Pitch Errors. When a thread has a pitch error it will only enter a nut of perfect form and pitch if the nut is made oversize. This is true whether the pitch error is positive or negative, and thus, whatever pitch error is present in a screw plug gauge, the gauge will reject work which is near the low limit of size.

Consider a thread with a cumulative pitch error of δp over a number of threads, i.e., its length is $np + \delta p$. If such a screw is engaged with a nut of perfect form and pitch they will mate as shown in fig. 2.29(*a*).

Consider an enlarged view of the thread flanks at A, as in fig. 2.29(*b*).

From the diagram

$$\tan \theta = \frac{\dfrac{\delta p}{2}}{\dfrac{\delta E_d}{2}}$$

$$= \frac{\delta p}{\delta E_d}$$

$$\therefore \ \delta E_d = \delta p \cotan \theta$$

where δp is the cumulative pitch error over

40

Fig. 2.29(b) Enlarged view at A.

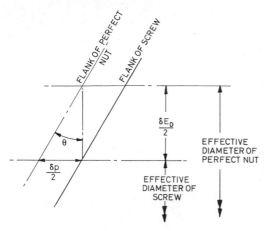

the length of engagement and δE_d is the equivalent increase in effective diameter.

The importance of this is emphasised when a Whitworth thread is considered, in which the flank angle θ is $27\frac{1}{2}°$ and cotangent $27\frac{1}{2}°$ = 1·920.

For Whitworth threads, $\delta E_d = 1·920 \ \delta p$
For Metric threads, $\delta E_d = 1·732 \ \delta p$

The pitch error is therefore almost doubled when the equivalent increase in effective diameter is calculated. A screw plug gauge having a cumulative pitch error of 0·006 mm will thus reject all work within 0·012 mm (approximately) of the low limit in the case of Whitworth threads, and within 0·01 mm in the case of Metric threads.

MEASUREMENT OF SIMPLE EFFECTIVE DIAMETER The simple effective diameter of a screw thread may be defined as the diameter of an imaginary cylinder co-axial with the thread axis which cuts the thread so that the distance between any pair of intercepts and adjacent flanks is half the pitch. This is explained more simply and diagrammatically in fig. 2.30.

Measurement of the simple effective diameter is carried out on the floating-carriage diameter measuring machine described on p. 34, the prisms used for measuring minor

diameter being replaced by steel wires, or cylinders, whose size is chosen so that they 'pitch' approximately at the effective diameter. Such cylinders are known as 'Best Size' wires and enable nominal values of pitch and flank angle to be used in subsequent calculations. Such cylinders can be purchased from most manufacturers of gauging equipment and their size is calibrated.

As for the minor diameter, a reading is taken *with the cylinders in place*, over a setting cylinder. A reading is then taken with the cylinders engaged in the thread. The difference in the readings is the difference between the diameter of the setting cylinder and the dimension T *under* the wires when engaged with the thread.

The geometry of this arrangement is shown in fig. 2.30, and is used in deriving the expression required to calculate the simple effective diameter.

From the diagram

$$E_d = T + 2x$$

In $\triangle$ ABC, $\tan \theta = \dfrac{BC}{AB}$

$$\therefore \ AB = BC \ \text{cotan} \ \theta$$

But by definition of the simple effective diameter, BC = $\frac{1}{4}$ pitch

$$\therefore \ AB = \frac{p}{4} \ \text{cotan} \ \theta \qquad \ldots (1)$$

In $\triangle$ ADE,

$$\sin \theta = \frac{DE}{AE}$$

$$\therefore \ AE = DE \ \text{cosec} \ \theta$$

But   DE = $\frac{1}{2}$ diameter of the measuring wires

$$\therefore \ AE = \frac{d}{2} \ \text{cosec} \ \theta$$

Now $x = AB - AF$
and AF = AE − EF

but EF also = $\dfrac{d}{2}$

41

Fig. 2.30 Calculation of simple effective diameter.

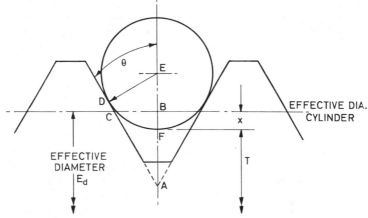

$$\therefore \ AF = \frac{d}{2} \ \text{cosec} \ \theta - \frac{d}{2}$$

$$AF = \frac{d}{2} \ (\text{cosec} \ \theta - 1) \dots (2)$$

Subtracting (2) from (1) to obtain x we get

$$x = \frac{p}{4} \ \text{cotan} \ \theta - \frac{d}{2} \ (\text{cosec} \ \theta - 1)$$

But $E_d = T + 2x$ and the term $2x$ is constant for any given thread if the nominal values of pitch and flank angle are used, as they may be if the best size wire is used. The term $2x$ is usually called P, and 'P values' can be tabulated for any pair of wires to cover the range of standard threads for which that pair are suitable.

$$\therefore \ P = 2x = \frac{p}{2} \ \cot \theta - (\text{cosec} \ \theta - 1)d$$

$$\therefore \ E_d = T + P$$

in which $T =$ measured dimension *under* the wires

$$P = \frac{p}{2} \ \cot \theta - (\text{cosec} \ \theta - 1)d$$

$p =$ nominal pitch
$d =$ wire diameter
$\theta =$ nominal flank angle
$\ \ \ =$ semi-angle of thread

Calculation of the 'Best Size' of Wire. Normally when measuring cylinders are pur-

chased they are of the best size wire for a given thread. However, if they are not available it is best to make them rather than use incorrect wire sizes, as these may incur large diametral errors due to flank angle errors.

In fig. 2.31, $AB = \frac{1}{2}$ wire diameter and $BC = \frac{1}{4}$ pitch.

$$\cos \theta = \frac{BC}{AB}$$

$$AB = \frac{BC}{\cos \theta}$$

$$\frac{d}{2} = \frac{p}{4 \cos \theta}$$

$$d = \frac{p}{2 \cos \theta}$$

Note. Study of this simple diagram may suggest a simple method of determining the simple effective diameter. This must *not* be

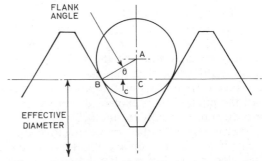

Fig. 2.31 'Best size' cylinder contacting thread at effective diameter.

used since the wire will rarely pitch on the effective diameter. The discrepancy will not sensibly affect the previous method if flank angle errors are present, but will have considerable effect if the incorrect simplified method is used.

Measurement over the Wires. If a measuring machine is not available, the simple effective diameter can be determined by measuring *over* three wires or, a better method, by the use of 'Ovee' gauges, which may be sprung over the thread as shown in fig. 2.32.

If the dimension T_1 *over* the wires is determined:

$$\text{then } E_d = T_1 + P_1 = T + P$$
$$\text{and } T_1 = T + 2d$$
$$\therefore \ P_1 = P - 2d = \frac{p}{2} \cot \theta - d (\operatorname{cosec} \theta - 1) - 2d$$
$$\text{or } P_1 = \frac{p}{2} \cot \theta - d (\operatorname{cosec} \theta + 1)$$

Corrections for Raking and Elastic Compression. The expression for simple effective diameter derived above is based on the assumption that the measurement is made over a plane section of the thread parallel to the thread axis, i.e., measurement is over a series of annular grooves of thread form. This of course is not so and the effect of measuring over a helix is to throw the measuring cylinders out slightly and increase the measured value by an amount C. At the same time measuring pressure applied to point contacts causes elastic deformation of both the wires and the thread flanks and reduces the measured value by an amount e. The correct value is obtained by applying corrections of $-C$ and $+e$.

$$\therefore \ E_d = T + P - C + e$$

The magnitudes of C and e are both normally very small and as they are of opposite sign their total effect is still less, so they may normally be disregarded. If it is required to determine their values for the measurement of reference gauges, readers are referred to the National Physical Laboratory Notes on Applied Science II, 'Measurement of Screw Threads', obtainable from H.M. Stationery Office.

VIRTUAL EFFECTIVE DIAMETER

It has been shown above that the effect of pitch and flank angle errors on a screw plug gauge is to cause a virtual increase in the effective diameter in the case of external screw threads. Thus the virtual effective diameter is defined as the effective diameter of the smallest nut of perfect form and pitch which the screw will enter. This is of course the vital dimension of a screw plug gauge and it is obtained by adding to the simple effective diameter amounts depending on the magni-

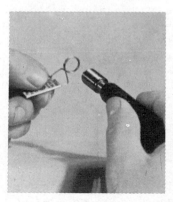

Fig. 2.32 Use of Ovee spring gauges. (Courtesy of the O-Vee Spring Gauges Ltd.)

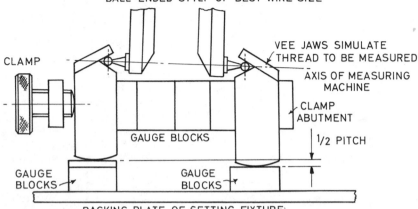

Fig. 2.33 Setting a measuring machine for determining simple effective diameter of an internal thread. Note the vee jaws offset by half pitch and the floating work stage allowing the fixture to swing into the attitude taken up by the thread.

ARMS OF MEASURING MACHINE CARRYING
BALL-ENDED STYLI OF "BEST WIRE" SIZE

VEE JAWS SIMULATE
THREAD TO BE MEASURED

AXIS OF MEASURING
MACHINE

CLAMP

CLAMP
ABUTMENT

GAUGE BLOCKS

1/2 PITCH

GAUGE
BLOCKS

GAUGE
BLOCKS

BACKING PLATE OF SETTING FIXTURE

tude of the pitch and flank angle errors.

∴ Virtual effective diameter
= Simple effective diameter
$$+ K_1 p(\delta\theta_1 + \delta\theta_2) + \delta p \cot \theta$$
in which $K_1 =$ a constant depending on the thread form
$p =$ thread pitch
$\theta =$ thread flank angle
$\delta p =$ pitch error over length of engagement

$\delta\theta_1$ and $\delta\theta_2$ are errors on RH and LH flanks in degrees, regardless of sign.

For a Metric thread
virtual effective diameter = simple effective diameter $+ 0.011\ 5p(\delta\theta_1 + \delta\theta_2) + 1.732\delta p$
and *for a Unified thread*
virtual effective diameter = simple effective diameter $+ 0.009\ 8p(\delta\theta_1 + \delta\theta_2) + 1.732\delta p$
and *for a Whitworth thread*
virtual effective diameter = simple effective diameter $+ 0.010\ 5p(\delta\theta_1 + \delta\theta_2) + 1.920\delta p$

MEASUREMENT OF SCREW RING GAUGES

The problems of measuring screw ring gauges are essentially the same as those for plug gauges but the difficulty is increased by the inaccessibility of the thread form and dimensions.

The pitch can be measured on a normal screw-pitch measuring machine, using a special attachment to allow entry of the stylus, rather like a boring bar.

The flank angle can only be measured by making a plaster cast of the thread, which must be of less than half the diameter of the thread and *lifted out*—not screwed out, or the cast may be distorted. The cast may then be projected in the normal way.

The simple effective diameter is measured by using ball-ended stylii, of 'best wire' size, in a measuring machine. The machine is set to a master, consisting of a pair of vee-notched arms analogising the thread (i.e., the master is built up so that the effective diameter of the vees is the nominal value for the thread to be measured), as shown in fig. 2.33.

These methods can only be used for fairly large threads. The only practicable method with very small screw ring gauges is to procure very accurate master screw plug gauges whose sizes differ by the gauge tolerance, and use them to test the gauge on a 'GO' or 'NOT GO' basis.

Fig. 2.34 Refraction. Note that the light is bent towards the normal on entry and away from the normal on leaving the glass.

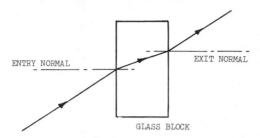

Fig. 2.35 Refraction of light through a glass prism.

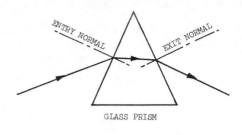

It should be noted that the effect of pitch and flank angle errors on a screw ring gauge is opposite to their effect on a screw plug gauge (i.e., these errors tend to *reduce* the simple effective diameter and the corrections for these errors must be subtracted and not added).

OPTICAL METHODS OF MEASUREMENT

OPTICAL PRINCIPLES

1. *Refraction.* If a ray of light passes from a less dense to a more dense material, e.g., from air to glass, it is 'bent' or *refracted* towards the more dense material, as shown in fig. 2.34. As it passes from the more dense to the less dense material it is again refracted as shown. If we pass the ray through a prism it is refracted as shown in fig. 2.35.

A series of prisms can be arranged as shown in fig. 2.36 to bring all the light rays to a point, or *focus*. In practice this series of prisms is made in one piece and called a *lens*, and the distance from the focus to the lens is called the *focal length*.

2. *Projection.* If an object is placed behind such a lens and illuminated from behind with a parallel beam of light its image will be *projected* by the lens, the extreme rays travelling the paths shown in fig. 2.37. By the properties of similar triangles:

$$\frac{\text{size of image}}{\text{size of object}} = \frac{l}{f}$$

where l = distance between lens and screen
f = distance between lens and object.

This is the principle of the optical projector. It requires a mounting for the work, a projection lens and a screen, and a lamp-

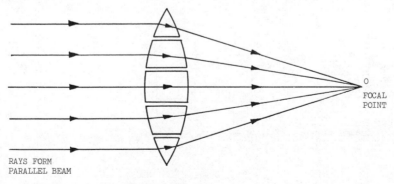

Fig. 2.36 A lens considered as a series of prisms. The light passing through the centre of the lens is not refracted.

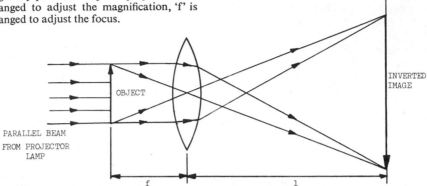

Fig. 2.37 Light ray path in an optical projector. 'l' is changed to adjust the magnification, 'f' is changed to adjust the focus.

house which projects a parallel beam of light. To vary the magnification it is necessary to adjust the distance between the lens and the screen, and to focus the instrument the work stage must be moved to adjust the distance between the object and the lens.

Such an instrument is shown in fig. 2.38 and has been described on p. 36 as applied to the measurement of screw-thread flank angles. It is also useful for projecting enlarged images of profile gauges and form tools. Modern projectors working on the same principle are more compact, using prisms and mirrors to turn the light path and project the image on

to a screen convenient to the operator and work stage so that all operations can be carried out from one position.

It must be emphasised that an optical projector will only enlarge linear dimensions; angles are not magnified. The lengths of the two faces making the angle are magnified and enable angular settings to be simplified, but the reading of the angle requires some other device such as the flank-angle protractor shown in fig. 2.23, or a microscope reading on a finely-divided angular scale. This is described in detail on p. 36.

3. *Reflection.* If a ray of light strikes a

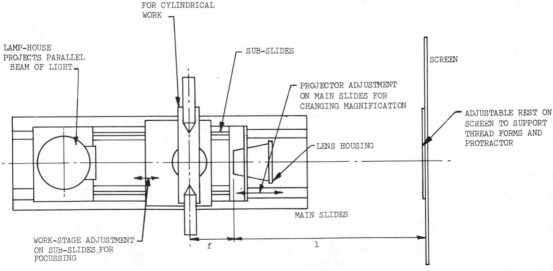

Fig. 2.38 Essentials of an optical projector shown in plan view.

46

mirror at an angle θ to the normal to the mirror, the reflected ray will also make the angle θ with the normal, as shown in fig. 2.39.

Fig. 2.39 Reflection from a plane surface.

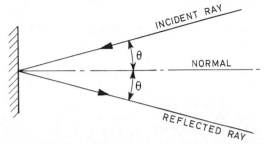

The angle of incidence is equal to the angle of reflection.

If now the reflector is turned through a small angle $\delta\theta$, the normal also turns through $\delta\theta$, making the angle of incidence $(\theta + \delta\theta)$.

The reflected angle will also be $(\theta + \delta\theta)$, as shown in fig. 2.40.

$\therefore$ Total angle between incident

$$\text{and reflected ray} = 2(\theta + \delta\theta)$$
$$= 2\theta + 2\delta\theta$$

Original angle between incident

$$\text{and reflected ray} = 2\theta$$

$\therefore$ Angle turned by reflected ray $= 2\delta\theta$

This is the principle of the *optical lever*.

If a mirror is turned through a small angle the reflected ray turns through twice that angle.

This principle is used in optical instruments to give a 'free' doubling of the magnification.

4. *Collimation and Auto-Collimation.* On referring again to fig. 2.36 it is obvious that if we reverse the situation, with a suitable lens, and place a point of light at the focal point, O, of the lens it will be projected as a parallel beam of light. Such a lens is called a *collimat-*

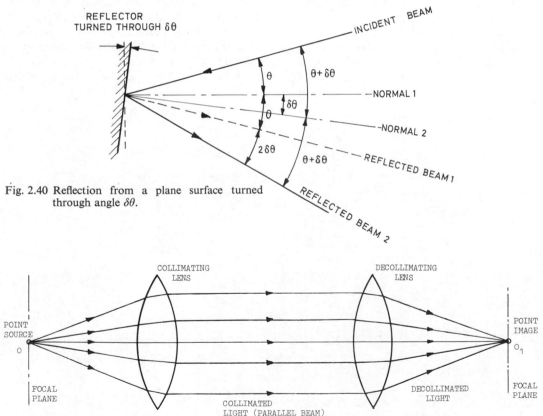

Fig. 2.40 Reflection from a plane surface turned through angle $\delta\theta$.

Fig. 2.41 Collimation and de-collimation of light.

47

ing lens. If the parallel beam of light projected from a collimating lens strikes a similar lens it is refocused or *decollimated* at point O_1 as shown in fig. 2.41.

If, instead of striking another lens, the parallel beam strikes a plane reflector it will be thrown back into the collimating lens which will refocus it at O. This is called *auto-collimation* and is shown in fig. 42(a). If the mirror is now tilted through a small angle δ, the reflected beam will turn through 2δ (see optical lever above) and will be refocused at point O_1, a distance x from the source, as shown in fig. 2.42(b). Thus the distance between the image and the source, x, is a measure of the angular displacement of the reflector and from fig. 2.42 (b):

In triangle POO_1,

$$\frac{OO_1}{OP} = \tan 2\delta$$

$$x = OO_1 = OP \tan 2\delta$$

OP is the focal length 'f' of the lens and as δ is small

$$\tan 2\delta = 2\delta \text{ radians}$$
$$\therefore \quad x = 2\delta f \text{ millimetres}$$

There are certain important points about this expression which are not immediately apparent. These are:

(a) The distance between the reflector and the lens has no effect on the separation x between source and reflected image.

(b) For high sensitivity, i.e., a large value of x for a small angular deviation δ, a long focal length is required.

(c) Although the distance of the reflector does not affect the reading x, if, at a given value of δ, the reflector is moved too far back, all the reflected rays will miss the lens completely and no image will be formed. Thus, for a wide range of readings, the minimum distance between lens and reflector is essential. This is particularly important where the principle is used in optical comparators, where it limits the maximum remoteness of the reflector if the full range of readings of the instrument is to be used.

Auto-collimators are essentially instru-

Fig. 2.42(a) Point source of light in focal plane of a collimating lens.

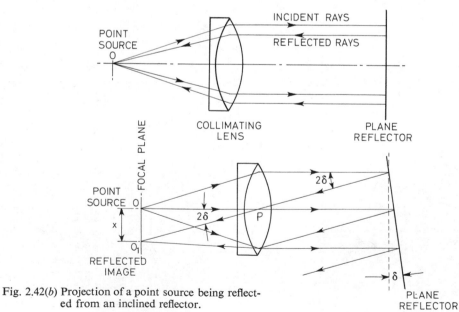

Fig. 2.42(b) Projection of a point source being reflected from an inclined reflector.

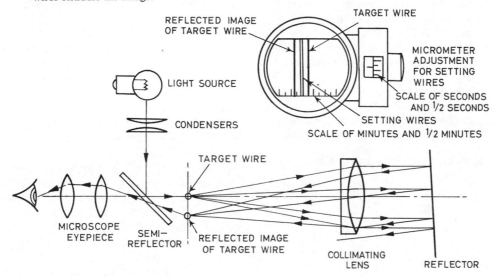

Fig. 2.43 Optical system and view through eyepiece of auto-collimator. A reading is taken by adjusting the micrometer until the setting wires straddle the image.

ments for the measurement of small angular displacements but, as will be seen, can be easily adapted to make an optical comparator for linear measurement. In all cases, the projection and reflection of a point source of light is impracticable and, depending upon the type of instrument, the image of a target wire or of an illuminated scale is projected.

THE MICROPTIC AUTO-COLLIMATOR

Since the idea of projecting the image of a point source of light is not practicable, in this instrument a pair of target wires in the focal plane of the collimating lens is illuminated from behind and their image is projected. Fig. 2.43 shows the optical arrangement of the instrument, the projected image striking a plane reflector and the reflection of the image being brought to a focus in the plane of the target wires.

The wires and their image are viewed simultaneously in an eyepiece, which also contains a pair of adjustable setting wires and a scale. The setting wires are adjusted by a micrometer until they straddle the reflected image

(not the target wire). The scale is read to the nearest $\frac{1}{2}'$ and the micrometer drum, which moves the wires $\frac{1}{2}'$ per revolution, is divided into 60 equal parts. Thus 1 division of the micrometer drum represents an angular deflection of the reflector of 0·5″ of arc. With care, and given a rigid mounting for the instrument, repeat readings of 0·2″ are possible.

The instrument normally has a range of readings of 10′ of arc up to a range of 10 m. It is invaluable in machine tool alignment testing or for any measurement involving small angular deviations.

THE ANGLE DEKKOR

In this application of the collimating principle, an illuminated scale is set in the focal plane of the collimating lens outside the field of view of a microscope eyepiece. It is then projected as a parallel beam and strikes a plane reflector below the instrument. It is reflected and refocused by the lens so that its image is in the field of view of the eyepiece. The image falls, not across a simple datum line, but across a similar fixed scale at right angles to the illuminated image. Thus the reading on the illuminated scale measures angular deviations from one axis at 90° to the optical axis, and the reading on the fixed scale gives the deviation about an axis mutually at right angles to the other two.

This feature enables angular errors in two planes to be dealt with or, more important, to ensure that the readings on a setting master and on the work are the same in one plane, the error being read in the other. Thus, induced compound-angle errors are avoided.

The optical system and the view in the eye-

Fig. 2.44 Optical system of an Angle Dekkor.

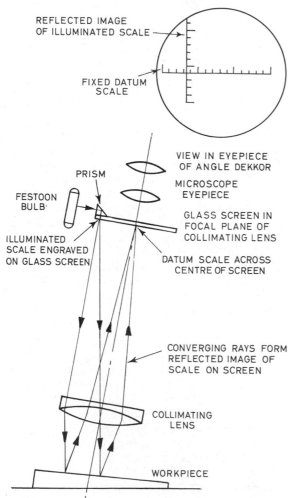

REFLECTED IMAGE OF ILLUMINATED SCALE

FIXED DATUM SCALE

PRISM

VIEW IN EYEPIECE OF ANGLE DEKKOR

MICROSCOPE EYEPIECE

FESTOON BULB·

GLASS SCREEN IN FOCAL PLANE OF COLLIMATING LENS

ILLUMINATED SCALE ENGRAVED ON GLASS SCREEN

DATUM SCALE ACROSS CENTRE OF SCREEN

CONVERGING RAYS FORM REFLECTED IMAGE OF SCALE ON SCREEN

COLLIMATING LENS

WORKPIECE

piece are shown in fig. 2.44. The physical features simply consist of a lapped flat and reflective base above which the optical details are mounted in a tube on an adjustable bracket.

Although the Angle Dekkor is not as sensitive as the auto-collimator it is extremely useful for a wide range of angular measurements at short distances. It therefore finds its application in toolroom-type inspection. Readings direct to 1′ over a range of 50′ can be taken and, by estimation, readings down to about 0·2′ are possible.

THE OPTICAL COMPARATOR If an Angle Dekkor is used in conjunction with a reflector whose angular position depends on the position of a measuring plunger as shown in fig. 2.45, when the plunger is raised a small distance h and is at a distance y from the reflector pivot,

$$\text{Angle } \delta = \frac{h}{y} \text{ radians}$$

Applying the auto-collimator principle, the displacement x of the scale image is

$$x = 2\delta f$$

$$= \frac{2h}{y} \cdot f$$

The magnification is in the ratio of the scale movement to the plunger movement, i.e.,

$$\text{Magnification} = \frac{x}{y} = \frac{2hf}{y} \times \frac{1}{h}$$

$$= \frac{2f}{y}$$

This is increased further by the magnifying power of the eyepiece and thus:

Overall magnification

$$= \frac{2f}{y} \times \text{eyepiece magnification.}$$

In practice, the reflector is built into the instrument and a prism is used to give a horizontal eyepiece, as shown in fig. 2.46. To avoid eye strain, most instruments of this type do not use an eyepiece but project the image of the scale and datum on to a screen.

An advantage of optical comparators over other types of comparator is that they can be read clearly under poor lighting conditions. Also, very little can go wrong with them, since the only moving parts are the plunger and the reflector.

ANGULAR MEASUREMENT

The ability to control and measure angles to high degrees of accuracy is just as important as the control and measurement of length. Just as working standards of length are necessary, so are standards of angle required, to form a basis for angular measurements and comparisons. There are available

to engineers three standards of angle, those derived from combinations of lengths, e.g., the *sine bar*; the angular equivalents of gauge blocks, or *combination angle gauges*; and certain natural standards of angle such as the circle, the right angle, and the flat 180°.

ANGLES DERIVED FROM COMBINATIONS OF LENGTH The most common form of angular setting device or measuring instrument using derived angles is the sine bar. In Book 1 various types of sine-bar equipment were shown and it is not proposed to repeat these descriptions. There are, however, certain possibilities of error arising from the misuse of a sine bar which should be avoided as much as possible.

(*a*) *Magnitude of Angle.* Consider the

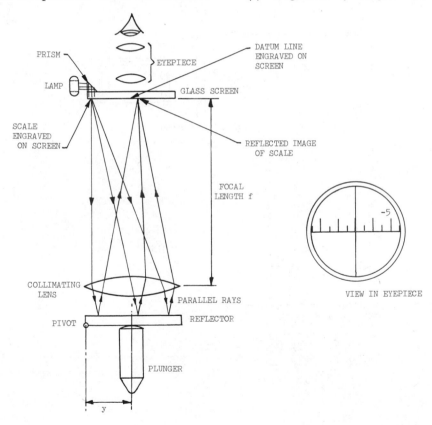

Fig. 2.45 Diagram of optical comparator.

effect of an error in the height of the gauge blocks used in setting a sine bar for different angles, say 15°, 45° and 70°. To exaggerate the effect, assume a catastrophic error of 1·0 mm in the height of the gauge blocks used.

Let angle $\theta = 15°$
$$\sin 15° = 0·258\ 82$$
Gauge block height $= 200 \times 0·258\ 8$
(for 200 mm sine bar)
$$h = 51·76\ \text{mm}$$
Due to error
Actual height $h = 52·76\ \text{mm}$

$$\text{Actual } \sin \theta = \frac{52·76\ \text{mm}}{200\ \text{mm}}$$
$$= 0·263\ 8$$
Actual angle $\theta = 15°\ 18'$
Error in angle $\theta = 18'$

Let angle $\theta = 45°$
$$\sin \theta = 0·707\ 1$$
$$h = 141·42\ \text{mm}$$
Actual height $h = 142·42\ \text{mm}$
Actual $\sin \theta = 0·712\ 1$
$$\theta = 45°\ 24'$$
Error in angle $\theta = 24'$

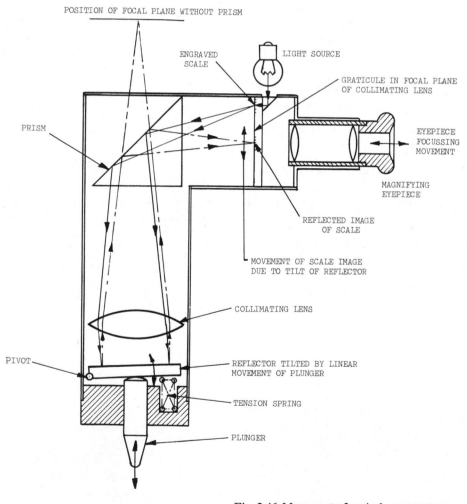

POSITION OF FOCAL PLANE WITHOUT PRISM

ENGRAVED SCALE

LIGHT SOURCE

GRATICULE IN FOCAL PLANE OF COLLIMATING LENS

PRISM

EYEPIECE FOCUSSING MOVEMENT

MAGNIFYING EYEPIECE

REFLECTED IMAGE OF SCALE

MOVEMENT OF SCALE IMAGE DUE TO TILT OF REFLECTOR

COLLIMATING LENS

PIVOT

REFLECTOR TILTED BY LINEAR MOVEMENT OF PLUNGER

TENSION SPRING

PLUNGER

Fig. 2.46 Movement of optical comparator.

Let angle $\theta = 70°$
$\sin \theta = 0.939\ 7$
$h = 187.94$ mm
Actual height $h = 188.94$ mm
Actual $\sin \theta = 0.944\ 7$
$\theta = 70°\ 52'$
Error in angle $\theta = 52'$

Thus, as the nominal angle increases the error increases, even though the gauge block error remains constant. If the above procedure is repeated at intervals of 10° for all angles between 0° and 90° a graph can be plotted of error in angle against nominal angle. It will then be found that for angles over 45° the increase in error is excessive. For this reason, measurement of such angles should be avoided and, where possible, the work should be turned through 90° and the complement of the angle used.

(b) *Alignment Errors.* If the workpiece is not accurately aligned with the sine bar, a compound angle results, giving rise to error. Many sine bars are fitted with a bar along one edge to enable correct alignment to be maintained. For conical work, sine bar centres should be used.

Other cases where the measured angle is determined from a combination of lengths are in the measurement of angles of taper of taper plug gauges, taper ring gauges and taper bores.

MEASUREMENT OF TAPER PLUG GAUGES The angle of taper of a taper plug gauge can usually be determined by using sine centres but if these are not available the angle can be determined by making diametral measurements at known distances along the gauge.

The measurements are normally made over calibrated precision rollers of equal diameter, the separation of the individual measurements being controlled by gauge blocks. This arrangement is shown in fig. 2.47.

In triangle ABC, h is the height of the gauge blocks and $BC = (M_2 - M_1)/2$, in which M_1 and M_2 are the measurements over the

Fig. 2.47 Measurement of a taper plug gauge.

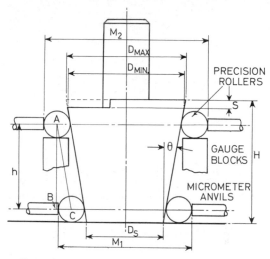

rollers.

$$\tan \theta = \frac{BC}{AB} = \frac{M_2 - M_1}{2h} \quad \ldots(1)$$

Thus the semi-angle of taper can be determined by direct measurement.

To find the maximum and minimum diameters at the top and bottom of the step it is first necessary to determine D_s, the diameter at the small end. Fig. 2.48 represents the small end of the gauge during the measurement of M_1.

Fig. 2.48 Measurement of the diameter of the small end of a taper plug gauge.

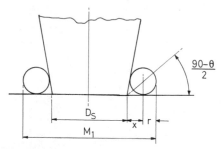

From fig. 2.48
$$M_1 = D_s + 2r + 2x$$
$$\tan\frac{(90 - \theta)}{2} = \frac{r}{x}$$

53

$$\therefore \ x = r \times \text{cotangent} \ \frac{(90 - \theta)}{2}$$

$$\therefore \ M_1 = D_s + 2r \left(1 + \cot \frac{90 - \theta}{2}\right)$$

$$\text{or } M_1 = D_s + d \left(1 + \cot \frac{90 - \theta}{2}\right)$$

where d = roller dia.

$$\therefore \ D_s = M_1 - d \left(1 + \cot \frac{90 - \theta}{2}\right)$$

Referring to equation (1) above, $\tan \theta$ is in fact equal to the increase in radius per unit of height.

$\therefore$ Increase in diameter per unit height
$$= 2 \tan \theta$$
$$\therefore \ D_{max} = D_s + 2H \tan \theta$$
$$\text{and } D_{min} = D_s + 2(H - S) \tan \theta$$
where H is the height of the gauge and S is the height of the step.

If a measurement M_3 is taken at some intermediate height between the positions for M_1 and M_2, two further values of θ can be determined. If all these values of angle are not the same then the taper is not a true cone, i.e., its sides are not straight. A check on roundness can also be made by carrying out the measurements M_1, M_2, and M_3, at different positions around the gauge.

Fig. 2.49 Measurement of a taper ring gauge.

MEASUREMENT OF TAPER RING GAUGES The procedure for measuring taper ring gauges is similar to that used for taper plug gauges, the measurements being made with precision calibrated balls and gauge blocks.
Again
$$\tan \theta = \frac{M_1 - M_2}{2h}$$

But in this case
$$D_L = M_1 + d \left[1 + \cot \frac{90 - \theta}{2}\right]$$

(where d = ball dia.)
$$\text{and } D_{max} = D_L - 2(H - S) \tan \theta$$
$$D_{min} = D_L - 2H \tan \theta$$

MEASUREMENT OF TAPER BORES The procedure described above can only be used where the taper bore is of large enough diameters to allow easy access of balls and gauge blocks. For smaller diameter tapers, angular and diametral measurements can be made by the arrangement shown in fig. 2.50, in which the heights at which balls of different diameters seat directly on the taper are measured.

The centre distance LM between the balls will be
$$LM = h_2 - h_1 - r_1 + r_2$$

$$\sin \frac{\theta}{2} = \frac{NL}{LM} = \frac{r_1 - r_2}{h_2 - h_1 - r_1 + r_2}$$

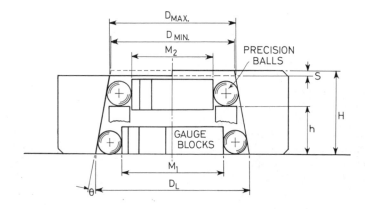

Fig. 2.50 Measurement of a taper bore.

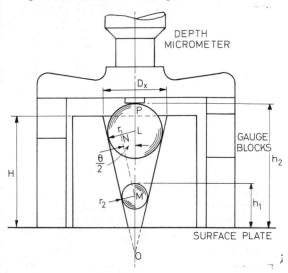

The semi-angle of the taper having been found, its uniformity may be determined by taking a further measurement on a ball of such diameter that it rests approximately mid-way along the length of the taper, and repeating the calculation for the new measured values obtained.

To find the diameter D_x at the large end of the taper:

$$\frac{OL}{LM} = \frac{r_1}{r_1 - r_2}$$

and $OP = OL + PL$

and $D_x = 2 \left(OP \tan \frac{\theta}{2} \right)$

The practical difficulties of this method of measurement are perhaps even more severe than in the previous case, especially if the taper has a small angle. The wedging effect of the balls and the consequent elastic deformation of both the balls and the gauge can cause appreciable errors in the measured values of h_1 and h_2, to give rise to related errors in the calculated angle. On no account should the balls be dropped into the taper. It is better if they are gently rolled into position with the axis of the taper lying almost horizontal.

Again, here is a case where practical experience of such measurement allows one to overcome the difficulties involved.

COMBINATION ANGLE GAUGES

Just as comparators for linear measurement are set to working standards of length, gauge blocks, so are some comparators for angular measurement set to working standards of angle known as combination angle gauges. These angle gauges have many similarities to gauge blocks; their working faces are flat and lapped to a wringing finish so that they can be combined by wringing together. Gauge blocks, however, can only be added but, by reversing their position relative to each other, combination angle gauges can also be subtracted, as shown in fig. 2.51.

Fig. 2.51 Addition and subtraction of combination angle gauges.

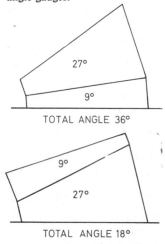

The gauges are made in sets consisting of thirteen gauges and a square block. The values of the angles used are arranged in a modified geometric progression with a common ratio of 3, as shown in the following table, and from this set any angle between 0° and 90° can be set up in steps of 0·05′ (3″). All gauges are marked < to indicate the 'thin' end. This may not be necessary with the larger angles, but a taper of 0·3′ or less is difficult to detect, even with a micrometer.

Degrees	Minutes	Decimal Minutes
1	1	0·05
3	3	0·1
9	9	0·3
27	27	0·5
41	square	block

Comparisons of angles by the use of an Angle Dekkor and combination angle gauges are quite simple. The nominal angle is made up with a suitable combination of angle gauges and the instrument is adjusted to obtain a reading from them, the gauges being adjusted on the table so that the illuminated scale crosses the fixed scale at approximately the mid-point. The gauges are then replaced by the workpiece, whose position is adjusted so that the reading on the fixed scale is the same. The reading on the illuminated scale is again noted and the difference in the two readings is the difference in the angle between the base and the face of the work, and the angle made by the combination angle gauges.

The work surface must be optically flat and reflective, but few work faces are made to this condition. It is therefore usually necessary to place a parallel reflector on the work surface. A gauge block serves this purpose admirably.

This method is ideally suited to relatively small workpieces. For example, the angles of a small vee block can be tested quickly, easily, and to an order of accuracy of 0·2′ by using an Angle Dekkor. Compare this with other possible methods and the advantages are quickly seen.

NATURAL STANDARDS OF ANGLE

Certain angles may be considered natural standards in that to determine their errors no standard is necessary and the measurement is direct rather than comparative. These angles are 90°, or the right angle, and 180°, or parallelism.

TESTING RIGHT ANGLES (90°)

The principle involved in testing a right angle without reference to a standard can be illustrated by considering a draughtsman's set square. If the square is placed against a tee square and a line drawn down the vertical face, the square turned over and another line drawn as shown in fig. 2.52, any angle between the lines is *double* the error in the right angle. This simple principle of reversal is used in almost all cases of testing squareness, the equipment used being mechanical, mechanical with an optical indicator or optical.

(a) Mechanical Squareness Tester. This instrument can be easily made and no great precision is required. It consists of an angle plate carrying a dial gauge at the top and a stop at the bottom separated by a known length L as shown in fig. 2.53. A reading R is taken on the parallel block to be tested in position (a), the block is reversed and a second reading taken in position (b). The reversal has the effect of doubling the error and the squareness error over the length L is half the difference in the readings.

Correction of Squareness Error. It is of little value knowing the error in squareness of a workpiece if unable to correct it. Fortunately this correction is not difficult.

Referring again to fig. 2.53 let us assume that the difference in dial gauge readings is 0·12 mm, i.e., the block is out of square by 0·06 mm over the length L. Correcting this value for the complete length of surface let us say that the block is out of square by 0·075 mm. To correct this, the block must be re-faced, with 0·075 mm of metal removed at A and C down to no metal removal at D and B.

If the block is set up on a surface grinding machine with face AD uppermost, a 0·075 mm cut can be taken across this face to within about 2·5 mm of D, as shown in fig. 2.54(a).

The block is now turned over as in fig.

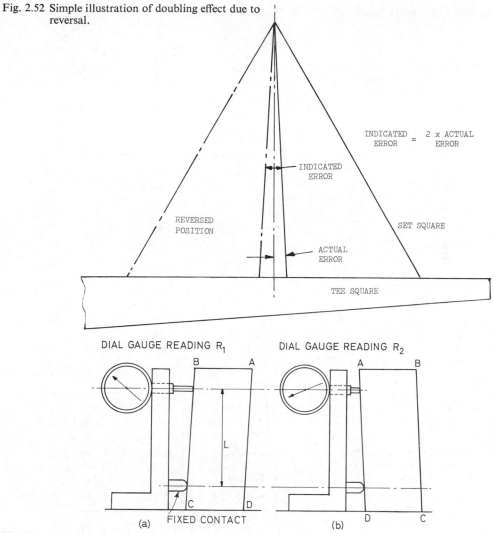

Fig. 2.52 Simple illustration of doubling effect due to reversal.

INDICATED ERROR = 2 x ACTUAL ERROR

INDICATED ERROR

REVERSED POSITION

SET SQUARE

ACTUAL ERROR

TEE SQUARE

DIAL GAUGE READING R₁

DIAL GAUGE READING R₂

B   A

A   B

L

C   D

D   C

(a)   FIXED CONTACT

(b)

Fig. 2.53 Dial gauge fixture for testing squareness. Squareness error $= \frac{1}{2}(R_1 - R_2)$ over length L.

2.54(*b*) and a cut is taken to clean up face BC, which is thus corrected by the required amount and is therefore square with reference to AB and CD.

It now only remains to grind AD parallel to BC again for all four faces to be 'true', i.e., adjacent faces square and opposite faces parallel.

(*b*) *Mechanical Squareness Tester for use*

with an Auto-Collimator. A similar principle is involved in a simple fixture for use with an auto-collimator or Angle Dekkor. As with so many simple, yet extremely effective, metrological devices, credit must be given to the National Physical Laboratory for its design.

This squareness tester consists simply of a bar pivoted at a convenient point and carrying

Fig. 2.54 Method of correcting squareness.

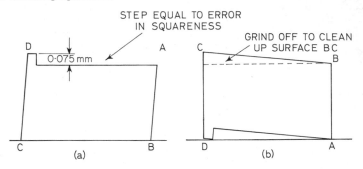

Fig. 2.55 Squareness testing using an auto-collimator.
Squareness error $= \frac{1}{2}(R_1 - R_2)$.

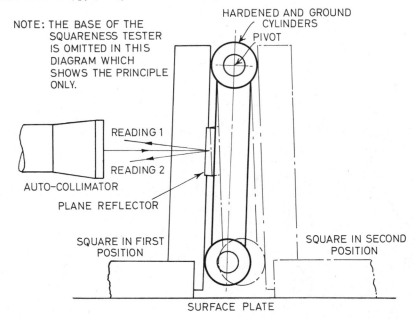

a pair of hardened and ground steel cylinders of precisely the same size. The bar also has mounted upon it a plane reflector and the instrument is set up on a flat reference plane of suitable degree of accuracy, usually a Grade A surface plate.

The arrangement is shown in fig. 2.55.

A reading is taken by the auto-collimator with the square in the first position shown. The square is then moved to the second position and the auto-collimator reading is again noted. The angular error in squareness is *half*

the difference in the two readings.

It should be noted that apart from errors in reading the auto-collimator and human failings such as not properly cleaning contact surfaces, the only possibility of error by this method would be due to cylinders of unequal diameter. This error could be eliminated by exchanging the cylinders and repeating the process.

The actual error in squareness would then be the mean of the two results.

(*c*) *Direct Optical Measurement of a Right*

Angle. We have seen that an auto-collimator or Angle Dekkor projects the image of a target wire or scale as a parallel beam of light. This beam of light consists of an infinite number of parallel rays, each of which is itself a minute image of the scale.

If we project the beam from an Angle Dekkor at an internal right angle, for instance a vee block as shown in fig. 2.56, the rays striking reflector (*a*) directly are reflected across to reflector (*b*) and back into the instrument, thus forming a reflected image of the scale. Due to the additional reflecting surface involved this will be a mirror image of the scale. Similarly the rays striking reflector (*b*) directly are reflected across to reflector (*a*) and back into the instrument, forming another mirror image.

If the angle is a perfect right angle only one mirror image will be observed in the eyepiece, but if the angle is in error *two* mirror images will be seen, as shown in fig. 2.57. The error in squareness is *half* the offset of the scale images, again due to a built-in reversal process.

Fig. 2.58 shows a similar set-up for checking an external angle. It should be noted that in neither case is the alignment of the instrument important. As long as it is directed at the angle so that the projected beam is split

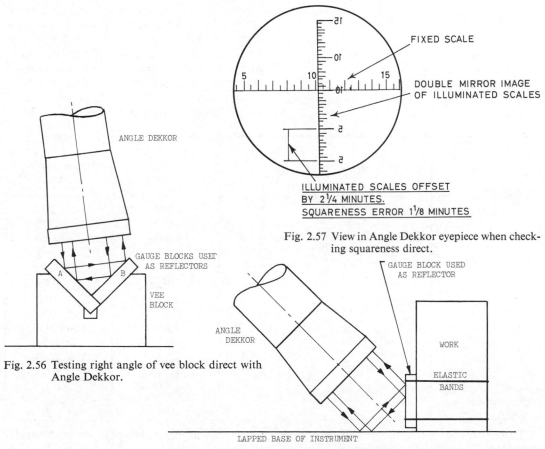

FIXED SCALE

DOUBLE MIRROR IMAGE OF ILLUMINATED SCALES

ILLUMINATED SCALES OFFSET BY 2¼ MINUTES.
SQUARENESS ERROR 1⅛ MINUTES

Fig. 2.57 View in Angle Dekkor eyepiece when checking squareness direct.

ANGLE DEKKOR

GAUGE BLOCKS USED AS REFLECTORS

VEE BLOCK

Fig. 2.56 Testing right angle of vee block direct with Angle Dekkor.

GAUGE BLOCK USED AS REFLECTOR

ANGLE DEKKOR

WORK

ELASTIC BANDS

LAPPED BASE OF INSTRUMENT

Fig. 2.58 Testing external right angle direct with Angle Dekkor.

between the two reflectors the double image will result.

TESTING A 180° ANGLE (PARALLELISM)
If a workpiece is to be checked

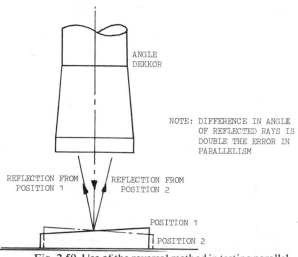

ANGLE DEKKOR

NOTE: DIFFERENCE IN ANGLE OF REFLECTED RAYS IS DOUBLE THE ERROR IN PARALLELISM

REFLECTION FROM POSITION 1

REFLECTION FROM POSITION 2

POSITION 1

POSITION 2

Fig. 2.59 Use of the reversal method in testing parallelism.

for parallelism it can simply be measured for thickness at each end. If, however, the error is required as an angle it can be determined by taking a reading by Angle Dekkor on the table and then on the workpiece, the difference in readings giving the angular error in parallelism directly.

Alternatively, a reading can be taken on the work surface, the work then being turned through 180° and a repeat reading taken. Again, due to the reversal process, the difference in readings is *double* the error in parallelism. This is shown in principle in fig. 2.59.

CIRCULAR DIVISION TESTING
Many situations arise in industry where a workpiece has to be turned through a complete circle by a number of equal steps or subdivisions. Such a process is called *indexing*, and the angular accuracy of the workpiece produced will depend upon the accuracy of the device used for indexing. This may be a rotary table, a dividing head, or an indexing fixture such as a rotary index plate with a

Position	Reading (′)	Reading (″)	Cumulative Error (″)	Correct for Zero (″)	Actual Error (″)
0	4	53	0	0	0
1	4	45	− 8	+ 0·25	− 7·75
2	4	38	− 15	+ 0·50	− 14·50
3	4	36	− 17	+ 0·75	− 16·25
4	4	39	− 14	+ 1·00	− 13·00
5	4	42	− 11	+ 1·25	− 9·75
6	4	48	− 5	+ 1·50	− 3·50
7	4	59	+ 6	+ 1·75	+ 7·75
8	5	08	+ 15	+ 2·00	+ 17·00
9	5	09	+ 16	+ 2·25	+ 18·25
10	5	01	+ 8	+ 2·50	+ 10·50
11	4	56	+ 3	+ 2·75	+ 5·75
12 (Repeat 0)	4	50	− 3	+ 3·00	0

This tabulation presupposes that the polygon is perfectly accurate. No polygon is absolutely accurate of course but, so long as the angular error at each face is known, allowance can be made for it.

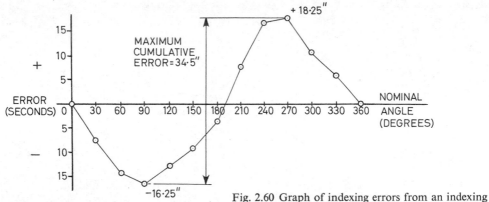

Fig. 2.60 Graph of indexing errors from an indexing device having an eccentric mounting.

number of equally-spaced slots into which a spring-loaded plunger locates.

The simplest means of calibrating an indexing device, such as a dividing head, is to refer it to a precision polygon.

This consists of a hardened and stabilised piece of steel whose reflecting faces are accurately lapped so that they are normal to equal divisions of a circle. The largest polygon made has 72 facets at intervals of nominally 5°. Normally a polygon having 12 sides at intervals of 30° is suitable for most work.

The polygon is mounted on the indexing device, and an auto-collimator is set up to give a reflection and reading from one facet of the polygon. If the device is now indexed through 30° or $\frac{1}{12}$ of a circle, the reading should be repeated in the auto-collimator. If this is not so, the difference between the readings is the error in indexing. Similarly, the difference between all readings and the first one are the errors in indexing through the total angle, while the errors between individual indexing motions are obtained by subtraction.

Normally a repeat reading is taken on the original facet of the polygon and any error in repetition is evenly distributed among the separate indexing motions.

The table opposite is for a set of readings on a milling machine dividing head set for simple indexing, the results being set out in graphical form in fig. 2.60.

STRAIGHTNESS AND FLATNESS TESTING

The auto-collimator can be used for the measurement of straightness by taking advantage of the fact that the distance between the reflector and the lens does not affect the reading. If the reflector is mounted on a small angle bracket which is moved along a non-flat surface any deviation from straightness in its path will result in a change of angle, and hence a change of reading in an auto-collimator sighted on the reflector.

In fig. 2.61 the reflector mount is shown in position 0–1 and the reading R_1 obtained in this position is a measure of the angle, relative to the auto-collimator axis, of points 0 and 1 on the surface. This line is taken as a datum, and all other readings are referred to it. The reflector stand is now moved so that its front feet are in the position previously occupied by its back feet, i.e., it is moved through its own base length, and reading R_2 is taken. The difference between R_2 and R_1 is the angle turned by the reflector through the non-flatness of the table in this position, and the base length L of the reflector enables the height h_2 to be obtained from

$$h_2 = L \times (R_2 - R_1) \text{ radians}$$

L is usually chosen to give an easy con-

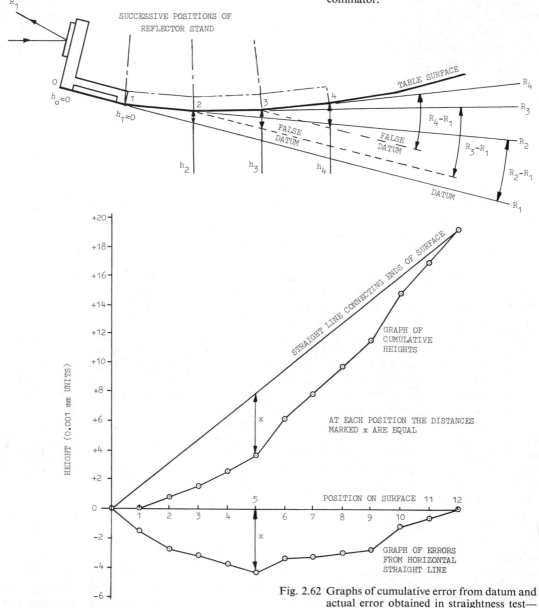

Fig. 2.61 Geometry of straightness test with auto-collimator.

Fig. 2.62 Graphs of cumulative error from datum and actual error obtained in straightness test—metric units. (See table p. 63.)

version from angle to height, and if $L = 103 \cdot 5$ mm a change in angle of $1'$ represents a change in height of $0 \cdot 03$ mm. The reflector is moved to its next position and reading R_3 is taken.

If we subtract R_1 from R_3 we obtain the angle $(R_3 - R_1)$ shown in fig. 2.61, *measured relative to the dotted line drawn parallel to the datum*, since the line of reading R_3 starts

Tabulated calculation for a hogged surface. Note the increase in readings indicating that the surface is hogged.

(1) Position on surface	(2) Readings	(3) Difference from 1st reading (")	(4) Change in height (μm)	(5) Cumulative height (μm)	(6) Correct to horizontal (μm)	(7) Error (μm)
0	3′ 14″	0	0	0	0	0
1	3′ 14″	0	0	0	+ 1·6	+1·6
2	3′ 15·6″	− 1·6	− 0·8	− 0·8	+ 3·2	+2·4
3	3′ 15·4″	− 1·4	− 0·7	− 1·5	+ 4·8	+3·3
4	3′ 16·2″	− 2·2	− 1·1	− 2·6	+ 6·4	+3·8
5	3′ 16·4″	− 2·4	− 1·2	− 3·8	+ 8·0	+4·2
6	3′ 18·8″	− 4·8	− 2·4	− 6·2	+ 9·6	+3·4
7	3′ 17·4″	− 3·4	− 1·7	− 7·9	+11·2	+3·3
8	3′ 17·6″	− 3·6	− 1·8	− 9·7	+12·8	+3·1
9	3′ 17·8″	− 3·8	− 1·9	−11·6	+14·4	+2·8
10	3′ 20·4″	− 6·4	− 3·2	−14·8	+16·0	+1·2
11	3′ 18·4″	− 4·4	− 2·2	−17·0	+17·6	+0·6
12	3′ 18·4″	− 4·4	− 2·2	−19·2	+19·2	0

Fig. 2.63 Cumulative and actual error —tabulation of data shown in fig. 2.62.

at point 2 (not point 1). Thus h_3 is the height from this false datum to point 3. The false datum is at a height h_2 above the real datum and to obtain the height of point 3 above the real datum we must accumulate the results, i.e., use $h_2 + h_3$.

Similarly the height h_4 at position 4 is the height obtained from a false datum and the height from the real datum is $h_2 + h_3 + h_4$.

This calculation is best carried out in tabular form and the columns in the table shown above are as follows.

Column 1 Position on table. Note that in fig. 2.61 four readings have been taken but there are 5 positions of the feet on the table. This is corrected by tabulating position 0 as well as position 1. These are both given the same reading R_1 since they both lie on the datum.
Column 2 Reading (minutes and seconds)

Note that position 0 and position 1 have the same reading.
Column 3 Difference from first reading (seconds). Position 0 and position 1 will both be $(R_1 - R_1) = 0$.
Column 4 Convert to height The values in column 3 are converted to height values h at, for a base length of 103·5 mm, the rate of $1' = 0·03$ mm or $1'' = 0·000\ 5$ mm.
Column 5 Cumulative height. To obtain the value of the heights from the true datum the values in column 4 must be accumulated, i.e., each one is added to the previous total with due regard to sign.

The final value will only be zero if, by chance, the datum chosen coincides with the line joining the end points of the table. If we plot a graph of the results in column 5 against position in column 1, the plotted line will be as shown in fig. 2.62. The actual flatness error at a given point is the distance marked x between the point and the straight line connecting the ends. This actual error can be found by adding two extra columns to the tabular calculation.

Column 6 Adjustment to bring both ends to zero. The final value of the cumulative error is $-19\cdot2\ \mu$m and values at intermediate points for the straight line will be proportionate amounts of this. Thus if we wish to make position $12=0$ we must add $+19\cdot2\ \mu$m to the cumulative error:

$$-19\cdot2+19\cdot2=0.$$

At position 1 we must add

$$\frac{19\cdot2}{12}=1\cdot6$$

At position 2 we must add

$$2\times\frac{19\cdot2}{12}=3\cdot2$$

and so on.

Fig. 2.64 Simple test for sign convention when testing straightness with an auto-collimator.

Thus column 6 gives proportionate amounts of the final figure in column 5 but of opposite sign.

Column 7 Error from Straight Line. This is the actual error and is obtained by adding, with due regard to sign, columns 5 and 6.

The graph of these actual errors is shown in fig. 2.62 and it can be seen that the values marked x are the same for each position in both cases.

DETERMINATION OF SIGN CONVENTION In any of these calculations an incorrect sign convention leads to misleading results, a 'hogged' surface being shown as hollow and vice-versa. The author finds it difficult to remember a sign convention and in any case a different convention occurs under different conditions. A simple test enables the correct sign convention to be determined. Fig. 2.64(*a*) shows the extreme positions of a reflector moving over a hogged surface, the smaller diagram showing the changes in reflector position that give the same change in reading by simply tilting the

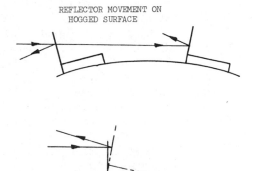

REFLECTOR MOVEMENT ON
HOGGED SURFACE

REFLECTOR MOVEMENT ON
HOLLOW SURFACE

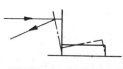

TILTING TOP OF REFLECTOR
STAND BACK = HOGGING

TILTING TOP OF REFLECTOR
STAND FORWARD = HOLLOW

(a)

(b)

stand. If the top of a reflector is tilted back then it represents a hogged surface. If a reading is taken in the auto-collimator while this is done the change in readings can be noted. Let us assume that tilting the top of the reflector back gives an *increase* in readings. Obviously then an increase in readings during a test indicates that the surface is hogged and a decrease in readings indicates that the surface is hollow.

Note: This test to determine a sign convention should be carried out for each set of readings taken.

This basic method of testing can be applied to straight edges, machine tool slideways and the flatness of machine tables and surface tables.

TESTING MACHINE TOOL SLIDE-WAYS In Book 1 it was shown that a lathe will produce a true cylinder only if the tool motion is straight and parallel to the work axis. The tool motion will only be straight if:

(*a*) both slideways are straight,
and (*b*) the two slideways are parallel.

Most lathes have a vee front slide and a flat rear slide, and the vee slide must be straight in both the horizontal and vertical planes. A slight modification to the reflector mount allows it to be used for both vee and flat slides, as shown in fig. 2.65.

The parallelism of the slideways vertically cannot be tested with an auto-collimator. It is necessary to use a precision spirit level for this purpose, readings being taken at both ends of the bed. The level can be used directly on a flat bed lathe as long as it will span the slide ways. To test the parallelism of vee and flat slides, a bridge piece as shown in fig. 2.66 is needed.

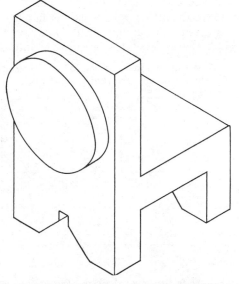

Fig. 2.65 Reflector mount suitable for testing inverted vee slides.

Fig. 2.66 Testing machine slides for wind or twist.

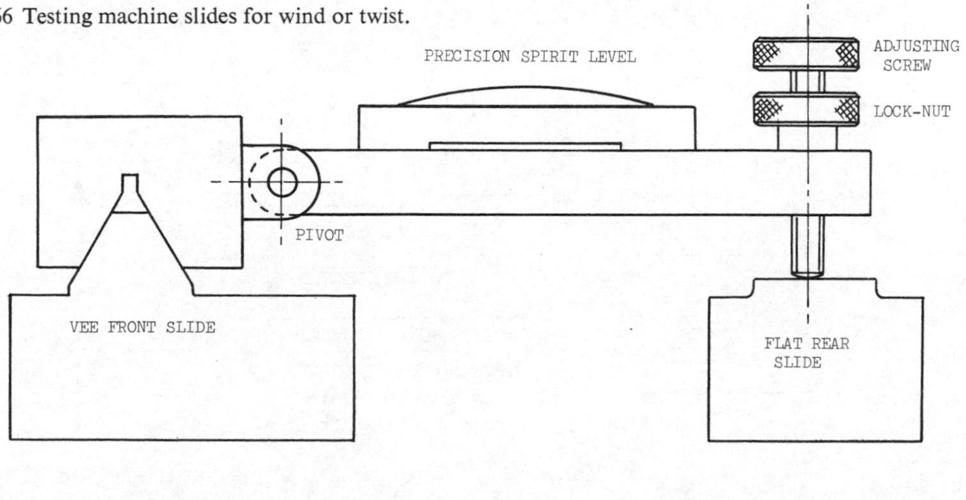

PRECISION SPIRIT LEVEL

ADJUSTING SCREW

LOCK-NUT

PIVOT

VEE FRONT SLIDE

FLAT REAR SLIDE

TESTING THE FLATNESS OF SUR-FACE TABLES The tests outlined on pp. 61-65 are only tests of straightness and if applied to a surface table test only the straightness along one line of the table. To check flatness over the whole area of the table a number of such lines of test must be covered and the results correlated. The minimum number of such lines of test is eight, arranged in a pattern as shown in fig. 2.67, and not only is the error along each line determined but also the height of each line relative to the others. A detailed discussion of this method can be found in *Metrology for Engineers* by J. F. W. Galyer and the author.

Fig. 2.67 Minimum number of lines of test for testing flatness as distinct from straightness.

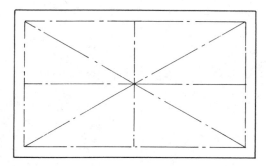

Fig. 2.68 Tests for spindle concentricity and alignment with guide-ways.

MACHINE TOOL ALIGNMENT TESTING

In Book 1 the alignments required to enable various machine tools to function correctly and to the desired degree of accuracy were discussed. Here we shall consider the tests required to check such alignments. In most cases a straight-line motion of tool or work is essential and can only be obtained if the machine tool slides are themselves straight and parallel. The testing of slideways for these conditions has been explained in previous pages, but it is not only necessary that the motion shall be truly linear, for it must also be correct in relation to another part or parts of the machine. The principles of testing these relative alignments are similar for all machine tools and it is these principles which will be outlined here, not the detailed test for each specific machine tool. Details of such tests are available in the book *Testing of Machine Tools* by Dr G. Schlesinger and in *Acceptance Test Charts for Machine Tools*, prepared jointly by the Institution of Mechanical Engineers and the Institution of Production Engineers.

The major alignments to be tested are that:

1. Machine spindle-nose taper axis is concentric with the axis of rotation (taper 'runs true').
2. Machine spindle axis is parallel to the

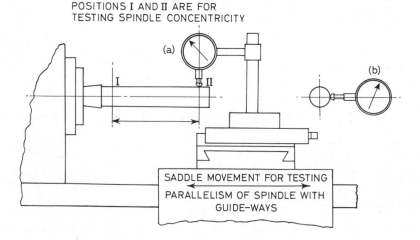

POSITIONS I AND II ARE FOR TESTING SPINDLE CONCENTRICITY

(a)

(b)

SADDLE MOVEMENT FOR TESTING PARALLELISM OF SPINDLE WITH GUIDE-WAYS

tool or work motion

3. Machine spindle axis is normal to the table surface.

4. Table surface is parallel to own motion.

1. *Running Accuracy of the Spindle-nose Taper.* This test is carried out by inserting an accurately-made hardened and ground test bar in the machine spindle nose and testing it with a dial gauge at positions I and II, fig. 2.68, with the spindle slowly rotating. This test applies to all rotating spindle machines.

2. *Machine Spindle Parallel to Tool or Work Motion.* The same test bar can be used for this test. The spindle remains stationary and the machine saddle or table is moved. The test is carried out in two planes (*a*) and (*b*) as shown in fig. 2.68. This test applies to lathe saddles, milling machine cross-slide table motions, vertical milling machine vertical slide motions, horizontal boring machines etc.

3. *Machine Spindle Axis Normal to Work Table.* A test bar is used to support a dial gauge at a suitable radius of rotation so that the plunger bears on the table surface as shown in fig. 2.69. As the spindle is slowly rotated, variations in dial gauge readings indicate non-squareness of the table to the axis of rotation. Note that this test is another application of the reversal principle discussed

previously. The test applies to drilling machines, vertical-spindle milling machines, jig boring machines, etc.

4. *Table Surface Parallel to its Own Motion.* A dial gauge is mounted on a fixed member of the machine with the plunger bearing on the machine table and the table is slowly traversed under the gauge as shown in fig. 2.70. If the table surface is not parallel with its own motion it produces a change in dial gauge reading and, more important, non-parallel work. This test applies to milling machines, surface grinding machines, jig boring machines, horizontal boring machines, and shaping machine tables.

5. *Machine Table Tee Slots.* Table tee slots, which are used to locate many fixtures in correct alignment with machine spindles, can be tested for these alignments using similar methods to 3 and 4 above.

MEASUREMENT OF SURFACE ROUGHNESS

The necessity to work to higher degrees of accuracy has brought with it the necessity to produce surfaces of better quality. It is of little use specifying a tolerance on the size of a part to the order of $\pm 0.000\,3$ mm if the local variations in height which constitute the surface finish are of the order of $0.001\,5$

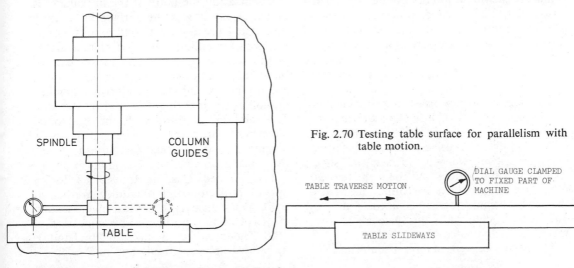

Fig. 2.70 Testing table surface for parallelism with table motion.

Fig. 2.69 Testing a drilling-machine spindle for squareness with the table.

mm. Furthermore, the nature of the surface may influence the functioning of the part. If a shaft is subject to reversals of load it becomes *fatigued* and its life can be greatly reduced. Failure due to fatigue often starts at the sharp root of a surface irregularity, and it follows that the better the surface finish the longer will be the fatigue life.

Wear is another problem confronting the engineer. The useful life of an assembly is often governed by the rate of wear of its component parts, and the rate of wear depends on the surface area in contact. A rough surface with large peaks and valleys will have less contact area than a smooth one and its rate of wear will be greater.

If the surface finish of a part is to be specified for a given function it must be possible to measure (assess is a better word) the surface quality and give it a numerical value. Visual assessment and assessment by touch are both used but these are subjective, i.e., they allow surfaces to be compared but only on the basis of an opinion as to which is the rougher.

A numerical assessment is better so that we can say that the surface to which the larger value is assigned is the rougher. This numerical assessment is usually obtained by means of an instrument in which a stylus is drawn slowly over the surface, and the stylus movements are measured to provide the numerical assessment. This method, however, raises a problem concerned with the geometry of surfaces. Most surfaces are not only rough but they are also non-flat. We do not wish to measure the non-flatness, but only the roughness, and the two must be separated. For this reason all surface measuring instruments of this type have a skid or shoe which rests on the surface and controls the instrument movement over the surface. As the measuring head is drawn over the surface the shoe follows the undulations and the stylus movements are measured *relative* to the shoe. Thus the only height variations measured are due to the roughness of the surface and any waviness is eliminated.

The stylus movements are usually ampli-fied to provide a trace from which the numerical assessment is obtained. It should be emphasised that all such traces are distorted and do not give a true picture of the surface. The vertical magnification is much greater than the horizontal magnification and a typical trace is shown in fig. 2.71, in which the horizontal magnification is only $\times 20$ but the vertical magnification is $\times 2\,000$.

THE TOMLINSON SURFACE METER This instrument uses mechano-optical magnification methods and was designed by Dr Tomlinson of the National Physical Laboratory, its essentials being shown in fig. 2.72.

The skid is attached to the body of the instrument, its height being adjustable to enable the diamond-tipped stylus shown to be positioned conveniently. The stylus is restrained from all motion except a vertical one by a leaf spring and a coil spring, the tension in the coil spring P causes a corresponding tension in the leaf spring. These forces hold a cross roller in position between the stylus and a pair of parallel fixed rollers as shown in the plan view. Attached to the cross roller is a light spring steel arm carrying at its tip a diamond which bears against a smoked glass screen.

In operation the body of the instrument is drawn slowly across the surface by a screw turned at 1 rev/min by a synchronous motor, the glass remaining stationary. Irregularities in the surface cause vertical movements of the stylus which cause the cross roller to pivot about point A and thus produce a magnified motion at the marking diamond on the arm. This motion, coupled with the horizontal movement, produces a trace on the glass magnified in the vertical direction at $\times 100$, there being no horizontal magnification.

The smoked glass is transferred to an optical projector and magnified further at $\times 50$, giving an overall vertical magnification of $\times 5\,000$ and a horizontal magnification of $\times 50$. The trace may be taken off by hand or by photographic methods and analysed.

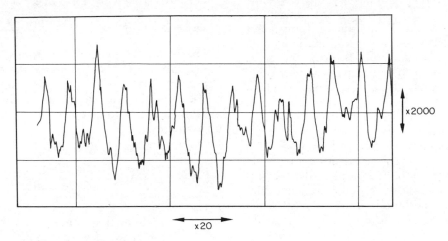

Fig. 2.71 Trace of surface. C.L.A. reading = 3·65 μm.

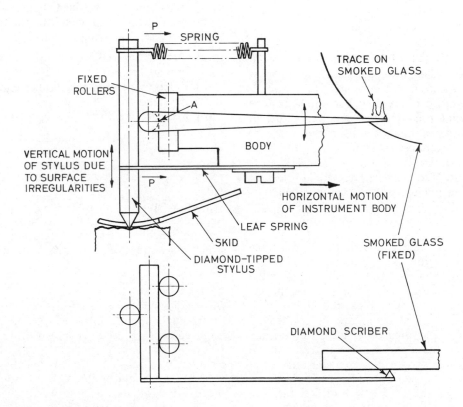

Fig. 2.72 Tomlinson Surface Meter.

THE TAYLOR–HOBSON 'TALY-SURF'

The Talysurf is an electronic instrument which works on the same basic principles as the Tomlinson instrument but the methods of magnification and recording the trace are different. It gives the same information much more rapidly and probably more accurately. It can be, and is, used on the factory floor or in the laboratory, whereas the Tomlinson instrument is essentially for use in the laboratory.

The measuring head again consists of a stylus, and a shoe which controls the movement of the instrument head across the surface. In this case the stylus movements relative to the shoe produce an electrical signal which can be used to produce a trace and a numerical assessment, the whole operation taking about two minutes. With some Talysurf instruments, no recorder is provided and the instrument simply gives a numerical assessment directly on a dial.

THE CENTRE-LINE AVERAGE INDEX

The numerical assessment most commonly used in this country is the Centre-Line Average Index or C.L.A. number. The C.L.A. index is defined as the average height from a mean line of all ordinates of the surface, regardless of sign.

Thus, referring to fig. 2.73, if equally-spaced ordinates are erected at $1, 2, 3, 4, \ldots n$ whose heights are $h_1, h_2, h_3 \ldots h_n$, then

$$\text{C.L.A.} = \frac{h_1 + h_2 + h_3 + \ldots h_n}{n}$$

To determine a C.L.A. index from a trace by the erection of ordinates would be a laborious process, and if an unfortunate ordinate spacing was chosen significant points on the surface might not be included. However, if an irregular area is divided by its length, the value obtained is the average height of the area. Such an area can be measured readily by a planimeter and if the total area enclosed by the trace and the mean line is divided by the length of the trace the average height of the trace from the mean

line is obtained.

Thus, referring to fig. 2.74 (where $A =$ area):

$$\text{Average height of trace} = \frac{A_1 + A_2 + A_3 + \ldots A_n}{L}$$

This value obtained is for the *trace*, not the surface under test. To obtain the C.L.A. index for the surface the value must be divided by the vertical magnification and multiplied by 10^3 to give the C.L.A. index in micrometres.

C.L.A. Index (in micrometres)

$$= \frac{A_1 + A_2 + A_3 + \ldots A_n}{L} \times \frac{10^3}{\text{Vertical mgn.}}$$

where the sum of the values of
$A =$ total area in mm^2
$L =$ length of trace in mm

Before the area is measured, the position of the mean line must be fixed. This can again be done by using a planimeter, by the following procedure. Referring to fig. 2.75:

(a) Draw a line AB parallel to the general line of the trace.
(b) Enclose the area by parallel end lines AA$_1$ and BB$_1$.
(c) Measure the total area by planimeter.

$$\text{Then } h = \frac{\text{Total area}}{\text{Length}}$$

where h is the distance of the mean line from AB.

This technique to analyse the trace is required for the Tomlinson instrument. The Talysurf incorporates an integrating device which gives the result directly on an Average Meter.

EFFECT OF LENGTH OF TRACE

Most machined surfaces consist of a number of irregularities of different spacing superimposed on each other as shown in fig. 2.76. It is clear that if a short length l_1 of surface is tested it will only include irregularities of a total height h_1 and a low C.L.A. index will result. If a greater length of surface l_2 is tested, all irregularities of both spacings will

70

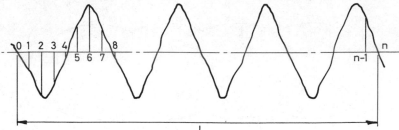

Fig. 2.73 Determination of C.L.A. index by measuring ordinates.

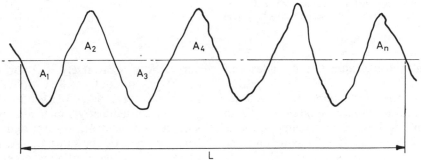

Fig. 2.74 Determination of C.L.A. index by measuring areas.

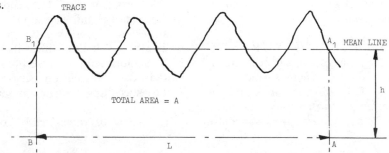

TRACE

B_1 A_1 MEAN LINE

TOTAL AREA = A   h

B   L   A

Fig. 2.75 Fixing the position of the mean line of a surface trace.

$$h = \frac{TOTAL\ AREA}{L}$$

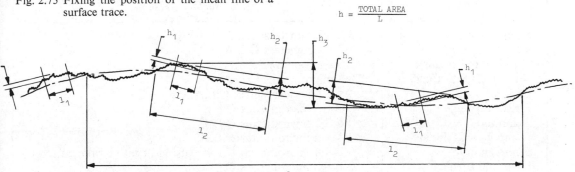

Fig. 2.76 Effect of sample length of surface on numerical assessment.

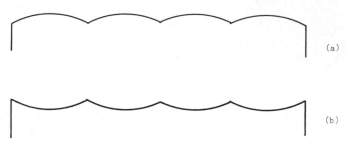

Fig. 2.77 Two surface textures having identical C.L.A. values but opposite mechanical characteristics.

be included and a greater C.L.A. index will result.

It follows that for comparison purposes the length of trace used must be stated. These sample lengths have been standardised at 0·25 mm, 0·80 mm and 2·50 mm, and are known as *Cut-off Wavelengths*. The most used Cut-off Wavelength is 0·80 mm and if not stated can usually be assumed. It ought, however, to be given.

EFFECT OF TYPE OF SURFACE
Consider the diagrams of two surfaces shown in fig. 2.77(*a*) and (*b*). These surfaces will obviously be totally different in character and a surface such as (*b*) would wear very rapidly since the contact area would increase

very slowly. Conversely, the surface shown at (*a*) has a contact area which increases rapidly as wear takes place and the rate of wear is consequently much less. These two surfaces are of identical form and will therefore have exactly the same C.L.A. Index, but one is the inverse of the other and has opposite characteristics.

It follows that the C.L.A. Index alone does not give enough information to enable surface qualities to be sensibly compared, and the trace also is valueless unless its magnification in both horizontal and vertical directions is stated. The information necessary for completely specifying a surface is therefore:

1. *Method of manufacture:* only compare

Process	Expected surface finish
Rough turning	6·3 micrometres C.L.A.
Rough grinding	3·2 micrometres C.L.A.
Shaping and planing	1·6 micrometres C.L.A.
Milling (H.S.S. tools)	0·8 micrometres C.L.A.
Drilling	0·8–12·5 micrometres C.L.A.
Finish turning	0·4–6·3 micrometres C.L.A.
Reaming	0·4–3·2 micrometres C.L.A.
Commercial grinding	0·4–3·2 micrometres C.L.A.
Finish milling	0·2–1·6 micrometres C.L.A. (using negative rake cutters)
Diamond turning	0·1–0·8 micrometres C.L.A.
Finish grinding	0·05–0·4 micrometres C.L.A. (precision work)
Honing and lapping	0·025–1·6 micrometres C.L.A.

surfaces produced by similar methods.

2. *C.L.A. Index*[1]
3. *Cut-off Wavelength:* only compare C.L.A. values obtained from the same sample length of surface.
4. *Trace:* magnifications should be stated and comparisons made only between traces of similar magnifications. If this is not possible the ratio between horizontal and vertical magnifications should be the same, e.g., $\times 5\,000$ vertical and $\times 50$ horizontal may be compared with $\times 2\,000$ vertical and $\times 20$ horizontal.

QUALITIES OF SURFACE FINISH

The quality of surface produced by a process depends on many features. A turned surface, for instance, will be rougher if the feed is coarse than if a fine feed is used. A very coarse grit wheel used for rough grinding will produce a rougher surface than a wheel used for finish grinding, which may indeed produce a finer surface finish than coarse lapping.

The table opposite shows the range of surface finish values which can be expected from various machining processes. Where a single figure is given it is the best surface finish that can be expected from the process. When a surface texture is specified on a drawing a single value is usually given, not the limits between which the finish produced must lie. In this case the finish stated is the WORST that may be allowed.

[1] It is likely that in the near future the abbreviation C.L.A. will be replaced by the symbol R_a.

SUMMARY

The control of modern manufacturing processes to give the quality and accuracy of work required makes the ability to measure to a high degree of precision an absolute necessity. There is only one exact length, the metre, which is currently specified as 1 650 763·73 wavelengths of a particular light. The technique used to measure length in terms of the wavelength of light need not concern us here but it is important to realise that all other measurements contain errors. The causes of these errors should be controlled and eliminated as far as possible but as complete elimination is impossible the accuracy of determination should be estimated and stated.

The equipment used to enable these measurements to be made to a high enough degree of precision requires more complex methods of amplification of size and angle than those encountered previously and study of these methods requires a basic knowledge of mechanical, optical, pneumatic and electrical techniques. These fundamentals having been grasped, their application to more specialised measurements can be studied. Particular cases which occur frequently in engineering are the measurement of screw threads, flatness, straightness and surface finish. If the geometry of a part is incorrect its size cannot be constant and therefore cannot be stated accurately to any degree of precision.

Metal Cutting

In Book 1 we considered the metal cutting process from an essentially practical standpoint and showed that for metal cutting to take place:

1. The tool must have adequate but not excessive clearance[1] and the clearance angle depends largely on the geometry of the workpiece.

2. The tool must have a rake[1] angle which depends largely on the material being cut.

3. The machine must provide the tool motions and the forces necessary to cause a shearing action to take place and the chip to be removed.

In this chapter the mechanics of metal removal will be examined more closely and some of the more sophisticated types of tool available to the engineer will be discussed.

THE MECHANICS OF METAL CUTTING

A discussion of the mechanics of metal cutting requires an examination of the forces exerted by the tool on the work and vice-versa. For purposes of simplicity, only *orthogonal cutting* will be considered in detail, rather than the more usual oblique cutting adopted in practice.

Orthogonal cutting is a particular case where only two forces are measured and the cutting edge is at right angles to the direction of feed. A typical case is that of machining the end of a tube as shown in fig. 3.1(a) and the forces which can be measured are:

1. Tangential force F_t, tangential to the work surface. In association with the cutting speed this is the main power-consuming force.

2. Axial force F_a, parallel to the work axis

[1] It is assumed that at this stage the student is familiar with the definitions of the terms used.

and resisting the feed motion. In association with the feed motion this also consumes power, but as the feed rate is usually very slow compared with the cutting speed, the power consumed by F_a is normally very small.

If the cutting edge is not at right angles to the direction of feed, as is more usual, a third force:

3. Radial force F_r is measured, which tries to force the tool out of the work and is resisted, in the case of a lathe, by friction in the cross slide and its lead screw. As no motion is associated with F_r it does not consume power but influences F_a.

The three-force, or oblique, cutting system, is shown in fig. 3.1(b).

MEASUREMENT OF TOOL FORCES

It has been emphasised above that the forces F_t and F_a can be *measured*. They are chosen because they are at right angles and can be easily resolved, using a triangle of forces, to find the *resultant* force R which is, in fact, the only real force acting. It is convenient simply to measure these forces, using a tool-force dynamometer, determine R and resolve R into pairs of forces at right angles to each other which are of interest.

Many forms of dynamometer are available, all working on the same basic principle. Due to the forces applied, the tool deflects, and if its deflections are measured they can be related to the forces which produce them. The differences in dynamometers are largely in the methods of measuring these deflections.

The instrument shown in fig. 3.2(a) carries the tool in a holder mounted on the front of a disc or diaphragm which is clamped to the main body of the dynamometer. The back of

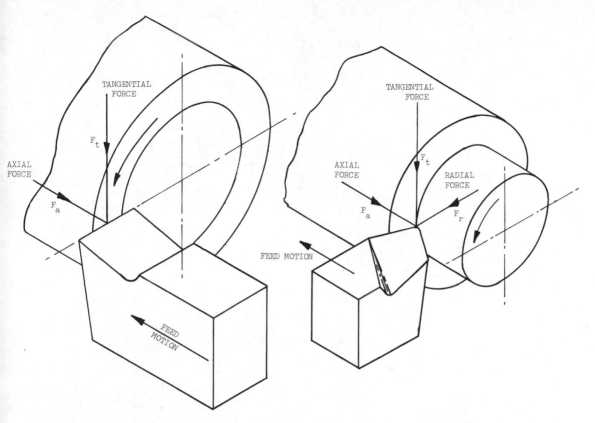

the diaphragm supports a bar against which dial gauges bear to detect the movements of the bar caused by the tool forces deflecting the diaphragm. A third dial gauge (not shown), operating in the horizontal plane, can be used to measure the third force F_a if necessary.

The tool is first replaced by an adaptor carrying a ball which is then loaded by known dead weights and a graph or calibration chart is made of load against deflection as shown in fig. 3.2(*b*). In operation, the tool should project a fixed amount so that its point is in the position of the ball centre. Its deflections are noted during cutting and by referring these deflections back to the calibration chart the forces involved can be determined.

SIMPLE ANALYSIS OF FORCES IN ORTHOGONAL CUTTING If we use a two-force dynamometer to measure the forces F_t and F_a, we can determine by means of a triangle of forces the resultant force R exerted by the work on the tool, as shown in fig. 3.3.

Note: In all the force diagrams the tool is shown as if mounted on a shaping machine, i.e., moving horizontally from right to left.

A simple way of finding any two components of R at right angles to each other is based on the fact that the angle subtended at the periphery of a semi-circle from its diameter is always a right angle. If the force F parallel to the rake face and the force N normal to the rake face are required, we extend the rake face to meet the circle and from this

75

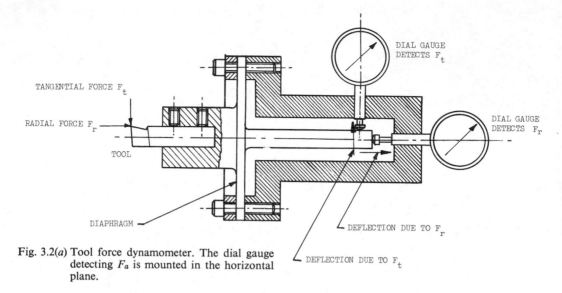

Fig. 3.2(*a*) Tool force dynamometer. The dial gauge detecting F_a is mounted in the horizontal plane.

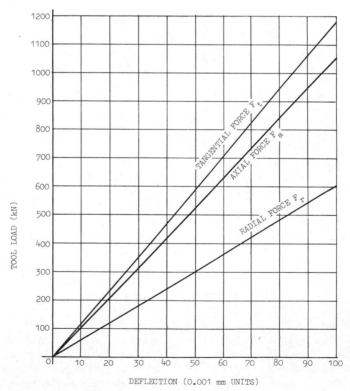

Fig. 3.2(*b*) Calibration chart for use with a cutting tool dynamometer.

76

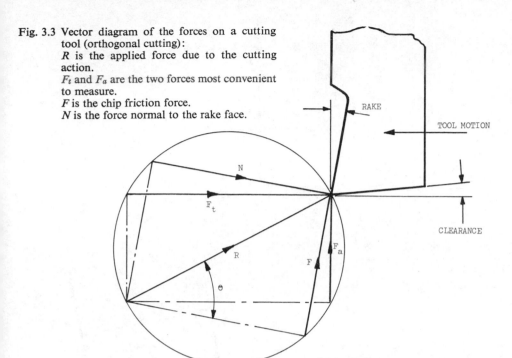

Fig. 3.3 Vector diagram of the forces on a cutting tool (orthogonal cutting):

R is the applied force due to the cutting action.

F_t and F_a are the two forces most convenient to measure.

F is the chip friction force.

N is the force normal to the rake face.

point draw to the other end of R (the diameter). These two vectors to scale represent forces F and N.

The force F is equal and opposite to the force of friction which must be overcome to move the chips along the rake face and N is the force, normal to the rake face, producing that friction.

The ratio $\dfrac{F}{N}$ is the coefficient of friction

$$\tan \theta = \frac{F}{N} = \mu$$

What is the effect of changing the coefficient of friction? Let us assume that the normal force N remains constant but, due to a reduced coefficient of friction, F is reduced. We can now reverse the above procedure and use the friction force F and the normal force N to find the resultant, and hence find new values for F_t and F_a, as shown in fig. 3.4. We find that both F_t and F_a are reduced because the resultant R is reduced. Recalling that F_t is the power-consuming force it

follows that a reduced friction coefficient between the chip and the tool rake face reduces the power consumption and the heat generated. This, then, produces a better cutting process and higher rates of metal removal may be employed.

A similar analysis can be used for examining the effect of an increase in rake angle but before we do this we must consider the effect of the rake angle on the angle at which the metal shears ahead of the tool. This is shown in fig. 3.5(a) and (b). The metal may be considered to shear along a line slightly steeper than the direction of N, the normal to the rake face. If the rake angle is increased, the angle at which shearing occurs is also increased, thus reducing the length of the shear line.[1] As the length of the shear line is reduced

[1] This is a simplified version of the work carried out by two men, Ernst and Merchant of the Cincinnati Milling Machine Co. Later researchers hold that shearing is not along a line but that a zone of deformation occurs ahead of the tool. For purposes of simplicity we will assume that shearing takes place along a line.

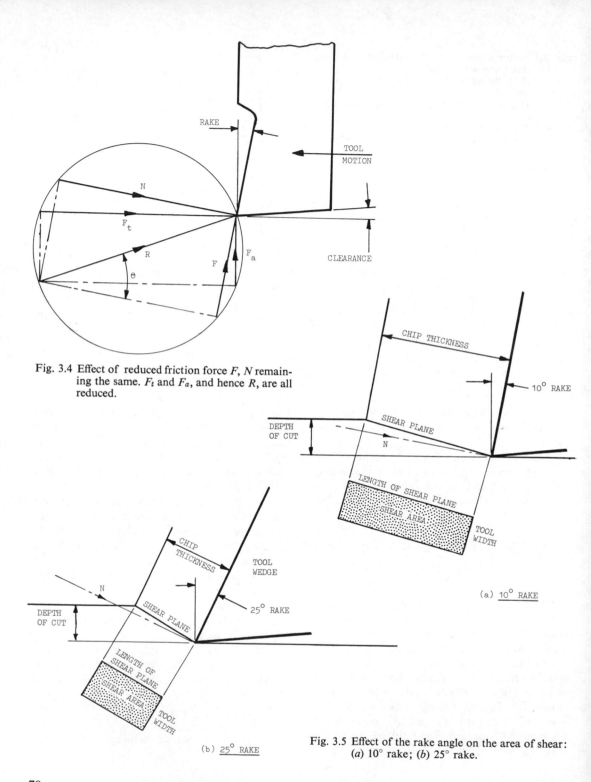

RAKE

TOOL
MOTION

CLEARANCE

N

F_t

R

F

F_a

θ

Fig. 3.4 Effect of reduced friction force F, N remaining the same. F_t and F_a, and hence R, are all reduced.

CHIP THICKNESS

10° RAKE

DEPTH
OF CUT

SHEAR PLANE

N

LENGTH OF SHEAR PLANE

SHEAR AREA

TOOL
WIDTH

(a) 10° RAKE

CHIP
THICKNESS

TOOL
WEDGE

N

SHEAR PLANE

25° RAKE

DEPTH
OF CUT

LENGTH OF
SHEAR PLANE

SHEAR AREA

TOOL
WIDTH

(b) 25° RAKE

Fig. 3.5 Effect of the rake angle on the area of shear:
(a) 10° rake; (b) 25° rake.

78

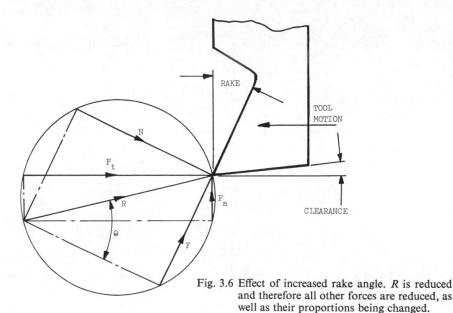

Fig. 3.6 Effect of increased rake angle. *R* is reduced and therefore all other forces are reduced, as well as their proportions being changed.

the shear area is correspondingly reduced and since

$$\text{Shear force} = \text{Shear strength} \times \text{shear area}$$

the shear force is reduced. Thus the forces necessary to produce cutting and the resulting force F are reduced (note that the ratio F/N remains the same). Using the circle method we can again draw in the forces, as in fig. 3.6, which shows that F_t and F_a are reduced. As F_t is the power-consuming force, the power consumption and heat generated will both be less.

It would appear then that the greater the rake angle the better will be the cutting conditions. While this is true up to a point it must be noted that as we increase the rake angle the force N, normal to the rake face, is operating in such a direction that it is likely to break off the tool point and that, for a given depth of cut, as the strength of the work material increases so does N increase. Furthermore, as the rake angle is increased the tool is weakened and therefore if the rake angle is made too steep and a tough material is being cut, early failure of the tool will result through the tool tip breaking off.

CHIP FORMATION IN METAL CUTTING

There are three fundamental types of chip produced in the metal cutting process, as shown in fig. 3.7:

    (*a*) the continuous or ribbon-type chip
    (*b*) the continuous chip with a built-up edge
    (*c*) the discontinuous chip.

(*a*) The continuous chip is produced by the metal ahead of the tool becoming greatly compressed and flowing across the rake face of the tool. Before the metal fails completely it compresses the next portion and so on. Examination of the chip illustrates this, the underside in contact with the rake face becoming highly polished or burnished and the top of the chip having minute serrations where partial failure has occurred. This form of chip indicates good cutting conditions with low chip friction, long tool life, good surface finish and low power consumption. It usually occurs when cutting a ductile material at high speed and fine feed, with a large rake angle, polished tool face and good lubrication.

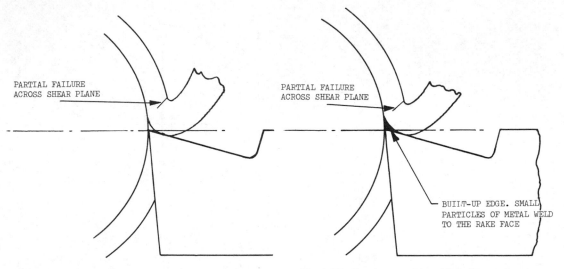

PARTIAL FAILURE
ACROSS SHEAR PLANE

Fig. 3.7(a) Continuous chip.

PARTIAL FAILURE
ACROSS SHEAR PLANE

BUILT-UP EDGE. SMALL
PARTICLES OF METAL WELD
TO THE RAKE FACE

Fig. 3.7(b) Continuous chip with built up edge.

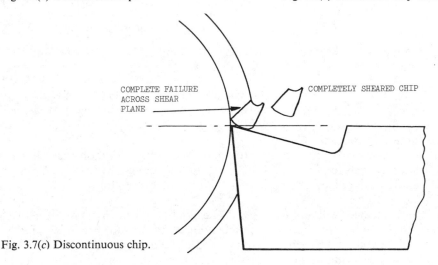

COMPLETE FAILURE
ACROSS SHEAR
PLANE

COMPLETELY SHEARED CHIP

Fig. 3.7(c) Discontinuous chip.

(b) The continuous chip with the built-up edge is formed in a similar manner but due to intense pressure and high temperature small pieces of work metal become welded to the tool tip. Due to the extreme pressure this weldment becomes work-hardened and brittle so that it eventually breaks off and is carried away by the chip over the tool. Being very hard it is also extremely abrasive, and causes rapid tool wear since the process of build-up and breakdown is repeated with very high frequency. The built-up edge usually occurs when a ductile material is being cut under conditions causing extreme heat and pressure, conditions such as poor tool-face finish, poor lubrication and too small a rake angle.

(c) The discontinuous chip occurs when the force involved in bending the chip causes complete breakdown of the shear zone and individual segments of metal come away separately. This can be due to the material itself being discontinuous, e.g., grey cast iron, where the discontinuities caused by the graphite flakes break the structure of the

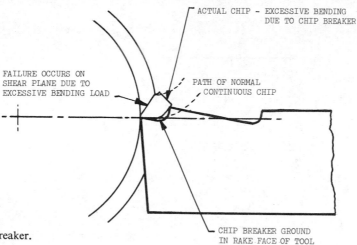

ACTUAL CHIP - EXCESSIVE BENDING
DUE TO CHIP BREAKER

FAILURE OCCURS ON
SHEAR PLANE DUE TO
EXCESSIVE BENDING LOAD

PATH OF NORMAL
CONTINUOUS CHIP

CHIP BREAKER GROUND
IN RAKE FACE OF TOOL

Fig. 3.8 Chip breaker.

metal, or can occur with a material such as brass whose shear strength is relatively low compared with the force required to bend it. With these materials a good surface finish results and the forces involved, and hence the power consumption, are low.

This type of chip can also occur with a ductile material if the cutting speed is too low and the rake angle too small. It is often induced deliberately in repetitive operations to give easy separation of the swarf from the work and to make the swarf itself easy to remove in large quantities. A step, called a *chip breaker*, is ground behind the cutting edge, as shown in fig. 3.8, which causes excessive bending of the chip and hence premature fracture. It should be noted that use of a chip breaker produces larger cutting forces and hence higher power consumption but these disadvantages are outweighed by simplified swarf clearance.

TOOL FAILURE AND TOOL LIFE

Under modern cutting conditions a tool usually fails in one of two ways:

(*a*) A land is worn on the clearance face, thus destroying the clearance angle and giving rise to rubbing, as shown in fig. 3.9(*a*).

(*b*) A crater is worn in the rake face behind the tool edge.

If the crater is allowed to develop, the cutting condition changes to one of high positive rake, giving rise to weakness and a calamitous tool failure, as shown in fig. 3.9(*b*).

Either of these conditions can demand an excessive amount of tool regrinding and in the case of cemented-carbide tipped tools is an expensive business. A tool is therefore considered to have failed when either:

(*a*) the wear land exceeds 0·25 mm
or (*b*) at the onset of cratering.

Modern production methods require that the tool life should be known and ideally last longer than one work shift, but a complete new set of pre-set tools is kept ready to be fitted into the machine with the minimum of difficulty. At the end of the shift the old tools are removed *before* they have failed, and are replaced by the set of new ones, for the next shift. This avoids replacing individual tools at irregular intervals, with a consequently greater machine 'down time'.

The tool life under the known cutting conditions can be found by testing under these conditions. It is fortunate that there is a mathematical relationship between the tool life T in minutes and the cutting speed V in metres per minute. The relationship is given

81

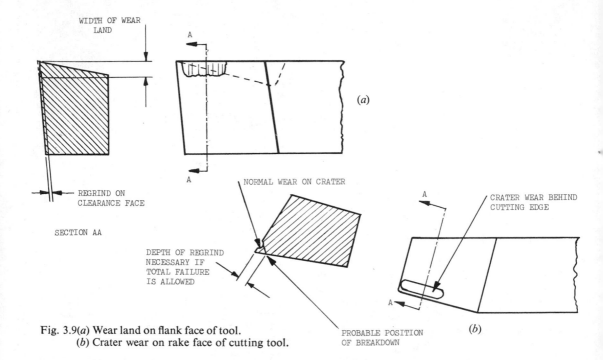

WIDTH OF WEAR
LAND

A

REGRIND ON
CLEARANCE FACE

SECTION AA

NORMAL WEAR ON CRATER

DEPTH OF REGRIND
NECESSARY IF
TOTAL FAILURE
IS ALLOWED

A

CRATER WEAR BEHIND
CUTTING EDGE

PROBABLE POSITION
OF BREAKDOWN

(a)

(b)

Fig. 3.9(a) Wear land on flank face of tool.
(b) Crater wear on rake face of cutting tool.

by

$$VT^n = C$$

where n and C are constants depending on the conditions, i.e., depth of cut, feed rate, coolant, etc.

Because the tool life and cutting speed are related in this way the tests can be accelerated by running at much higher speeds than occur in practice. From the values obtained for n and C in these tests a value for V can be found to give an adequate tool life T.

It must be emphasised that the value of T is the *actual cutting time*, not the time the tool is in the machine. Thus a tool life of 100 min could well be equivalent to a 240 min work shift in a capstan lathe where each tool is only used for part of the work cycle.

Consider a tool whose required tool life is 100 min. Tests carried out under the cutting conditions show that with a cutting speed of 200 m/min the tool life is 25 min, and with a cutting speed of 270 m/min the tool life is

15 min. The cutting speed which will give the required tool life of 100 min can now be calculated.

$$VT^n = C$$
$$\therefore \ \log V + n \log T = \log C.$$

Substitute known values,
$$\log 270 + n \log 15 = \log C$$
$$\log 200 + n \log 25 = \log C$$
$$2\cdot431\ 4 + (n \times 1\cdot176\ 1) = \log C \qquad \ldots (1)$$
$$2\cdot301\ 0 + (n \times 1\cdot397\ 9) = \log C \qquad \ldots (2)$$

Subtract $0\cdot130\ 4 - (n \times 0\cdot221\ 8) = 0$

$$\therefore \ n = \frac{0\cdot130\ 4}{0\cdot221\ 8}$$

$$n = 0\cdot589$$

Substitute in (1)
$$2\cdot431\ 4 + (0\cdot589 \times 1\cdot176\ 1) = \log C.$$
$$2\cdot431\ 4 + 0\cdot689 = \log C$$
$$\therefore \ \log C = 3\cdot120\ 4$$
$$C = 1\ 319.$$

In practice the value of C is not required,

82

since the values of n and $\log C$ are used to find the new value of the cutting speed V.

$$\log V + n \log T = \log C \qquad \log C = 3 \cdot 120\ 4$$
$$T = 100 \text{ min}$$
$$\log T = 2$$
$$n = 0 \cdot 589.$$

Substitute:
$$\text{Log } V + (0 \cdot 589 \times 2) = 3 \cdot 120\ 4$$
$$\log V = 3 \cdot 120\ 4 - 1 \cdot 178$$
$$= 1 \cdot 942\ 4$$
$$\therefore\ V = 87 \cdot 6 \text{ m/min}$$

An alternative solution can be used if we re-arrange the equation

$$\log V + n \log T = \log C$$
$$\text{to } \log V = -n \log T + \log C$$

in which n and $\log C$ are constants for a given set of conditions. This equation is therefore of the form $y = -mx + C$.

This is the equation to a straight-line graph with a negative slope.

Thus if we plot $\log V$ against $\log T$ for our known values, as in fig. 3.10, and draw a straight line through them, the required value of $\log T = \log 100 = 2$ can be inserted and the corresponding value of $\log V = 1 \cdot 945$ obtained. The required cutting speed is found from antilog V.

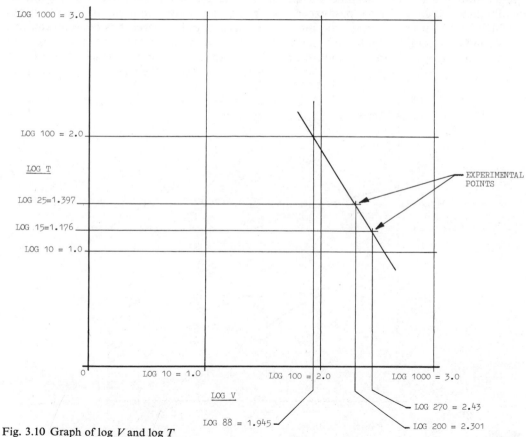

Fig. 3.10 Graph of log V and log T
  V = Cutting speed in metres/min.
  T = Tool life in minutes.

A word of warning on experimental method is important here. A straight-line graph can only be drawn through two experimental points if it is known that they conform to a straight-line law. In this case the work of many experimenters ensures us that this is so, but unless the law is known to operate these methods must not be used.

In practice it is unlikely that a speed of precisely 87·6 m/min could be obtained. The cutting speeds available depend upon the work diameter and the speed range available from the machine and the nearest *lower* speed should be used. This gives a further assurance that the tool life required will be exceeded.

It is not usually necessary to conduct tests on all the tools for a given machine set-up. Generally it can be decided from past experience which tool is working under the most arduous conditions and this tool is tested, the remainder working at suitable and convenient speeds.

CUTTING TOOL MATERIALS

The development of cutting tool materials has been essentially a search for materials able to withstand the high temperatures generated at high cutting speeds. Ideally, a cutting tool should have the following properties:

(*a*) hardness to resist abrasion

(*b*) the ability to retain this hardness at high temperatures

(*c*) toughness to withstand any shock loads imposed, particularly during an interrupted cut

(*d*) the ability to provide a good surface finish to reduce the chip/tool friction.

In practice it has been found impossible to arrange for a given material to have all these properties and research has concentrated on (*b*), the hot hardness, other means having been found to overcome the deficiencies of the material so far as the other desirable proper-

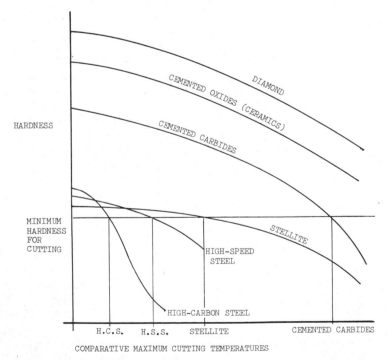

Fig. 3.11 Comparative values of maximum cutting temperatures for various tool materials.

ties are concerned.

The hardness of different tool materials can be plotted against temperature on a graph, as shown in fig. 3.11, across which can be drawn the line of the minimum hardness required for efficient cutting. The line then shows the comparative maximum temperatures at which the different tool materials can be used and although the graph cannot be used directly to determine cutting speeds it does indicate the relationship between cutting speeds and tool materials.

PLAIN HIGH-CARBON STEEL

This material has been discussed at length in Book 1. Here it is only necessary to point out that the steel has the property of softening as its temperature is increased. This process, known as *tempering*, is most useful in many applications but is a limitation as far as metal cutting is concerned. Cutting speeds with high-carbon steel tools are about one third of those with high-speed steel tools and the usefulness of high-carbon steel as a cutting tool material is largely limited to hand tools and other cutting tools operating at low cutting speeds.

HIGH-SPEED STEEL

Again, this material has been discussed at length in Book 1. Fig. 3.11 shows that its hardness does not drop below that required for cutting until a much higher temperature than that for plain carbon steel has been reached. This ability to remain hard at high temperatures is largely due to the inclusion of tungsten as an alloying element. The commonest high-speed steel is known as 18–4–2 H.S.S., these being the percentages of tungsten, chromium and vanadium present in a steel containing 0·7% carbon. The tungsten and chromium, in association with the carbon, form very hard carbides which themselves associate to form double carbides of high stability at high temperatures, hence the hot hardness. The vanadium has the effect of refining the grain structure and improving the shock resistance of the material.

High-speed steel is still probably the most common cutting tool material for use in machine tools. It is an extremely good material in the medium speed ranges, the cutting speed for its use on low carbon steel work material being approximately 30 m/min. Regrinding is a simple operation; cooling of the tool during grinding is necessary but not so critical as with plain carbon steel tools.

STELLITE

This is the proprietary name of a non-ferrous cast alloy of cobalt, chromium and tungsten, containing iron only as an impurity. It is hard in the as-cast condition and cannot be further hardened or softened by heat treatment. Fig. 3.11 shows that it retains its hardness up to higher temperatures than high-speed steel and it will in fact cut when red hot. It is also tough enough to be used as a tool bit or drill without having to be brazed as a tip on a tough steel shank. Stellite as a cutting tool material has been rather overshadowed by the cemented carbides but due to its extreme hot hardness it is said to have the ability to 'drill holes in hardened steel'. Actually this is not strictly true. Holes can be made in hardened material because this is locally softened by the heat generated by the drill friction. The work is clamped to the machine table, the drill run at high speed and pressed against the work until both work and drill become hot. This softens the work locally but not the drill which, although it may be glowing a dull red, proceeds to cut as soon as the work is soft enough. Obviously no coolant must be used in this process.

Apart from the specialised application outlined above, the main use of Stellite is now not in the metal cutting field. It can also be deposited on steel as a hard facing by a process similar to welding and is thus used for repairing tools which do not cut but are subject to friction and wear at high temperatures. A typical example is a pressure diecasting tool where the hot metal moving at high speed erodes the die, particularly at the point of entry. This wear is made up by the deposition of Stellite. Stellite can only be finished by grinding, of course, since it cannot be softened to enable it to be cut by conventional tools.

CEMENTED CARBIDES Carbides of certain metals, notably tungsten and boron, are extremely hard but are not in themselves tough enough to stand up to the rigours of the metal cutting process. They are therefore bonded together by another material just as bricks are cemented together by mortar, hence the term cemented carbides. In this case the bonding material is the metal cobalt. The tungsten carbide, or boron carbide, is milled to a fine powder and mixed in the desired proportions with powdered cobalt. The mixture is then placed in a mould and heated under pressure to form a slug of the material. At this stage it is crumbly or friable and is in what is known as the 'biscuit' form. It can, however, be handled and is then heated to a very high temperature in the presence of hydrogen. The hydrogen atmosphere prevents damage by atmospheric oxygen and the now-familiar cemented-carbide tool tip is produced. Fig. 3.11 gives some indication of its hardness values, which may be as high as Rockwell 85C. Increases in temperature reduce the hardness slowly but at 800°C the hardness is about Rockwell 65C, harder than fully-hardened high-speed steel at room temperature.

For many years cemented carbides were used as tips brazed to a tough medium-carbon steel shank but later developments include the clamped-tip tool discussed in detail in a subsequent section.

As a general guide, the cutting speed for a given material using cemented-carbide tools is about three times that for high-speed steel with the same material. Certain precautions must be observed in the use of cemented-carbide tools, notably:

(a) The machine must be rigid and free from vibration;

(b) The power and speeds available must be adequate to allow the tool to be used at high rates of metal removal;

(c) The tool must not be allowed to rub and it is better to withdraw the tool while the feed is still engaged rather than disengage the feed first;

(d) It is well worth while stoning the rake face of the tool to a high degree of surface finish.

Regarding (a) and (b), it is remarkable how many tools of this type are used on unsuitable machines because it is the done thing to use carbide-tipped tools. They are expensive to produce and maintain and should not be used where high-speed steel would do equally well. Regarding cutting speed, it will be found that if the cutting speed is too low a good but dull matt surface finish is produced. If the speed is raised, a point will be reached where the finish is equally good but brilliant and shining. The speed is then about right.

CERAMIC TOOLS The word 'ceramic' is derived from a Greek word meaning 'of the earth' and referred originally to earthenware products of the potter. With the growth of the electrical industry the same processes were used for electrical insulators[1] and as these developed it was realised that certain of the materials had the basic properties required for cutting tools, i.e., hardness and the ability to retain that hardness at high temperatures.

The most common ceramic material used for cutting tools is aluminium oxide, Al_2O_3. This is an abrasive or cutting constituent of grinding wheels but for the conventional metal cutting process a much denser form is required. The grit is milled to a very fine powder, mixed with very small amounts of bonding material and pressed into shape in moulds. The slugs produced are then fired in kilns at extremely high temperatures to

[1] A spark plug manufacturer kindly provided the author with some specially formed sticks of his insulator material which successfully cut mild steel at 300 m/min surface speed.

produce the tool tips used for cutting. They are so hard as to be almost unmachineable and are finished by light grinding with a diamond wheel.

The material is weak in bending strength and extremely brittle, so must consequently be well supported. The introduction of these ceramic tips led to the use of clamped throw-away-tip tools, since regrinding is extremely difficult and they cannot be brazed to tool steel shanks.

These tips are particularly well suited to finish-turning at very high speeds with low feed rates, the cutting speed being of the order of ten times that used with high-speed steel. They particularly lend themselves to negative-rake cutting.

NEGATIVE RAKE CUTTING We have seen that the modern tool materials, cemented carbides and ceramics, have the basic properties of abrasion resistance and hot hardness, but are extremely brittle and will not withstand shock or bending loads well. They must be well supported and designed so that the applied loads do not give rise to conditions which cause early failure.

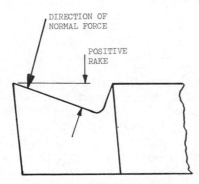

Fig. 3.12(*a*) Positive rake cutting tool.

Fig. 3.12(*a*) for positive-rake cutting shows that the force N normal to the rake face acts towards the unsupported part of the tool and tends to break off the tip.

If the rake angle is made negative as in fig. 3.12(*b*), the normal force N is inclined back-

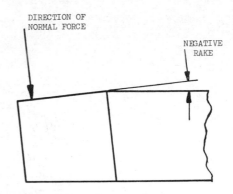

Fig. 3.12(*b*) Negative rake cutting tool.

wards into the body of the tool and the tip is in direct compression, which is a form of loading it is better equipped and supported to withstand.

Due to the much higher cutting speeds used with these tool materials, conditions in the cutting zone are different from those in conventional cutting. The action is so rapid that the heat generated by chip friction does not have time to pass into the work or the tool and almost all the heat is concentrated in the chip. The chip becomes much more plastic and a thin continuous chip results from a rake angle which would undoubtedly give a thicker discontinuous chip at lower speeds.

CLAMPED-TIP TOOLS If the tool used has a negative rake angle equal to the clearance angle, the angle between the rake and clearance faces is 90°. Thus a square slug of material with a suitable nose radius on each corner can be used directly as the cutting medium. Such a tool is shown in fig. 3.13. The tip is clamped in position, well supported to resist the cutting forces and with a minimum amount of tip overhang. The shank is so designed that the tip is inclined about an axis along the cutting edge, this inclination providing rake and clearance, and the cutting edge is thus at constant height over the whole depth of cut.

When the edge is worn the tip is turned through 90° to bring a new edge into action.

Fig. 3.13 Throw-away type clamped tip tool

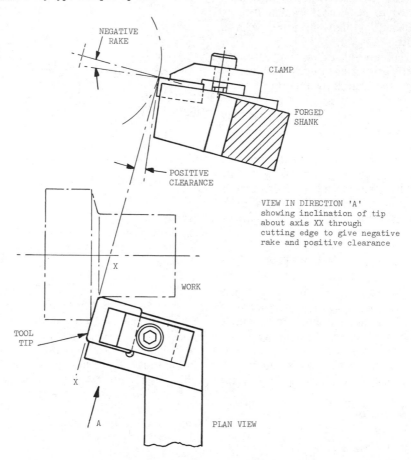

NEGATIVE RAKE

CLAMP

FORGED SHANK

POSITIVE CLEARANCE

VIEW IN DIRECTION 'A'
showing inclination of tip
about axis XX through
cutting edge to give negative
rake and positive clearance

WORK

TOOL TIP

X

A

PLAN VIEW

When all four top edges are worn the tip is turned over to reveal four new edges, giving a total of eight in all. When all the edges are worn the tip is disposed of, hence the name 'throw-away' tip.

A similar development has taken place with milling cutters. Until recently, inserted-tooth face mills had a series of brazed tips set into the body as shown in fig. 3.14(a). When the tips were worn, the regrinding and resetting of the teeth were critical to get all the tip points at the same height. Modern cutters employ throw-away tips which are accurately located in the body and, when replaced, position themselves accurately. Such a cutter is shown in fig. 3.14(b).

These milling cutters, usually face mills, are used at much higher speeds than conventional cutters, with a fine feed, to give very high rates of metal removal. As with turning tools, machine rigidity, power and speed are extremely important and these milling cutters should only be used under suitable conditions, not on an old, underpowered machine just for the sake of using this type of tool.

THE GRINDING PROCESS
Grinding is essentially a true metal-cutting process. That this is so is illustrated by fig. 3.15, which is a magnified photograph of the 'dust' obtained from grinding. The metallic particles are typical of metal-cutting swarf,

Fig. 3.14(a) Face milling cutter with negative-rake
tips brazed to shanks.

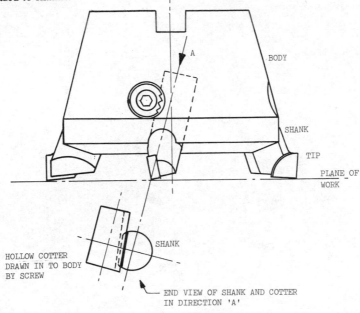

BODY

SHANK

TIP

PLANE OF
WORK

A

HOLLOW COTTER
DRAWN IN TO BODY
BY SCREW

SHANK

END VIEW OF SHANK AND COTTER
IN DIRECTION 'A'

NOTE SERRATIONS IN SHANK AND COTTER
TO PROVIDE POSITIVE POSITIONAL LOCKING

Fig. 3.14(b) Face milling cutter with negative-rake
throwaway-type tips.

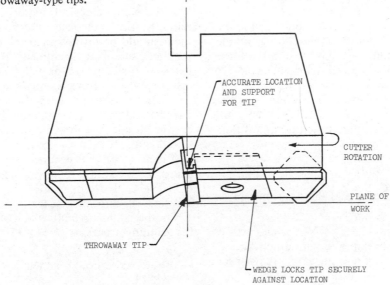

ACCURATE LOCATION
AND SUPPORT
FOR TIP

CUTTER
ROTATION

PLANE OF
WORK

THROWAWAY TIP

WEDGE LOCKS TIP SECURELY
AGAINST LOCATION

89

Fig. 3.15 Enlarged photograph of grinding dust. Note the similarity to swarf produced by conventional cutting processes.

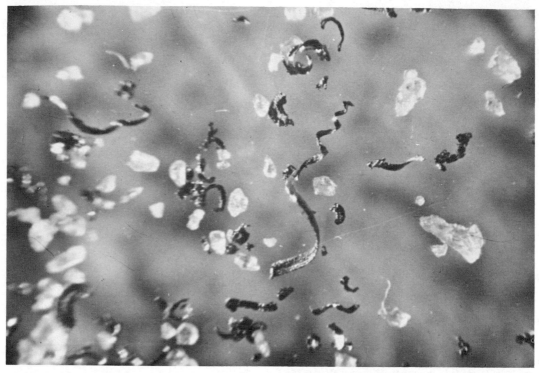

other materials present being the abrasive particles removed from the wheel.

A grinding wheel has two constituents, the abrasive particles which do the cutting and the bond which holds the abrasive in the form of a wheel or disc. The abrasive particles project slightly from the disc and, being sharp-edged, have a clearance angle and negative rake. As the edge of the particle becomes dull the loads imposed upon it increase and it fails in one of two ways:

(a) It is torn out of the bond, thus disclosing other particles;
or (b) It is shattered and the fragments have sharp edges which continue cutting.

This is known as the *self-sharpening* action of a grinding wheel and if a grinding wheel is operating correctly it is inevitable that wheel wear occurs.

GRINDING FAULTS In the grinding process many chips of material are being removed simultaneously and ideally all of them should be thrown clear of the work. In practice some are retained in the gaps between the abrasive particles and clog or *load* the wheel. If the loading becomes excessive the abrasive particles do not protrude enough and the process changes from one of cutting to one of rubbing and excessive heat is generated.

If wheel loading occurs, a higher wheel speed and reduced feed may help, or changing the wheel to one with a softer[1] bond and finer grit size will improve matters.

The other major fault which can occur in the grinding process is *glazing*. Glazing occurs

[1] 'Softer' in this context means a weaker bond. A 'soft' wheel has a weak bond and a 'hard' wheel a strong bond.

when the abrasive particles become blunt and lose their edges and the cutting load is not high enough to remove them from the bond. Again, the process changes from cutting to rubbing, with increased heat generation.

An obvious cure is to change to a softer (weaker bond) wheel, but the condition can be alleviated by increasing the amount of work each grain has to do, thus increasing the load and improving the self-sharpening action. If the wheel speed is reduced or the work speed increased, the amount of metal removed per grain is increased and the likelihood of removing blunted grains is correspondingly increased, with a resulting improvement in action.

The opposite fault to glazing is excessive wheel wear, due to grains being removed before they become blunt. It follows that if the opposite remedial action is taken the work done by each grain is reduced. Thus, in this case, the wheel speed is increased and the work speed reduced.

Whichever fault occurs, and whichever remedy is chosen, the wheel should always be dressed by a diamond to restore its cutting action. No change in conditions will unclog a loaded wheel or re-form an excessively worn wheel.

SELECTION OF GRINDING WHEELS If a grinding wheel is correctly selected in the first place and its conditions of use are correct, none of the above faults should arise. The factors affecting the choice of a grinding wheel are:

(*a*) workpiece material
(*b*) angle of contact between work and wheel
(*c*) condition of machine
(*d*) wheel speed
(*e*) work speed.

The types of grinding wheel available must be considered in the light of these factors and the characteristics of the wheels must be balanced against the operating conditions. The characteristics of the wheel are indicated by the code on the cardboard pad on the side of the wheel. This follows a British Standard (BS 1814: 1952) and may be interpreted as follows:

A = Type of abrasive
60 = Grit size
N = Grade
8 = Structure
V = Type of bond

Type of Abrasive. Two types of abrasive are generally used; aluminium oxide, signified by the letter A, and silicon carbide, signified by the letter C. Aluminium oxide is the slightly softer and should be used for grinding harder materials. Aluminium oxide wheels are usually white but may be red or brown in colour. Silicon carbide is a green material and wheels of this abrasive are known as green grit wheels.

Grit Size. The abrasive grains used are accurately graded so that all grains in a wheel are of the same size. This is achieved by sieving or, with the finer grains, by centrifugal separation. The number indicates the number of meshes per unit length of the sieve they will just pass through, thus a large number indicates a fine grit and vice-versa. The grain sizes generally used are as follows:

Roughing work	8–24
Commercially-accepted finish	30–60
Fine finish	70–180
Very fine finish	220–600

Grade of Wheel. This indicates the bond strength, a weak-bond wheel being known as a soft wheel and a strong-bond wheel as a hard one. A low letter of the alphabet indicates a soft wheel and a high letter a hard one. Thus the grading is as follows:

Very soft	A, B, C, D, E
Soft	F, G, H, I, J, K
Medium	L, M, N, O, P
Hard	Q, R, S, T, U
Very hard	V, W, X, Y, Z.

Structure. The structure of a wheel is an

indication of the proportion of bond to abrasive. An open-structure wheel may have up to 30% bond while a close wheel may have only 10%. The structure is indicated by a simple numerical scale as follows:

Dense	0, 1, 2, 3	finishing
Medium	4, 5, 6, 7	general purpose
Open	8, 9, 10, 11, 12 etc.,	high metal removal rates.

Type of Bond. The final letter indicates the type of bond used in the wheel, as follows:

Vitrified bond	V	Most used for general work
Resinoid bond	B	For fettling castings
Rubber bond	R	Strongest type. Used for thin cut-off wheels
Shellac bond	E	Thin wheels with a fine finish
Silicate bond	S	Mild action. Used for fine-edged tools. Very large wheels.

Thus, the wheel grade A 60 N 8 V indicates an aluminium oxide (A) wheel of medium grit size (60), of medium hardness (N), having an open structure (8) and with a vitrified bond (V).

This information must now be balanced against the operating conditions. A good general rule is

Harder work—softer wheel.

This applies to both bond strength and type of abrasive. If, therefore, we are grinding a hardened tool steel, an aluminium oxide wheel should be used. If a soft material is being ground, a silicon carbide wheel is generally used, simply to achieve the desired accuracy and finish. The harder grit retains its sharpness longer while the soft bond allows the relatively low loads to remove dull grains before glazing occurs.

Angle of Wheel Contact. This depends largely on the type of work being carried out and fig. 3.16 shows the variation in contact area between different machine set-ups. The rule is

Large angle of contact—softer wheel.

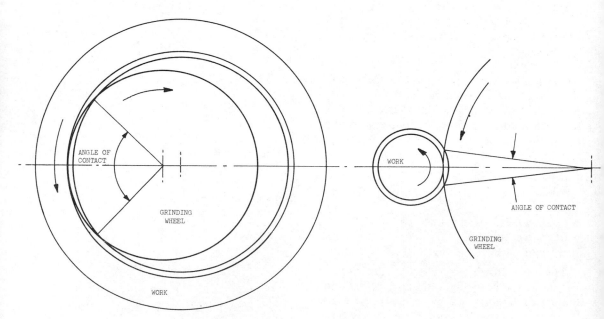

Fig. 3.16 Effect of type of work on angle of contact.

Machine Condition. This refers generally to the rigidity of the machine and the amount of vibration present. The rule is

Good rigid machine—softer wheel.

Wheel Speed. If the wheel speed is high, the work moves only a small distance while the abrasive grain passes. Thus at high wheel speeds each grain removes only a small piece of material and is therefore lightly loaded. The rule is

High wheel speed—softer wheel.

Work Speed. If the work speed is high, a grain of abrasive will be called upon to remove more material, each time it passes, than if the work speed is low. It follows that the rule is

High work speed—harder wheel.

Consider now a situation where a large inside diameter is being rough-ground in a hardened steel die ring. Because of the large diameter, the surface speed of the work will be relatively high and that of the wheel will be relatively low. The angle of contact will be large and we can decide from the known conditions that the type of grinding wheel required must be as follows:

Factor	Conditions	Decision
(a) Wheel material	Hard work	Al_2O_3
(b) Grit size	Roughing	Coarse
(c) Wheel grade	High work speed	Hard
	Large contact angle	Soft
	Low wheel speed	Hard
	Old machine	Hard
(d) Wheel structure	Roughing	Open
(e) Type of bond	General	Vitrified bond

Thus we need an *Aluminium oxide* wheel of *coarse grit* with a *hard bond* of *open structure* and a *vitrified bond.* Such a wheel would be specified by

A   20   Q   10   V.

SUMMARY

In these days of high productivity it is not enough for the technician to know how to grind a tool on an offhand grinding machine. He must know of the forces involved in cutting and thus understand the reasoning behind applications of the tools with which he is familiar. He must know why it may be more economic to run a tool at less than its most efficient speed for the benefit of tool life. Particularly the operating conditions must be appreciated and the fallacy of using more sophisticated tool materials where high-speed steel would do as well must be recognised. The reasoning behind the choice of a grinding wheel must be clear, as also must be the way to correct any operating faults which may arise.

4

Turning and Boring

The relative proportion of cylindrical work and other solids of revolution manufactured in modern industry can be assessed by noting the number of machines devoted to work of this nature in a well-equipped toolroom. Usually the lathes outnumber the rest of the machines put together, including vertical and horizontal boring machines, and jig boring machines. These boring machines also are used to machine holes, outside diameters and flat faces on work which cannot be con-

veniently machined in a lathe because of the size, shape or accuracy required. It is interesting to note that in workshops where these specialist machines are not available, such work is usually done on a lathe but with less convenience and greater cost.

In Book 1, Chapter 8, the alignments of the centre lathe were discussed, as were the basic principles of work-holding, screw-cutting and boring of holes to a high degree of positional accuracy. At this stage the student

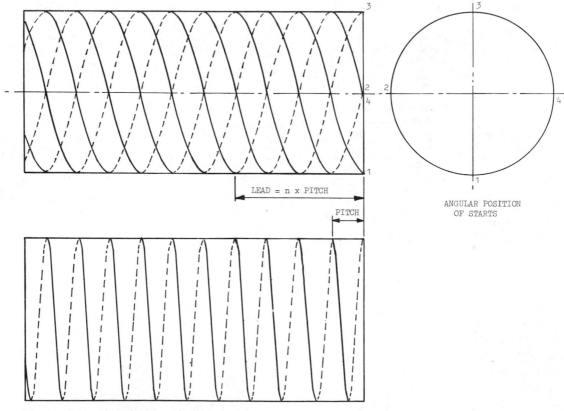

Fig. 4.1 Comparison between single and multi-start threads.

should, by his studies and practical experience, be familiar with these principles and they will not be repeated here. This Chapter will deal with certain more advanced operations which may be carried out on a centre lathe, notably the production of special screw threads. It will also deal with the principles involved in the uses of the specialist machines mentioned above.

MULTI-START SCREW THREADS

Many instances occur in industry of a multi-start screw thread, i.e., a cylinder on which a number of identical screw threads are cut equally spaced, so that a casual examination gives the impression of a single thread. In all cases the effect is to give a lower velocity ratio and mechanical advantage but a greater movement of the nut for a single turn of the screw.

One turn of a single-start screw of 5 mm pitch moves the nut the same distance, 5 mm. One turn of a three-start screw of 5 mm pitch moves the nut three times this distance, i.e., 15 mm.

Note that:

(a) Pitch = distance from a point on one thread to a similar point on the next thread
(b) Lead = distance moved by the nut for one turn of the screw
= $n \times$ pitch where n = number of starts.

A comparison of two such threads is shown in fig. 4.1.

Multi-start threads are used where a large axial movement of the screw or nut is required for a small angular movement. Typical examples range from the thread on a fountain pen cap to the screw of a fly-press. Other examples are two- and three-start worms, oil grooves in bearings and the rifling of a gun barrel. The principles involved in cutting multi-start threads are the same as those outlined in Book 1 for single-start threads but there are three additional problems to be overcome:

(a) Calculation and setting up of gear trains
(b) Indexing to obtain the correct spacing of the starts
(c) Grinding the tool.

GEAR TRAIN CALCULATIONS

In Book 1 it was shown that the formula used to find the gears for a single-start thread was

$$\frac{\text{No. of teeth on DRIVER}}{\text{No. of teeth on DRIVEN}}$$

$$= \frac{\text{T.P.I. on lead screw}}{\text{T.P.I. on work}}$$

$$= \frac{\text{Pitch of work}}{\text{Pitch of lead screw}}$$

In the case of a multi-start thread the tool movement must be equal to the LEAD, not the pitch. It follows that the expression used for calculating the gears must be modified to:

$$\frac{\text{DRIVER}}{\text{DRIVEN}} = \frac{\text{LEAD of work}}{\text{LEAD of lead screw}}$$

Example. Calculate the gears required, and show their relative positions with the aid of a diagram, to cut a FOUR-start thread of 2 mm pitch on a lathe with a lead screw of 5 mm pitch.

$$\frac{\text{Driver}}{\text{Driven}} = \frac{\text{lead of work}}{\text{lead of lead screw}} = \frac{4 \times 2\,\text{mm}}{5\,\text{mm}}$$

$$\frac{\text{Driver}}{\text{Driven}} = \frac{8\,\text{mm}}{5\,\text{mm}}$$

$$= \frac{80}{50}$$

The arrangement of the gears is shown in fig. 4.2. Note that as the lead of the work is *greater* than that of the lead screw the work will rotate more slowly than the lead screw and therefore the driver will be the larger gear.[1]

[1] Avoid preconceived notions about the positions of the gears. A student asked the author's assistance in this matter, having calculated the correct gear train but finding that it cut a fine thread. On being asked

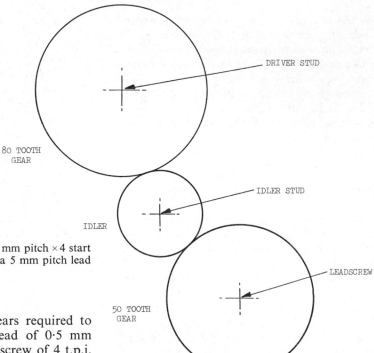

80 TOOTH
GEAR

IDLER

DRIVER STUD

IDLER STUD

LEADSCREW

50 TOOTH
GEAR

Fig. 4.2 Gear train for cutting a 2 mm pitch × 4 start thread on a lathe having a 5 mm pitch lead screw.

Example. Calculate the gears required to cut a three-start metric thread of 0·5 mm pitch on a lathe with a lead screw of 4 t.p.i.

$$1 \text{ mm} = \frac{1}{25 \cdot 4} \text{ in}$$

$$\therefore \text{ Pitch of work} = \frac{0 \cdot 5}{25 \cdot 4} \text{ in}$$

$$\text{Lead of work} = \frac{3 \times 0 \cdot 5}{25 \cdot 4} \text{ in}$$

$$\frac{\text{Driver}}{\text{Driven}} = \frac{\text{Lead of work}}{\text{Lead of lead screw}}$$

$$= \frac{\dfrac{3 \times 0 \cdot 5}{25 \cdot 4} \text{ in}}{\frac{1}{4} \text{ in}}$$

$$= \frac{3 \times 0 \cdot 5 \times 4}{25 \cdot 4}$$

$$\frac{\text{Driver}}{\text{Driven}} = \frac{6}{25 \cdot 4} \times \frac{5}{5}$$

$$= \frac{30}{127}$$

where he put the gears on the lathe he pointed out that, '. . . the smallest gear is always the driver.' It is not; the driver is the gear calculated as the driver in the expression used.

The required gear train is shown in fig. 4.3. It may be recalled from Book 1 that, in the absence of a 127-tooth gear, a 63-tooth gear may be used as a *driver* to give an approximate gear train with an error of only 1 part in 8 000.

$$\frac{\text{Driver}}{\text{Driven}} = \frac{30}{127}$$

let driver = 63

$$\frac{63}{\text{Driven}} = \frac{30}{127}$$

$$\text{Driven} = \frac{63 \times 127}{30}$$

$$= \frac{8\,001}{30} \simeq \frac{8\,000}{30}$$

$$\therefore \frac{\text{Driver}}{\text{Driven}} = \frac{63}{8\,000/30} = \frac{63 \times 30}{8\,000}$$

$$\frac{\text{Driver}}{\text{Driven}} = \frac{63 \times 30}{80 \times 100}$$

These gears are arranged as shown in fig. 4.4.

It may well be that neither a 63- nor a 127-tooth gear is available. In this case a close approximation to the gear train can be found by the use of continued fractions. The procedure to be followed is set out step by step below but the mathematical reasons for these steps are not explained in detail.

(*a*) Required gear train $= \dfrac{30}{127}$

(*b*) Arrange for division with the fraction inverted i.e., $\dfrac{127}{30}$

(*c*) Proceed as in normal long division but, after each division, divide the *remainder* into the previous divisor until there is no remainder.

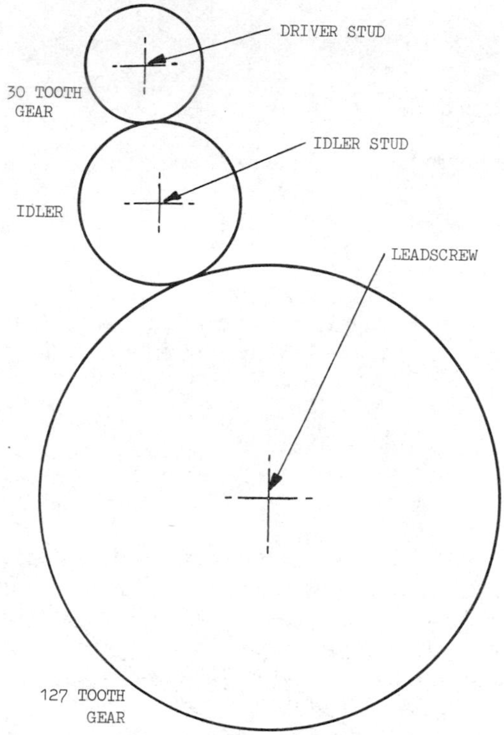

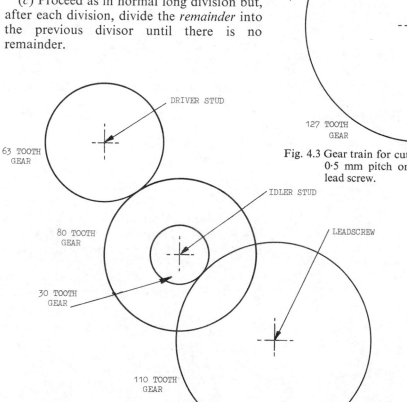

Fig. 4.3 Gear train for cutting a three-start thread of 0·5 mm pitch on a lathe having a 4 t.p.i. lead screw.

Fig. 4.4 Gear train for cutting a 3 start thread of 0·5 mm pitch on a lathe having a 4 t.p.i. lead screw using a 63-tooth gear as a driver.

$$30)\ \overline{127}\ (4$$
$$\underline{120}$$

remainder $\overline{7)\ 30}\ (4$
$\underline{28}$

remainder .... $\overline{2)\ 7}\ (3$
$\underline{6}$

remainder .... $\overline{1)\ 2}\ (2$
$\underline{2}$

remainder .... $\overline{0}$

(*d*) The quotients (in this case 4, 4, 3, 2) are now set out as a *continued fraction* as follows:

$$\cfrac{1}{4+\cfrac{1}{4+\cfrac{1}{3+\cfrac{1}{2}}}}$$

(*e*) Take this continued fraction a step at a time. It will be found that as more of the stages are included the fractions calculated become closer approximations of 30/127, i.e., they converge on the true value and are known as *convergents*.

1st convergent

$$=\frac{1}{4}$$

2nd convergent

$$=\frac{1}{4+\frac{1}{4}}=\frac{1}{\frac{17}{4}}=\frac{4}{17}$$

3rd convergent

$$=\frac{1}{4+\cfrac{1}{4+\frac{1}{3}}}=\frac{1}{4+\cfrac{1}{\frac{13}{3}}}=\frac{1}{4+\frac{3}{13}}=\frac{1}{\frac{55}{13}}=\frac{13}{55}$$

4th convergent

$$=\frac{1}{4+\cfrac{1}{4+\cfrac{1}{3+\frac{1}{2}}}}=\frac{1}{4+\cfrac{1}{4+\frac{2}{7}}}=\frac{1}{4+\frac{7}{30}}=\frac{30}{127}$$

The last convergent is not available as a gear train but its calculation checks that the

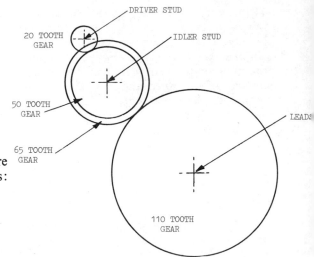

Fig. 4.5 Gear train calculated using continued fractions.

continued fraction is correct. The nearest approximation is 13/55

$$\therefore\ \frac{\text{Driver}}{\text{Driven}}=\frac{13}{55}=\frac{2\times6\cdot5}{5\times11}$$

$$=\frac{20}{50}\times\frac{65}{110}$$

This gear train can be set up as shown in fig. 4.5, and, being an approximation, will give rise to a pitch error which should now be calculated to determine whether it will be acceptable or not.

The actual lead cut can be found by referring the ratio 13/55 back to the expression

$$\frac{\text{Driver}}{\text{Driven}}=\frac{\text{Lead of work}}{\text{Lead of lead screw}}$$

$$\frac{13}{55}=\frac{\text{Lead of work }(x)}{\text{Lead of lead screw }(\frac{1}{4}\text{ in})}$$

$$x=\frac{13}{55}\times\frac{1}{4}\text{ in}$$

$$=\frac{13}{55}\times\frac{1}{4}\times25\cdot4\ \text{mm}=\frac{330\cdot2}{220}$$

$$=1\cdot500\ 9\ \text{mm}[1]$$

As this error is only 9 parts in 10 000 the thread would almost certainly be acceptable for commercial work.

Example. Calculate the gear train required to cut a four-start thread with a pitch of 3 mm on a lathe whose lead screw has a pitch of 5 mm.

Lead of work $= 3$ mm $\times 4 = 12$ mm

$$\frac{\text{Driver}}{\text{Driven}} = \frac{\text{Lead of work}}{\text{Lead of lead screw}}$$

$$= \frac{12 \text{ mm}}{5 \text{ mm}}$$

$$= \frac{12}{5} = \frac{4 \times 3}{2 \cdot 5 \times 2}$$

$$= \frac{40}{25} \times \frac{30}{20}$$

In this case, as both the work and the lead-screw are of metric pitch the calculation is quite straightforward, no translation gear nor approximation being necessary. The gear train is shown in fig. 4.6.

INDEXING TO OBTAIN THE CORRECT SPACING OF STARTS

Referring back to fig. 4.1, we can see that when the first-start thread has been completely cut, the correct relative position of the tool and the work for the second-start thread can be fixed by either of two basic methods:

1. Move the tool axially one pitch with the work remaining stationary.
or 2. Index the work through $1/n$ starts with the saddle remaining stationary.

1. AXIAL MOVEMENT OF TOOL
This is easily accomplished by using the compound top slide, which must of course be

---

¹ This calculation is to determine a small error and should not be carried out on a slide rule. Since the error is in the fifth significant figure, six-figure logarithms would need to be used for a logarithmic solution. Such calculations should therefore be made longhand.

set accurately parallel to the work axis. Unfortunately, on many lathes the accuracy of the compound top slide and dial leaves a lot to be desired. This can be overcome by using the lead screw to move the top slide and measuring the movement by a gauge block and a dial gauge as shown in fig. 4.7. The dial gauge is set to read zero against the gauge block, which is held against a convenient surface of the top slide. The gauge block is now removed and the top slide is advanced until the dial gauge again reads zero. On modern machines this is probably the most-used method when the machine is fitted with a Norton gearbox.

2. INDEXING THE WORK Probably a more accurate method of indexing to obtain the correct spacing of the starts is to rotate the work through $1/n$ revolutions, everything else being fixed, where n is the number of starts.

If the work is held between centres and much of this work is done, it is worth while making up a special catch plate as shown in fig. 4.8. This has twelve equally-spaced slots and after each start is cut the work is removed

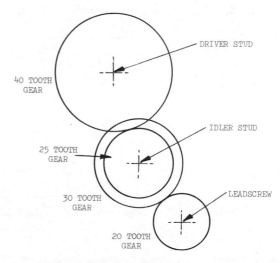

Fig. 4.6 Gear train for cutting a 4 start thread of 3 mm pitch on a lathe having a lead screw of 5 mm pitch.

and then replaced with the driving dog located in the correct slot for the next start. Twelve is a useful number of slots as it enables 1, 2, 3, 4 and 6 starts to be cut.

If the work is held in a chuck, or if the quantity of work is such that the manufacture of a special catch plate is not justified, the old method of marking the gear train may be used. The angular position of the headstock spindle relative to the lead screw must be fixed, and the lead screw itself must be locked by engaging the saddle half-nuts. Two teeth on the driven gear and the single tooth which they span on the idler gear are marked with chalk. Now two teeth on the idler and the tooth which they span on the driver are similarly marked with chalk. The number of teeth on the driver is now divided by the number of starts and teeth are marked at the required intervals as shown in fig. 4.9.

The idler can now be removed, but as it is marked relative to the lead screw it can be put back in exactly the same position. With the idler removed the headstock can be indexed

as required until, when the idler is re-assembled in the correct position relative to the driven gear, the driver gear is in the correct position relative to the idler, and has therefore been indexed through the required part of a revolution.

This method has the limitation that on modern lathes the screw-cutting gear train is not accessible, being part of a Norton gear-box. Further, the number of teeth on the driver must be divisible by the number of starts and the method is rather laborious and messy. On the whole, one of the two previous methods is to be recommended although this gear-marking technique is probably the most accurate.

GRINDING THE TOOL
Most multi-start threads, oil grooves, etc., have a steep helix angle as shown in fig. 4.10. If a tool ground for a square thread has the normal 5°–7° side clearance as shown in cross-section (a), it will foul on the leading edge and have excessive clearance on the

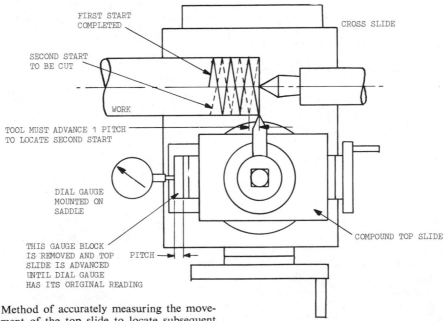

Fig. 4.7 Method of accurately measuring the movement of the top slide to locate subsequent starts.

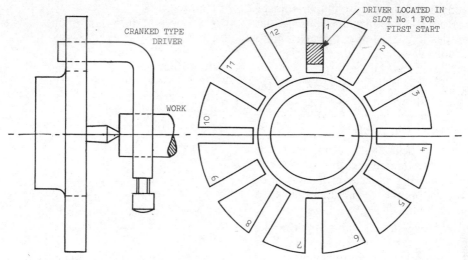

Fig. 4.8 Special catch plate for indexing work to locate subsequent starts.

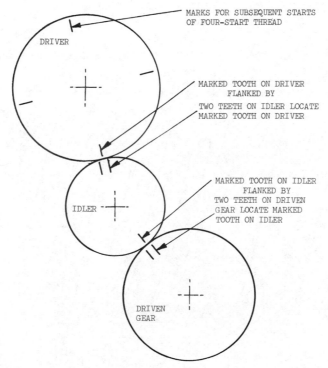

Fig. 4.9 Marking screwcutting change wheels to locate subsequent starts.

trailing edge. The tool should therefore be ground to coincide with the helix angle plus 5° on the leading edge and the helix angle minus 5° on the trailing edge to give the correct clearance, as shown in (b).

If the rake face is ground normal to the helix angle as shown in fig. 4.10(c), the tool width must be compensated for this angle or a narrow thread will result.

Note that the helix angle at the root of the thread is steeper than at the crest. It is therefore the root helix angle which should be used in calculating the tool angles rather than the crest helix angle.

Example. Design a tool with suitable angles for cutting a square thread which has four starts of 5 mm pitch and an outside diameter of 50 mm.

Tool width
$$= 2 \cdot 5 \text{ mm (half pitch)}$$
Thread depth
$$= 2 \cdot 5 \text{ mm}$$
Root diameter
$$= 50 \text{ mm} - (2 \times 2 \cdot 5 \text{ mm})$$
$$= 45 \text{ mm}$$
Root circumference
$$= \pi \times 45 \text{ mm} = 141 \cdot 5 \text{ mm}$$

Referring to fig. 4.11:
$$\tan \theta = \frac{\text{lead}}{\text{root circumference}}$$
$$(\theta = \text{helix angle.})$$
$$= \frac{4 \times 5 \text{ mm}}{141 \cdot 5}$$
$$= 0 \cdot 141$$
$$\therefore \ \theta = 8° \ 3'$$
Leading edge angle
$$= 8° + 5° = 13°$$
Trailing edge angle
$$= 8° - 5° = \ 3°$$

Fig. 4.10 Section of 2-start square thread showing the effect of the helix angle on the tool angles.

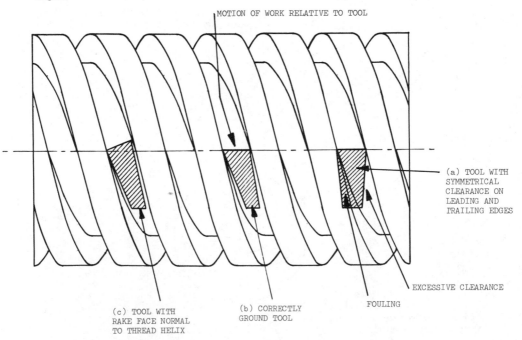

(a) TOOL WITH SYMMETRICAL CLEARANCE ON LEADING AND TRAILING EDGES

EXCESSIVE CLEARANCE

FOULING

(c) TOOL WITH RAKE FACE NORMAL TO THREAD HELIX

(b) CORRECTLY GROUND TOOL

MOTION OF WORK RELATIVE TO TOOL

Fig. 4.11 Calculation of the helix angle θ.

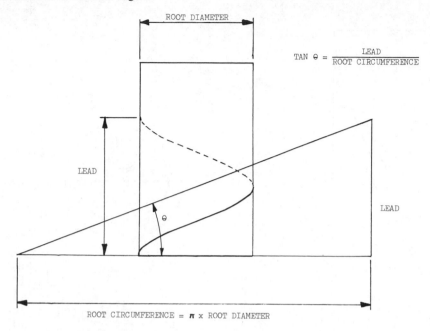

$$TAN\ \Theta = \frac{LEAD}{ROOT\ CIRCUMFERENCE}$$

ROOT CIRCUMFERENCE = π x ROOT DIAMETER

Other angles are as for a normal square cutting tool as shown in fig. 4.12.

If the helix is carried to an extreme such as that shown in fig. 4.13, the helix angle is so steep that it is more nearly parallel with the axis than normal to it. This raises the point that the tool motion is then a far greater component of the cutting speed than is the work rotation. For this reason, the main power requirement is in the tool feed motion rather than in the work rotation. On lathes which were specially designed for this purpose, such as gun rifling lathes, the motor drive was via a gear box to the lead screw and the headstock was rotated by the screw-cutting change wheels rather than vice-versa, as on a conventional lathe.

THREAD WHIRLING

This is a modern process for the production of large screw threads and worms, be they single or multi-start. One of the problems with screw cutting is that either a great many cuts have to be taken to complete the thread

Fig. 4.12 Cutting tool for a square thread of 50 mm outside diameter and 5 mm pitch having 4 starts.

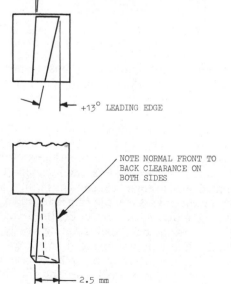

-3° TRAILING EDGE

+13° LEADING EDGE

NOTE NORMAL FRONT TO BACK CLEARANCE ON BOTH SIDES

2.5 mm

103

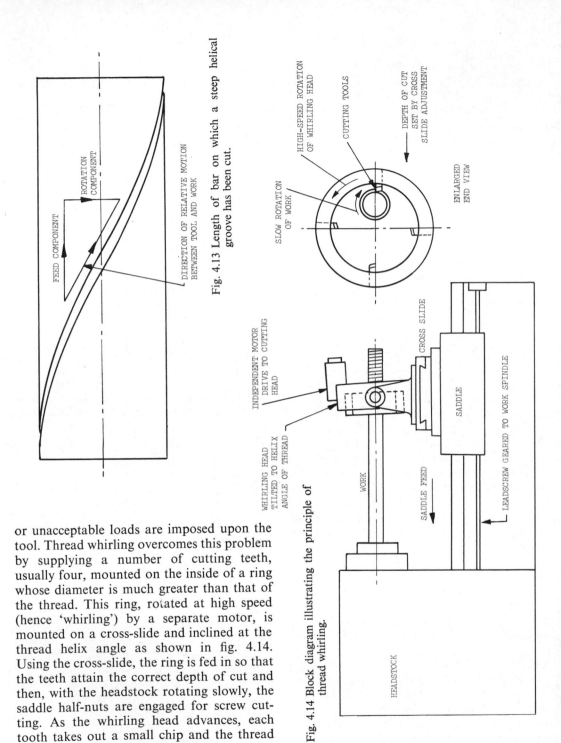

FEED COMPONENT

ROTATION COMPONENT

DIRECTION OF RELATIVE MOTION BETWEEN TOOL AND WORK

Fig. 4.13 Length of bar on which a steep helical groove has been cut.

HIGH-SPEED ROTATION OF WHIRLING HEAD

CUTTING TOOLS

DEPTH OF CUT SET BY CROSS SLIDE ADJUSTMENT

SLOW ROTATION OF WORK

ENLARGED END VIEW

INDEPENDENT MOTOR DRIVE TO CUTTING HEAD

WHIRLING HEAD TILTED TO HELIX ANGLE OF THREAD

WORK

SADDLE FEED

CROSS SLIDE

SADDLE

LEADSCREW GEARED TO WORK SPINDLE

HEADSTOCK

Fig. 4.14 Block diagram illustrating the principle of thread whirling.

or unacceptable loads are imposed upon the tool. Thread whirling overcomes this problem by supplying a number of cutting teeth, usually four, mounted on the inside of a ring whose diameter is much greater than that of the thread. This ring, rotated at high speed (hence 'whirling') by a separate motor, is mounted on a cross-slide and inclined at the thread helix angle as shown in fig. 4.14. Using the cross-slide, the ring is fed in so that the teeth attain the correct depth of cut and then, with the headstock rotating slowly, the saddle half-nuts are engaged for screw cutting. As the whirling head advances, each tooth takes out a small chip and the thread

104

finish is really a series of very small curved facets rather than a smooth surface. This is not so marked as to be noticeable. If Acme threads or worms are to be cut, the teeth in the whirling head can be arranged so that two teeth gash the work to depth and the third and fourth teeth clean up the flanks. This process enables very large threads and worms to be cut in one pass, using a high-speed cutter and a very slow feed motion.

VERTICAL BORING MACHINES

Consider a casting of 2 m outside diameter by 0·7 m inside diameter and 0·5 m long made of cast iron of relative density 7·2. The total mass of such a casting can be calculated as follows:

Volume

$$= \frac{\pi}{4} \times \text{length} \times (D^2 - d^2)$$

$$= \frac{\pi}{4} \times 0 \cdot 5 \times (2^2 - 0 \cdot 7^2) \text{ m}^3$$

$$= \frac{\pi}{4} \times 0 \cdot 5 \times (4 - 0 \cdot 49) \times 10 \times 10 \times 10 \text{ dm}^3$$

As mass in kilogrammes = Volume in dm³ × relative density

$$\text{Mass} = \frac{\pi}{4} \times \frac{0 \cdot 5 \times 3 \cdot 51 \times 7 \cdot 2 \times 100^3}{1\ 000} \text{ kg}$$

$$= 9\ 925 \text{ kg}$$

$$\simeq 10\ 000 \text{ kg}$$

Fig. 4.15 Block diagram showing the main features of a vertical boring machine.

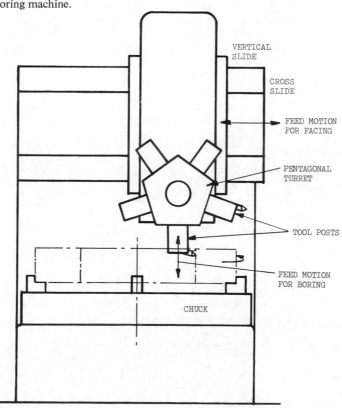

VERTICAL SLIDE

CROSS SLIDE

FEED MOTION FOR FACING

PENTAGONAL TURRET

TOOL POSTS

FEED MOTION FOR BORING

CHUCK

Consider now the difficulties of bolting such a casting to a lathe faceplate in such a way that it is accurately positioned and held while it is machined. Apart from these problems the loads imposed on the headstock bearings by an overhanging load of this nature would be far too great and by its nature the lathe is the most flexible of machine tools. Such a load would cause machine deflections which would introduce unacceptable misalignments.

The solution is to stand the lathe on its headstock so that the bearings are only taking small radial loads and the thrust load due to the weight of the casting can be taken by a thrust bearing properly designed and equipped to carry it. Such a machine is the vertical boring machine shown in diagrammatic form in fig. 4.15. It may be fitted with a single vertical slide carrying a five-sided turret which can be indexed to bring different types of tool into use or, in the case of larger machines, two independent vertical slides may be fitted, each carrying tool posts so that one can be boring while the other is either facing or turning the outside diameter of the work.

Typical boring machine work with which the author has been associated has been the machining of very large dies for press tools used for deep drawing. In heavy industry the vertical boring machine may be used for machining very large blanks for gears such as those used in the reduction sets of ships' propulsion machinery.

BALANCING OF FACEPLATE WORK

Faceplate work, either on a lathe or on a vertical boring machine, is often not symmetrical in nature and hence out-of-balance forces are developed, causing vibrations and excessive bearing loads which can become dangerous. Sometimes the operator fits balance weights which are selected by trial and error until the lathe stops jumping up and down! By then the damage may be done.

If an out-of-balance mass of W kilogrammes is moving in a circular path with

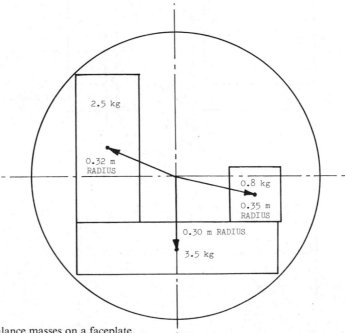

Fig. 4.16 Out-of-balance masses on a faceplate.

an angular velocity of ω radians per second at a radius r metres, a radial force of $\dfrac{W\omega^2 r}{g}$ newtons is generated. This force is always radial and when the centre of gravity of the mass is at the top of its path the force is vertically upwards, while at the instant the mass is at the bottom of its path the force is vertically downwards. This force can be balanced by an equal and opposite force $\dfrac{W_1\omega^2 r_1}{g}$ newtons, produced by a mass of W_1 kilogrammes placed at a radius r_1 metres diametrally opposite the centre of gravity of the out-of-balance mass W.

Therefore
$$\frac{W\omega^2 r}{g} = \frac{W_1\omega^2 r_1}{g}$$
and $\quad Wr = W_1 r_1$

The balance weight of mass W_1 is often determined by the weights available and the radius r_1 at which it must be fitted can now be calculated.

The above case is the simplest one of a single out-of-balance mass. In most cases the workpiece and the ancilliary equipment, such as an angle plate, necessary to mount it on the faceplate give a more complex situation. Consider the situation in fig. 4.16. The three rectangular blocks represent various parts of a turning fixture whose masses and positions of centres of gravity are as shown. In this case the balance weights available are of mass 1 kg, 2 kg, 3 kg and 4 kg, and it is required to select a suitable balance weight and decide upon the radius and position at which it must be attached to the faceplate.

The force[1] diagram showing the various values of Wr is shown in fig. 4.17(a) and the vector diagram is shown in fig. 4.17(b). The closure of the vector diagram is, to scale, equal to the value of $W_b r_b$ and its direction indicates the angular position of the balancing

[1] These are not forces but are proportionate to the forces acting. The actual force exerted by each out of balance mass is $W\omega^2 r/g$ but as ω^2/g is constant for all cases it cancels out and can be ignored.

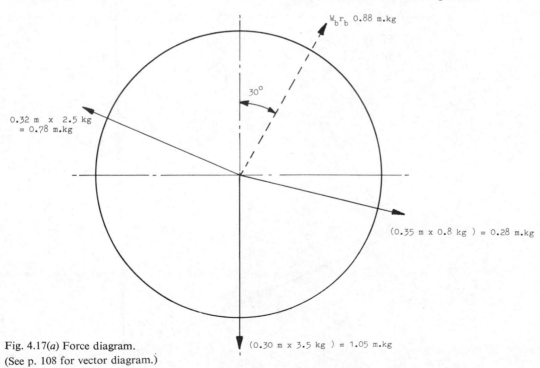

Fig. 4.17(a) Force diagram.
(See p. 108 for vector diagram.)

mass relative to the vertical datum used. From the diagram:

$$W_b r_b = 0.88 \text{ m kg}$$

If the 2 kg balance weight is used:

$$r_b = \frac{0.88 \text{ m kg}}{2 \text{ kg}}$$

$$r_b = 0.44 \text{ m}$$

It must be remembered that balancing does not remove the forces but prevents vibration by adding an equal and opposite force. At high speeds the faceplate is under considerable stress of a tensile nature and cast iron, from which faceplates are made, is weak in tension. It is therefore advisable to keep speeds down to avoid danger through failure of the faceplate.

THE HORIZONTAL BORING MACHINE

To machine the bores, flanges and other holes of the casting shown in fig. 4.18 would present almost insurmountable difficulties on the lathe because, apart from the difficulties of holding and mounting, the work would have to be repositioned on the faceplate to machine each bore.

The horizontal boring machine, whose alignments are shown in fig. 4.19, is designed for such work as this. It has a horizontal table

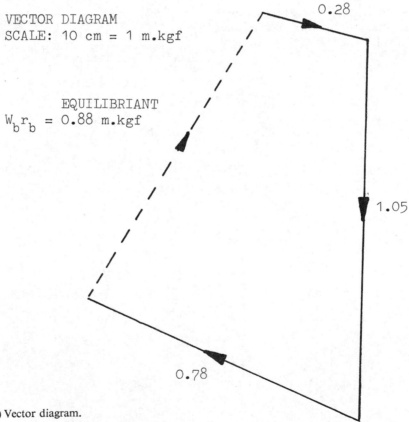

VECTOR DIAGRAM
SCALE: 10 cm = 1 m.kgf

EQUILIBRIANT
$W_b r_b$ = 0.88 m.kgf

0.28

1.05

0.78

Fig. 4.17(*b*) Vector diagram.

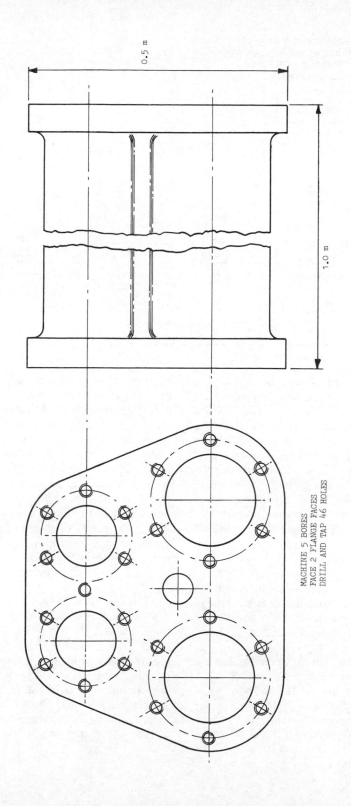

0.5 m

1.0 m

MACHINE 5 BORES
FACE 2 FLANGE FACES
DRILL AND TAP 46 HOLES

Fig. 4.18 Typical casting to be machined on a horizontal boring machine.

Fig. 4.19 Block diagram showing the main features of
a horizontal boring machine with a boring
bar in position for through boring.

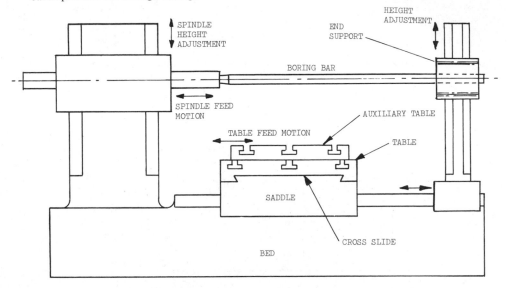

which can be moved across the bed and a
horizontal spindle whose bearings are
mounted on vertical slides. Thus the position
of the axis of rotation of the spindle relative
to the work can be adjusted accurately in
two co-ordinate directions. Feed is obtained
either by a longitudinal movement of the
table or by an axial movement of the boring
bar. For long holes, a boring bar is passed
through the work and supported in a bearing
mounted on the vertical slides of the movable
headstock, as shown.

For boring short or blind holes a stub
boring bar is used, as shown in fig. 4.20. The
boring head carries a radial slide on which the
bar is mounted and radial adjustment is made
by means of a micrometer screw so that the
required diameter of work is achieved easily
and accurately.

Facing of flanges can be done by using a
facing head, carrying a single-point tool on a
radial slide which can be fed radially while
the machine is running. Alternatively, the
facing of large areas can be achieved by using
a facing cutter and traversing the table across

the bed in a similar manner to the use of a
facing cutter on a milling machine. If the
area cannot be covered in one pass, a series of
cuts can be taken with the spindle set at
different heights.

An important accessory to the basic horizontal boring machine is the auxiliary table.
It is in effect a rotary table, square in plan,
with tee slots for bolting work down. It can
be located and locked at any of the four main
positions or any intermediate position. Thus
if the casting shown in fig. 4.16 had cross
holes to be bored, the table could be rotated
without removing and resetting the work.

JIG BORING MACHINES

These machines were developed to enable
holes to be bored to a high degree of positional accuracy in location plates for jigs,
fixtures, and press tools. Currently they are
used for many hole-boring applications where
high precision is essential and are often used
for repetition work of this nature.

Essentially, the machine has a table which
can be accurately positioned along the bed.

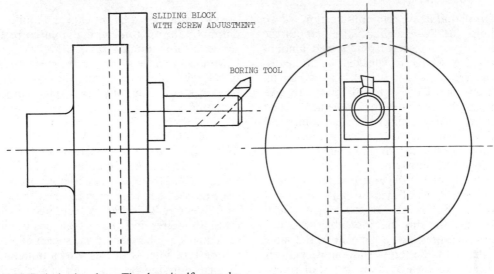

SLIDING BLOCK
WITH SCREW ADJUSTMENT

BORING TOOL

Fig. 4.20 Stub boring bar. The bar itself may be
replaced by others of different lengths.

Fig. 4.21(*a*) Block diagram of cross-rail type of jig
boring machine.

SPINDLE
HEAD

TRANSVERSE POSITIONAL
ADJUSTMENT ACCURATELY
AT 90° TO TABLE SLIDES

VERTICAL
SLIDES

CROSS
SLIDES

HEIGHT
ADJUSTMENT

TABLE
SLIDES

TABLE

SPINDLE
FEED MOTION

BED

The vertical head is carried on horizontal cross slides over the bed so that the co-ordinate positioning of the spindle relative to the work is attained by table movements along the bed and spindle-head movements across the rails (see fig. 4.21(*a*)). Alternatively, open-fronted machines are made on which the spindle head is fixed and both co-ordinate movements X and Y are achieved by moving the table as in fig. 4.21(*b*).

The accuracy which can be achieved with these machines is due in part to the care taken

111

in their manufacture and construction. As an example, the Société Genévoise scrapes the table slideways to a predetermined amount of hogging which is checked by an auto-collimator. The weight of the table on assembly then flattens the slideways to give an acceptable straight-line movement. Heat treatment of the castings to give stability and avoid warping due to internal stresses takes up to two weeks, the cooling being carefully controlled at a steady rate.

The heart of the accuracy of the machine lies in the method of measuring the table and cross-slide movements. In the past, the lead screw used for moving the table was also used to measure that movement in the same way that a lathe cross-slide movement is produced and measured by the lead screw. The errors in the lead screw were therefore directly transmitted to the table movements. This was overcome in the past by fitting a lead-screw correction bar. The correction bar was a plate cam cut to a graph of the lead-screw errors. As the table moved, the follower

position was varied by the cam and moved the datum on the micrometer dial, thus correcting the lead-screw pitch errors.

Modern methods divorce the measurement of the table movement from the screw which produces it. Basically two methods are available.

1. LENGTH BAR AND MICRO-SCOPE This is the system used on the modern Swiss-type jig-borers made by the Société Genévoise and is based on a divided scale built into the machine table and running its full length. This scale is accurately divided into millimetres and at any table position one scale mark can be seen on the screen of a projection type microscope as shown in fig. 4.22. A corresponding external scale is attached to the machine bed and can be read against an external index attached to the machine table. This index can be adjusted to allow the operator to work from a convenient datum.

Assume that the operator is called upon to bore two holes at a centre distance of 54·404

Fig. 4.21(*b*) Block diagram of open-fronted type of jig boring machine.

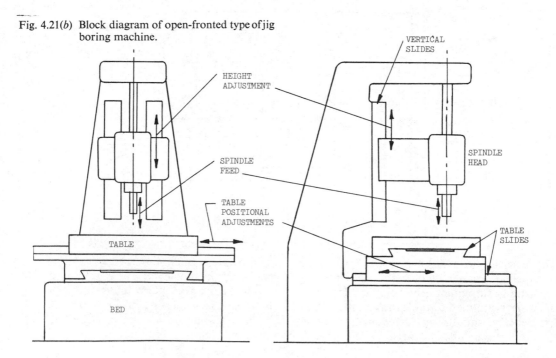

mm and that the first hole has been bored at a datum scale setting of 20·000 mm. It follows that the scale reading for boring the second hole must be 74·404 mm. The operator would adjust the table until the reading on the external scale was between 74·00 and 75·00 mm. He would then adjust the micrometer shown in fig. 4.22 until it read 0·400 mm direct and 0·004 mm on the vernier scale. The table position would now be adjusted using the slow-motion handwheel until the scale line seen on the projection screen was midway between the index marks. The table position reading would now be 74·404 mm and the table would have been moved 54·404 mm.

This method of measuring table move-ments has the advantage that the divided scale is completely enclosed and therefore completely protected from damage and furthermore the setting system, being optical, has no contact faces which may wear or become damaged.

INCREMENTAL LENGTH STAN-DARDS
The Newall Engineering Com-pany's jig boring machines are of the open-fronted type, both co-ordinate movements being applied to the table. A row of rollers[1] whose diameter is $25 \pm 0.000\ 5$ mm is posi-

[1] Although made to within $\pm 0.000\ 5$ mm on dia-meter, these rollers are graded and selected to cancel out any cumulative inaccuracy.

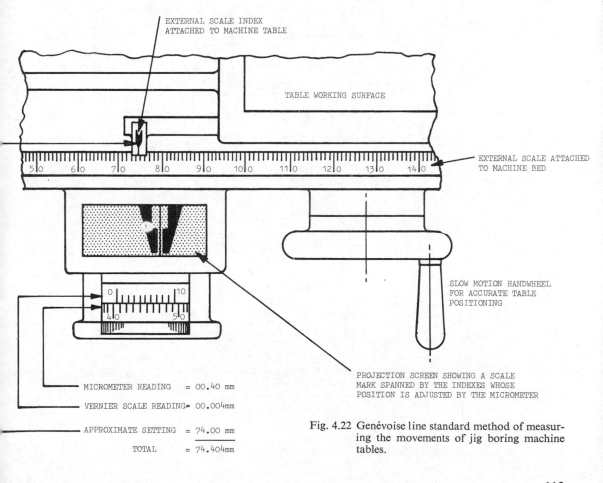

Fig. 4.22 Genévoise line standard method of measur-ing the movements of jig boring machine tables.

tioned in a channel so that the rollers are revealed by the table as it moves on its slides (see fig 4.23). A micrometer head reading to 0·002 mm is mounted on a block so that it locates on the rollers and can thus be moved in 25 mm increments, which are sub-divided by the micrometer. The micrometer anvil bears against a dial gauge mounted on the table. Thus, to bore a pair of holes at a spacing of 161·6 mm the table is adjusted so that the dial gauge reads zero when in contact with the micrometer which at this stage may be reading 3·234 mm. The first hole is bored and the micrometer head moved back 6

rollers (150 mm). The micrometer reading is adjusted to (161·6 – 150) + 3·234 mm, i.e., 14·834 mm and the table moved until the dial gauge again reads zero. The table has been moved 161·6 mm and the second hole may now be bored.

This method of measuring the table movement is applied to both movements at right angles to each other so that co-ordinate positions of the work can be accurately fixed.

ROTARY TABLES The versatility of the jig boring machine is greatly increased by the fitting of a rotary table. Once the work is

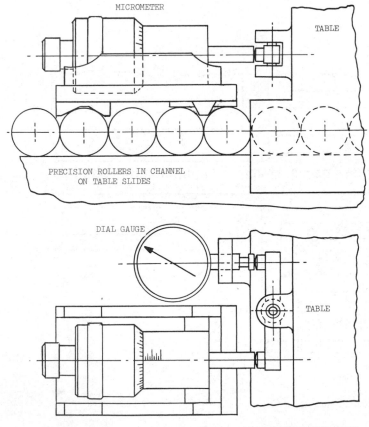

Fig. 4.23 Newall Micro-locator method of measuring
the movements of jig boring machine tables.

centralised on such a table a series of holes can be bored to a high degree of positional accuracy expressed as a pitch-circle radius and an angular position from a datum. As with the main table, the measurement of the movement of the rotary table is divorced from the worm and wheel which produces the movement, the angular displacement being measured optically.

WORK SETTING It is of little use being able to bore holes at accurate centre distances if the position of the first hole relative to the work datum is inaccurate. Thus it is necessary to be able to position the machine spindle accurately relative to a datum which may be an edge of a workpiece or the centre of rotation of a rotary table.

To position the spindle centre over the edge of a workpiece, a small angle block is provided and is placed against the edge of the workpiece, as shown in fig. 4.24. This block has a datum line scribed on its top surface accurately over face *A* which is located against the work datum. A microscope is provided which, when fitted into the machine spindle,

has its optical axis coincident with the spindle axis. In the eyepiece can be seen a pair of hair lines and the spindle is turned until these hair lines are parallel with the scribed line on the setting block. The table is now adjusted until the hair lines span the scribed line, when the spindle axis is accurately positioned over the edge of the workpiece.

Where the work is mounted on a rotary table the spindle axis must be accurately positioned over the centre of the rotary table. The table usually has a Morse taper hole in the centre for this purpose, into which a test bar is fitted. A dial gauge attached to the spindle is now brought to bear on the test bar until the dial gauge reading remains constant as the spindle is rotated. This device is shown in fig. 4.25.

It now remains to mount the work on the rotary table and adjust it so that its axis coincides with that of the rotary table, i.e., adjust its position so that it 'runs true'.

DIMENSIONING FOR JIG BORING
In Book 1 the importance of dimensioning by rectangular co-ordinates was discussed in

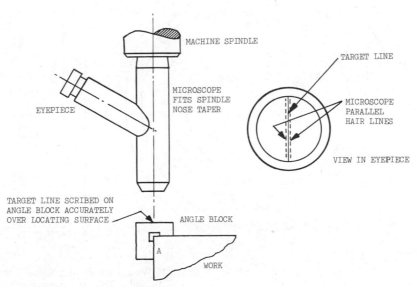

Fig. 4.24 Method of positioning the spindle axis over the work datum face.

Fig. 4.25 Method of aligning axis of rotary table
under machine spindle axis.

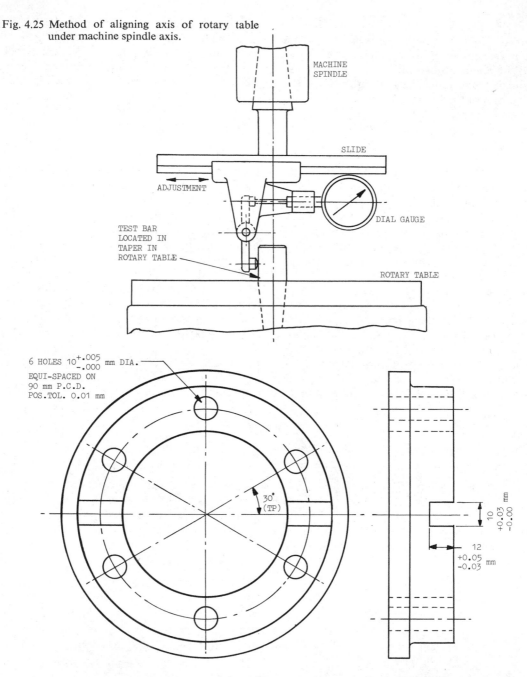

MACHINE
SPINDLE

SLIDE

ADJUSTMENT

DIAL GAUGE

TEST BAR
LOCATED IN
TAPER IN
ROTARY TABLE

ROTARY TABLE

6 HOLES $10^{+.005}_{-.000}$ mm DIA.
EQUI-SPACED ON
90 mm P.C.D.
POS.TOL. 0.01 mm

30°
(TP)

$10^{+0.03}_{-0.00}$ mm

$12^{+0.05}_{-0.03}$ mm

Fig. 4.26 Workpiece suitable for jig boring using the
rotary table and dimensioned accordingly.
Note that the slots may be milled on the jig
borer.

Chapter 7, in connection with the use of the compound-table drilling machine. If, as in fig. 4.26, a part has a number of holes dimensioned by polar co-ordinates about a single centre datum, the part can be machined from these dimensions on the rotary table, particularly if the component is cylindrical. If, on the other hand, two pitch circles of holes about different centres are required as in fig. 4.27, they would be better machined on the standard table from calculated rectangular co-ordinates as shown. Working on the rotary table would require resetting of the workpiece, with a consequent risk of inaccuracy.

The method of rectangular co-ordinates lends itself to automatic control for repetition work, particularly on a machine such as the Société Genévoise with the optical measuring system. A recording device is supplied which has two knobs, each of which can be set to any of twenty positions, giving 400 positions available. The table movements are made by hand adjustment on the first component and at each hole position the knobs are moved to a different setting and a 'record' button is pressed. This records on magnetic tape the position of that hole. Subsequent components are placed in the same location on the table and the knobs moved to the setting for the first hole. Another button is pressed and the table moves automatically to that position, the process being repeated for each hole position. The Société Genévoise guarantees a positional accuracy of 0·005 mm over 1·4 m of table movement on their largest machine, this being the worst possible error in the centre distance of any pair of holes.

Fig. 4.27 Workpiece suitable for jig boring using the co-ordinate positioning of the table and dimensioned accordingly.

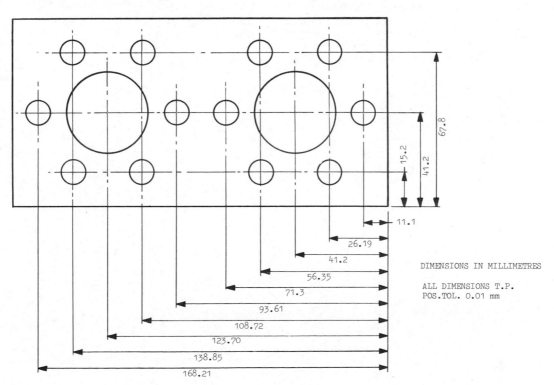

DIMENSIONS IN MILLIMETRES

ALL DIMENSIONS T.P.
POS.TOL. 0.01 mm

The accuracy attainable with jig boring machines is such that by replacing the spindle with measuring equipment they can be used as inspection machines, so they are now being modified in this fashion and sold as measuring equipment for checking large workpieces in the aircraft and aero-space industries.

SUMMARY

A great deal of the work manufactured in industry is cylindrical in form. This is for the simple reason that cylinders produced as solids of revolution can be more readily made to fit each other and will rotate one within the other to provide bearings. Forms produced as solids of revolution may be much more complex than simple right cylinders and to produce forms such as multi-start threads on a lathe requires not only a knowledge of the machine but also of the geometry of the work to be produced.

For more specialised work special machines have been developed. These include thread whirling machines, for the production of large threads and worms, and vertical boring machines, which are basically lathes standing on their headstocks, for large heavy work-pieces.

The boring machines have been developed in turn for two purposes. The horizontal boring machine is used for work whose shape and size make it almost impossible to swing the work about an axis. The tool is therefore rotated and moved axially to provide the motions necessary to produce the cylinder required. The jig boring machine utilises highly accurate co-ordinate table movements in the horizontal plane under a precision vertical spindle to give the high degree of positional accuracy of hole centres required by some work.

It is important that the technician engineer should be aware of all these processes, and of their capabilities and limitations. In understanding the basic features of the processes he should be better equipped to deal with any unusual problems the future may hold for him.

5

Capstan and Turret Lathes

INTRODUCTION

For the performance of repetitive turning, drilling and other operations, the centre lathe has certain limitations. These include the following:

(*a*) *Manual Skill.* Each dimension is arrived at by the skill of the operator in measuring the workpiece and manipulating the machine controls to give the desired size.

(*b*) *Tool Changing.* The number of tools mounted in the toolpost is severely limited and to perform a large number of operations involves virtually resetting the machine each time the tools are changed.

(*c*) *Tailstock Operations.* Only one tool can be mounted at a time in the tailstock and to perform a sequence of operations such as centre-drilling, drilling, reaming and tapping would require four changes of tool, and the depth of drilling would have to be controlled by the operator.

(*d*) *Speed Changing.* Very few centre lathes have provision for changing quickly the spindle speed or reversing its directions of rotation. The machine must be stopped if gnashing of gear teeth and possible damage are to be avoided.

If a lathe is required for repetitive work, certain modifications of it must be made to eliminate the above deficiencies. These modifications, which resulted in the development of capstan and turret lathes for repetitive production, are as follows:

(*a*) *Sizing Methods.* If the manual skill is to be eliminated, the size required must be produced by pre-setting the machine. All slideways are equipped with stops and the sliding member is fed in until the stop is reached.

(*b*) *Tooling Set-ups.* The cross-slide is equipped with a multi-tool post at the front which can be rapidly indexed into position. A single rear toolpost is also fitted.

(*c*) *Tailstock Tooling.* To facilitate the mounting of a larger number of tools which can be fed along the axis of the work, the tailstock is replaced by a hexagonal turret which has six tooling stations. Each station has its own stop so that the depth of feed can be controlled, and power feed is available.

(*d*) *Speed Changing.* The headstock is fitted with a constant-mesh gear box, i.e., the gears are always in mesh and the required speed is selected, forward or reverse, by engaging clutches which can be thrown in or out of mesh without stopping the machine. A later development has been the introduction of 'plugboard control', in which the speeds are changed by an electro-pneumatic system. The required speed for each turret position is selected on a plugboard and as the turret is indexed a set of micro-switches brings in the appropriate circuit to engage the pre-selected clutch and so give the desired speed.

Thus the lathe has now taken on a new configuration, as shown in fig. 5.1, and is known as a *capstan* or *turret lathe*. In a capstan lathe the turret is mounted on a sub-slide which can be adjusted and locked in position along the bed, but the length of travel of the turret is limited by the length of the sub-slide. The turret of the turret lathe is mounted directly upon the lathe bed and its length of travel is therefore limited only by the length of the main slideways. Also shown in fig. 5.1 are the arrangements of the length stops on the saddle, cross-slide, and turret.

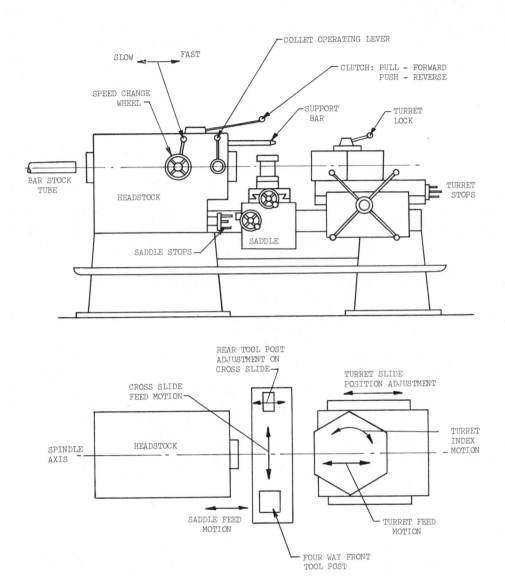

COLLET OPERATING LEVER

CLUTCH: PULL - FORWARD
PUSH - REVERSE

SLOW   FAST

SPEED CHANGE
WHEEL

SUPPORT
BAR

TURRET
LOCK

BAR STOCK
TUBE

HEADSTOCK

TURRET
STOPS

SADDLE STOPS

SADDLE

REAR TOOL POST
ADJUSTMENT ON
CROSS SLIDE

TURRET SLIDE
POSITION ADJUSTMENT

CROSS SLIDE
FEED MOTION

SPINDLE
AXIS

HEADSTOCK

TURRET
INDEX
MOTION

SADDLE FEED
MOTION

TURRET FEED
MOTION

FOUR WAY FRONT
TOOL POST

Fig. 5.1 Block diagram of capstan lathe showing
main controls, motions and adjustments.

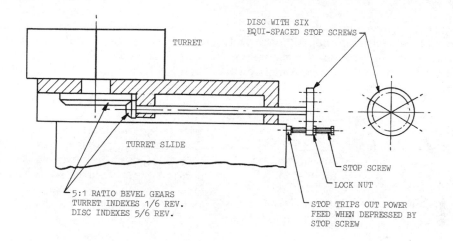

TURRET

DISC WITH SIX
EQUI-SPACED STOP SCREWS

TURRET SLIDE

STOP SCREW

LOCK NUT

STOP TRIPS OUT POWER
FEED WHEN DEPRESSED BY
STOP SCREW

5:1 RATIO BEVEL GEARS
TURRET INDEXES 1/6 REV.
DISC INDEXES 5/6 REV.

ARRANGEMENT OF TURRET SLIDE STOPS

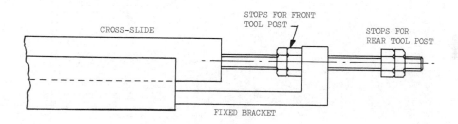

CROSS-SLIDE

STOPS FOR FRONT
TOOL POST

STOPS FOR
REAR TOOL POST

FIXED BRACKET

ARRANGEMENT OF CROSS-SLIDE STOPS

121

CAPSTAN LATHE TOOLING

As the capstan lathe evolved, specialised tooling set-ups were developed to enable its full capabilities to be used. Most of the tools used in the cross-slide toolpost are of the standard type of turning tool, although knife tools with zero plan-approach angle are frequently used to save a second operation to square up and clean out corners. The main development in tooling for the capstan lathe has been in turret-mounted equipment, so that the turret has not only replaced the tailstock for co-axial machining operations such as drilling and reaming, but is also used for turning and boring operations.

CROSS-SLIDE OPERATIONS Most of the cross-slide work is straightforward turning, facing and parting off, a normal set of turning tools being used. Where a complex form which it is not practicable to generate is required, a form tool can be used.

Two common types of form tool used are the *radial* type, shown in fig. 5.2(*a*), and the *tangential* type, fig. 5.2(*b*). In both cases it is essential that the tool is re-ground and set correctly or an error of form will result. To give precise height adjustment and rigidity, the radial tool is mounted on a serrated wedge-type toolpost and the tangential tool is usually gripped in a dovetail. Both tools are sharpened by grinding the rake face; obviously it would be too costly to re-grind the form. The extra length of the tangential tool gives it a longer life than the radial tool.

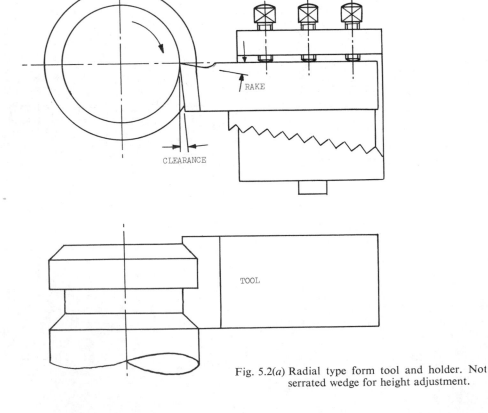

Fig. 5.2(*a*) Radial type form tool and holder. Not serrated wedge for height adjustment.

122

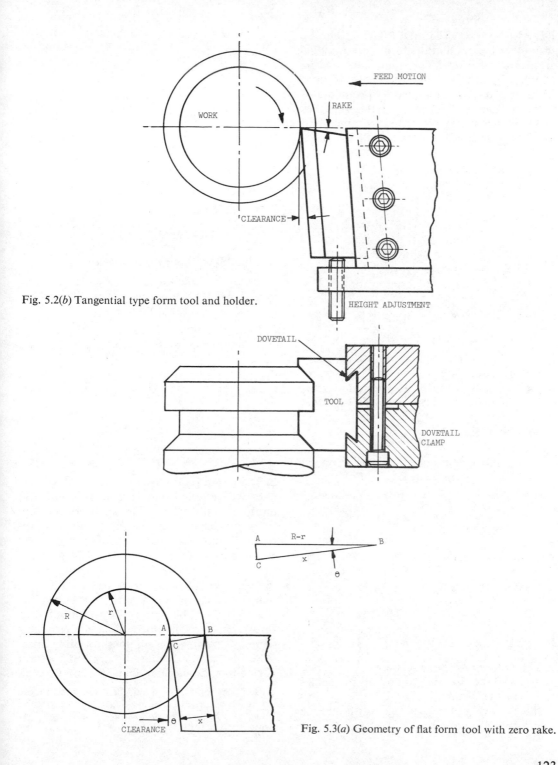

FEED MOTION

RAKE

WORK

CLEARANCE

HEIGHT ADJUSTMENT

Fig. 5.2(*b*) Tangential type form tool and holder.

DOVETAIL

TOOL

DOVETAIL
CLAMP

A $\quad$ R-r $\quad$ B

C $\quad$ x

θ

R $\quad$ r

A $\quad$ B

C

CLEARANCE $\quad \theta \quad$ x

Fig. 5.3(*a*) Geometry of flat form tool with zero rake.

123

FORM TOOL GEOMETRY It can be seen from fig. 5.3 that the form on the tool is ground parallel to the clearance face and its depth is not the same as the depth of form which it produces on the work. The depth of form on the tool depends on the depth of form on the work, the clearance angle and the rake angle, and it must be calculated.

(a) Flat form tool with zero rake angle
This is the simplest case, shown in fig. 5.3(*a*)

If R = outside radius of work
  r = root radius of work
  $(R - r)$ = depth of form on work
  θ = clearance angle
  x = depth of form on tool

Then $\cos \theta = \dfrac{x}{(R - r)}$

and $x = (R - r) \cos \theta$

(b) Flat form tool with positive rake angle
In this case, shown in fig. 5.3(*b*), the geometry is more complex as correction must also be made for the rake angle. The solution is in three stages.
(i) In triangle ABC

  AB = length of rake face in contact with the work
Angle ABC = $(\alpha + \theta)$, where α = rake angle

$$\frac{x}{\text{AB}} = \cos (\alpha + \theta)$$

$$x = \text{AB} \cos (\alpha + \theta) \qquad \cdots (1)$$

To find AB, use triangle AOB

  Angle OAB = $(180° - \alpha)$
  OA = r
  OB = R

The remaining two stages are:
 (ii) Use the sine rule to find all the angles in the triangle.
 (iii) Knowing all angles, again use the sine rule to find AB.

(ii) $\dfrac{R}{\sin \text{A}} = \dfrac{r}{\sin \text{B}}$

  $\sin \text{B} = \dfrac{R}{r \sin \text{A}} \qquad \cdots (2)$

(iii) $\dfrac{\text{AB}}{\sin \text{O}} = \dfrac{R}{\sin \text{A}}$

  $\text{AB} = \dfrac{R \sin \text{O}}{\sin \text{A}}$

But O = $(\alpha - \text{B})$
  A = $(180 - \alpha)$

$\therefore \ \text{AB} = \dfrac{R \sin (\alpha - \text{B})}{\sin (180° - \alpha)} \qquad \cdots (3)$

in which B is found from stage (ii)
  α = rake angle
  R = outside radius of work
  θ = clearance angle

Note also that $\sin (180° - \alpha) = \sin \alpha$
Summarising stages (i), (ii), and (iii) we have

(i) $x = \text{AB} \cdot \cos (\alpha + \theta) \qquad \cdots (1)$

(ii) $\sin \text{B} = \dfrac{R}{r \sin \alpha} \qquad \cdots (2)$

(iii) $\text{AB} = \dfrac{R \sin (\alpha - \text{B})}{\sin \alpha} \qquad \cdots (3)$

Substitute in (i) to calculate x.

It will be noted that in these solutions the terms R and r occur. The shape of the tool therefore depends on the radius of the work and will only produce accurate forms on bar of the correct diameter. If a tool is designed to produce a vee groove on a bar of 20 mm diameter but is used on a bar of 100 mm diameter, neither the depth nor the angle of the groove will be correct. However, as most form tools are designed for one particular component this problem does not often arise.

Similar methods must be applied to form correction for circular form tools.[1] In each

[1] Circular form tools should be dealt with in more detail in the subject 'Engineering Construction and Materials'. See *Theory of Machine Tools*, by J. W. Browne (Cassell), Book 2, Chapter 2.

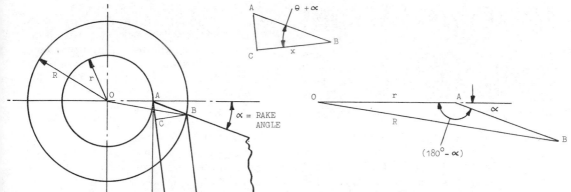

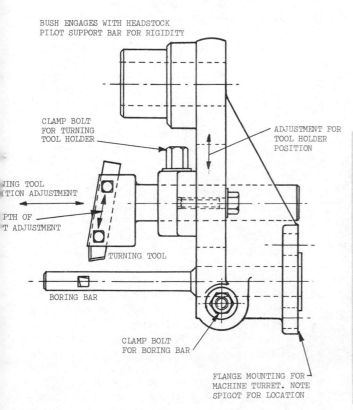

Fig. 5.3(b) Geometry of flat form tool with positive
rake.

R r O A B
α = RAKE
ANGLE

Θ
CLEARANCE
ANGLE

C x

O r A α B
R
(180° - α)

A Θ + α B
C x

BUSH ENGAGES WITH HEADSTOCK
PILOT SUPPORT BAR FOR RIGIDITY

CLAMP BOLT
FOR TURNING
TOOL HOLDER

ADJUSTMENT FOR
TOOL HOLDER
POSITION

JING TOOL
TION ADJUSTMENT

PTH OF
T ADJUSTMENT

TURNING TOOL

BORING BAR

CLAMP BOLT
FOR BORING BAR

FLANGE MOUNTING FOR
MACHINE TURRET. NOTE
SPIGOT FOR LOCATION

Fig. 5.4 (a) Elevation of knee toolholder.

Fig. 5.4 (b) Knee-turning toolholder—note pro-
vision for fitting with boring bar.
(Reproduced by kind permission of
H. W. Ward & Co.)

125

case it is advisable to determine first the length AB of the rake face in contact with the work.

TURRET OPERATIONS

The major proportion of the work on a capstan lathe is carried out with turret-mounted tooling, the tools being mounted in sequence and the turret automatically indexing as it is withdrawn by the operator.

TURNING FROM THE TURRET

The machining of external diameters falls into two categories, depending on the method of work holding.

(a) *Chuck-held work*. Work which is held in a chuck or turning fixture is usually fairly rigid and needs no additional support while cutting takes place. Such turning is usually carried out with a *knee tool holder*, as shown in figs. 5.4(a) and 5.4(b). Note that the rigidity of this type of tool holder can be increased by using the overhead support bar protruding from the headstock. This engages the guide bush shown on the tool holder and maintains the alignment of the turret *and* the spindle axis, preventing deflection of the turret by the cutting force applied.

Fig. 5.5 (b) (Reproduced by kind permission of H. W. Ward & Co.)

A boring bar can also be fitted so that a hole can be machined at the same time as the external surface. The chuck or fixture should be fitted with a guide bush to pilot the end of the boring bar and again maintain the geometry of the workpiece by reducing tool deflections.

A further development of the knee tool holder is the *combination tool holder*, shown in fig. 5.5(a), which can be fitted with two turning tools and a boring bar. Thus, simultaneous machining operations are possible. Indeed, by increasing the number of tools mounted in the boring bar, as shown in fig. 5.5(b), multi-diameter bores can be machined at the same time. Such set-ups involve more complex and time-consuming toolsetting and are only economic where the time saved in machining outweighs the setting time. The machine down-time for setting can be reduced by the use of pre-set tooling, i.e., by having two combination tool-holders, one in the machine and the other out for tool maintenance. When the tools have been reground they are pre-set in position and the complete toolholder is changed. Pre-setting of boring tools is facilitated by the use of a boring bar cutter micrometer, as shown in fig. 5.6.

Comparing the knee-type toolholder with the combination-type tool-holder, although the knee type only has provision for one turning tool it has a greater range of adjustment, for the tool post can be moved up the body of the holder. The adjustment in the combination-type toolholder is merely that of the tool overhang in the toolpost.

(b) *Bar Work*. When work is produced from bar stock it is usually not as firmly supported by the chuck and is itself rather less rigid than the castings and forgings which comprise much of chuck and fixture-held work. Thus some form of steady is required to prevent deflection of the work through the cutting load. For such work, therefore, a *roller steady box* is generally used on which is mounted, as well as the tool, a pair of rollers which bear against the work and resist the cutting load,

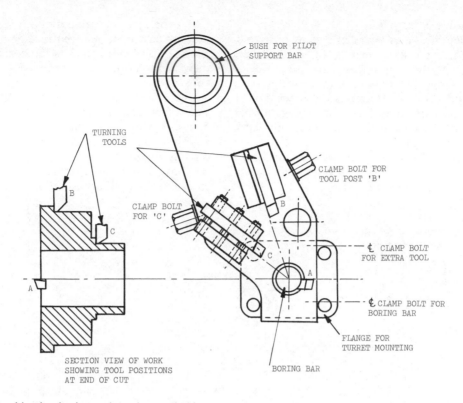

BUSH FOR PILOT
SUPPORT BAR

TURNING
TOOLS

CLAMP BOLT FOR
TOOL POST 'B'

CLAMP BOLT
FOR 'C'

₵ CLAMP BOLT
FOR EXTRA TOOL

₵ CLAMP BOLT FOR
BORING BAR

FLANGE FOR
TURRET MOUNTING

BORING BAR

SECTION VIEW OF WORK
SHOWING TOOL POSITIONS
AT END OF CUT

Fig. 5.5 Combination boring and turning toolholder.
(a) Front view showing relative positions of
tools, machine axis and pilot support bar
axis.

Fig. 5.6 Boring bar setting micrometer.

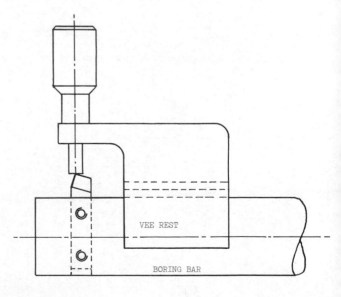

VEE REST

BORING BAR

as shown in fig. 5.7.

The rollers may be either leading or following the tool, as shown in fig. 5.8. Rollers following the tool are used when the operation is the first reduction in diameter on a new bar. Obviously leading rollers cannot be used on non-round bar, and even round bar may have irregularities and cause problems. A further advantage of using following rollers is that their pressure produces a burnishing effect and the roller finish is to some extent reproduced on the turned bar.

If a diameter has already been turned and the bar has to be reduced in diameter for a short length, leading rollers can be used. They then help to ensure that the two diameters are concentric.

Figs. 5.9(*a*) and 5.9(*b*) illustrate a roller steady box and show the adjustments. Small boxes usually fit into the turret by means of a shank, as shown, but larger boxes bolt directly on the turret, locating in a register, and have a hole through the body of the box to enable longer bars to be turned.

Fig. 5.7 Geometry of roller box showing forces on tools and rollers.

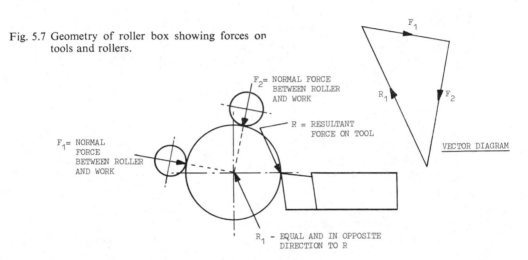

Fig. 5.8 Alternative positions of rollers in relation to tool.

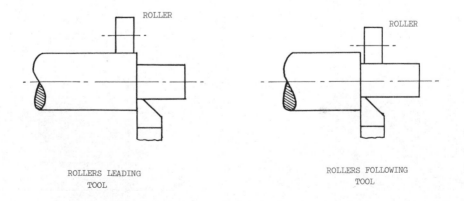

HOLE PRODUCTION The method used for machining holes in capstan and turret lathe work, as in any other machining process, depends on the accuracy required. Thus holes with large tolerances are simply centred and drilled. Drilling, however, is not only prone to errors of size but the drill can wander and give rise to a non-straight hole. Where accuracy of diameter is required the hole can be reamed, but a reamer is a sizing tool and will not correct all geometrical errors and rather tends to follow the drilled hole. Thus, for the highest degree of accuracy, the hole must be centred, drilled, bored and finally reamed.

Centring. Centre holes for starting a drill can be produced with a centre drill. These tools are, however, notoriously delicate and easily broken. A better method is to use a short flat drill as shown in fig. 5.10. This is extremely stiff and has less tendency to wander or break.

Fig. 5.9 (*a*) (Reproduced by kind permission of H. W. Ward & Co.)

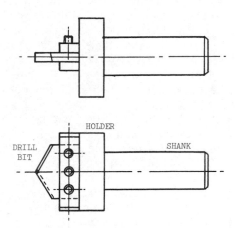

Fig. 5.10 Flat or spade drill for starting holes.

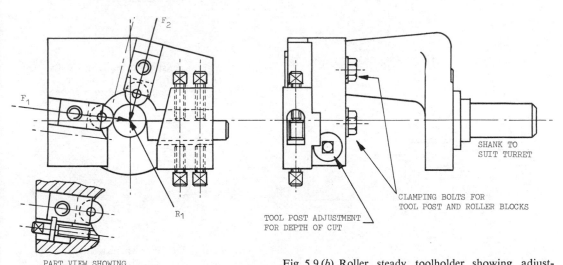

PART VIEW SHOWING
ROLLER BLOCK ADJUSTMENT

Fig. 5.9 (*b*) Roller steady toolholder showing adjustments. Forces F_1, F_2 and R_1 refer to fig. 5.7.

129

Drilling. Normal twist drills are used for capstan lathe work. They can, even with the smaller sizes, be obtained with a taper shank to fit the hole in the drill holder mounted on the turret. Where straight shank drills are used an adaptor with a clamping bush, as shown in fig. 5.11, is used. This method of holding can also be used for taps and reamers.

Deep holes present a problem in getting the swarf out of the hole and the cutting fluid into the cutting area. For this reason, larger drills are formed initially with straight flutes so that holes can be drilled up the solid part of the drill. They are then twisted hot to the required helix angle before being hardened and finish ground. In operation, cutting fluid is forced down the holes under pressure to cool the cutting edge and flush the swarf out.

Reaming. If a hole has been bored prior to reaming, the reamer can be held rigidly in a taper adaptor or a drill holder as shown in fig. 5.11. If a drilled hole is to be reamed, however, and the hole is not straight, or is eccentric, a rigidly held reamer might be broken. In these circumstances the reamer must be mounted in a floating reamer holder, fig. 5.12, which allows enough free movement for the reamer to follow the hole.

Recessing. If a blind hole is to be tapped or a stepped hole is to have a squared-out shoulder, a recessing operation may be necessary. This can be accomplished with the recessing attachment shown in fig. 5.13. The tool is mounted on a dovetail slide so that it can be moved across the face of the turret by the lever shown. The operator enters the tool into the work with the handle drawn towards him, the slide thus being moved away, advances the turret to the stop and pushes the handle away from him to form the recess. The handle is then pulled back and the turret withdrawn.

TAPER AND PROFILE BORING

Form tools cannot very well be used for

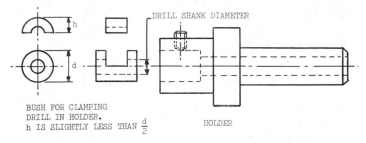

BUSH FOR CLAMPING DRILL IN HOLDER.
h IS SLIGHTLY LESS THAN $\frac{d}{2}$

HOLDER

Fig. 5.11 Adaptor for straight shank drills. The same clamping arrangement may be used in tapping attachments and reamer holders.

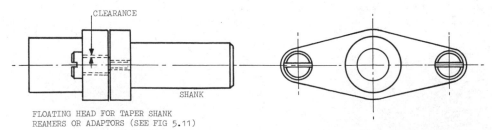

FLOATING HEAD FOR TAPER SHANK REAMERS OR ADAPTORS (SEE FIG 5.11)

Fig. 5.12 Simple floating reamer holder. Clearance between the shoulder screws and holes in the front flange allows the reamer to float.

130

machining bores. If a straight taper is required the machine may be fitted with a taper-turning attachment similar to that used on a normal centre lathe If this is not available, an attachment similar to the recessing attachment is used, with the slide connected by a link and roller to a cam plate mounted on the cross-slide, as shown in fig. 5.14. The depth of cut is set by the cross-slide and when the operation is completed the turret is withdrawn so that the roller clears the slot. The turret can then be indexed in the normal way.

This device can also be used for external turning to avoid a second operation. A case in point is the machining from copper of spot-welding tips as shown in fig. 5.15. Originally these were straight-turned, threaded, and parted off, the machining of the taper being a second operation. Forming the taper by a

form tool was impossible since, due to the weak nature of the work material, the component broke off before forming was completed. By using the cam plate the taper was turned by a series of fine cuts and the component was finally parted off when completed.

STOCK LENGTH STOP When parts are being machined from bar stock it is necessary to control the stock length fed from the chuck. This can be done by means of a simple piece of bar held in the turret and adjusted by the turret stop. A better method is to use a stop bar with a screw and locknut, as shown in fig. 5.16. This makes for easier fine adjustment and control of the length fed from the collet.

An alternative which saves the use of an

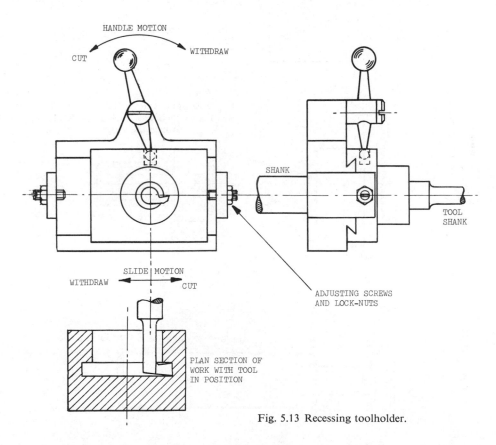

Fig. 5.13 Recessing toolholder.

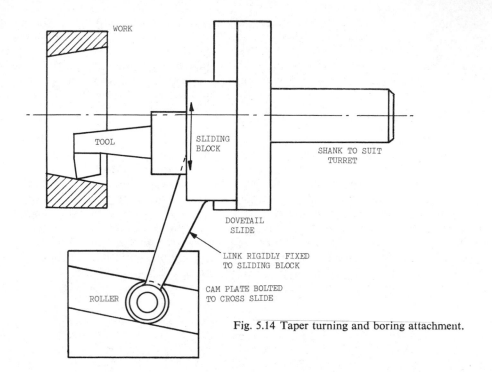

WORK

TOOL

SLIDING
BLOCK

SHANK TO SUIT
TURRET

DOVETAIL
SLIDE

LINK RIGIDLY FIXED
TO SLIDING BLOCK

CAM PLATE BOLTED
TO CROSS SLIDE

ROLLER

Fig. 5.14 Taper turning and boring attachment.

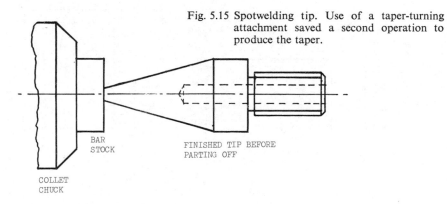

Fig. 5.15 Spotwelding tip. Use of a taper-turning attachment saved a second operation to produce the taper.

BAR
STOCK

FINISHED TIP BEFORE
PARTING OFF

COLLET
CHUCK

Fig. 5.16 Adjustable stop for bar work.

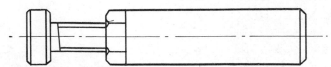

extra turret station and indexing movement is to combine the length stop with a centre drill holder on a swinging arm. With the stop in position the stock is fed to length and the collet locked The turret is now withdrawn to allow the centre drill to be brought into position and then advanced for centre drilling. This attachment is shown in fig. 5.17.

SCREW THREAD MANUFACTURE
Much of the work carried out on capstan and turret lathes involves a threading operation, either externally or internally.

EXTERNAL THREADS These can be produced by a screwcutting process like that used with centre lathes but with the following difference. The capstan lathe is usually fitted with a simple gear box with ratios of 1 : 1, 2 : 1 and 4 : 1 with the spindle, from which interchangeable leader screws are driven. Thus to cut a thread of 2 mm pitch a leader screw and nut of 8 mm pitch would be fitted and driven using the 4 : 1 ratio. Since the gearbox only has these ratios, the problem of picking up the thread using a chasing dial does not arise. This method is generally used only on large diameter work. For threads up to about 40 mm, *self-opening dieheads* or *thread rolling boxes* are used.

If one considers cutting an external thread with a button die in a special holder, one must realise that after the die has been screwed on it must also be screwed off by reversing the machine. Since this work is carried out at low speed it would be much more efficient if the threading device could be withdrawn directly along the thread without reversing the machine. The self-opening diehead enables this to be done by cutting the thread by four equally-spaced chasers, as shown in fig. 5.18, which can be withdrawn clear of the thread crests when the end of the thread is reached. The diehead is then withdrawn.

The chasers fit into slots in the body of the diehead and are surrounded by a cam plate. As the cam plate is rotated in a clockwise direction (from the back of the machine), i.e., the handle is pushed away from the operator, the cams close the chasers to the correct depth of cut, the cam plate being held in position by a spring-loaded pin or detent pin. The diehead is fed to the work by the operator who then allows it to feed itself along the work and follows up with the turret. The turret stop is set slightly short and when the axial movement of the turret is arrested the front portion of the diehead continues to feed forward, under the self-feeding action of the chaser, until it is pulled clear of the detent pin. The diehead is then opened by springs (not shown in the diagram), the chasers being positively withdrawn by opening cams which engage in slots in the backs of the chasers.

Fig. 5.17 Combined bar stop and centre drill holder.

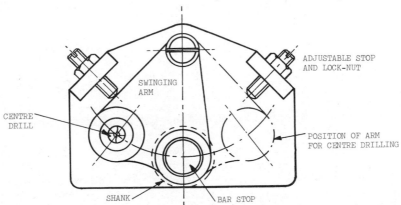

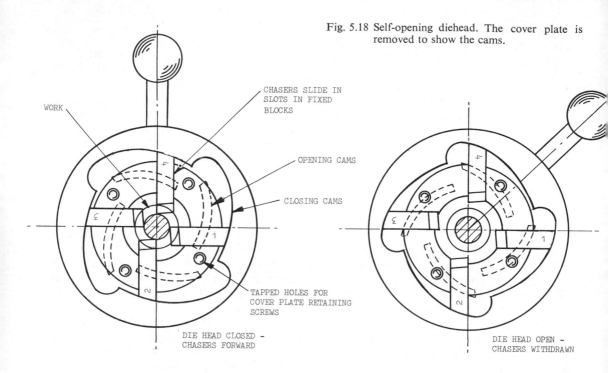

WORK

CHASERS SLIDE IN
SLOTS IN FIXED
BLOCKS

OPENING CAMS

CLOSING CAMS

TAPPED HOLES FOR
COVER PLATE RETAINING
SCREWS

DIE HEAD CLOSED -
CHASERS FORWARD

DIE HEAD OPEN -
CHASERS WITHDRAWN

It is important to note that the chasers are in fact sections of a thread and allowance must be made for the helix angle of the thread. They are therefore made in sets, each having its thread form offset by a quarter of one pitch. It is essential that they are fitted into the diehead in the correct order and to enable this to be maintained they are numbered as shown in fig. 5.18.

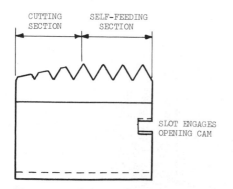

CUTTING
SECTION

SELF-FEEDING
SECTION

SLOT ENGAGES
OPENING CAM

Fig. 5.19 Radial-type chaser.

The chasers cut only on the front or cutting section shown in fig. 5.19. The remainder of the chaser, known as the self-feeding section, engages the thread already cut and provides the feed motion. Note that the chasers are radial. They are not suited to heavy loads which occur with coarser threads and may not be ground on the rake face. They are ground on the cutting portion of the clearance face in a jig, to ensure that they all contact the work at the same time and take an equal cutting load.

A general view of this type of diehead is shown in fig. 5.20.

Another form of diehead uses tangential chasers. The principle is similar but the chasers are presented to the work in a tangential manner as shown in fig. 5.21. Note that although these chasers are fed axially along the work they are essentially form tools and can be compared with those shown in figs. 5.3(a) and (b). In the tangential chaser the cutting force is directed into the body of

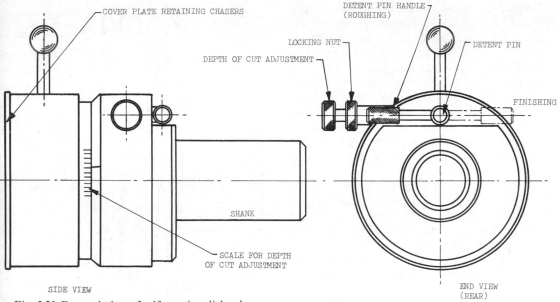

Fig. 5.20 External view of self-opening diehead.

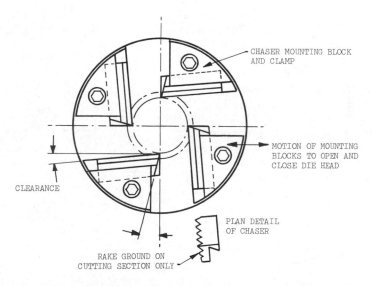

Fig. 5.21 Front view of tangential type of self-opening
diehead.

the chaser, rather than on to an overhanging section as with a radial chaser. Tangential chasers are therefore capable of withstanding heavier loads and are used for larger threads.

With both types of diehead it is unlikely that manufacturing precision would allow the chasers to be assembled and cut a thread of the correct diameter without adjustment. The knurled screw shown in fig. 5.20 adjusts the angular position of the cam plate when the

135

diehead is closed, which adjusts the depth of cut. When the adjustment is correct the adjusting screw is locked by the nut shown. Another feature of both types of diehead is the ability to cut threads in two passes, a roughing cut and a finishing cut. This is achieved by making the end of the detent pin into a form of cam. When the lever on the end of the pin is towards the operator the diehead is opened slightly for roughing, and when it is turned through 180° the diehead is closed to the finishing position.

Cutting threads with dieheads is essentially a slow-speed operation; cutting speeds range from 2 m/min for tough steel to 15 m/min for free-cutting steel, higher speeds being used for brass and aluminium.

A later technique combines the principle of the diehead with that of thread rolling in the *self-opening thread-rolling head*. The self-opening principles are similar to those of the dieheads described above but the chasers are replaced by free-running accurately machined rollers carrying the thread form. These are set at the helix angle of the thread and feed themselves along the bar, which is made slightly larger than the mean diameter of the thread. The rolling action forces excess material out of the thread valley to form the crest as shown in fig. 5.22, which shows two rollers operating. In practice, three rollers are used which are offset relative to each other by $\frac{1}{3}$ of the pitch.

A little thought will show that as the centroid of the crest area is at a greater radius than the centroid of the root area there is a greater volume of material above the mean line than below it. This extra material is provided by making the blank diameter slightly larger than the mean diameter of the thread. The actual blank diameter can be calculated by application of the theorem of Guldinus and Pappus, but as some trial and error is inevitable a good guide is to make the blank diameter equal to the mean thread diameter plus 0·1 mm. The blank requires a 30° chamfer to less than the thread root diameter and the speed used should be in excess of

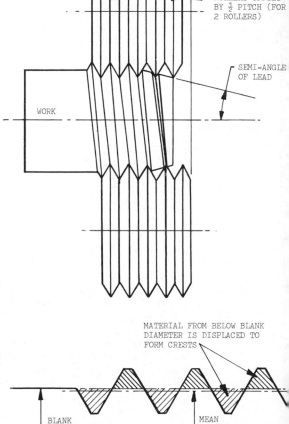

Fig. 5.22 Principle of thread rolling. In plan view the rolls are inclined to coincide with the helix angle of the thread.

1 000 rev/min. As the rolling head therefore moves along the bar very rapidly, the turret head must be fed at the required speed up to the blank. This looks almost brutal but the process produces accurate threads of high finish very rapidly. A further advantage is that the grain flow of the material follows the profile of the thread, giving a rather stronger thread than is produced by cutting, where the

lines of grain flow are cut by the thread form.

INTERNAL THREADS   These are produced by tapping and it is unfortunate that, in sizes below about 25 mm, a tap having been screwed in must be screwed out by reversing the machine. As reversal is not instantaneous some arrangement is required to enable the tap to rotate freely, and thus feed no further forward, until the operator can reverse the machine, when the tap is again prevented from rotating and screws itself out. Note that in both directions the tap is self-feeding, i.e., the full-form threads along the body of the tap provide the feed effect by engaging with the threads already cut by the cutting portion on the nose of the tap. In both forward and reverse directions the operator merely causes the turret to follow the natural motion of the tap.

The simplest device for tapping consists of a tap holder whose body is free to rotate. It is restrained from doing so by the operator gripping a knurled portion of the body and then releasing it, to allow free rotation, when the full depth is reached. He then reverses the machine and again grasps the tap holder to prevent rotation so that the tap screws itself

out. This device can only be used for small-diameter threads of fine pitch where the tapping torque can easily be provided by the grip of the operator.

A more common device is that shown in fig. 5.23, which consists of a tap holder mounted on the moving portion of a spring-loaded dog clutch. As with a diehead, the turret stop is set short so that the turret reaches the limit of its travel before the tap reaches the full depth of the hole. The tap continues to feed forwards and draws the clutch dogs out of engagement thus allowing the tap to rotate freely until the machine is reversed. The clutch on the tapping head shown has angled engaging faces and is spring loaded into engagement. If the tap meets an obstruction and the torque increases, the clutch is forced out of engagement, against the spring, before the tap breaks.

WORK-HOLDING METHODS

The method of holding the work in a capstan lathe depends largely on the type of work being carried out. This falls into two basic categories, work machined and parted-off from the bar, and work machined from a cut-

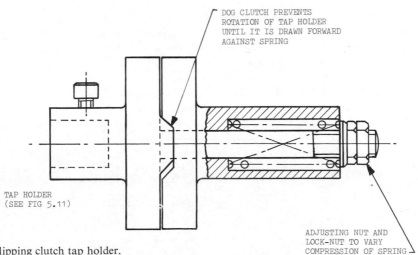

DOG CLUTCH PREVENTS
ROTATION OF TAP HOLDER
UNTIL IT IS DRAWN FORWARD
AGAINST SPRING

TAP HOLDER
(SEE FIG 5.11)

ADJUSTING NUT AND
LOCK-NUT TO VARY
COMPRESSION OF SPRING

Fig. 5.23 Slipping clutch tap holder.

off piece of material, or a casting or forging. In both cases first and second or subsequent operations must be considered separately as different conditions may apply and affect the work-holding method.

HOLDING BAR WORK   Much of the work machined on a capstan lathe consists of components machined from a bar and then parted off. The bar stock is usually held in a collet chuck with an automatic feed arrangement so that when the collet is opened the bar feeds forwards to the stop in the turret head. The type of collet used differs from that described in Chapter 8 of Book 1, where the collet is drawn back into a taper to close on the work. Such a draw-in collet would tend to pull the bar away from the bar-stop if used on a capstan lathe and, instead, a *dead-length collet* is used. In this case the collet is fixed in its location in the machine spindle and the closing taper moves axially along the tapered nose of the collet to close the collet on the work. Thus the collet does not move and the bar remains securely against the stop. A diagram illustrating a typical dead-length collet and its method of operation is shown in fig. 5.24.

Fig. 5.24 Diagram of dead-length type collet chuck.

In conjunction with the dead-length collet, a means of controlling the bar protruding from the back of the machine is required as well as a method of feeding the bar when the collet is opened. The bar is usually gripped at its outboard end in a holder mounted in a bearing so that it is free to rotate. The holder slides along support bars, and when the collet is opened it is pulled forwards by a system of weights and pulleys. The weights are suspended in a triple-sheave pulley block giving a velocity ratio of six to one, the free end of the cable being attached to the bar holder. Thus if the weights fall 0·5 m the bar holder moves 3 m. As the available fall is usually greater than 0·5 m, it provides ample movement for the normal 3 m length of bar stock.

Hand operation of the bar feed is sometimes used, a handwheel and cable at the rear of the headstock drawing the bar holder forward. Another form of bar feed utilises an air cylinder.

SECOND-OPERATION   COLLET WORK   Consider the component shown in fig. 5.25. Assuming that the first operation consisted of feed to stop, centre drill, drill,

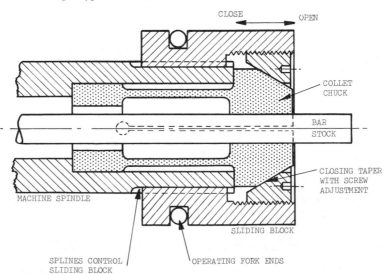

Fig. 5.25 Collet fitted with back stop for second operation work.

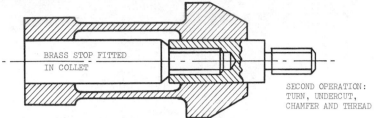

BRASS STOP FITTED IN COLLET

SECOND OPERATION: TURN, UNDERCUT, CHAMFER AND THREAD

tap, and part-off to length, the part must now be reversed in the collet to turn, undercut, chamfer, and thread. It must be positioned so that the correct length is left protruding from the collet, but in such circumstances the normal bar stop cannot be used. A soft steel or brass stop is therefore fitted into the back of the collet as shown in fig. 5.25.

Had the work been turned to a shoulder in the first operation the difficulty would not have arisen since the operator would then merely insert the work up to the shoulder before closing the collet.

HOLDING CUT-OFF BLANKS Another common type of work is the machining of a part from a solid disc which has previously been cut off a bar of large diameter which, due to its size, could not be fed through the headstock spindle. Such work is gripped in a self-centring three- or four-jaw chuck, but such a chuck has different requirements from that used on a centre lathe:

(a) Its operation must be rapid.

(b) Only a small jaw movement is required, sufficient to release and grip work which, for long runs, is all of the same diameter.

(c) Although the jaw movement need only be small the jaws must be adjustable to accommodate a wide range of work sizes.

Rapid operation can be obtained by limiting the jaw movement so that the jaws are opened or closed by half a turn of the key. The opening and closing are not operated by the usual scroll but by a cam ring operating against a key on the back of each jaw.

Adjustment for different diameters is arranged by making the jaws in two parts, the sliding block which is operated by the cam ring and always moves between the same limits, and the gripping jaw which is bolted to the sliding block but whose position can be adjusted. Positive positioning of the gripping jaw is arranged by having serrations on the rear of the jaw engaging with similar serrations on the sliding block. These details are shown in fig. 5.26.

By positioning the gripping jaws asymmetrically on the sliding blocks, work of irregular shapes can be held, or rectangular blocks can be held for the machining of holes and other features off-centre.

SECOND-OPERATION CHUCK WORK It is inevitable that much of the second-operation work performed in chucks is gripped on the surfaces machined in the first operation. For this reason soft jaws are used to avoid damaging the finished surface. It is also essential that the work is held so that turned diameters mate correctly without a step due to eccentricity. To ensure concentricity, a disc which is slightly less in diameter than that of the finished work is first gripped at the back of the jaws. The front of the soft jaws is then bored out to a suitable size to accommodate the finished outside diameter of the first operation. A typical component for such work would be the gear blank shown in fig. 5.27. The first operation would consist of face, face to step, centre-drill and turn, drill and chamfer, bore and chamfer. Before the second operation, soft

139

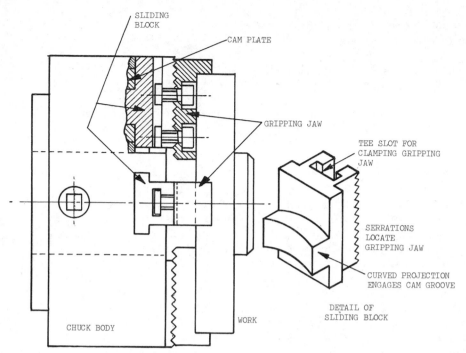

SLIDING
BLOCK

CAM PLATE

GRIPPING JAW

TEE SLOT FOR
CLAMPING GRIPPING
JAW

SERRATIONS
LOCATE
GRIPPING JAW

CURVED PROJECTION
ENGAGES CAM GROOVE

DETAIL OF
SLIDING BLOCK

CHUCK BODY

WORK

Fig. 5.26 Self-centring four-jaw chuck for a capstan
lathe. One jaw assembly is shown in
section.

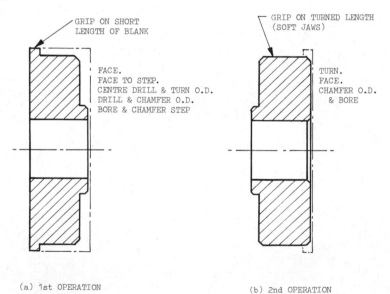

GRIP ON SHORT
LENGTH OF BLANK

FACE.
FACE TO STEP.
CENTRE DRILL & TURN O.D.
DRILL & CHAMFER O.D.
BORE & CHAMFER STEP

GRIP ON TURNED LENGTH
(SOFT JAWS)

TURN.
FACE.
CHAMFER O.D.
& BORE

(a) 1st OPERATION

(b) 2nd OPERATION

Fig. 5.27 Typical component for chuck work. The
chain-dotted outline shows the metal
removed in each operation.

jaws would be fitted and machined to suit the turned outside diameter, after which the second operation would be turn, face, chamfer hole and outside diameter. Figs. 5.27(*a*) and (*b*) show the blank at the two stages of manufacture.

PLANNING FOR CAPSTAN OPERATIONS

The capstan lathe is essentially a tool of the production engineer. It can do nothing that cannot be done on a centre lathe but it can perform repetitive operations much more quickly and is used where the savings in labour costs more than outweigh the increased tooling and setting costs. However, the capstan lathe will only be economic if used efficiently and it will only be used efficiently if the work is planned correctly. Planning for capstan lathes falls into three stages:

(*a*) Selection of machine;
(*b*) Operation layout;
(*c*) Estimation of operation time.

MACHINE SELECTION It is of little use proceeding with an operation layout if the work cannot be accommodated in the machine. For this reason manufacturers supply *capacity charts* for their machines which show the slide movements and adjustments available. A comparison of the work with the capacity chart enables the suitability of the machine for the job to be readily estimated.

OPERATION LAYOUTS The cost of a part often depends on whether the machine set-up is the most efficient for the part and although in many cases the sequence of operations is self-evident it is often necessary to prepare a tool layout. This is a plan view of the part and all the tooling in position.

It enables the planning engineer to decide precisely what tools are required and to ensure that they are available before the job is begun. A comparison with the capacity chart will show whether or not the machine will accommodate the job and when the machine and layout have been decided the operating time can be estimated.

Typical layouts are shown in fig. 5.28 for bar work, and in 5·29 for chuck work. The tooling shown on the layout is stylised, rather than a true representation. Thus in fig. 5.28 the rollers and tool in the roller box are correctly positioned and the overall dimensions of the box are correct but the full details are not shown. In fig. 5.29 the knee turning tools are shown in the horizontal position rather than in the vertical position normally used. This enables the cutting tools to be shown in the correct position relative to the work, but the knee tool guide bushes are not shown.

The amount of detail shown is really a matter of individual taste, but the actual position of the cutting tools and overall dimensions of the equipment should be correct.

ESTIMATION OF OPERATION TIME The time required to machine a part depends upon the cutting speeds and feeds used for the various operations, and also upon the non-productive operations which, although vital, do not directly contribute to the value of the part, e.g., load and unload, change speed, feed stock to stop, index turret, etc. The actual cutting time can be accurately calculated from a knowledge of the cutting speeds and feeds used.

To illustrate the calculations of cutting times consider a length of bar of 25 mm diameter to be turned down to 20 mm diameter for a length of 75 mm, using a knee turning tool with tungsten-carbide tooling. The material is free-cutting mild steel, allowing a cutting speed of 150 m/min and a feed rate of 30 cuts/cm.

Note that the cutting speed is the peripheral or surface speed in metres per minute and the feed rate indicates the number of revolutions the work must make as the tool advances 1 cm.

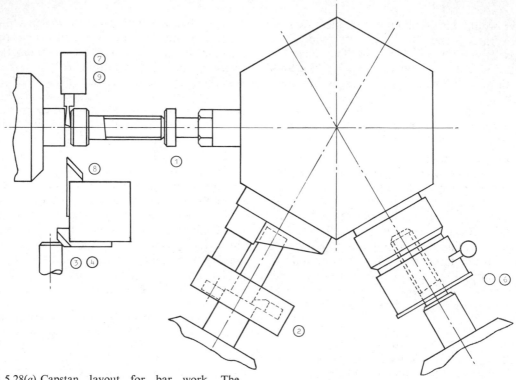

Fig. 5.28(*a*) Capstan layout for bar work. The numbers indicate the operation sequence.

Circumference of bar

$$= \pi \times \text{diameter}$$

$$= \pi \times 25 \text{ mm}$$

$$= 78 \cdot 5 \text{ mm}$$

Work speed in revolutions per minute

$$= \frac{\text{Cutting speed in metres per minute}}{\text{Circumference in metres}}$$

$$= \frac{150 \text{ m/min}}{78 \cdot 5/1\,000 \text{ m}}$$

$$= \frac{150 \times 1\,000 \text{ rev/min}}{78 \cdot 5}$$

$$= 1\,910 \text{ rev/min}$$

It is unlikely that the machine would have this precise speed available so for considerations of tool life the next nearest speed *downwards* is chosen. Assume a speed of 1 800 rev min.

Length of work
$$= 75 \text{ mm} = 7 \cdot 5 \text{ cm}$$
Feed rate $= 30$ cuts/cm
Number of revolutions
$$= \text{length in centimetres} \times \text{feed rate in cuts per centimetre}$$
$$= 7 \cdot 5 \text{ cm} \times 30 \text{ cuts/cm}$$
$$= 225 \text{ rev}$$

Cutting time

$$= \frac{\text{No: of revolutions}}{\text{Speed in revolutions per minute}}$$

$$= \frac{225 \text{ rev}}{1\,800 \text{ rev/min}}$$

$$= 0 \cdot 125 \text{ min}$$

Operation sheet for bar work — PART NO. _____ PART NAME: BOLT

1 OPERATN. NO.	2 OPERATION	3 TOOLING	4 TURRET OR X SLIDE	5 SPEED M/MIN	5 SPEED REV/MIN	6 FEED RATE CUTS/CM	7 TOTAL REVS	8 CUTTING TIME, MIN.	9 NON-PRODUCTIVE TIME, MIN.	10 REMARKS
1	STOCK TO STOP	BAR STOP	–	–	–	–	–	–	0.105	
	INDEX & LOCK TURRET		–	–	–	–	–	–	0.100	
2	TURN 25mm x 75mm LONG	ROLLER BOX	T	50	600	30	225	0.375		ROLLERS LEADING H.S.S. TOOL
	INDEX & LOCK TURRET		–	–	–	–	–	–	0.100	
	POSITION X SLIDE & SET STOP		–	–	–	–	–	–	0.130	
3	CHAMFER TURNED END	45° R.H. TOOL	X	50	600	HAND	60	0.100		FRONT TOOL POST
	POSITION X SLIDE & SET STOP		–	–	–	–	–	–	0.130	READY FOR OP. 7
4	CHAMFER HEAD	45° R.H. TOOL	–	–	–	–	–	0.100		AS FOR OP. 3
	CHANGE SPEED		–	–	–	–	–	–	0.100	
5	ROUGH THREAD	S/O DIE HEAD	T	10	60	10	50	0.833		25mm x 1mm PITCH CHASERS
	WITHDRAW & RESET DIE HEAD		–	–	–	–	–	–	0.080	
6	FINISH THREAD	S/O DIE HEAD	T	10	60	10	50	0.833		AS FOR OP. 5
	INDEX TURRET 3 STATIONS	↑	–	–	–	–	–	–	0.200	
	POSITION X SLIDE & SET STOP		–	–	–	–	–	–	0.130	
7	CHANGE SPEED		–	–	–	–	–	–	0.080		READY FOR OP. 7
	PARTIAL PART-OFF	PARTING-OFF TOOL	X	25	150	HAND	30	0.200		
	INDEX FRONT TOOL POST		–	–	–	–	–	–	0.110	
8	CHAMFER HEAD	45° L.H. TOOL	X	25	150	HAND	15	0.100		SET RELATIVE TO P/O TOOL – NO SLIDE ADJUSTMENT
9	INDEX FRONT TOOL POST		–	–	–	–	–	–	0.110		READY FOR OP. 3
	FINISH PART-OFF	PARTING-OFF TOOL	X	25	150	HAND	30	0.200		AS FOR OP. 8
	REMOVE PART		–	–	–	–	–	–	0.04	
	CHANGE SPEED		–	–	–	–	–	–	0.100		READY FOR OP. 2
	TOTALS							2.741	1.515	TOTAL TIME/PART 4.256 min

Fig. 5.28(b) Operation sheet for bar work.

143

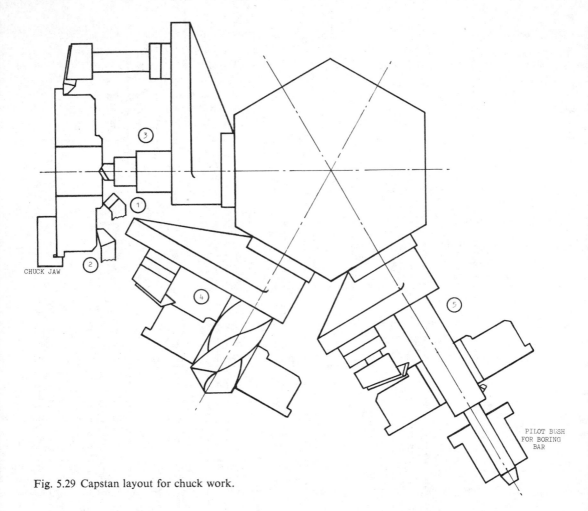

Fig. 5.29 Capstan layout for chuck work.

If the calculations for a series of operations were carried out as on p. 143, they would become hopelessly spread out and untidy. It is far better to set the calculations out in a tabular form. The table can include the times for non-productive operations and a total floor-to-floor time can be arrived at. Consider the bolt shown in fig. 5.28 (*a*), for which the table, or operation sheet, would be as shown in fig. 5.28 (*b*).

Columns 1, 2, 3 and 4 are self-explanatory.

Column 5 shows the cutting speed to be used and from this the work speed in revolutions per minute is calculated.

Column 6 is the feed rate in cuts per centimetre, which enables the number of revolutions required for the operations to be calculated.

Column 7 is the number of revolutions required for the operation and is obtained by multiplying the feed rate in column 6 by the length of work to be cut.

Column 8 is the time required for the cutting operations. The total revolutions are known and are divided by the revolutions per minute to give the cutting time in minutes.

Column 9 shows the time required for non-productive operations. These non-productive

144

times are known for different machines by work study engineers from past experience, those used here being for a medium-sized capstan lathe. A full list of them is not given but from the values used in fig. 5.28(*b*) the student could compile a useful basic table of such values. These he could augment by estimating times for other non-productive operations with which he is familiar.

Column 10 is a useful place to include any explanatory comments, as shown.

From the operation sheet, fig. 5.28(*b*), it would appear that a capstan operator, working under the conditions shown, could produce this part in 4·256 min, or 14·1 parts per hour or 112·8 such parts in an eight-hour shift. Allowances must be made, however, for unavoidable stoppages. Since the part is 100 mm long plus a parting-off allowance, about 105 mm is required per part. Thus, if the operator is using bars of 3 m length he must stop after every 28 parts and insert a new length of bar. Time must be allowed for this. Allowance must also be made for tool maintenance and for the operator to attend to the needs of nature. Unfortunately, these two contingencies rarely coincide.

Various organisations have their own arrangements and standards for these allowances but detailed descriptions of them form an important part of work study and would be out of place in this book. However, the student should be aware of the need for such allowances, and that the simple time-estimation sheet is not the whole story.

SUMMARY

The capstan lathe is designed to eliminate the skill required to produce a part on a centre lathe. It has a greater number of tooling stations and enables repetition work to be carried out without frequent tool changes and resetting. The skill largely rests on the tool setter who sets the machine up with suitable tools for the work in hand.

Turret lathes are larger and will accommodate a wider range of work. They are often used for smaller batches and the operator is a skilled man usually doing his own setting.

Cost estimating for capstan and turret lathes requires a considerable skill in planning and can be carried out to a high degree of accuracy of estimation of floor-to-floor time or cycle time.

The next logical development is to make the machine fully automatic and dispense with the operator. It is interesting to note that many single-spindle automatic lathes are indeed similar to capstan lathes but all the operations are controlled by cams and timing trips. The estimating for these machines is important to enable the cams to be designed and the timing settings calculated. The operation and cam design sheets are very similar to fig. 5.28(*b*) but are calculated in revolutions per operation for both cutting and non-productive operations so that the total revolutions can be calculated. The proportion of each cycle devoted to each operation can be calculated and the cam-layouts made accordingly.

It was shown in Book 1 that the milling machine is basically designed for the production of flat surfaces by either a generating or a copying process. With the addition of a rotary table or a dividing head the scope and range of work of the machine can be increased enormously. The machine discussed was the plain milling machine in both its horizontal- and vertical-spindle forms. Various modifications of the milling machine are available and are of two basic types:

(*a*) More specialised machines, for repetition work

(*b*) The universal milling machine, for more sophisticated and toolroom work.

SPECIALISED TYPES OF MILLING MACHINE

1. LINCOLN MILLING MACHINE

The basic alignments of this machine are similar to those of the plain horizontal machine in that the table surface is parallel to the spindle axis and the table motion is normal to the spindle axis. There the similarity ends. The table of the Lincoln machine cannot be raised or lowered, but has only a horizontal feed motion. The arbor is supported at each end as shown in fig. 6.1 and the cutters are positioned relative to the work by the spacing collars unless, as on some machines, a sideways table adjustment is provided. The depth of cut is set by vertical adjustment of the spindle.

This type of machine is especially useful for gang milling and heavy straddle milling of long workpieces.

2. DUPLEX MILLING MACHINE

This machine, whose basic form is shown in fig. 6.2, is similar to the Lincoln machine but has two horizontal spindles on which are mounted facing cutters. These can be adjusted vertically for position and horizontally for depth of cut. The Duplex machine is particularly suited to the facing of flanges and bosses on both sides of a casting at once.

The logical extension of the Duplex milling machine is the *Triplex* machine, which has a vertical spindle as shown in fig. 6.2, thus enabling the top face as well as two sides of a casting to be machined simultaneously.

Another development of the milling machine for high rates of metal removal is the *vertical-spindle rotary table machine*. With this, a continuously rotating horizontal table carries a number of fixtures which are unloaded and reloaded in turn as they pass the operator. Such machines are used for relatively small parts.

A machine for much larger parts is the *open-sided spar mill*. This has a horizontal spindle carrying a facing cutter which is used for machining large parts from the solid billet, usually in the aero-space industry.

Note that in all these machines the table has a single motion, the feed motion in the horizontal plane. This makes for extreme rigidity and high rates of metal removal by the use of modern tool materials such as those discussed in Chapter 3.

The latest developments of milling machines are entirely opposite in concept and purpose. One is the special-purpose machine designed solely for the single job for which it was made, the production quantities being such that the capital cost of the machine can readily be absorbed.

The other development is the automatically-controlled milling machine which is basically a plain vertical machine whose table motions are controlled by a magnetic tape produced by computer from a program derived from the form and dimensions of the part required.

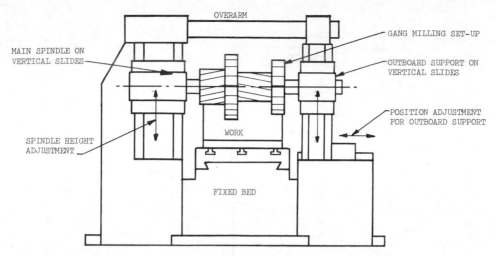

Fig. 6.1 Lincoln-type milling machine. Note the extreme rigidity obtained with the fixed bed construction.

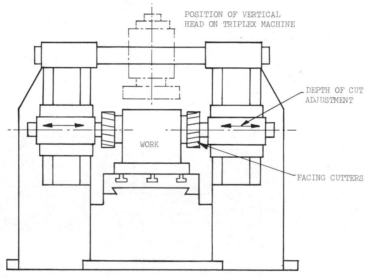

Fig. 6.2 Triplex and Duplex type milling machines.

These machines can produce economically in small batches the most complex forms and require very little operator skill. Many spar mills, also, are controlled in this manner.

THE UNIVERSAL MILLING MACHINE

A re-examination of the alignments of the plain horizontal milling machine discussed in Book 1 will show that the longitudinal table motion is fixed in direction and at right angles to the axis of the machine spindle. The only difference in the universal milling machine is that this alignment is not fixed, for the table *and its slideway* can be swung through an angle, as shown in fig. 6.3. This, with the aid

147

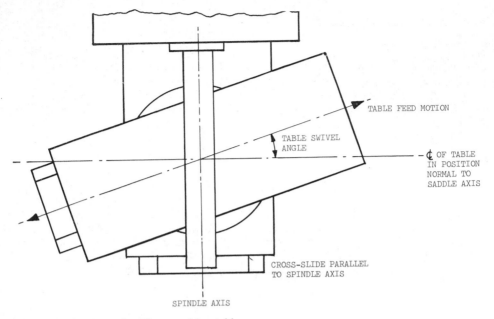

TABLE FEED MOTION

TABLE SWIVEL
ANGLE

₵ OF TABLE
IN POSITION
NORMAL TO
SADDLE AXIS

CROSS-SLIDE PARALLEL
TO SPINDLE AXIS

SPINDLE AXIS

Fig. 6.3 Universal horizontal milling machine table
adjustment.

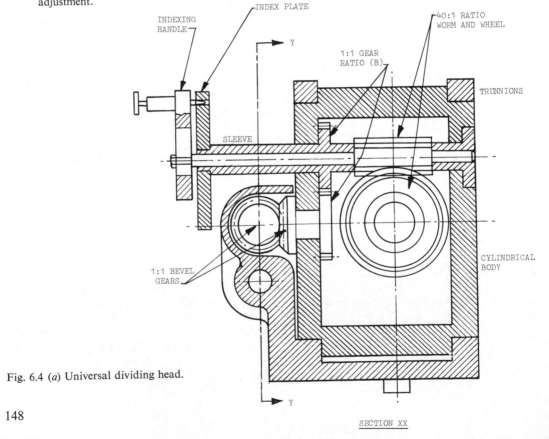

INDEXING
HANDLE

INDEX PLATE

40:1 RATIO
WORM AND WHEEL

Y

1:1 GEAR
RATIO (B)

TRUNNIONS

SLEEVE

CYLINDRICAL
BODY

1:1 BEVEL
GEARS

Y

Fig. 6.4 (a) Universal dividing head.

SECTION XX

148

of a dividing head, enables helical[1] milling to be carried out.

THE UNIVERSAL DIVIDING HEAD

The dividing head used in conjunction with a universal milling machine is more sophisticated than that discussed in Book 1. It still consists essentially of a work-holding device mounted on a spindle nose which can be rotated by a worm and wheel which give a 40:1 reduction ratio. Similar index plates and quadrants are used for simple indexing but the universal head has two important features not appearing in the simpler devices.

1. An auxiliary gear shaft is provided which, through the 1:1 gear ratio A (fig. 6.4), the 1:1 bevel gears, and the 1:1 gear ratio B,

[1] Sometimes incorrectly called *spiral* milling. A spiral is a two-dimensional curve like a hairspring, while a helix is three-dimensional as in a screw thread. Spiral milling will be discussed under Cam Milling.

Fig. 6.4(*b*)

drives the index plate. When the indexing plunger is withdrawn the index plate can rotate relative to the indexing handle. On the other hand, if the plunger is engaged and the auxiliary gear shaft is turned, the rotating index plate turns the indexing handle and hence the worm. In this case, rotation of the auxiliary gear shaft causes the work to rotate through the normal 40:1 reduction ratio. Note that all the gears connecting the index plate to the auxiliary gear shaft are of 1:1 ratio and the plate therefore rotates at the same speed as the shaft, the work spindle turning at 1/40th of this speed.

2. The other feature of this dividing head is that its spindle axis can be swung through 90° from the horizontal to the vertical position. To allow this, the whole cylindrical body of the dividing head, including the wormwheel drive and the work spindle, is carried in trunnions as shown in fig. 6.4. To enable the

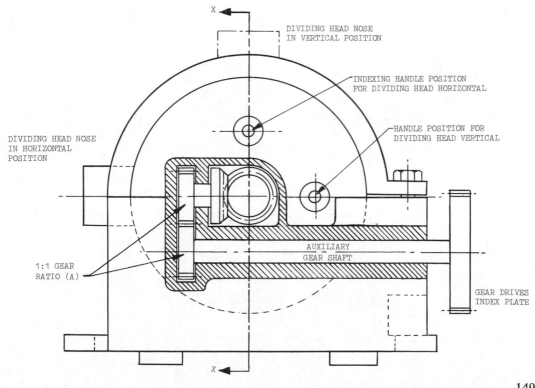

X

DIVIDING HEAD NOSE
IN VERTICAL POSITION

INDEXING HANDLE POSITION
FOR DIVIDING HEAD HORIZONTAL

HANDLE POSITION FOR
DIVIDING HEAD VERTICAL

DIVIDING HEAD NOSE
IN HORIZONTAL
POSITION

1:1 GEAR
RATIO (A)

AUXILIARY
GEAR SHAFT

GEAR DRIVES
INDEX PLATE

X

SECTION YY

auxiliary gear shaft to be geared to the table leadscrew, the auxiliary shaft must remain horizontal, which necessitates the gear train B and the bevel wheels. Gear train A is necessary to keep down the height of the auxiliary shaft so that the indexing handle can be moved into the position shown when the spindle is in the vertical position.

Summarising these points we can see that the universal dividing head has the following features:

(a) The auxiliary shaft can be used to turn the index plate.

(b) The auxiliary shaft can be geared to the table lead screw.

(c) The auxiliary shaft can be geared to the dividing-head spindle when the dividing-head spindle is in the horizontal position.

(d) The dividing-head spindle can be swung to any angle between the horizontal and the vertical.

The reasons for the provision of these facilities will now be considered.

HELICAL MILLING A helix may be defined as the locus of a point moving around a cylinder and at the same time moving parallel to the cylinder axis, the linear movement being proportional to the angular movement. A screw thread is a helix, and in order to produce a screw thread the cutting tool must move along the bar at the same time as the bar rotates, the ratio between the linear and angular velocities being constant.

If it is desired to mill a helical groove in a bar, the bar must rotate and at the same time move axially, the angular movement being proportional to the linear movement. On the milling machine the table feed provides the linear movement and the dividing head, if

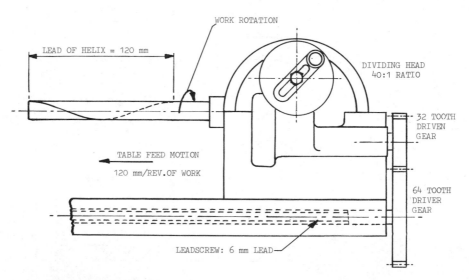

Fig. 6.5 Dividing head set up to produce a helix of 120 mm lead.
Note: This diagram shows only the essentials. The work-holding device and idler gears are not shown.

geared to the table leadscrew, provides the rotational movement.

Consider a helix with a lead of 120 mm being cut on a machine whose table lead-screw has a lead of 6 mm. To produce such a helix the work must make one complete revolution while the table advances 120 mm as shown in fig. 6.5. As has been stated, the lead screw is geared to the dividing head, but in such a manner that the leadscrew, through the gears, *drives the dividing-head plate*, and, as long as the indexing plunger is engaged with the plate, the worm and hence the wormwheel and work rotate.

Thus, for one revolution of the work:

$$\text{Revolutions of leadscrew} = \frac{120 \text{ mm}}{6 \text{ mm}}$$

Revolutions of dividing-head worm
$$= 40 \text{ (for 1 rev of work)}$$

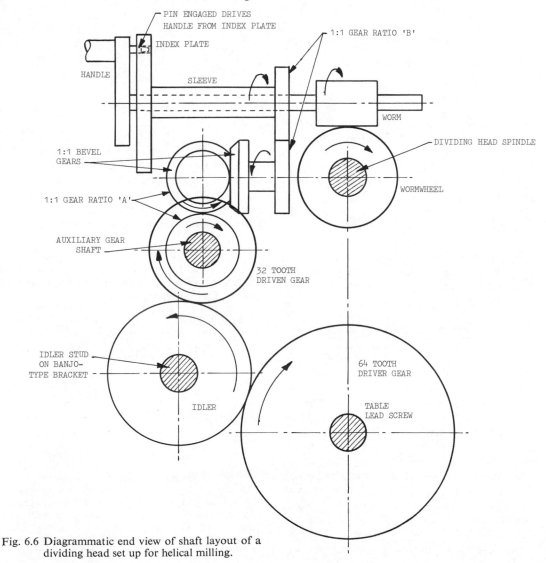

Fig. 6.6 Diagrammatic end view of shaft layout of a dividing head set up for helical milling.

As the dividing-head gear (driven) must, in this case, rotate faster than the lead-screw gear (driver), the driven gear will be the smaller and therefore:

$$\frac{\text{Driver}}{\text{Driven}} = \frac{6 \times 40}{120} = \frac{240}{120}$$

Idler gears are necessary between the driver and driven gears, the number of idler gears being chosen to give the correct direction of rotation for a right-hand or left-hand helix. A banjo-mounting is provided to enable the idler gears to be mounted as shown in fig. 6.6.

Returning to the expression

$$\frac{\text{Driver}}{\text{Driven}} = \frac{240}{120}$$

we can see that the numerator, 240, is the lead of the machine screw (6 mm) multiplied by the dividing head ratio (40 : 1), i.e., it is actually 240 mm. This is called the *lead of the machine*, since it is the distance the table advances when the leadscrew makes 40 rev. Thus, if a 1 : 1 gear ratio is used between the dividing head and the leadscrew, this is the lead of the helix produced on the work.

The denominator in the above expression is the lead of the work (120 mm) and we can thus produce a general expression to cover all cases of helical milling:

$$\frac{\text{Driver}}{\text{Driven}} = \frac{\text{Lead of machine}}{\text{Lead of work}}$$

in which lead of machine = lead of leadscrew × dividing head ratio.

It may be required to cut a number of equally-spaced helices, e.g., to cut a worm. The gears drive the index plate and the work is driven from the plate via the indexing handle plunger but, when the table is stationary, the plunger can still be withdrawn and the indexing handle turned to index the work to a fresh position, in the normal way. Thus, any convenient number of similar helices can be cut parallel to each other around the work.

Standard gears normally available for this purpose have the following numbers of teeth: 24 (two off), 28, 32, 40, 44, 56, 64, 72, 86 and 100 teeth. In addition, the following special gears can be supplied if required: 46, 47, 52, 58, 68, 70, 76 and 84 teeth.

Returning now to our expression

$$\frac{\text{Driver}}{\text{Driven}} = \frac{\text{Lead of machine}}{\text{Lead of work}}$$

If machine lead = 240 mm
and work lead = 120 mm

$$\frac{\text{Driver}}{\text{Driven}} = \frac{240}{120} = \frac{2}{1}$$

$$= \frac{64}{32}$$

or any other pair of gears giving the same ratio.

CALCULATION BASED ON HELIX ANGLE

In many cases the helix angle[1] rather than the lead is given. For instance, if a pair of helical gears are to mesh together they must be of the same helix angle, but if they are of different diameters they must have different leads.

Consider a groove of 70° helix angle to be cut to a mean diameter of 50 mm, i.e., the diameter midway between the root of the helix and the work periphery.

From fig. 6.7:

$$\tan \alpha = \frac{\text{lead of work}}{\text{mean circumference}}$$

$$= \frac{\text{lead of work}}{\pi \times \text{mean diameter}}$$

∴ lead of work = π × mean diameter × tan α

$$= \pi \times 50 \text{ mm} \times \tan 70°$$

$$= \pi \times 50 \times 2 \cdot 7475 \text{ mm}$$

lead of work = 431·58 mm

[1] In this work the definition of helix angle shown in fig. 6.7 is used, i.e., it is the angle between the generator of the helix and the line normal to the work axis. The author considers this to be the best definition but some confusion exists and, in many cases, the angle between the helix and the work axis is used.

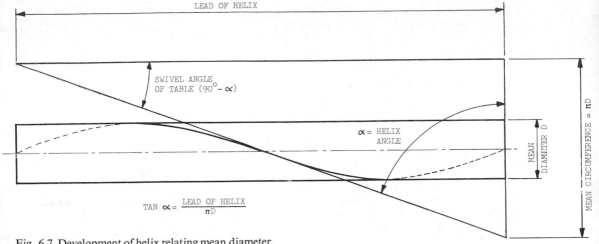

TAN $\alpha = \dfrac{\text{LEAD OF HELIX}}{\pi D}$

Fig. 6.7 Development of helix relating mean diameter, lead and helix angle.

$$\frac{\text{Driver}}{\text{Driven}} = \frac{\text{Lead of machine}}{\text{Lead of work}}$$

If the lead of the machine = 240 mm

then $\dfrac{\text{Driver}}{\text{Driven}} = \dfrac{240}{431 \cdot 58}$

By inspection it is clear that this ratio will not be a practicable one so we may approximate to

$$\frac{\text{Driver}}{\text{Driven}} = \frac{240}{432}$$

$$= \frac{1}{1 \cdot 8}$$

It is now necessary to find two gears to give this ratio and from those available we find

$$\frac{\text{Driver}}{\text{Driven}} = \frac{40}{72}$$

A simple way to find these gears is to use a slide rule to multiply the ratio, in this case 1·8, by the gear tooth numbers in turn until the answer is a whole number which matches one of the gears available. The two numbers used then give the gears required:

$1 \cdot 8 \times 24 = 43 \cdot 2$	$1 \cdot 8 \times 32 = 57 \cdot 6$
$1 \cdot 8 \times 28 = 50 \cdot 4$	$\mathbf{1 \cdot 8 \times 40 = 72}$

The approximation of 432 instead of 431·58 produces an error in the helix angle and the actual helix angle α cut can be found:

$$\tan \alpha = \frac{\text{lead of work}}{\text{mean circumference}}$$

$$= \frac{432}{\pi \times 50}$$

$$= 2 \cdot 751$$

$$\therefore \quad \alpha = 70^\circ \ 1 \cdot 4'$$

The error of 1·4′ may be considered negligible.

THE UNIVERSAL MILLING MACHINE TABLE

If, now, the actual motion of the work relative to the cutter during helical milling is considered, the need for the milling machine table to be able to swivel becomes apparent.

The motion of a point on the work surface, being a combination of linear motion and rotation, is not in line with the table, but approaches the cutter along the line of the helix. Thus the helix must be aligned with the cutter to produce an *approximately* correctly-formed slot, and this alignment is achieved by swinging the table through the complement to

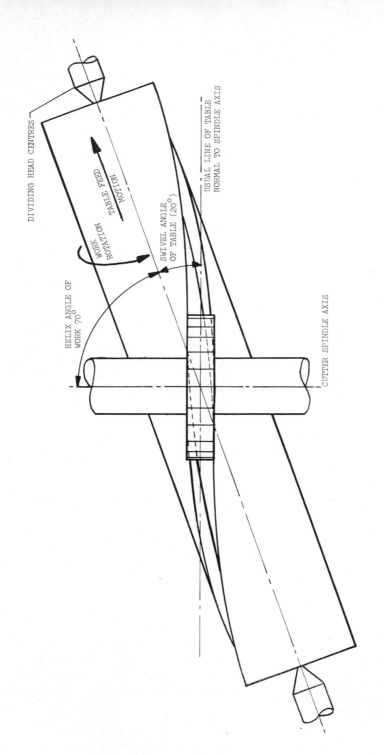

Fig. 6.8 Relative positions of machine spindle and table motion to produce a helix of 70° mean helix angle. The dotted lines show fouling zones ahead of and behind the cutter.

DIVIDING HEAD CENTRES

USUAL LINE OF TABLE NORMAL TO SPINDLE AXIS

TABLE FEED MOTION

WORK ROTATION

SWIVEL ANGLE OF TABLE (20°)

HELIX ANGLE OF WORK 70°

CUTTER SPINDLE AXIS

the helix angle; for the previously worked example the table is turned through $(90° - 70°) = 20°$, the machine setting being as shown in fig. 6.8.

If the table is not swung in this manner the groove produced takes the form of a projected view of the cutter along the line of the helix. This can be demonstrated by cutting a helical groove with the table set at right angles to the spindle axis and then another groove with the table correctly set. The effect is immediately apparent.

It has been emphasised above that the form of groove produced is only approximately that of the cutter form. It will not be exact in form for two reasons.

1. The helix angle at the bottom of the groove is different from that at the periphery of the work. The table can only be set at one angle: obviously, the *mean* helix angle is used and the setting is incorrect for all points above and below this.

2. Due to the depth of cut, the cutter intersects the work surface both ahead and to the rear of the point of full depth of cut. At these points the work is not approaching the cutter at the true helix angle and interference occurs. Thus a side-and-face cutter will not cut a square-sided groove but one with sides at an angle of slightly greater than 90° to the root. This effect can be clearly seen in fig. 6.8, where the dotted lines show the fouling zones ahead of and behind the cutter, the extent of the fouling depending on the diameter of the cutter and the depth of cut. The effect can be minimised by using the smallest diameter cutter possible. The point does not arise if an end mill is used, since the projected shape of an end mill is the same in all directions.

Consider again the last example, in which an approximation produced an error of 1·4′ in the helix angle. The machine table cannot in any case be set to this order of accuracy, which explains why this error is negligible.

Considering the earlier case, where the lead of the work was 120 mm, let this be for a groove to be cut in a bar 20 mm diameter with a groove depth of 6 mm.

Mean diameter of groove
$$= 20 \text{ mm} - 6 \text{ mm} = 14 \text{ mm}$$

$$\tan \alpha = \frac{\text{lead of work}}{\text{mean circumference}}$$

$$\text{where } \alpha = \text{helix angle}$$

$$= \frac{120 \text{ mm}}{\pi \times 14 \text{ mm}}$$

$$= 2 \cdot 72$$

Helix angle $\alpha = 69° 49′$

$\therefore$ Angle of swivel of table
$$= 90° - 69° 49′$$
$$= 20° 11′ \text{ or say } 20\tfrac{1}{4}°$$

Summarising:
$$\frac{\text{Driver}}{\text{Driven}} = \frac{\text{Lead of machine}}{\text{Lead of work}}$$

$$\tan \text{ helix angle } \alpha = \frac{\text{Lead of work}}{\text{Mean circumference}}$$

Swivel angle of table $= (90 - \alpha)°$

It is appropriate here to emphasise what *cannot* be done on the universal milling machine. If the table is swung to an angle the workface will not be machined at that angle because it is the *direction of the table motion* which is changed. The work simply moves obliquely relative to the cutter, which produces a form whose profile is that of the cutter projected along the line of the table motion, just the same as when the table of a plain horizontal machine is misaligned. This effect is explained and illustrated on pp. 206 and 207 of Book 1.

The only way to machine work at an angle in this manner is to retain the table setting normal to the spindle axis and mount the work on a swivel-base vice or rotary table.

CAM MILLING On page 149 it was shown that a facility of the universal dividing head is its ability to have the spindle axis swung through 90° from the horizontal to the vertical. Consider such a dividing head,

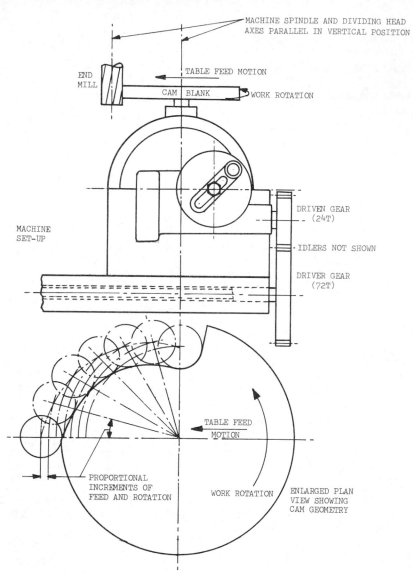

MACHINE SPINDLE AND DIVIDING HEAD
AXES PARALLEL IN VERTICAL POSITION

END
MILL

TABLE FEED MOTION

CAM BLANK

WORK ROTATION

MACHINE
SET-UP

DRIVEN GEAR
(24T)

IDLERS NOT SHOWN

DRIVER GEAR
(72T)

TABLE FEED
MOTION

PROPORTIONAL
INCREMENTS OF
FEED AND ROTATION

WORK ROTATION

ENLARGED PLAN
VIEW SHOWING
CAM GEOMETRY

Fig. 6.9 Cam milling set-up to give the maximum lift
per revolution of the cam with a given gear
train.

geared to the table leadscrew as in helical milling but set in the vertical position as shown in fig. 6.9, the work in this case being a disc. The machine is of the universal type with a vertical head fitted which can be inclined so that the end mill is set on the centre line of the work, the setting being such that the work and cutter axes are parallel. Ideally the cutter should be of the same diameter as the cam follower.

As the table is advanced, it feeds the cutter into the work. But, through the gearing between the dividing head and the table, the work is also rotating, and the increase in the depth of the cut is proportional to the angle of rotation. Thus a cam of true spiral form is produced, i.e., its lift is proportional to the angle of rotation, and the cam follower will have constant velocity if the cam rotates at constant speed.

Let the required cam have a lift of 20 mm in 90° of rotation.

Total lift per revolution of the cam

$$= 20 \text{ mm} \times \frac{360°}{90°}$$

$$= 80 \text{ mm}$$

Therefore for one revolution of the work the table must advance 80 mm. If the leadscrew has a lead of 6 mm:

$$\text{Revolutions of leadscrew} = \frac{80 \text{ mm}}{6 \text{ mm}}$$

But for one revolution of the work the driven gear, turning the dividing head worm, must make 40 rev. As this makes the more revolutions it requires the smaller gear and therefore the ratio of tooth numbers is given by:

$$\frac{\text{Driver (leadscrew gear)}}{\text{Driven (dividing head gear)}} = \frac{40}{80/6}$$

$$\frac{\text{Driver}}{\text{Driven}} = \frac{240 \text{ mm}}{80 \text{ mm}} = \frac{3}{1}$$

Note again that the numerator, 240 mm, is the *lead of the machine* while the denominator is the lift per revolution of the cam.

Thus a general expression can be written:

$$\frac{\text{Driver}}{\text{Driven}} = \frac{\text{Lead of machine}}{\text{Lift per revolution of cam}}$$

From the gears available the ratio required can be obtained from:

$$\frac{\text{Driver}}{\text{Driven}} = \frac{3}{1} = \frac{72}{24}$$

The 72 tooth gear is attached to the leadscrew and the 24 tooth gear to the dividing head, with suitable idlers.

This set-up, with both machine and dividing head spindles vertical, is the simplest case of cam milling which, for a given train of gears, gives the maximum lift per revolution of the cam. Consider now the dividing head and machine spindles swung to the horizontal position. The cam lift produced would be zero and, in fact, this would simply be an expensive method of turning a disc. This condition is shown in fig. 6.10.

If the vertical position gives the maximum lift per revolution of the cam and the horizontal position gives zero lift, then inter-

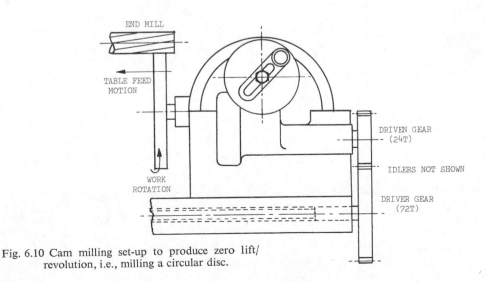

Fig. 6.10 Cam milling set-up to produce zero lift/revolution, i.e., milling a circular disc.

157

Fig. 6.11 Cam milling with inclined cutter and work
   axes.

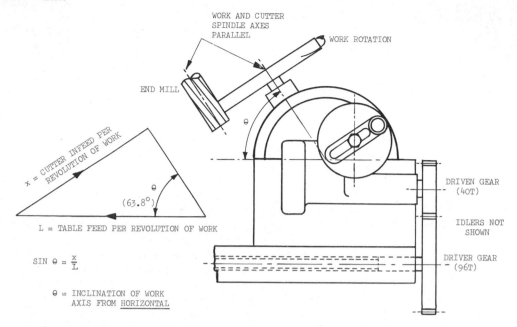

mediate angular positions produce inter-mediate cam lifts with the same train of gears. This condition is shown in fig. 6.11, the machine and dividing head spindle axes being turned through the same angle so that they remain parallel to each other.

From fig. 6.11:

Let table movement per revolution of cam

$$= L$$

and lift per revolution of cam produced $= x$

$$\text{Then } \frac{x}{L} = \sin \theta$$

$$\text{and } L = \frac{x}{\sin \theta}$$

But L will in fact be the maximum lift per revolution with a particular gear train.

$$\frac{\text{Driver}}{\text{Driven}} = \frac{\text{lead of machine}}{L}$$

$$= \frac{\text{lead of machine}}{x/\sin \theta}$$

$$\text{or } \frac{\text{Driver}}{\text{Driven}} = \frac{\text{lead of machine} \times \sin \theta}{x}$$

$$\therefore \sin \theta = \frac{x}{\text{lead of machine}} \times \frac{\text{Driver}}{\text{Driven}}$$

where $x =$ required lift per revolution of cam

If therefore a gear ratio is chosen which gives a *greater* lift per revolution of the cam than is required, the correct lift per revolution can be obtained by inclining the set-up through angle θ.

Consider a cam requiring a lift of 21·5 mm in 87° of rotation:

$$\text{Lift per revolution} = 21 \cdot 5 \text{ mm} \times \frac{360°}{87°}$$

$$= 88 \cdot 97 \text{ mm/rev}$$

This would obviously not be easily obtainable with the gears available so let us choose a convenient lift per revolution greater than this, say 100 mm.

Assuming a machine lead of 240 mm:

158

$$\frac{\text{Driver}}{\text{Driven}} = \frac{\text{lead of machine}}{\text{maximum lift per revolution}}$$

$$= \frac{240}{100}$$

$$\frac{\text{Driver}}{\text{Driven}} = \frac{96 \text{ teeth}}{40 \text{ teeth}}$$

$$\sin\theta = \frac{x}{\text{lead of machine}} \times \frac{\text{Driver}}{\text{Driven}}$$

where $x = 88{\cdot}97$ mm

$$= \frac{88{\cdot}97 \text{ mm}}{240 \text{ mm}} \times \frac{96}{40}$$

$$\sin\theta = 0{\cdot}8897$$

$$\theta = 63{\cdot}8° \text{ from the horizontal}$$

It is frequently required that a cam should have different rates of rise and fall over different parts of its periphery. In this case the gears can be calculated for the greatest lift required per revolution and then, using the same gears, the lesser lifts can be obtained by using different inclinations of the dividing head and machine spindle, i.e., different values of θ.

Consider a cam having the following details:

First lobe: Lift = 15 mm in 62°
Second lobe: Lift = 5 mm in 25°
Third lobe: Lift = 20 mm in 130°

For each case calculate the lift per revolution of the cam.

First lobe:

$$\text{Lift/rev} = 15 \text{ mm} \times \frac{360°}{62°} = 87 \text{ mm/rev}$$

Second lobe:

$$\text{Lift/rev} = 5 \text{ mm} \times \frac{360°}{25°} = 72 \text{ mm/rev}$$

Third lobe:

$$\text{Lift/rev} = 20 \text{ mm} \times \frac{360°}{130°} = 55{\cdot}4 \text{ mm/rev}$$

The greatest lift required per revolution of the cam is 87 mm and using a convenient value of 90 mm/rev we have:

$$\frac{\text{Driver}}{\text{Driven}} = \frac{\text{Lead of machine}}{\text{Maximum lift per revolution}}$$

$$= \frac{240}{90}$$

Convenient gears give

$$\frac{\text{Driver}}{\text{Driven}} = \frac{64}{24}$$

$$\sin\theta = \frac{\text{required lift per rev.}}{\text{lead of machine}} \times \frac{\text{Driver}}{\text{Driven}}$$

First lobe:

$$\sin\theta = \frac{87 \text{ mm}}{240 \text{ mm}} \times \frac{64}{24} = 0{\cdot}9667$$

$$\therefore \ \theta = 75{\cdot}2°$$

Second lobe:

$$\sin\theta = \frac{72 \text{ mm}}{240 \text{ mm}} \times \frac{64}{24} = 0{\cdot}8000$$

$$\therefore \ \theta = 53{\cdot}2°$$

Third lobe:

$$\sin\theta = \frac{55{\cdot}4 \text{ mm}}{240 \text{ mm}} \times \frac{64}{24} = 0{\cdot}6156$$

$$\therefore \ \theta = 38{\cdot}0°$$

Note that in all cases the angle θ is the inclination of the dividing head spindle *from the horizontal*, as shown in fig. 6.11.

INDEXING WITH THE UNIVERSAL DIVIDING HEAD

The simple dividing head discussed in Book 1 can be used for direct and simple indexing. With the normal range of index plates provided, such a dividing head is capable of a wide range of indexing movements. It may be recalled that the required turns of the indexing handle can be obtained from the following expressions:

(*a*) For *n* equal divisions

$$\text{No. of turns of handle} = \frac{40}{n}$$

(b) For angular indexing

$$\text{No. of turns of handle} = \frac{\text{Angle required}}{9°}$$

The index plates usually provided are, for single-sided index plates:

Plate No. 1: 15, 16, 17, 18, 19 and 20 holes

Plate No. 2: 21, 23, 27, 29, 31 and 33 holes

Plate No. 3: 37, 39, 41, 43, 47 and 49 holes

and for double-sided index plates:

1st Side: 24, 25, 28, 30, 34, 37, 38, 39, 41, 42 and 43 holes

2nd Side: 46, 47, 49, 51, 53, 54, 57, 58, 59, 62 and 66 holes.

Consider a gear wheel of 53 teeth which is to be cut on a dividing head equipped with the three single-sided index plates.

$$\text{No. of turns of handle} = \frac{40}{n} = \frac{40}{53}$$

It so happens that 53 is a prime number and the indexing movement cannot be obtained by simple indexing. This is true for all prime numbers which do not appear in the numbers of holes provided in the index plates or which are not a factor of one of the numbers. The problem can be overcome by one of two methods, *compound indexing* or *differential indexing*. Both involve the same principle; the number of turns of the handle is chosen to give an approximation to the required index and the correction is made by turning the plate the required amount backwards or forwards. Compound indexing was used in the past and consisted in effect of finding two index movements, one for the handle and one for the plate, using different hole rings in the index plate. These two movements, when added, gave the required indexing of the work

which could not be accomplished by a single movement. The method has largely fallen into disuse for three reasons:

(a) The complexity of the process gives rise to a greater chance of operator error.

(b) If the handle movement is forward and the plate movement is backward, it is easy to induce backlash.

(c) Prime numbers of divisions such as 53, greater than the number of holes in the index plate, still cannot be achieved accurately.

This method has therefore been largely superseded by the differential method.

DIFFERENTIAL INDEXING We have seen that for helical milling the dividing head index plate can be geared to the machine spindle. Consider now the index plate being geared to the *dividing head spindle* as shown in fig. 6.12. As the indexing handle of the dividing head is rotated it causes the worm, wormwheel and spindle to turn, and the gears from the spindle to the index plate cause the *index plate to rotate*, backwards or forwards depending upon the number of idlers used. In effect, this is an automatic method of compound indexing which overcomes the disadvantages mentioned above.

Consider now the problem of indexing 53 equal divisions.

$$\text{Turns of handle} = \frac{40}{53}$$

This, as we have seen, is not obtainable by simple indexing. If we make a rough approximation, then

$$\text{Turns of handle} = \frac{40}{48} = \frac{5}{6} = \frac{15}{18}$$

The indexing movement used is therefore 15 holes in the 18-hole ring in plate No. 1.

Note: The approximation chosen, in this case, 48, should contain a factor appropriate to one of the numbers of gear teeth available. If this is not done, it will not be possible to obtain a suitable gear train.

Fig. 6.12 Shaft layout of a dividing head set up to index 53 divisions by differential indexing. Note that two idlers are necessary to give the correct relative motion between plate and handle.

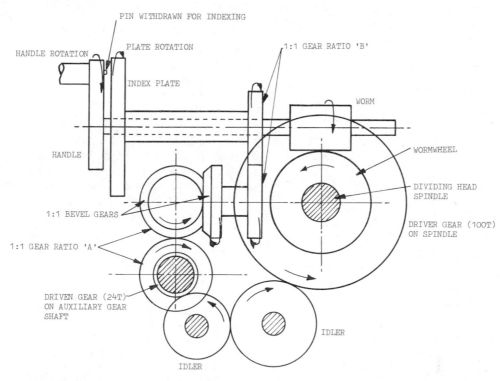

If 53 indexing movements are made of 15 holes in an 18-hole ring:

$$\text{Total handle movement} = \frac{15}{18} \times 53$$

$$= \frac{795}{18}$$

$$= 44\frac{3}{18} \text{ turns}$$

But for one revolution of the work the handle should make only 40 revolutions. The gears must therefore be arranged so that in one forward revolution of the dividing head spindle the index plate moves *backwards* $4\frac{3}{18}$ or $\frac{75}{18}$ revolutions.

$$\therefore \frac{\text{Driver}}{\text{Driven}} = \frac{75}{18} = \frac{25}{6}$$

$$= \frac{100}{24}$$

The driver gear is attached to the dividing head spindle and the driven gear to the stub spindle driving the index plate, as in fig. 6.12, the number of idler gears used being chosen to ensure that the plate moves in the opposite direction to the handle.

Thus the indexing procedure is the same as for simple indexing, viz., 15 holes in the 18-hole ring of a no. 1 plate, and the gears used give automatic compensation for the, in this case, excessive work rotation brought about by the approximate indexing movement.

As a further example consider a dividing head being used to mark off an angular vernier scale to read to units of 3', each

161

vernier division being compared with two of the degree units on the main scale. It was shown in Book 1 (page 83) that the smallest unit to which a vernier can be read is equal to the difference in the scale divisions and therefore the vernier scale divisions required must be marked off at an angle of 2° minus 3'.

$$\therefore \text{ Angular index} = 120' - 3' = 117'$$

For angular indexing:

$$\text{No. of turns of handle} = \frac{\text{No. of degrees}}{9°}$$

$$= \frac{\text{No. of minutes}}{540'}$$

$$\therefore \text{ No. of turns of handle} = \frac{117}{540} = \frac{13}{60}$$

Assuming that a dividing head with a double-sided plate is to be used it is clear that the numbers of holes available in the index plate do not allow for this movement. An approximation may be chosen and, again, it is advisable for the numbers in the approximation to be factors of the numbers of teeth available in the gears.

$$\text{Let approximate index} = \frac{14}{60}$$

$$\text{Turns of handle} = 7 \text{ holes in a 30-hole ring}$$

It is now necessary to determine the error in a complete revolution of the spindle. The exact number of divisions of 117' in a circle of 360° is equal to $\dfrac{360° \times 60'}{117'} = \dfrac{21\,600'}{117'}$.

If this number of movements of 7 holes in a 30-hole ring is made:

Total handle movement

$$= \frac{21\,600}{117} \times \frac{7}{30}$$

$$= 43\tfrac{1}{13} \text{ or } 40 + \frac{40}{13} \text{ turns}$$

But for one complete turn of the work the handle must only make 40 revolutions and therefore in one revolution of the spindle the index plate must make 40/13 revolutions backwards. The gear ratio required is therefore:

$$\frac{\text{Driver}}{\text{Driven}} = \frac{40}{13}$$

Examining the gears available, this ratio can be obtained by using

$$\frac{\text{Driver}}{\text{Driven}} = \frac{40}{13} = \frac{5 \times 8}{2 \times 6\cdot5} = \frac{70}{28} \times \frac{64}{52}$$

This is a compound gear train, set up as shown in fig. 6.13. An idler may again be required to ensure that, because the approximate index is too great, the plate moves in the opposite direction to the handle.

It should be noted that two of the special gears have been used in this gear train. If these were not available, continued fractions could be used either to obtain an approximate simple indexing movement or to obtain a suitable gear ratio using the standard gears. The method used is identical to that used in Chapter 4 to obtain an approximate gear ratio for screw cutting and again, the error induced should be calculated to ensure that it is not excessive.

(a) *Approximation to Use Standard Gears.* The ratio required is 40/13 and a continued fraction gives only two convergents, 40/13 and 3/1. As 40/13 is not obtainable the ratio

$$\frac{\text{Driver}}{\text{Driven}} = \frac{3}{1} \text{ is used}$$

$$\frac{\text{Driver}}{\text{Driven}} = \frac{72}{24}$$

Recalling that an indexing movement of 14 holes in a 60-hole circle is being used, then in one handle movement:

$$\text{Movement of handle} = \frac{14}{60} \text{ rev}$$

$$\text{Movement of spindle} = \frac{14}{60 \times 40} \text{ rev}$$

Fig. 6.13 Compound gear train for differential indexing. Again an extra idler gear is necessary to
give the correct direction of plate rotation.

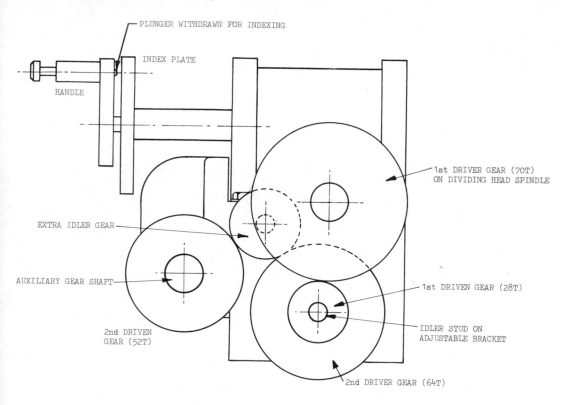

PLUNGER WITHDRAWN FOR INDEXING

INDEX PLATE

HANDLE

1st DRIVER GEAR (70T)
ON DIVIDING HEAD SPINDLE

EXTRA IDLER GEAR

AUXILIARY GEAR SHAFT

2nd DRIVEN
GEAR (52T)

1st DRIVEN GEAR (28T)

IDLER STUD ON
ADJUSTABLE BRACKET

2nd DRIVER GEAR (64T)

Movement of plate $=\dfrac{14}{60\times40}\times\dfrac{3}{1}$ rev

$$=\dfrac{14}{800}\ \text{rev}$$

$\therefore$ Actual handle movement

$$=\dfrac{14}{60}-\dfrac{14}{800}\ \text{rev}$$

$$=\dfrac{560}{2\,400}-\dfrac{42}{2\,400}\ \text{rev}$$

$\therefore$ Revolutions of handle

$$=\dfrac{518}{2\,400}$$

Revolutions of work

$$=\dfrac{518}{2\,400}\times\dfrac{1}{40}$$

Angular movement of work

$$=\dfrac{518}{2\,400}\times\dfrac{1}{40}\times360^\circ\times60'$$

$$=116{\cdot}55'$$

The error of $0{\cdot}45'$ would be acceptable for
most work, but not for the division of a
vernier scale.

163

(*b*) *Approximation to Use Simple Indexing.* The actual index required was 13/60. Again using continued fractions:

```
  13)60(4
      52
      ──
      8)13(1
         8
         ─
         5)8(1
            5
            ─
            3)5(1
               3
               ─
               2)3(1
                  2
                  ─
                  1)2(2
                     2
                     ─
                     0
```

The continued fraction is therefore:

$$\cfrac{1}{4+\cfrac{1}{1+\cfrac{1}{1+\cfrac{1}{1+\cfrac{1}{1+\cfrac{1}{2}}}}}}$$

1st convergent $=\dfrac{1}{4}$ 4th convergent $=\dfrac{4}{14}$

2nd convergent $=\dfrac{1}{5}$ 5th convergent $=\dfrac{5}{23}$

3rd convergent $=\dfrac{2}{9}$ 6th convergent $=\dfrac{13}{60}$

It is known that an index movement of 13/60 is not possible so consider 5/23, recalling that a double-sided index plate is being used in this problem. Reference to page 160 shows that an index of 10 holes in a 46-hole plate can be used.

$$\text{Turns of handle} = \frac{5}{23} \text{ rev}$$

$$\text{Turns of work} = \frac{5}{23} \times \frac{1}{40} \text{ rev}$$

$$= \frac{5}{23} \times \frac{1}{40} \times 360° \times 60'$$

$$= 117\cdot39'$$

In this case the error is less than that induced by an approximate gear train. This will not always be so and if the correct gears are not available both methods should be tried to see which gives the smaller error. Usually the approximate differential indexing method will be the more accurate, but not always, as has been shown.

THE CUTTER/WORK RELATIONSHIP

In this chapter we have seen how the simple milling machine has developed in two directions. The first is towards specialised machines such as the Lincoln and Duplex milling machines designed for high rates of metal removal, and the second is the universal milling machine which, when used in conjunction with a universal dividing head, is capable of a much wider range of toolroom-type operations. In either case the problem of metal removal rates is important and an improvement can be achieved by the use of cutters with inserted teeth made from modern cutting tool materials, as discussed in Chapter 3. A further improvement can be achieved, under certain conditions and using peripheral cutters, by reversing the cutter/work relationship. Thus instead of using conventional, or up-cut milling, the cutter is reversed on the arbor and its direction of rotation is reversed, but the direction of the work feed remains the same. This is called *down-cut milling*, or in some cases, *climb-cutting*.[1]

The relative motions of the cutter and work are shown in fig. 6.14 (*a*) and (*b*) for both up-cut and down-cut milling. An examination of the forces involved shows an immediate difference in the processes. If F_t is the force normal to the tooth, i.e., tangential to the

[1] The term *climb-cutting* is more usually applied to *hobbing*, a gear manufacturing process in which the work spindle is vertical and the cutter appears to 'climb' up the work.

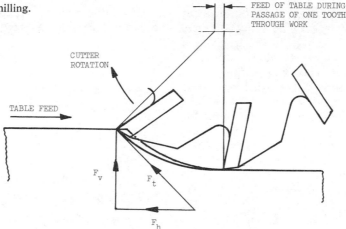

Fig. 6.14(*a*) Up-cut milling.

CUTTER
ROTATION

TABLE FEED

FEED OF TABLE DURING
PASSAGE OF ONE TOOTH
THROUGH WORK

F_v

F_t

F_h

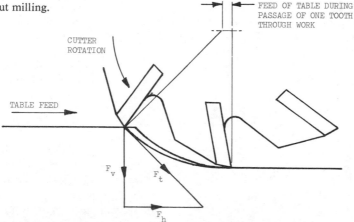

Fig. 6.14(*b*) Down-cut milling.

CUTTER
ROTATION

TABLE FEED

FEED OF TABLE DURING
PASSAGE OF ONE TOOTH
THROUGH WORK

F_v

F_t

F_h

cutter, the horizontal component F_h is in opposition to the direction of feed and the vertical component F_v is upwards in the case of up-cutting. Thus the horizontal component, operating against the leadscrew, takes up any backlash while the vertical component tends to lift the work off the table against the clamping force.

In down-cut milling, the horizontal force is in the direction of the feed motion and any backlash in the leadscrew will allow the work to be dragged into the cutter. This effectively increases the feed per tooth causing over-loading of the cutter and probably breakage. This would appear to eliminate down-cut milling as a method of cutting but, because of other advantages, machines have been developed in which the leadscrew backlash can be eliminated, the cost of the mechanism required being offset by the increased metal removal rates possible. Note also that the vertical force F_v is downwards, thus assisting the work-clamping forces.

The reason for the increased metal removal rates is shown in fig. 6.14. The rate at which metal can be removed depends on the cutting speed and feed rate used, and an increase in these will contribute to reduced tool life. In up-cut milling, at the start of the cut the depth of cut is zero, rubbing tends to occur and causes a high rate of cutter wear. In down-cut milling, however, by the time a tooth engages the work the table has fed forwards, giving a definite cut as the tooth engages the work and a gradual run-out. This reduces the rate of cutter wear, enabling higher speeds and feeds to be used between cutter regrinds. The author has no figures available for milling but for hobbing, a process with a similar cutting action, increases of 20% in cutting speed plus 10% in feed rate, with an increased tool life of the order of 30%, have been reported, with an improvement in surface finish.

It must be emphasised that only machines on which backlash can be eliminated from the table feed mechanism should be used for down-cut milling. Machines with a hydraulic table feed are eminently suitable but those with the leadscrew-and-nut type of feed drive must be fitted with a backlash eliminator, or serious damage may be done to the cutter.

OPTIMUM CUTTING CONDITIONS

For any cutting process on a given machine there is a metal removal rate which is the most economic that can be achieved under the prevailing conditions. It will depend on:

(a) Tool life between regrinds;
(b) Power available.

(a) TOOL LIFE We have seen in Chapter 3 that the tool life T is related to the cutting speed V by a law of the form

$VT^n = C$ where n and C are constants depending upon the conditions.

Thus, if we require a certain tool life we can ascertain the cutting speed required to give that life.

(b) POWER AVAILABLE It can be shown that under given conditions of work material and cutting tool material the volume of work material which can be removed per minute with one kilowatt of power is almost constant.

Let the width of cut be W millimetres, the depth of cut be d millimetres and the feed rate be f millimetres per minute. Then:

Volume removed per minute
$$= W \times d \times f \text{ cubic millimetres}$$

If the volume removed per minute for the expenditure of 1 kW is the constant K:

Power required, P,

$$= \frac{\text{Volume to be removed per minute}}{\text{Volume removed per minute per kilowatt}}$$

$$P = \frac{Wdf}{K} \text{ kilowatts}$$

As the width of cut, W millimetres, is usually fixed either by the width of the work or the width of the cutter, and the depth of cut is usually such that we wish to remove the metal at one pass, it follows that f, the feed rate in millimetres per minute, must be calculated to allow this to be done with the power available, and the power required, P kilowatts, must not exceed this.

Therefore feed rate $f = \dfrac{P \times K}{W \times d}$ mm per minute

Work material	Cutter material	Type of cutter	K $mm^3/min\,kW$
Medium carbon steel	H.S.S.	Slab mill	20 000
	H.S.S.	Face mill	35 000
	Tungsten carbide	Negative-rake face mill	20 000
Cast iron	H.S.S.	Slab mill	40 000
	H.S.S.	Face mill	60 000

Approximate values of K in cubic millimetres per minute per kilowatt of power supply are given in the preceding table. It must be emphasised that they are average values of K and in practice they will vary according to the condition of the machine, the condition of the cutter, the coolant used and other factors.

For a given operation the actual value of K can be found by performing a test on a milling machine with a wattmeter wired into the machine circuit.

Consider now the face milling of a piece of medium-carbon steel 100 mm wide with a H.S.S. cutter, the depth of cut being 5 mm and the optimum power available 5 kW.

$$\text{Feed rate } f = \frac{KP}{Wd} \text{ millimetres per minute}$$

$$= \frac{20\,000 \times 5}{100 \times 5}$$

$$\therefore \ f = 200 \text{ mm/min}$$

It has been found that to give the required tool life a cutting speed of 20 m/min is suitable for a cutter of 120 mm diameter.

Spindle speed in revolutions per minute

$$= \frac{\text{cutting speed in metres per minute}}{\text{circumference of cutter in metres}}$$

$$= \frac{20 \text{ m/min}}{\pi \times 120/1\,000 \text{ m}}$$

Spindle speed

$$= 53 \text{ rev/min}$$

Feed in millimetres per revolution

$$= \frac{200 \text{ mm/min}}{53 \text{ rev/min}}$$

$$= 3 \cdot 75 \text{ mm/rev}$$

If the cutter has 15 teeth, then the feed per tooth can be found as:

feed per tooth

$$= \frac{3 \cdot 75 \text{ mm/rev}}{15 \text{ teeth/rev}}$$

$$= 0 \cdot 25 \text{ mm/tooth}$$

This would be suitable for roughing, which is required, since we are concerned with optimum rates of metal removal.

Another situation for a similar calculation would be to ensure that a large surface could be finish machined at one pass, using a large enough cutter. Alternatively, if a lot of material had to be removed and the required finish demanded a feed of no more than 0·06 mm/tooth, what would be the maximum allowable depth of cut? Could the surface be machined in one cut or would a roughing cut followed by a fine-feed finishing cut be preferable?

This type of calculation need not be restricted to milling operations. By experiment values of K could be found for turning operations and drilling processes, in fact for any metal-cutting process where high metal removal rates are required.

CALCULATION OF CUTTING TIMES

Examination of a milling machine shows that, unlike the lathe, the table feed rate is independent of the spindle speed. On a lathe, the feed rate is usually quoted in cuts per centimetre, i.e., the number of revolutions the spindle makes for a centimetre of traverse. On a milling machine, the table feed-rate is given directly in millimetres per minute irrespective of the spindle speed. Thus it would appear that a workpiece 200 mm long, with a table traverse speed of 50 mm/min, would take 4 min to machine. This, however, does not take into account the fact that a milling cutter does not attain its full depth of cut immediately it makes contact with the work. A distance x is required for the cut to build up at the start. This can be seen in fig. 6.15 for peripheral milling, i.e., using a slab mill, slot cutter, or side-and-face cutter, and in fig. 6.16 for face milling.

Consider fig. 6.15.

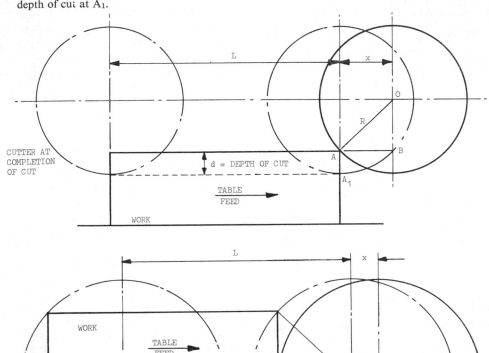

Fig. 6.15 Approach factor for peripheral milling. Cutter makes contact at A and reaches full depth of cut at A_1.

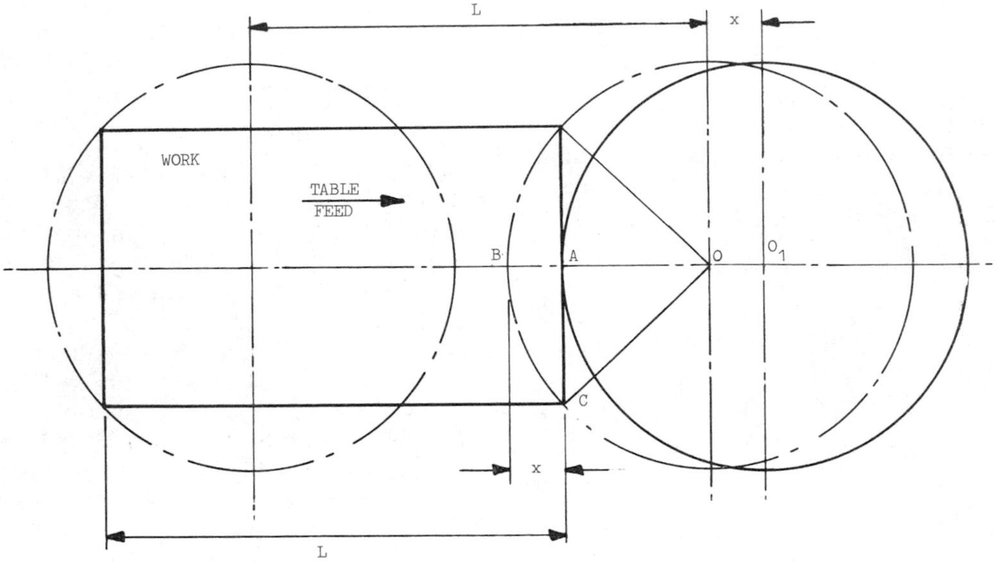

Fig. 6.16 Approach factor for face milling. Cutter makes contact at A with centre at O and reaches full width of cut when centre reaches O_1.

In triangle OAB,
OA = cutter radius R
AB = approach factor x
OB = $R - d$, where d = depth of cut

Using the theorem of Pythagoras,

$$(OA)^2 = (OB)^2 + (AB)^2$$
$$(AB)^2 = (OA)^2 - (OB)^2$$
$$x^2 = R^2 - (R - d)^2$$
$$= R^2 - (R^2 - 2Rd + d^2)$$
$$= R^2 - R^2 + 2Rd - d^2$$
$$= 2Rd - d^2$$

168

$$x^2 = d(2R - d)$$
but $2R =$ cutter diameter D
$\therefore \quad x^2 = d(D - d)$

and approach factor $x = \sqrt{[d(D - d)]}$ where $d =$ depth of cut and $D =$ cutter diameter.

The full length of traverse is therefore $L + x$. It might appear that it should be $L + 2x$, an allowance being made for the cutter to clear the work at the end. This is not so, because once the spindle centre line has passed the edge of the work all the metal has been removed.

The conditions for face milling are shown in fig. 6.16, in which x is again the approach factor and R the radius of the cutter. In this case the width of the work, W, must be considered.

From fig. 6.16,

$$x = \text{AB} = \text{OB} - \text{OA}$$

But $\text{OB} = R$, the cutter radius.

In triangle OAC

$$\text{OC}^2 = \text{OA}^2 + \text{AC}^2$$
$$\text{OA}^2 = \text{OC}^2 - \text{AC}^2$$

But OC also $= R$

and $\text{AC} = \dfrac{W}{2}$

$$\therefore \quad \text{OA}^2 = R^2 - \frac{W^2}{4}$$

$$\text{OA} = \sqrt{(R^2 - W^2/4)}$$

and
$$x = \text{OB} - \text{OA}$$
$$= R - \sqrt{(R^2 - W^2/4)}$$

But $D =$ cutter diameter, then

$$x = \frac{D}{2} - \sqrt{\left(\frac{D^2}{4} - \frac{W^2}{4}\right)}$$

$$= \frac{D}{2} - \frac{1}{2}\sqrt{\left(D^2 - W^2\right)}$$

and therefore

Approach factor $x = \frac{1}{2}[D - \sqrt{(D^2 - W^2)}]$

Again no allowance need be made for run-out, indeed the cutter should be cleared away from the work as rapidly as possible to avoid rubbing. In fact, in face milling the spindle can be inclined so that the rear of the cutter clears the work by about 0·05 mm to avoid rubbing.

In both cases, then, the total traverse is given by

Total traverse $= (L + x)$ millimetres
   where $L =$ work length (millimetres)
   $x =$ approach factor (millimetres)
and
cutting time $= \dfrac{L + x}{f}$ minutes

$f =$ feed rate in millimetres per minute.

SUMMARY

In this chapter we have seen how the plain milling machine, discussed in Book 1, has developed in two directions to give extremely rigid machines capable of high rates of metal removal in one case, and in the other case the universal milling machine which, with a universal dividing head, is capable of an extremely wide range of operations.

By the use of modern tool materials and unconventional methods, the productivity of the machine can be increased. The optimum cutting conditions for a given class of work can be obtained by quite simple calculations.

As with other productive processes, it is necessary to be able to calculate cutting times and also the times for loading and unloading the machine, but with milling machines the variety of work-holding methods is so great that the latter have not been considered in detail.

7

Abrasive Machining Processes

The functional requirements of many components demand qualities of working surface that cannot be produced by the usual metal-cutting tools, even those made from modern cutting tool materials such as cemented carbides, as discussed in Chapter 3. The outstanding requirements which preclude such finishing processes are:

(*a*) A high degree of surface finish
(*b*) A high degree of accuracy
(*c*) Hardness to resist wear.

Good surface finish and dimensional accuracy are complementary. A high degree of accuracy in dimensions demands a good surface finish and although a good surface finish can be provided even when high accuracy is not essential, such a finish is comparatively expensive and probably unnecessary.

Three processes are used to achieve the above requirements, all using abrasive cutting methods. These are grinding, honing and lapping. The cutting action of an abrasive was discussed in Chapter 3 and only the machining processes using abrasive cutting techniques will now be considered.

GRINDING PROCESSES With few exceptions, the geometric form of a component consists of one of, or a combination of, three basic shapes, flat, cylindrical, or conical. Thus a grinding machine must provide the relative motions between the work and wheel to enable such shapes to be produced. The machines available fall into four categories, surface grinding machines, cylindrical grinding machines, universal grinding machines and cutter grinding machines. Other specialised types which will not be discussed here are

thread grinding machines and centreless grinding machines.

SURFACE GRINDING MACHINES

This type of grinding machine is used for producing flat, and usually parallel, surfaces and can be considered in many ways as being equivalent to the milling machine. It may have a horizontal wheel spindle, grinding with the periphery of the wheel, or a vertical spindle, in which case the grinding is done by the wheel face. In either case there are certain fundamentals common to both machines:

1. The table motion must be straight both longitudinally and transversely, in order to produce flat surfaces.

2. The table surface must be parallel to its own motion, in order to produce parallel surfaces.

3. The adjustment to set the depth of cut must be sensitive enough to enable increments of 0·001 mm to be achieved either directly or by estimation.

In order to maintain accuracy, the machine must be extremely rigid, which is achieved by having the table on a fixed bed, the vertical adjustment being made by raising and lowering the wheelhead. Again, the similarity to the fixed-bed milling machine may be noted, where rigidity is a major requirement, although for a different reason.

An essential accessory for the surface grinding machine is the magnetic chuck, which enables flat workpieces to be held for grinding without mechanical clamping methods which might damage a finished work surface. Since the chuck is clamped to the machine table and the work is held magnetically on the upper surface of the chuck, the

Fig. 7.1(*a*) Permanent magnet type chuck in on
         position.

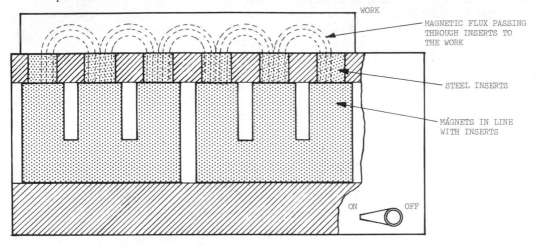

Fig. 7.1(*b*) Permanent magnet type chuck in off
         position.

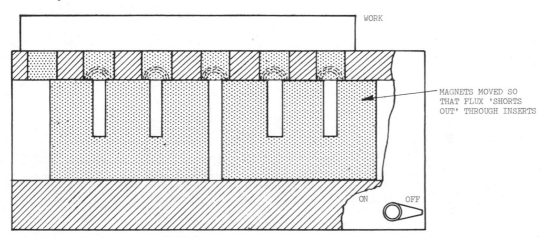

surface and the base of the chuck must be parallel and this parallelism must be maintained. The two surfaces must therefore be treated with care so that their parallelism is not destroyed by small burrs raised by mishandling. Non-ferrous parts cannot be held on a magnetic chuck and for these and for ferrous parts which are not suitable for magnetic holding, a vice can generally be used.

Magnetic chucks may be of the permanent magnet type shown in fig. 7.1, or of the electro-magnetic type, containing coils to energise the magnets, which is operated by simply switching the electric current on or off. This type has the disadvantage that a d.c. supply is necessary, requiring a rectifier. It must also be carefully sealed so that coolant does not get into the wiring. The permanent-magnet type illustrated is the one most commonly used.

The working face of a permanent-magnet chuck is made of a non-magnetic alloy in which steel inserts are fitted to line up with the pole faces of the magnets. Movement of the 'switch' causes the magnets to move sideways so that in the 'on' position the pole pieces are in line with the inserts and the magnetic flux passes through the work as shown in fig. 7.1(*a*). In the 'off' position the inserts are each in contact with two poles of the magnets and the flux is effectively 'shorted out', as shown in fig. 7.1(*b*), so that none passes through the work, which can then be removed.

It is often a serious disadvantage for a workpiece to become permanently magnetised and unfortunately hardened steel, which often has to be ground, retains a considerable amount of magnetism after being held on a magnetic chuck. This residual magnetism can be removed by placing the workpiece in an alternating magnetic field, and demagnetisers operating on this principle are available.

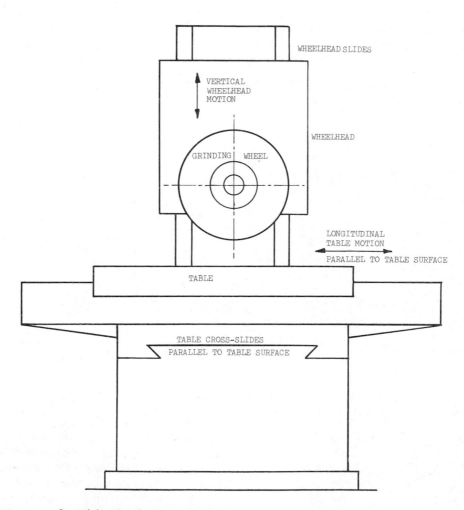

Fig. 7.2 Layout of peripheral wheel-type surface grinding machine.

THE HORIZONTAL–SPINDLE SUR-
FACE GRINDING MACHINE This
machine is illustrated in fig. 7.2, its alignments
being similar to those of the plain horizontal
milling machine. It can be used for straightforward surface grinding, in which case the
table is traversed longitudinally and the wheel
is gradually fed across the work to cover the
complete surface. The cross-feed may be hand-
controlled or automatically controlled, in
which case it can be varied from 0·2 mm to
2 mm per stroke of the table.

Alternatively, the machine can be used to
grind the sides and bases of slots and grooves.
For this type of operation the workpiece must
be aligned with the table traverse motion and
the wheel must also be positioned accurately
across the work. Thus on this type of grinding
machine the cross-feed adjustment must be
equally as sensitive as the vertical adjustment
of the wheel head. It should be noted that for
grinding the vertical sides of a workpiece, or
a groove, the sides of the wheel must be
relieved by dishing as shown in fig. 7.3. On
small workpieces, it may be better to perform
this type of operation on a small tool-and-
cutter grinder, but for large workpieces the
peripheral machine is quite suitable.

Wheel dressing is normally carried out with
the traverse motion locked, a diamond in a
holder being gripped on the magnetic chuck
as shown in fig. 7.4 and passed back and forth
across the wheel. Note the position of the
diamond relative to the direction of rotation
of the wheel. If for any reason the diamond
becomes loose, the rotation of the wheel will
throw it clear rather than drag it under the
wheel and create a hazard.

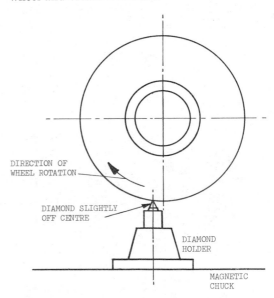

Fig. 7.4 Wheel dressing on surface grinder.

An examination of the configuration of the
peripheral-wheel machine shows that the
wheel spindle overhangs the work table. This
is not a very rigid form of construction and
this type of machine is more suited to work
of high accuracy, requiring sensitive control
than it is to work requiring high rates of metal
removal. Furthermore, a number of passes

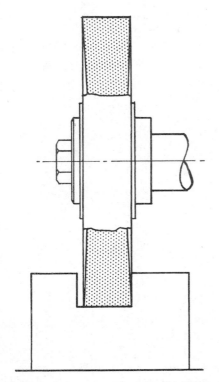

Fig. 7.3 Sides of wheel relieved for grinding groove
faces.

are necessary to cover a complete work surface and the machine is therefore slower than the vertical-spindle machine.

THE VERTICAL-SPINDLE SURFACE GRINDING MACHINE

The configuration of this machine is shown in fig. 7.5 and it will be noted that the machine cuts with the face of a cup wheel and not with the periphery. This lends itself to greater rigidity of the wheel spindle and higher metal-removal rates, the width of the work being less than the wheel diameter so that the work can be ground all over at one pass. Frequently the motor is made integral with the wheel spindle.

Many such machines do not have a table cross-feed, so the normal traverse, set to run slowly, is used for wheel dressing, the diamond holder again being held on the magnetic chuck or bolted direct to the table. The wheel is then lowered and the diamond traversed back and forth across the wheel face.

Unlike the horizontal-spindle machine, the vertical-spindle surface grinding machine is suitable only for grinding large flat surfaces but at much higher rates of metal removal.

CYLINDRICAL GRINDING MACHINES

The cylindrical grinding machine performs similar functions to the lathe in that it may be used for generating cylindrical, conical (tapered) and flat work-faces, the cutting tool being the grinding wheel. Unlike the lathe, the cutting tool (grinding wheel) is not traversed to produce cylindrical work, the generating motion being confined to the work table. Thus, in order to produce cylindrical and flat work surfaces, the following alignments are necessary.

1. Table motions must be truly straight
2. Longitudinal table feed must be parallel to the work spindle axis or line of centres.
3. Wheel in-feed motion must be truly normal to the line of centres.

These are the only motions available on a plain cylindrical grinding machine. To pro-

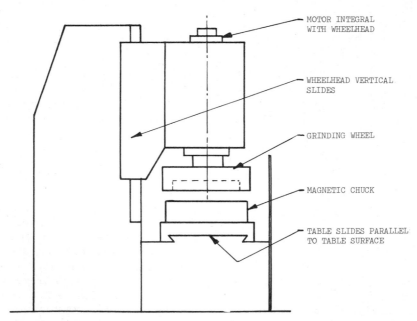

MOTOR INTEGRAL WITH WHEELHEAD

WHEELHEAD VERTICAL SLIDES

GRINDING WHEEL

MAGNETIC CHUCK

TABLE SLIDES PARALLEL TO TABLE SURFACE

Fig. 7.5 Layout of vertical spindle surface grinder (end view).

Fig. 7.6 Configuration of plain cylindrical grinding machine.

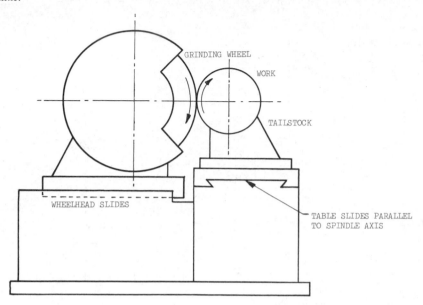

THE PLAIN CYLINDRICAL GRINDING MACHINE The configuration of this machine is shown in fig. 7.6, the machine consisting basically of a bed on which are mounted the table and table slideways. At the back of the machine is the wheelhead, mounted on slideways at right angles to the table slides to provide the infeed of the wheel to set the depth of cut.

duce tapered workpieces, a universal machine is used, in which the workhead can be set at an angle to the table motion.

THE PLAIN CYLINDRICAL GRINDING MACHINE The configuration of this machine is shown in fig. 7.6, the machine consisting basically of a bed on which are mounted the table and table slideways. At the back of the machine is the wheelhead, mounted on slideways at right angles to the table slides to provide the infeed of the wheel to set the depth of cut.

Mounted on the table are the workhead and the tailstock, positioned so that the workspindle axis and the line of centres are both accurately parallel to the table feed motion. Thus any work generated by the work spindle rotation and the table feed will be truly cylindrical.

Facing operations can be carried out by using the side of the wheel as long as two important points are noted.

1. The side of the wheel must be relieved so that it only contacts on an edge of small area.

2. If the facing is done on a shouldered workpiece the corner should be undercut.

These conditions are shown in fig. 7.7.

Cylindrical grinding can be done by using the normal longitudinal feed provided the wheel width is less than the length of the work. In this case the longitudinal rate of feed is important. If the feed per revolution of the work is one-third of the wheel width or less, the outer edges of the wheel will do all the cutting and wear will be concentrated at the edges, causing the wheel to wear to a convex profile. The centre portion of the wheel periphery, which does little cutting, rapidly becomes glazed. If, on the other hand, the work feed per revolution is about two-thirds of the wheel width, then on the rightward motion of the work the cutting will be done by the left-hand two-thirds of the wheel, and on the reverse stroke by the right-hand two-thirds. A little thought will show that these areas overlap and therefore the middle third of the wheel does twice as much cutting as the

175

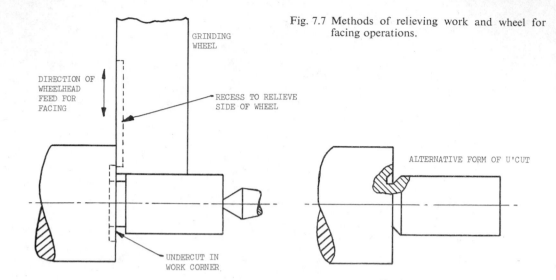

DIRECTION OF WHEELHEAD FEED FOR FACING

GRINDING WHEEL

RECESS TO RELIEVE SIDE OF WHEEL

UNDERCUT IN WORK CORNER

ALTERNATIVE FORM OF U'CUT

Fig. 7.7 Methods of relieving work and wheel for facing operations.

portions on either side. The wheel tends to wear to a concave profile, which is to be preferred. At the end of the stroke the wheel should not clear the work, but about one-third of its width should be allowed to run off.

If the work width is less than the wheel width, the work can be ground by the plunge-feed method. The wheel is carefully dressed and fed slowly and radially into the work, with no longitudinal feed in the usual sense. To reduce localised wheel-wear, the table should be reciprocated back and forth about 5 mm during cutting. This method, without the table oscillation, lends itself to form grinding.

WORK HOLDING METHODS

Work to be ground can be held in a conventional chuck or between centres. It is interesting to note that a major cause of errors of concentricity (work running out of truth) on a lathe is the headstock or live centre running out of truth, so that the work does not rotate on a fixed axis. This is overcome on the grinding machine by having both centres stationary. A method of driving the catchplate about a dead centre is shown in fig. 7.8.

The centre spindle passes right through the work head and has two flanges. In each flange is a hole through which a screw can be fitted. With the screw in position 'A', as shown, the centre spindle is locked and cannot rotate. This is the condition normally used, the work-holding device being screwed on the spindle nose extension which is integral with the pulley unit.

If it is necessary to have the centre rotating (normally only for grinding centres) the screw is removed from position 'A' to position 'B'. The second flange is then locked to the driving pulleys and rotates with them, thus driving the centre spindle.

It must be realised that fig. 7.8 is a much simplified diagram and, as drawn, the workhead cannot be assembled nor is provision made for adjusting end play. A useful design problem might be to redraw this workhead with the necessary modifications.

It should also be noted that the tailstock spindle is spring-loaded to take up any expansion of the work as its temperature rises during the grinding operation.

GRINDING STEADIES Just as in turning, so in grinding, a long slender work-

Fig. 7.8 Simplified diagram of workhead for cylindrical grinding machine.

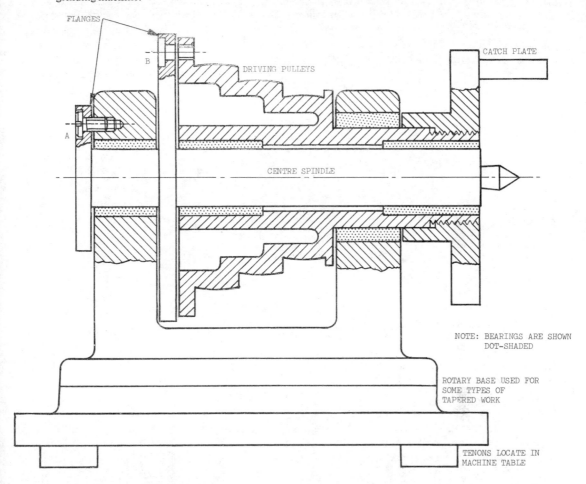

FLANGES

B

A

DRIVING PULLEYS

CATCH PLATE

CENTRE SPINDLE

NOTE: BEARINGS ARE SHOWN DOT-SHADED

ROTARY BASE USED FOR SOME TYPES OF TAPERED WORK

TENONS LOCATE IN MACHINE TABLE

piece tends to be deflected away from the grinding wheel by the forces set up during grinding. The deflection tends to increase as the forces move away from the reactions of the headstock and tailstock centres and reaches a maximum at the midpoint of the work. As the cut is reduced by the work deflection, the work produced becomes slightly barrel-shaped. It is of interest to note that a workpiece supported between centres and resisting applied cutting loads is one of the few genuine cases of a simply-supported beam occurring in practice.

The forces applied by the wheel to the work are shown in fig. 7.9 and they are seen to be, as in other cutting methods, a horizontal force F_h which deflects the work away from the wheel, and a vertical force F_v which, by deflecting the work downwards, also reduces the depth of cut. It would appear, therefore, that the shoes of the work steady should be positioned on the horizontal and vertical centre lines but this is not so. Consider a non-round workpiece with a protrusion at 'A', as shown. When the high point contacts the steady, the work is pressed into the wheel and

177

metal is removed from a point opposite 'A', creating a low point. When this low point contacts the steady block it relieves pressure on the high point 'A' which is not therefore removed. Thus, if the steady blocks are on the centre lines, non-roundness may be exaggerated.

By positioning the steady blocks off-centre at P_1 and P_2 as shown, this condition is avoided and the action becomes self-rounding.

The construction of a grinding steady is shown in fig. 7.10. The steady blocks are made of hardwood and are adjusted independently, pressure being applied first by the

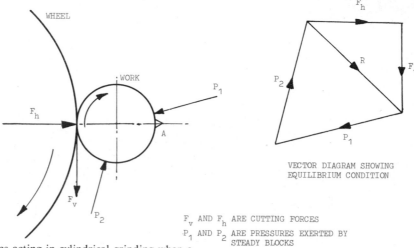

Fig. 7.9 Forces acting in cylindrical grinding when a steady is used.

VECTOR DIAGRAM SHOWING EQUILIBRIUM CONDITION

F_v AND F_h ARE CUTTING FORCES
P_1 AND P_2 ARE PRESSURES EXERTED BY STEADY BLOCKS
R IS THE RESULTANT OF F_v AND F_h

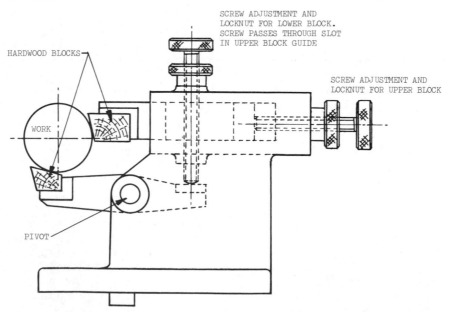

Fig. 7.10 Grinding steady.

lower block which is then locked. The upper block, which may be spring-loaded, is then fed forward until sufficient pressure is applied to the work. Either the spring loading compensates for the reduction in diameter as grinding proceeds, or adjustments are made to the blocks.

THE UNIVERSAL GRINDING MACHINE

The plain cylindrical grinding machine is limited to the external grinding of parallel cylindrical work. The universal machine can be adapted for internal grinding and the alignments can be adjusted to enable tapers to be ground.

Where a great deal of internal grinding is to be done, a machine built solely for the purpose is used, but if a universal machine is to be used it can be adapted in two ways. The internal grinding spindle can be mounted at the back of the wheel head which is then swung through 180° to bring the internal grinding spindle into use. Alternatively, the internal spindle may be mounted on the front of the wheelhead on a special bracket. In either case, to attain normal cutting speeds of the order of 800–1 000 m/min at the wheel surface, with wheels of 25 mm diameter or less, rotational speeds of the order of 10 000–12 000 rev/min are necessary. These speeds are achieved by driving the spindle from a large-diameter aluminium pulley to a small pulley on the internal spindle extension. A lightweight woven-linen belt is generally used to keep centrifugal effects to a minimum and to ensure that the belt and small pulley remain in contact. Even so, the author has seen such a belt, run at too high a speed, expand under the influence of centrifugal force until, just before it flew off, it was completely clear of both pulleys.

TAPER GRINDING In order to grind tapered or conical work, the axis of rotation of the work must be at an angle to the longitudinal feed motion of the table. This can be achieved in three ways. For tapers up to about 20° included angle, the table surface can be swung relative to the table feed motion, as shown in fig. 7.11.

Steeper angles of taper can be ground by inclining the workhead relative to the table motion as in fig. 7.12(a). Alternatively, it may be more convenient to turn the wheelhead slides through the semi-angle of taper and set the wheelhead so that its axis is parallel with the slides, as shown in fig. 7.12(b). In this case the wheelhead feed motion is used to traverse the wheel across the work in the direction of the arrow and the cut is applied by a slight adjustment of the longitudinal table stop. Note that it may be necessary to dress the

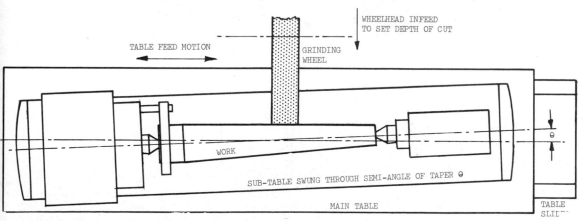

Fig. 7.11 Block diagram of set-up for grinding shallow angle of taper.

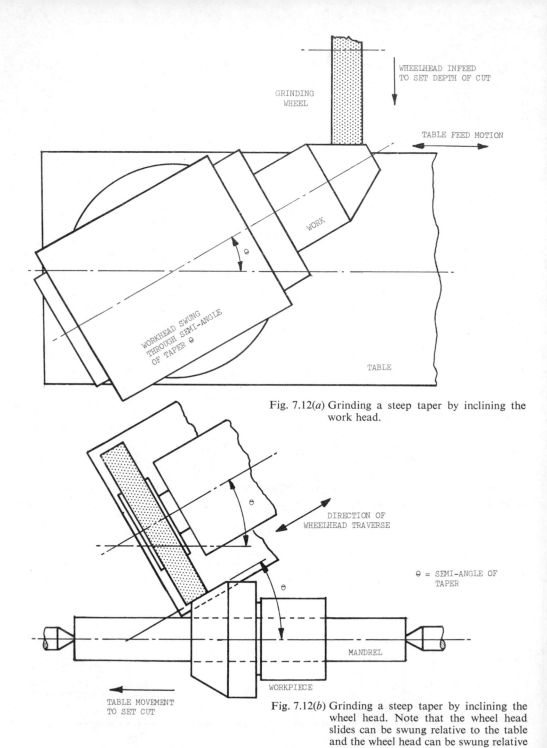

WHEELHEAD INFEED
TO SET DEPTH OF CUT

GRINDING
WHEEL

TABLE FEED MOTION

WORK

θ

WORKHEAD SWUNG
THROUGH SEMI-ANGLE
OF TAPER θ

TABLE

Fig. 7.12(*a*) Grinding a steep taper by inclining the work head.

θ

DIRECTION OF
WHEELHEAD TRAVERSE

θ = SEMI-ANGLE OF
TAPER

θ

MANDREL

TABLE MOVEMENT
TO SET CUT

WORKPIECE

Fig. 7.12(*b*) Grinding a steep taper by inclining the wheel head. Note that the wheel head slides can be swung relative to the table and the wheel head can be swung relative to its slides.

wheel in order to avoid fouling of the cylindrical portion of the work.

The methods of grinding tapers described above are all generating methods and, as has been stated, in order to generate a taper the feed motion of the wheel relative to the work must be at an angle to the axis of rotation of the work. Instead of being generated, short tapers can be copied either by dressing the wheel to the angle required or, more frequently, by swivelling the wheel or workhead and *plunge grinding*, that is feeding the wheel slowly and directly into the work. This method is normally used only for chamfers and relieving sharp corners.

THE TOOL AND CUTTER GRINDING MACHINE

The grinding of cutting tools and especially of milling cutters is a specialised process for which special grinding machines have been developed. A common type is one in which the table has longitudinal slides and cross slides as shown in fig. 7.13. The double-sided wheelhead is mounted on a vertical column, which also carries the motor, so that the head can be raised, lowered and swivelled without any complicated driving arrangement. There is usually no power feed to the table motions but the hand controls are duplicated so that the operator can work from either the front or rear of the machine.

GRINDING SINGLE-POINT TOOLS

Consider the relatively simple problem of grinding the plan approach angle and the side clearance simultaneously on a single-point tool. Fig. 7.14(*a*) shows that, starting with a rectangular block of tool steel, the block must be tilted in two planes. It must be tilted back at the plan approach angle and to one side to give the side clearance, the shaded area showing the finished clearance face. A similar

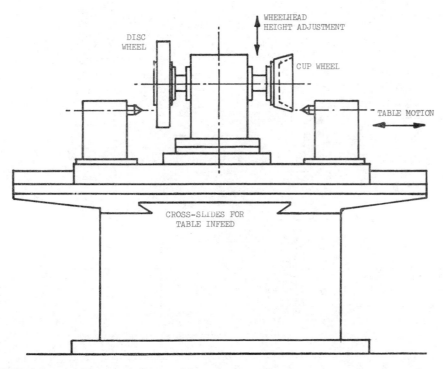

Fig. 7.13 Block layout of cutter grinding machine.

Fig. 7.14 Grinding a single-point tool. The shaded
faces must be horizontal during grinding.
(a) Clearance face; (b) Rake face.

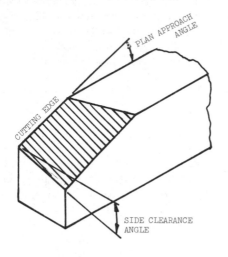

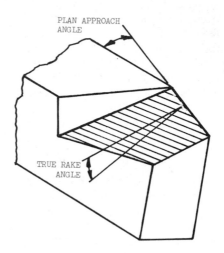

(a) CLEARANCE FACE

(b) RAKE FACE

process must be used for the plan relief or
trail angle, where clearance is also required.
If a straight-edged tool is required, with true
rake ground at right angles to a horizontal
cutting edge (see fig. 6.8 of Book 1) the tool
must be swung about this edge. Thus the

block must now be turned in the horizontal
plane and tilted through the rake angle so
that a horizontal grinding motion removes the
material to give the rake face shown shaded
in fig. 7.14(b).

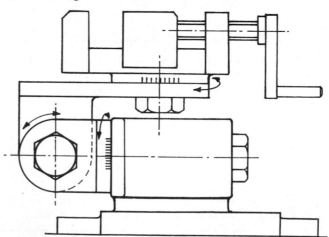

Fig. 7.15 Universal grinding vice with 3 axes of tilt.

182

It follows that a tool grinding vice must have the facility of being swung through angles in three planes. It usually takes the form shown in fig. 7.15, to enable the necessary compound angles to be produced.

GRINDING MILLING CUTTERS If a milling cutter is to be sharpened, a set-up must be arranged so that each tooth can be passed across the grinding wheel in turn, with the same amount of material being removed from each tooth. This necessitates a method of indexing. At the same time, the set-up must be so arranged that the correct angle is produced on the cutter, to give the correct cutting action when the cutter is in use.

The method of indexing used depends on the type of cutter being ground, and the relative positioning of the cutter and wheel produces the correct cutting angles.

Whatever type of cutter is being ground, it is advisable to take a series of only light cuts, the same cut being taken on all teeth before

feeding in the cutter to remove further material. If the cut is too heavy, local overheating and possible damage to the cutter may occur and the cutter will then require regrinding again in a short time.

METHOD OF INDEXING THE CUTTER The cutter must not rotate during the grinding of each tooth, and rotation is prevented by locating one of the teeth against a metal stop or *tooth rest*. The cutter is held against this tooth rest by hand pressure and the tooth rest is often spring-loaded to facilitate the indexing of the cutter for the grinding of successive teeth. The tooth rest is generally positioned so that the force due to the grinding wheel rotation holds the cutter-tooth against it. This is not always possible and figs. 7.16(a) and (b) show the two conditions. In fig. 7.16(a) the clearance face of a side-and-face cutter is being ground; the tooth rest locates on the tooth being ground and the rotation of the grinding wheel helps

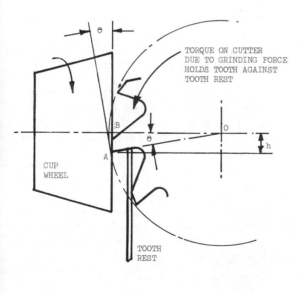

(a) GRINDING CLEARANCE FACE

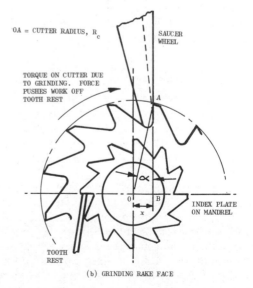

(b) GRINDING RAKE FACE

Fig. 7.16 Cutter grinding.

to hold the cutter against it. If the cutter is badly worn it may not be possible to locate against the rake face in which case a separate index plate is mounted on the cutter mandrel and the tooth rest locates in the notches of the index plate. This location is shown in fig. 7.16 (b) where the rake face of a cutter is being ground and the cutter must be held against the tooth rest by hand pressure against the torque exerted by the pressure of the grinding wheel. The student might like to consider the effect of locating against a rake face when the rake face is being ground.

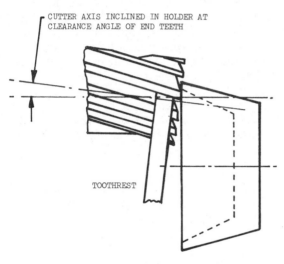

CUTTER AXIS INCLINED IN HOLDER AT CLEARANCE ANGLE OF END TEETH

TOOTHREST

Fig. 7.17 Regrinding clearance faces on an end mill.

If the end teeth of an end mill or shell end mill are to be reground it will be necessary for the cutter to overhang and be inclined, as shown in fig. 7.17, in which case it is mounted in a special fixture whose axis can be given the necessary inclination.

Note that in all the above cases the teeth being ground are straight teeth, so the tooth rest holder is clamped to the machine table and moves with the cutter.

If a helical-toothed cutter is to be ground, the tooth rest must be fixed and not move with the cutter, in order to obtain the combination of rotational and linear movements required to follow the helix. The tooth rest is

therefore attached to the wheel head and is not spring-loaded, but it must be wider than the wheel so that the cutter is fully controlled throughout its contact with the wheel. Due to its width, the tooth rest must be inclined to coincide with the helix angle of the wheel as shown in fig. 7.18. For indexing, the cutter is simply fed clear of the tooth rest and rotated until the next tooth can be located.

SETTING THE CUTTER TO PRODUCE THE CORRECT ANGLES

It is sometimes found that in order to set the cutter 'correctly' relative to the wheel, the grinder works by trial and error, adjusting the setting on successive teeth until the grinding marks register all over the existing face being ground. This is not good practice because if the cutter is already incorrect the error is perpetuated. Further, such a method can progressively increase errors in cutting angles. It is much better to calculate the setting required to produce the correct angle, irrespective of any errors which may already exist, and thus grind the cutters correctly.

GRINDING CLEARANCE FACES

The clearance face of a side-and-face cutter or a slitting saw can either be ground on the periphery of a disc wheel or on the face of a cup wheel.

A helical-toothed cutter is usually ground on the periphery of a wheel, in which case the clearance angle is obtained by raising the wheelhead so that the wheel centre is above the cutter centre.

The cutter and wheel centres are first aligned, a gauge often being provided with the machine for this purpose. The height of the tooth rest is then adjusted so that the cutting edge is at the same height as the cutter centre. The wheel head is then raised to give the correct clearance angle θ.

Referring to fig. 7.19:

In triangle OAB

$$\sin \theta = \frac{OB}{OA} = \frac{h}{R_w}$$

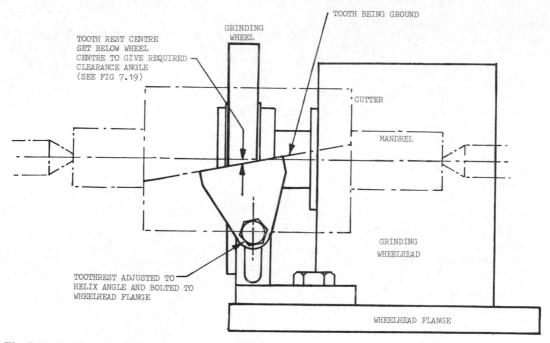

Within the figure:

TOOTH BEING GROUND

GRINDING WHEEL

TOOTH REST CENTRE SET BELOW WHEEL CENTRE TO GIVE REQUIRED CLEARANCE ANGLE (SEE FIG 7.19)

CUTTER

MANDREL

GRINDING WHEELHEAD

TOOTHREST ADJUSTED TO HELIX ANGLE AND BOLTED TO WHEELHEAD FLANGE

WHEELHEAD FLANGE

Fig. 7.18 Grinding clearance on a helical milling cutter. The cutter is 'ghosted' to allow details of the tooth rest to be shown.

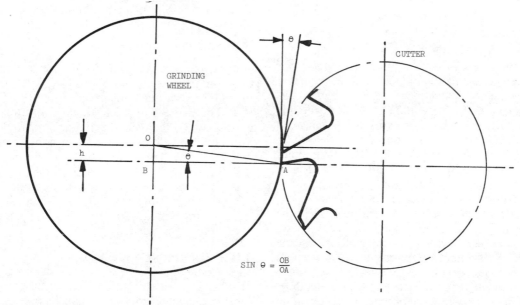

Within the figure:

GRINDING WHEEL

CUTTER

θ

O

h

B

θ

A

$$\text{SIN } \theta = \frac{OB}{OA}$$

Fig. 7.19 Grinding clearance using the wheel periphery.

185

and $\qquad h = R_w \sin \theta$

where h = height by which wheel centre is
raised above cutter centre
R_w = radius of wheel
θ = clearance angle.

This method gives hollow-ground teeth and is not recommended except for helical slab mills, end mills, etc., which are difficult to grind in any other way.

To grind the clearance angle of a side-and-face cutter on a cup wheel as shown in fig. 7.16(a), the cutter is again set on the tooth rest so that the cutting edge is on the horizontal centre line of the cutter. The tooth rest is now lowered a distance h to give the required clearance angle.

From Fig. 7.16(a):

In triangle OAB

$$\sin \theta = \frac{AB}{OA} = \frac{h}{R_c}$$

and $\qquad h = R_c \sin \theta$

where R_c = radius of cutter

h = distance by which cutting edge is *lowered* below cutter centre
θ = clearance angle.

In some cases the tooth rest holder has a screw adjustment, with graduations to enable the height adjustment to be made conveniently. If such equipment is not available the setting can be done with a height gauge.

GRINDING RAKE FACES Sometimes a cutter requires grinding on the rake face. If a side-and-face cutter is ground too frequently on the clearance face the clearance land becomes too wide and can then be reduced by grinding the rake face. Also, continuous clearance grinding reduces the cutter diameter and hence the chip space, and it becomes necessary to regash the cutter to give adequate chip clearance. Certain cutters, notably form-relieved cutters, must be ground on the rake face only and the rake angle must be correct or the cutter will not produce the correct form.

To grind the rake face, a saucer-shaped wheel is used, as shown in fig. 7.16(b). The machine is set so that the wheel face is beyond the cutter centre line by an amount x to give the correct rake angle α. The cut is then set by lowering the tooth rest until the teeth contact the wheel face.

From fig. 7.16(b):

In triangle OAB

$$\sin \alpha = \frac{OB}{OA} = \frac{x}{R_c}$$

$$x = R_c \sin \alpha$$

where x = horizontal displacement of tooth edge when finished.
R_c = cutter radius
α = rake angle.

Other multi-toothed cutters such as taps and reamers are ground in a similar manner and for all such work the following points are emphasised.

1. Light cuts only must be taken to avoid overheating and softening the tool or cutter.

2. Care must be taken to obtain the correct angles on the cutter to give an efficient cutting action.

3. Certain cutters, notably form-relieved cutters, reamers and taps, must be ground only on the rake face so that the form or diameter is not made incorrect.

4. To ensure that all teeth take an equal cutting load, the depth of grinding cut should not be changed until all teeth have been ground at the one setting.

5. In all this work and particularly in the case of small cutters, the operator's hand is close to the grinding wheel which, of necessity, may be unguarded. Concentration is necessary to avoid accidents.

THE LAPPING PROCESS
The production of fine surfaces by lapping is an ancient one, carried out for centuries by lapidaries, who shape and polish precious stones. In engineering it is a process used to produce a very fine surface finish and in some

cases, the required close fit between mating parts.

The abrasive used is not bonded in the form of a stick or wheel but is suspended in a fluid or grease which is applied to the parts being lapped, which are then rubbed against each other. By using very fine abrasive powders, extremely fine surface finishes can be produced and, since the metal removal rate can be very low, a high degree of dimensional accuracy is possible.

The lap, or lapping plate, is softer than the workpiece and becomes impregnated with the abrasive whose grains, held stationary as the workpiece is moved relative to the lap, cut minute chips from the surface.

If a flat surface is to be lapped, obviously the lapping plate must be flat. Usually the plates are made in threes, and are lapped together in alternate pairs until all three register over their whole surface.[1] They must then be flat. Such lapping plates are usually made of grey cast iron, either rectangular or circular in shape, and have grooves about 1 mm wide by 1 mm deep cut at right angles across their surface at intervals of about 10 mm. These grooves act as channels for the surplus abrasive which, for hand lapping of flat surfaces, is normally suspended in a grease. The grit size used is about 200 for metal removal purposes and 400 for finishing, although much finer grits may be used for special purposes such as the final lapping of gauge blocks to a wringing finish.

CYLINDRICAL LAPPING Cylindrical parts such as gudgeon pins can be machine lapped as a production process. The pins are held between two plates which are mounted on vertical spindles, the pins being retained in position between the plates by a cage so that the axis of the pins is at about 15° to the radius of the plate, as shown in fig. 7.20. The top plate remains stationary while the lower one rotates and the cage is oscillated. The pins are caused to rotate by the relative motion of the plates and, due to their angular position, some

[1] See Whitworth principle—page 91, Book 1.

sliding motion takes place between the surfaces. It is this which produces the cutting action.

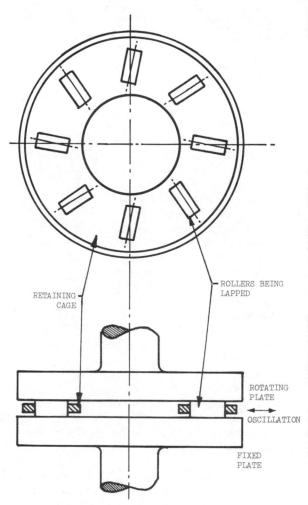

Fig. 7.20 Machine lapping cylindrical parts. Note that the work axes are not radial relative to the plates.

LAPPING ALLOWANCE Lapping is a slow method of removing metal and the less material to be removed the better. It is also true since lapping is essentially a process for correcting the geometry and improving the finish of the workpiece, the better the condition of the ground surface prior to lapping

187

the less metal will have to be removed. For normal surfaces the lapping allowance should be 0·007 mm to 0·015 mm, or 0·015 mm to 0·030 mm on a diameter. On well-finished ground surfaces, 0·005 mm, or 0·010 mm on diameter, is sufficient.

HONING

The honing process differs from lapping in that a stick of abrasive is pressed against the surface to be finished, relative motion between the surface and the honing stick producing the cutting action, and the work areas being flooded with a flow of paraffin or light oil to wash away the chips and abrasive particles.

The process is commonly used for finishing the bores of internal combustion engines. The hones are mounted in holders held in a cylindrical body which is oscillated back and forth along the bore and at the same time rotated. Each single particle of abrasive, in one oscillation, produces a helical scratch but through the repeated oscillations and the rotation the paths of the particles cross and recross, producing a random scratch pattern which is an excellent bearing surface for reciprocating parts.

The rotary motion is imparted to the hone body through universal joints so that the hones are guided by the bore being finished. Since the hones are pressed against the bore either by spring or hydraulic pressure, there is some corrective action for both taper and non-roundness.

Much smaller honing machines with horizontal spindles are used for honing ring gauges and the barrels of diesel engine injector units, the workpiece being held and moved along the hone by hand. Again the hone follows the existing hole, corrects it for size and produces the required surface finish, but does not correct its geometry. It follows that the machining process prior to honing must be geometrically correct.

The peripheral speed of rotation of the hone should be 65–100 m/min and the average axial speed 20–25 m/min. The working stroke is normally equal to the length of the stones, and the over-run, or the amount the stones protrude at each end of the stroke, should not exceed 0·2 of the length of the stone.

SUPERFINISHING

This is a modification of the honing process developed in the 1930s by the Chrysler Corporation of America to overcome a bearing problem. When cars are transported long distances by transporter their wheels remain stationary but they receive similar vibrations and loads to those occuring when they are running. This used to cause a fault in the wheel hub bearings known as 'Brinelling', a permanent indentation of the bearing tracks by the rollers in the taper-roller bearings used. It was found that if, before assembly, the ground tracks were finished by a particular form of honing this Brinelling effect no longer occurred. The method of honing used was developed and became known as *superfinishing*. It is now used a great deal for finishing bearing surfaces in the motor industry.

The process consists of rubbing fine-grit hones over the surface as it rotates while the hone is oscillated rapidly back and forth. The amplitude of oscillation is about 5 mm at a frequency of 2 000–3 000 cycles per minute. For parts up to about 75 mm in length the stones are made the same length as the part and the oscillation is the only axial motion. For longer parts the oscillation is superimposed on a feed motion of about 5 mm per revolution of the work, which has a surface speed of 5–15 m/min for roughing and 20–35 m/min for finising operations.

Apart from overcoming the Brinelling problem it has been proved that, by superfinishing, the initial wear of rubbing surfaces is reduced, thus reducing the running-in period for new machinery and vehicles. Friction losses also are reduced and any localised softening due to overheating during grinding can be detected. The soft spots show up as grey zones on the super-finished surface.

SUMMARY

Surfaces are produced by abrasive cutting processes where high degrees of accuracy and surface texture are required or where the work is too hard to be machined by conventional cutting processes.

The machine alignments necessary to produce flat, cylindrical and conical surfaces are similar to those used where such forms are produced on other machines, but generally the accuracy of alignment and sensitivity of control must be of a higher order. Work-holding methods must be designed so that they maintain these alignments and do not damage the finished surfaces.

Cutter grinding is a specialised process and a special range of machines and techniques has been developed to carry out the various operations. Apart from his knowledge of these methods, the technician must also be able to make the calculations necessary to maintain the accuracy of cutters, in terms of both form and cutting angles, to give efficient cutting.

Lapping, honing and superfinishing are three abrasive cutting processes which rely on the form of the part being substantially correct before they are applied. Lapping will correct geometrical form but excessive metal removal by this method is expensive. These processes should be regarded as sizing and surface-finishing operations, each having its own application in modern technology. The mechanical engineering technician should be aware of the methods, their applications and their limitations.

8

Welding Processes

INTRODUCTION

The joining of metals by welding has been practised by man for about three thousand years. In those early days all welding was done by blacksmiths and was only practicable with iron. The parts to be welded were heated to about 1 000°C until they were plastic and then hammered together. At these temperatures the iron oxide on the surface of the iron is fluid and the hammering was done in such a manner that the oxide was squeezed out of the weld, giving metal-to-metal contact.

Later, as man's technology developed, methods became available of heating metals locally until they fused and the two parts which were being welded flowed into each other while molten, solidifying into a continuous joint. Losses and reinforcement were made up by the use of a filler rod of similar composition to the metals being joined. Thus developed the modern welding process.

Note that, unlike a soldered or brazed joint, a welded joint has the following characteristics:

1. A continuous joint is made, there being no foreign material 'sticking' the two parts together.
2. The continuity extends to the grain structure of the weld which, ideally, should be indistinguishable from that of the joined parts.
3. If a filler rod is used it simply makes good any losses and builds up the weld. It does not stick the parts together.

It follows that two basic methods of welding are available:

(a) *Pressure welding*, in which the parts are heated to a plastic condition and the weld is formed by mechanical pressure.

(b) *Fusion welding*, in which the parts are melted and run into each other, giving a continuous joint.

Variations available in these basic methods of welding are largely in the methods of heating used, fig. 8.1 showing those to be discussed in this work. It must be realised that these by no means exhaust the methods available. Modern techniques which will not be discussed here include arc-image welding, laser-beam welding, electron-beam welding, cold pressure welding, ultrasonic welding, explosive welding and many others.

METHODS OF FUSION WELDING

To produce a weld by fusing the two parts together requires an extremely intense and localised source of heat, so that the parts are melted locally and are little affected outside the weld area. Such intense high-temperature sources of heat can be obtained by the combustion of suitable gases or by an electric arc.

1. GAS WELDING Burning a fuel gas with air, as in a simple gas blow torch, will not give high enough temperatures for welding. Consequently the gas is burned with oxygen, the most common fuel gases being acetylene, hydrogen and propane, with flame temperatures as follows:

Oxygen—acetylene 3 250°C
Oxygen—hydrogen 2 800°C
Oxygen—propane 3 100°C

OXY-ACETYLENE WELDING Two systems are available for oxy-acetylene welding, (a) *low pressure* and (b) *high pressure*.

The low-pressure system is generally used where the welding process is carried out at fixed points on a production line and large

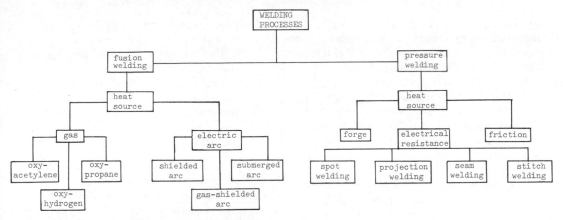

Fig. 8.1 Summary of welding processes discussed in
text.

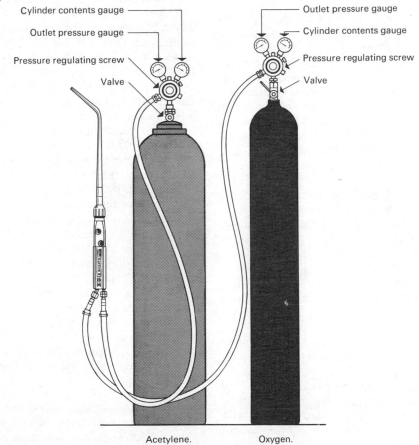

Acetylene.   Oxygen.
(cylinder painted maroon)(cylinder painted black)

Fig. 8.2 High pressure welding outfit. (Reproduced by
courtesy of British Oxygen Co. Ltd)
Note: Latest Continental practice is to use
blue cylinders for oxygen.

quantities of acetylene are required. The acetylene is produced in a generator and piped to the work stations, a special injector type of blowpipe being required.

The high-pressure system is used in general engineering, maintenance and garage work. It has the great advantages that it is portable, requires no power supplies and the capital cost of equipment is relatively low. The equipment required is as follows (see fig. 8.2).

(*a*) *Oxygen Cylinder*. The oxygen is supplied at high pressure, approximately 120 atmospheres, in a steel cylinder fitted with a high-pressure valve. Oxygen cylinders are painted BLACK.

(*b*) *Acetylene Cylinder*. Acetylene becomes unstable if compressed to a greater pressure than 2 atmospheres and is then liable to explode. The gas may be dissolved safely at higher pressures in liquid acetone, which will dissolve 25 times its own volume of acetylene for each atmosphere of pressure. The gas is therefore dissolved at about 15 atmospheres pressure and a cylinder when full contains $15 \times 25 = 375$ times its own volume of gas. Acetylene cylinders are painted RED and have a flat end.

(*c*) *Pressure Regulators*. Before the gases are fed to the blowpipe their pressures must be reduced by a pressure regulator. When the cylinder stop-valve is turned on, gas is supplied to the underside of a spring-loaded diaphragm. The gas pressure, if in excess of the spring pressure, holds the valve closed. If the pressure screw is now turned until the spring pressure exceeds the gas pressure, the diaphragm deflects, opens the valve and releases gas, whose pressure depends upon the amount by which the spring is compressed. Points to note are:

(i) Oxygen regulators have right-hand threads with plain nuts and acetylene regulators have left-hand threads, with notched hexagon nuts so that they cannot be confused.

(ii) Oxygen regulators should never be greased. Grease in contact with high-pressure oxygen is liable to cause an explosion.

(iii) The regulator is *closed* by *unscrewing* the regulating screw.

(iv) The regulators have two gauges; the high-pressure gauge shows the quantity (pressure) of gas remaining in the cylinder, while the low-pressure gauge shows the output pressure from the regulator.

(*d*) *The Blowpipe*. The gas blowpipe has two connections, one for the outlet union of each regulator. Each screw thread has the same hand as the corresponding cylinder and regulator so that the connections cannot be confused. The oxygen hose is black and the acetylene hose maroon. The welding nozzles of the blowpipes are interchangeable, varying in diameter from 1·0 mm for thin sheet work to 4·0 mm for heavy duty work. Gas is supplied from both regulators at the same pressure, and the adjustments on the blowpipe control the quantity of each gas supplied. Apart from mixing the gases, the blowpipe also contains a means of preventing flashback of the flame up the supply hoses.

To light the blowpipe, both regulators are adjusted to the same pressure, depending upon the tip size being used. This varies from 13 kN/m² for the smallest tip to 50 kN/m² for the large tips. The acetylene adjustment on the blow-torch is opened first and the flame started with a spark lighter. This flame is simply one of acetylene burning in air and is bright yellow and long, and gives off black smuts. The oxygen adjustment is now opened gradually and as the quantity of oxygen increases the flame shortens and takes on a typical blue colour.

By suitably adjusting the oxygen control on the blowpipe, three types of flame can be produced:

(i) Oxydising flame—excess oxygen
(ii) Carburizing flame—excess acetylene
(iii) Neutral flame—complete combustion with the minimum necessary oxygen.

Fig. 8.3 shows these flames diagram-

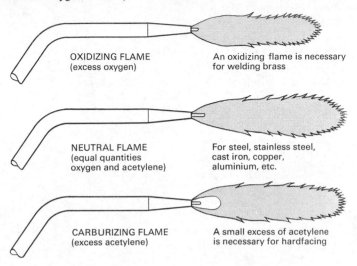

Fig. 8.3 Welding flame conditions. (Reproduced by courtesy of British Oxygen Co. Ltd)

OXIDIZING FLAME (excess oxygen)

An oxidizing flame is necessary for welding brass

NEUTRAL FLAME (equal quantities oxygen and acetylene)

For steel, stainless steel, cast iron, copper, aluminium, etc.

CARBURIZING FLAME (excess acetylene)

A small excess of acetylene is necessary for hardfacing

matically. The correct adjustment for a neutral flame is attained when the haze due to excess acetylene just disappears. If the oxygen supply is increased, the cone shortens and the flame is oxidising in nature. If the oxygen supply is reduced, a feather of acetylene becomes more prominent and a carburising flame is produced.

For most purposes a neutral flame is desirable. If a carburising flame is used when welding steel the carbon content of the weld becomes greater than that of the parent metal and the weld becomes brittle.

A carburising flame is used for depositing Stellite, i.e., in hard-facing work, while an oxidising flame is used when welding alloys containing zinc, e.g., brass.

WELDING TECHNIQUES Two methods are employed for producing a weld by gas welding. These are illustrated in fig. 8.4(a) and (b) and are called *leftward* and *rightward* welding.

Leftward, or forward, welding is carried out with the torch in the right hand, the movement being from right to left, with the flame pointing into the unwelded portion of the work. This method gives better visibility for the operator but is limited to work of 4–5 mm thickness or less.

Rightward, or backward, welding uses the opposite technique, with the flame playing over the weld already produced. This reduces the cooling rate and has an annealing effect, improving the ductility of the weld. The method is used for thicker materials.

Fig. 8.5 relates the metal thickness to the edge preparation, filler rod diameter, technique to be used and the rate of welding in millimetres per minute for various thicknesses of metal.

FLAME CUTTING If iron or steel is heated almost to melting temperature and a stream of oxygen is then played upon it, the metal is rapidly oxidised. The melting temperature of the iron oxide is less than that of the metal from which it is formed so the oxide, being in a liquid state, is blown away from the zone by the stream of oxygen being used.

It follows from this that the oxy-acetylene *cutting* blowpipe has two functions. It must:

(a) provide a suitable flame for preheating

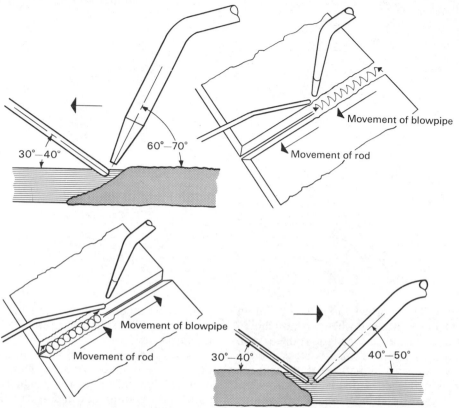

Fig. 8.4 Rightward and leftward welding. (Reproduced by courtesy of British Oxygen Co. Ltd)

the metal and (b) provide a stream of oxygen for cutting.

The cutting torch therefore has three controls as shown in fig. 8.6. The acetylene control and the heating oxygen control provide the combustible gas mixture which burns at the annular jet surrounding the main central oxygen jet. The third control supplies pure oxygen to the central jet and is of the lever type, the supply of oxygen being cut off when the lever is depressed. The lever can be locked down by the cutting oxygen control.

To start the blowpipe, both oxygen valves should be closed and the acetylene valve opened, the gas jet issuing from the outer passage then being lit. The heating oxygen valve is opened and adjusted to give a suitable flame. The cutting jet is now started by opening the cutting oxygen valve, but the oxygen supply is cut off by depressing the central lever.

A guide clamped to the jet is rested on the work and, with the control lever depressed, the work is rapidly heated to white heat. The lever is released and the stream of pure oxygen impinging on the work starts the cutting action. The torch can now be drawn slowly along the work to produce the cut.

With hand-held equipment, metal up to 600 mm thick can be cut. By machine cutting, metal up to 850 mm thick can be cut and greater thicknesses than this can be cut using an oxygen lance.

194

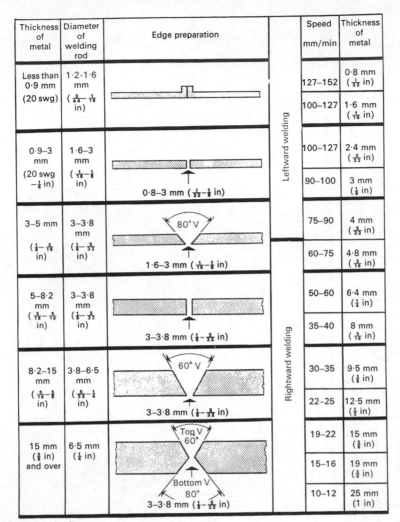

Thickness of metal	Diameter of welding rod	Edge preparation		Speed mm/min	Thickness of metal
Less than 0·9 mm (20 swg)	1·2–1·6 mm ($\frac{3}{64}$–$\frac{1}{16}$ in)		Leftward welding	127–152	0·8 mm ($\frac{1}{32}$ in)
				100–127	1·6 mm ($\frac{1}{16}$ in)
0·9–3 mm (20 swg –$\frac{1}{8}$ in)	1·6–3 mm ($\frac{1}{16}$–$\frac{1}{8}$ in)	0·8–3 mm ($\frac{1}{32}$–$\frac{1}{8}$ in)		100–127	2·4 mm ($\frac{3}{32}$ in)
				90–100	3 mm ($\frac{1}{8}$ in)
3–5 mm ($\frac{1}{8}$–$\frac{3}{16}$ in)	3–3·8 mm ($\frac{1}{8}$–$\frac{5}{32}$ in)	80° V 1·6–3 mm ($\frac{1}{16}$–$\frac{1}{8}$ in)		75–90	4 mm ($\frac{5}{32}$ in)
				60–75	4·8 mm ($\frac{3}{16}$ in)
5–8·2 mm ($\frac{3}{16}$–$\frac{5}{16}$ in)	3–3·8 mm ($\frac{1}{8}$–$\frac{5}{32}$ in)	3–3·8 mm ($\frac{1}{8}$–$\frac{5}{32}$ in)	Rightward welding	50–60	6·4 mm ($\frac{1}{4}$ in)
				35–40	8 mm ($\frac{5}{16}$ in)
8·2–15 mm ($\frac{5}{16}$–$\frac{5}{8}$ in)	3·8–6·5 mm ($\frac{5}{32}$–$\frac{1}{4}$ in)	60° V 3–3·8 mm ($\frac{1}{8}$–$\frac{5}{32}$ in)		30–35	9·5 mm ($\frac{3}{8}$ in)
				22–25	12·5 mm ($\frac{1}{2}$ in)
15 mm ($\frac{5}{8}$ in) and over	6·5 mm ($\frac{1}{4}$ in)	Top V 60° Bottom V 80° 3–3·8 mm ($\frac{1}{8}$–$\frac{5}{32}$ in)		19–22	15 mm ($\frac{5}{8}$ in)
				15–16	19 mm ($\frac{3}{4}$ in)
				10–12	25 mm (1 in)

Fig. 8.5 Edge preparations. (Reproduced by courtesy of British Oxygen Co. Ltd)

HYDROGEN AS A FUEL GAS As stated previously, if acetylene is compressed to above two atmospheres it becomes unstable and likely to explode. For this reason it cannot be used for underwater work, where a higher pressure is needed to force the gas out of the blowpipe against the water pressure. For underwater work, therefore, hydrogen is used. Although its flame temperature is lower than that of an oxy-acetylene flame, it can be used for normal cutting processes by divers working underwater.

The torch used for this work is similar to the normal cutting torch except that it has an additional annular jet or bell around the jet. This is supplied with compressed air to hold the water away from the flame and cutting area.

2. ELECTRIC-ARC WELDING In this, as in gas welding, the parts to be welded are melted locally and filler rod is cast into the

195

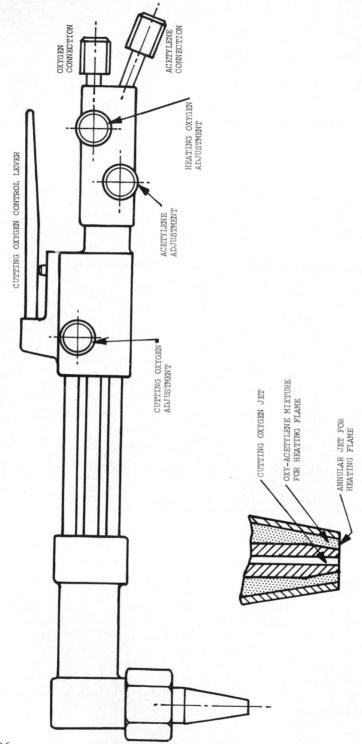

OXYGEN CONNECTION

ACETYLENE CONNECTION

HEATING OXYGEN ADJUSTMENT

CUTTING OXYGEN CONTROL LEVER

ACETYLENE ADJUSTMENT

CUTTING OXYGEN ADJUSTMENT

CUTTING OXYGEN JET

OXY-ACETYLENE MIXTURE FOR HEATING FLAME

ANNULAR JET FOR HEATING FLAME

Fig. 8.6 Flame cutting torch.

molten pool thus formed to build up and form an integral part of the weld. The localised heating is, however, produced by an electric arc struck either between the filler rod and the work, or between a separate electrode and the work.

The technique was first used in 1881, carbon electrodes being used to produce the arc, with a separate filler rod as in gas welding. In 1888 a bare steel wire was used as the electrode by a Russian, N. G. Slavianoff, the electrode also acting as the filler rod. This technique was used until the 1930s but it was difficult to strike and maintain the arc, and the weld was seriously contaminated by atmospheric oxygen and nitrogen. These difficulties have been overcome by covering the electrode with a thick coating of flux which shields the arc with large volumes of the gas given off, covers the weld with a layer of slag and controls the arc.

Later developments have been to flood the weld area with an inert gas to give gas-shielded arc welding, and to perform the weld under a deep layer of granulated flux, this method being known as submerged-arc welding.

Arc welding can be performed with either a.c. or d.c. electric power supply. Direct current requires the use of a motor-generator set or a transformer-rectifier, which are more complex electrically than the transformer used with alternating-current sets. For most purposes, therefore, a.c. welding sets are used but, as will be shown, direct current is used for certain gas-shielded processes.

An electric arc of the type used in welding is an intense source of ultra-violet rays. These can be dangerous if viewed directly and can produce an extremely painful condition called *arc eyes*, particularly if the eyes are unshielded when the arc is struck. The arc welding process should never be observed without a suitable shielding arrangement for the eyes. If a flash is observed directly, it may be several hours before the full effects are felt, a feeling that the eyes are full of sand and a tendency to avoid light.

Bathing the eyes in a solution of boracic acid in distilled water with a little glycerine added gives relief and an affected person will do well to lie in a dark room with a damp cloth over the eyes until the effects have passed.

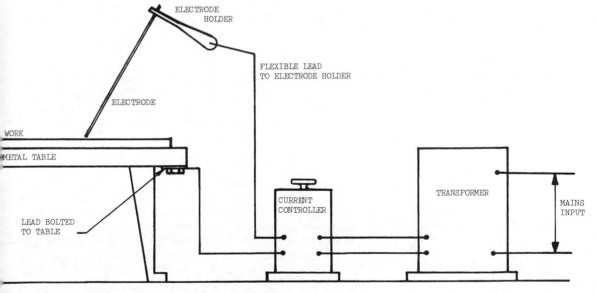

Fig. 8.7 Block diagram of electric arc welding set-up

It is far better, however, to avoid flashes by keeping away from the process unless personally involved, and then using only the correct type of glass shield. Special glass is required and ordinary smoked or tinted glass is not satisfactory.

METHODS OF ELECTRIC ARC WELDING

1. SHIELDED-ARC WELDING The equipment used consists of a transformer to step-down the supply voltage and a regulator to allow the current to be adjusted to suit the requirements of the work. One connection from the regulator is made to the work and the other to the electrode holder, as shown in fig. 8.7.

The electrode is coated with a flux which, during welding, forms a cup in the end of the electrode and stabilises the arc. As the electrode is consumed, the coating gives off an inert gas which envelops the weld and prevents atmospheric attack. At the same time, other constituents form a slag which solidifies over the weld and gives a slow cooling rate and, again, prevention from atmospheric attack. If a weld requires more than one pass this slag must be chipped away, as it normally is from a finished weld. During welding, metallic particles are carried from the electrode into the weld as shown in fig. 8.8. This metal carry-over is due to the processes involved rather than gravity, which means that vertical and overhead welding can be readily accomplished.

The currents used vary from 50–100 V and up to 750 A for a.c. welding, depending upon the diameter of the electrode and the work in hand.

To start the weld, the operator strikes the end of the electrode against the work rather like striking a match. The electrode is then withdrawn some 3 mm to 6 mm away from the work and, with the arc established, the rod is drawn slowly and evenly across the work to produce the weld.

Due to the intensely localised heating of the parent metal the arc-welding technique can be used on castings without any need for preheating except for castings of intricate form. This is a considerable advantage over gas welding, where preheating of castings is normally essential.

Thin work, up to 6 mm thick, can be welded with one pass. For greater thicknesses, edge preparation is necessary as shown in fig. 8.9(a), and a sealing run is also needed if the work is done only from one side. For still greater thicknesses a number of runs are required on both sides, using different electrode thicknesses for the various runs. Fig. 8.9(b) shows a sequence of weld runs in a single-vee weld in a plate 25 mm thick. Comparison with fig. 8.9(c) shows the economy achieved by double-vee welds.

2. GAS SHIELDED ARC WELDING[1] Certain materials, notably those which oxidise readily, are extremely difficult to weld by conventional gas or electric-arc welding processes. To overcome the problems of attack by atmospheric oxygen the idea was conceived of using a non-consumable tungsten electrode to strike an arc and produce the melting temperatures required, and at the same time to flood the area of the weld with a continuous stream of inert gas.

Initially the gas used in America, where the process was developed, was helium and this welding method was called the *heli-arc* process. America was the only place where helium was readily available and in other areas argon was used. This gradually came to be preferred generally and the process is now called *argon-arc* welding.

The equipment is more complex than for conventional arc welding. Ideally, direct current would be used with the electrode made positive, as under these conditions any oxide formed is dispersed by the action of the arc. However, this tends to cause overheating of the electrode, which melts at the tip and contaminates the weld. In practice, a.c. supply is

[1] Often called TIG (Tungsten Inert Gas) welding.

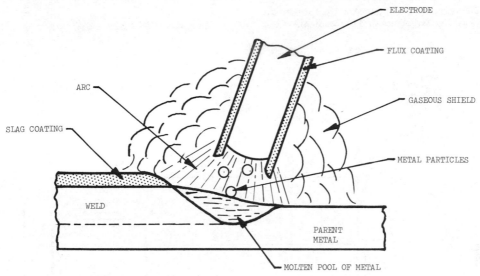

Fig. 8.8 Diagram of shielded arc weld in progress.

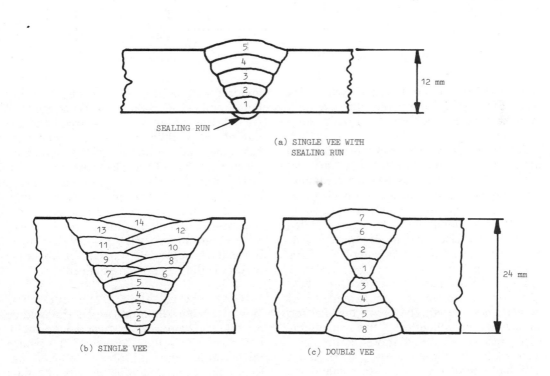

Fig. 8.9 Sequence of runs for different conditions.

Fig. 8.10 Block diagram of gas-shielded tungsten-arc
welding (argon arc or TIG welding).

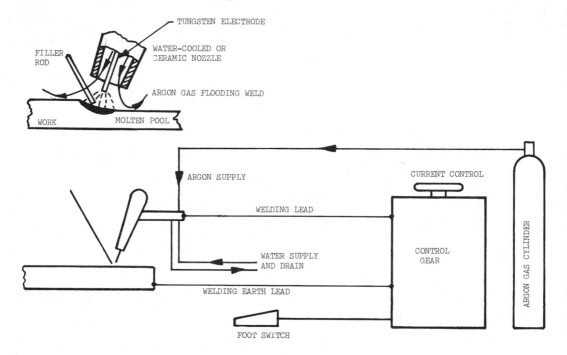

TUNGSTEN ELECTRODE

WATER-COOLED OR
CERAMIC NOZZLE

FILLER
ROD

ARGON GAS FLOODING WELD

WORK

MOLTEN POOL

ARGON SUPPLY

CURRENT CONTROL

WELDING LEAD

WATER SUPPLY
AND DRAIN

CONTROL
GEAR

ARGON GAS CYLINDER

WELDING EARTH LEAD

FOOT SWITCH

generally used, the positive half-cycle giving
oxide removal and the cooler negative half-
cycle keeping the electrode at a lower average
temperature.

A high-frequency starter unit is required to
initiate the arc since the electrode must not
touch the work and thus become contaminated. Nor must it be touched by the filler rod.

A supply of argon is obviously required and,
as this must flood the weld area, it is fed
through the electrode holder around the
electrode, an outline of the equipment being
shown in fig. 8.10.

When the arc has been started it is held
stationary for a few seconds until a molten pool
of metal has formed. The end of the filler rod
should be kept within the argon stream all the
time, since constant withdrawal and replace-
ment of the filler rod can disturb the argon
flow and entrain air which will contaminate
the weld. Correct choice of filler wire size is

important and a leftward technique is used to
flow argon ahead of the weld. When the weld
is complete the arc can be stopped but the
flow of gas should be continued until the weld
has cooled sufficiently for there to be no danger of oxidation of the weld area.

The process can be used to weld materials
from 0·5 mm to 50 mm thick but high
thermal conductivity may limit the maximum
thickness that can be welded. Flux must not
be used and the materials to be welded must
be clean before welding starts. A feature of the
process is the clean finish obtained.

3. GAS-SHIELDED METAL-ARC
WELDING[1] Although argon-arc welding
has many advantages for some types of welding, particularly the absence of flux which
might cause corrosion after welding, it was
found to have limitations. A separate filler

[1] Often called MIG (Metal Inert Gas) welding.

rod meant that the welder had two items to manipulate, while visibility and access to some joints tended to be poor. A later development was *gas-shielded metal-arc welding*, in which the filler rod becomes the electrode and is therefore consumable. This fact allows a direct-current system to be used, with the electrode as the positive pole, to give the desirable self-cleansing action mentioned earlier. The wire used is between 0·75 mm and 2 mm diameter and, being so thin, can be wound on a spool to give a continuous feed so that the operator does not have to keep stopping to change electrodes. A diagram of the set-up for this process appears in fig. 8.11. Arrangements can be made for the arc length to be automatically controlled and the method therefore lends itself to complete automation.

4. CO_2 ARC WELDING OF STEEL The gas-shielded processes discussed previously have considered only the inert gas argon as a shielding agent. Such a gas is necessary for shielding the welding of aluminium, stainless steel etc. but it is very expensive and the cost of the quantities required precludes its use for welding plain-carbon steel and cast iron, which can be successfully welded with the normal flux-coated electrode. However, the gas-shielded process does lend itself to automatic welding and for this reason the process has been modified to use carbon dioxide as the shielding gas for welding ferrous materials.

Flux-cored filler wires are used, varying in diameter from 1 mm to 4 mm. The wire is coiled on a spool and automatically fed through the welding 'torch' by rollers, the torch being water-cooled in heavy applications.

The speed of welding is very high, up to 500 mm/min, which largely eliminates distortion. Labour costs are claimed to be up to 50% less than for conventional manual arc welding.

5. SUBMERGED-ARC WELDING
The slag coating produced in manual arc welding is beneficial in that it protects the weld from atmospheric attack and also insulates it to give a reduced cooling speed. If these advantages are to be retained in automatic welding, problems arise in passing the current from the electrode guides, through the coating, to the electrode metal. These problems have been successfully overcome but it has been found better to feed the flux in powdered form from a hopper ahead of the electrode. The arc is therefore submerged[1] under a layer of flux which melts to

[1] Submerged-arc welding has nothing to do with underwater welding.

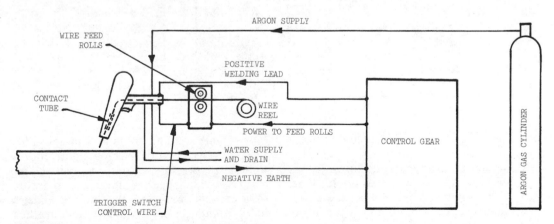

Fig. 8.11 Block diagram of gas-shielded metal-arc welding (MIG welding).

Fig. 8.12 Submerged-arc welding.

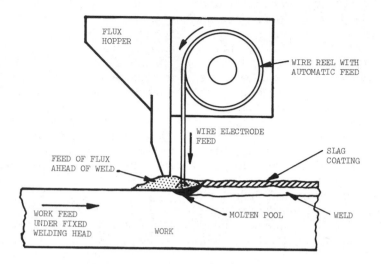

Fig. 8.13 Electro-slag welding.

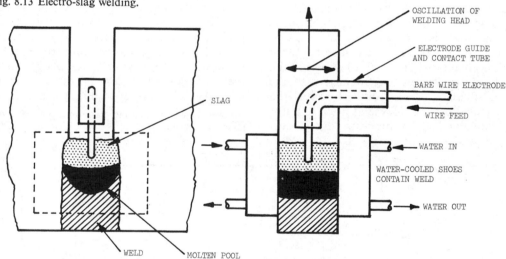

form a slag over the molten pool and protects it.

A diagram of the process is shown in fig. 8.12. The wire is bare and needs no flux core as in CO_2 welding, but is copper-coated to prevent corrosion in storage and ensure good electrical contact with the electrode guide.

This method lends itself to downhand (horizontal) welding of mild and low-alloy steels. It is widely used in shipbuilding, for the welding of pressure vessels, in pipe welding etc. The welding head is moved over the work on a carriage, or the work is moved under a fixed welding head, the latter method generally being used in pipe welding, where the joint is revolved under the head.

6. ELECTRO-SLAG WELDING

As metal thicknesses increase, multi-run welds using automatic methods become uneconomical but if a large current is used to make the weld in one pass the molten pool tends to be uncontrollable and run ahead of the electrode. To overcome this, the plates to be welded are turned into the vertical position as shown in fig. 8.13 and water-cooled shoes are provided to contain the molten pool and prevent the slag from running away.

The wire electrode used passes through a bath of molten slag on top of the weld pool. This is not an arc welding process in the accepted sense. The heat is generated by the passage of the electric current through the molten slag, the slag bath also shielding the weld. As the electrode is consumed the depth of the molten pool increases and the water-cooled guides are raised. The process is similar to continuous casting.

The process is faster than submerged-arc welding for plates greater than 50 mm thick but the mechanical properties of the weld are slightly inferior.

COMPARISON OF FUSION WELDING PROCESSES

The list below compares the processes discussed above and indicates briefly the applications of each process with the features peculiar to it.

1. *Oxy-Acetylene Welding*. Manual general-purpose process. Equipment of low capital cost and readily portable.
2. *Oxy-Hydrogen Welding*. As above but with lower flame temperature. Can be used under water.
3. *Shielded-Arc Process*. Faster than gas welding. Equipment more expensive and not so readily portable.
4. *Gas-Shielded Arc Welding* (TIG welding). Non-consumable tungsten electrode. Used for welding aluminium and magnesium alloys and stainless steel.
5. *Gas-Shielded Metal Arc Welding* (MIG welding). Consumable electrode. Lends itself to automatic welding.
6. *CO_2 Welding*. As for 5. Used on ferrous metals.
7. *Submerged-Arc Welding*. Automatic process for ferrous metals giving better slag protection than 6.
8. *Electro-Slag Welding*. As for 7 but can weld thicker sections.

DISTORTION AND STRESSES IN WELDS

If steel is loaded when cold, up to the elastic limit, it will deform until the load is removed, when it will return to its original shape. If the elastic limit is exceeded, the steel takes on a permanent set.

If the load is applied when the steel is at a temperature greater than 550°C, the steel does not exhibit any elasticity and any deformation due to the load will be permanent.

During welding, when the steel is heated to 1500–1600°C, it is therefore non-elastic. The non-uniform heating and cooling produce forces due to expansion and contraction, causing distortion which is per-

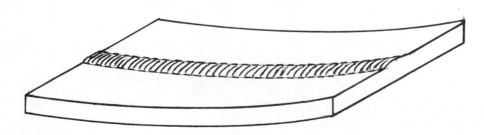

Fig. 8.14 Longitudinal distortion.

manent.

Furthermore, as the weld cools after solidi-fication, further distortion occurs which, if restrained, causes residual stresses to be retained in the welded structure.

Consider a simple butt weld in thin material. The welded face of the material is heated to the plastic phase and has a much higher temperature than the underside. The forces of contraction are therefore much greater on the upper face and the plate bows upwards as shown in fig. 8.14. This is called longitudinal distortion.

When a weld is being made where the edges have previously been prepared in the form of a vee, the inner faces of the vee expand inwards. When the weld is completed, a contraction in the same direction occurs, due to cooling of the deposited weld material. The distortion then takes place in an angular manner as shown in fig. 8.15(*a*). This can be overcome by presetting the parts at an estimated equal and opposite angle as shown in fig. 8.15(*b*), or by making a double-vee weld, where the contraction will be sym-metrical.

Similarly the contraction of the weld fillets in a tee-joint can cause the cross-piece to bow as shown in fig. 8.16(*a*). Again this can be avoided by distorting the part as shown in fig. 8.16(*b*) prior to welding.

An alternative to presetting the parts is to restrain them by holding them in position in fixtures, or by the use of clamps, or by preliminary tack welding. This reduces dis-tortion but the contraction forces are still present and, being resisted, set up residual stresses. Such stresses can be relieved by reheating the complete assembly, where feasible, or by locally reheating selected areas in the case of large structures.

If the heat input can be further localised by limiting the welding to a small length or area at a time, the amount of distortion will be reduced. Two methods of achieving this are (*a*) *step-back welding* and (*b*) *skip welding*.

In both cases the welding is done in short lengths along the work. In step-back welding, adjacent lengths of weld are made, each beginning where the next one will end, with the direction of deposit in opposition to the general direction of progression of the weld. This will be more clearly understood by referring to fig. 8.17(*a*). The technique used is rightward welding but the sections of weld are carried out in the numerical order shown, the arrows indicating the direction of deposition.

Skip welding is rather similar. A short length of weld is made at position 1, the next a short distance away at position 2 and so on as shown in fig. 8.17(*b*), the numbers again

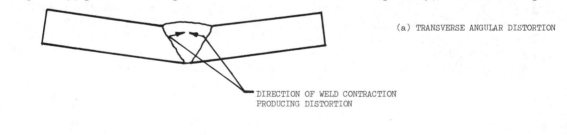

(a) TRANSVERSE ANGULAR DISTORTION

DIRECTION OF WELD CONTRACTION
PRODUCING DISTORTION

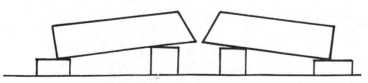

(b) PRE-SETTING TO CORRECT DISTORTION

Fig. 8.15(*a*) Transverse angular distortion. (*b*) Pre-setting to correct distortion.

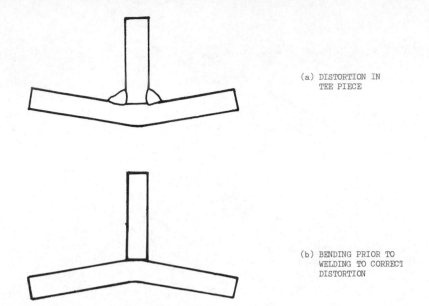

(a) DISTORTION IN
    TEE PIECE

(b) BENDING PRIOR TO
    WELDING TO CORRECT
    DISTORTION

Fig. 8.16(*a*) Distortion in Tee piece. (*b*) Bending prior
to welding to correct distortion.

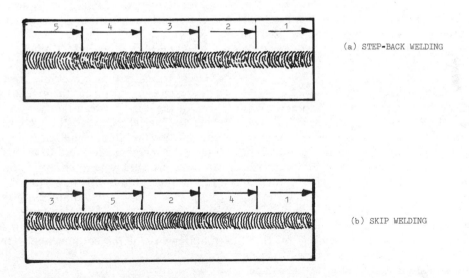

(a) STEP-BACK WELDING

(b) SKIP WELDING

Fig. 8.17(*a*) Step-back welding. (*b*) Skip welding.

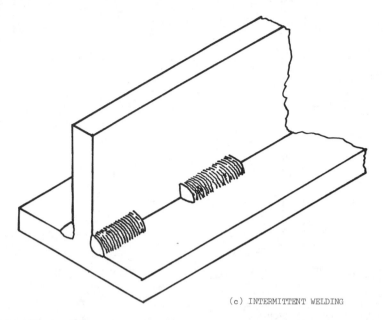

(c) INTERMITTENT WELDING

Fig. 8.17(c) Intermittent welding.

indicating the sequence and the arrows the direction.

Where a continuous weld is not essential intermittent lengths of weld can be used to advantage to reduce distortion, as shown in fig. 8.17(c).

PRESSURE WELDING

In the introduction to this Chapter it was mentioned that the earliest welding was performed by heating the metal, usually wrought iron, into the plastic temperature range and hammering the two parts together. The faces to be welded were usually curved, as shown in fig. 8.18, so that welding started at the centre and squeezed the oxide out.

This process is little used today and has been replaced by fusion welding of thick material, except in specialised cases such as flash butt welding, and by electrical-resistance welding such as spot, stitch, seam and projection welding for thinner materials. These latter processes have found extremely wide application in motor vehicle body manufacture, where the body is fabricated from sheet steel and the individual panels are spot welded to form the complex body structure of the modern automobile.

ELECTRICAL- RESISTANCE WELDING

An electrical-resistance weld is formed by passing an electric current through a localised area of the joint between the two parts to be welded. The resistance to the passage of the current at the joint between the surfaces raises the temperature there to a level which allows a pressure weld to be formed.

The localisation of the area of current passage is achieved by compressing the work between a pair of water-cooled copper electrodes as shown in fig. 8.19. Note that the requirements of the equipment for this type of weld are:

(a) A suitable electric current. This requires a transformer to step down the mains voltage and increase the current flowing.

(b) A means of applying pressure between the electrodes, by air or hydraulic pressure.

Fig. 8.18 Joint preparations for pressure welding.

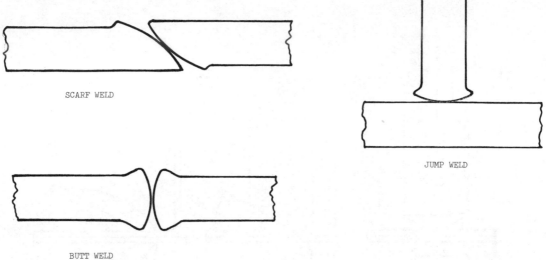

SCARF WELD

JUMP WELD

BUTT WELD

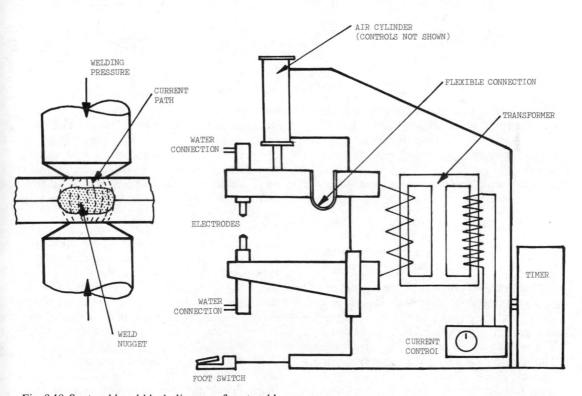

WELDING
PRESSURE

CURRENT
PATH

AIR CYLINDER
(CONTROLS NOT SHOWN)

FLEXIBLE CONNECTION

TRANSFORMER

WATER
CONNECTION

ELECTRODES

WATER
CONNECTION

WELD
NUGGET

TIMER

CURRENT
CONTROL

FOOT SWITCH

Fig. 8.19 Spot weld and block diagram of spot welding machine.

Fig. 8.20 Spot welding electrodes and their applications.

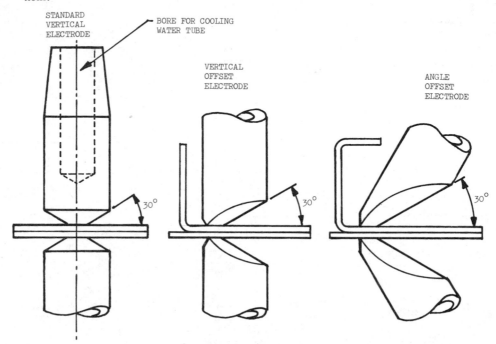

STANDARD VERTICAL ELECTRODE

BORE FOR COOLING WATER TUBE

VERTICAL OFFSET ELECTRODE

ANGLE OFFSET ELECTRODE

30°

30°

30°

Simple spring-loaded devices can be used but are not common nowadays.

(c) A suitable timing device to give the correct sequence and length of events during welding.

The heat generated by the passage of an electric current is given by the expression:

$H = I^2RT$, where H is the heat in joules
I is the current in amperes
R is the resistance in ohms
T is the time in seconds.

Thus, the heat produced can be varied by:

(a) *Varying the current flow*. This is the least sensitive change which can be made, since the heat generated varies as the current squared. It is usually achieved by using a transformer whose tapping is changed by simply moving a control.

(b) *Varying the resistance*. The resistance to the flow of the current depends upon the pressure between the faces and the area through which the current flows. The area depends on the electrode size, which is decided by the metal thickness and cannot therefore be changed readily. The pressure used is that required to form the weld after heating has taken place and therefore cannot readily be altered.

(c) *Varying the time of current flow*. The heat generated depends directly upon the length of time through which the current flows, and this is the most sensitive control of the heat generated. The current time is measured in cycles of the a.c. supply at 50 Hz (hertz, formerly cycles per second) and modern timers can give a required time ±0·25 Hz.

The foregoing is true for all types of resistance welding. Variations in the technique have been developed for different purposes as follows.

208

METHODS OF ELECTRICAL RE-SISTANCE WELDING 1. *Spot Welding*. This process is illustrated in fig. 8.19, the two parts to be welded being pressed together between a pair of water-cooled electrodes, as shown. Usually, each spot weld is made individually, the spacing being determined by the operator although the approximate distance between spots should be given in the job specification to ensure adequate strength.

The electrode tip size varies, depending upon the thickness of the material, a guide to the tip diameter being:

$$D = \sqrt{t}$$

where D = electrode tip diameter in millimetres and t = thickness of material in millimetres with which the electrode is in contact.

A commonly-used design of electrode is shown in fig. 8.20, the tapered shank being used to hold the electrode in the electrode holder. An alternative type uses a threaded connection. The hole shown must be large enough to accept freely a tube from which cooling water can circulate.

An accepted figure for welding pressures is 70 MN/m² based on the electrode tip diameter. This pressure, often applied as an impact, or suddenly applied load, rapidly causes distortion of the electrode tip, which spreads, increases the contact area and reduces the intensity of pressure. It is therefore important to keep the electrode dressed to the correct form and diameter.

Ideally the weld should form a nugget as shown in fig. 8.19, the diameter of which is at least $0.8\sqrt{t}$, with the nugget equally distributed in the two materials. Faulty welds may be due to a number of causes, listed below. An indication of faulty welds is an enormous stream of sparks from the weld area. This usually indicates an excessive expulsion of metal from the weld area, giving a firework display which, although spectacular, often results in a weak weld of poor appearance.

Causes of faulty welds, in the order in which it is reasonable to check, are:

(*a*) Scaly or dirty material
(*b*) Electrodes improperly dressed
(*c*) Electrodes badly aligned
(*d*) Badly made parts. The electrode pressure is for welding, not correcting bad presswork.
(*e*) Welding pressure incorrect (usually too

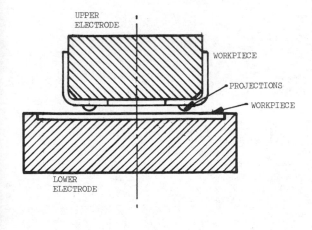

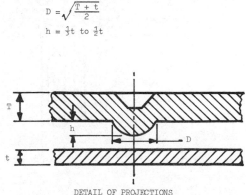

$$D = \sqrt{\frac{T + t}{2}}$$

h = $\tfrac{1}{3}$t to $\tfrac{1}{2}$t

DETAIL OF PROJECTIONS

Fig. 8.21 Projection-welding sheet metal components. Note location in electrodes.

209

low).

(*f*) Welding current incorrect (usually too high).

Spot welding is normally used for the production of individual welds between two sheet metal parts. If a solid part is to be welded to a sheet metal component or a number of welds are to be made simultaneously, the projection welding process is used.

2. *Projection Welding.* A requirement of all methods of resistance welding is that the area through which the current passes, and hence the heated area, is localised. In spot welding this is achieved by using small electrodes. If, however, a small area of one component is raised to form a projection a similar effect can be obtained. The electrodes are in this case shaped to suit the component and may assist in locating the parts.

If two sheet metal parts are welded in this manner, a number of welds can be formed simultaneously and the spacing of the welds can be closely controlled. The projections are produced by pressing during manufacture of the part and are of the form shown in fig. 8.21.

A typical case of welding a solid part to a sheet metal component occurs in the production of oil filters for automobiles, where an oil-tight connection is required. The boss is made of the form shown in fig. 8.22 and the annular projection collapses to form an oil-tight weld.

The production of long fluid-tight welds such as the seams of fuel tanks is not feasible by this method since the area of metal in contact is too great. For these purposes another method of resistance welding, seam welding, is employed.

3. *Seam Welding.* To produce a water-tight seam by resistance welding, the two parts together are passed between a pair of discs which form the electrodes through which the current flows and between which the pressure is applied. As the discs rotate they roll the work between them and the current is passed in pulses to form a series of overlapping spot welds, as shown in fig. 8.23. Cooling is generally done by flooding the work from an external water supply.

If it is not necessary for the joint to be watertight, the speed of rotation of the discs

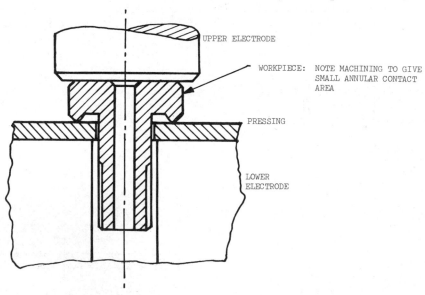

Fig. 8.22 Projection-welding machined boss to sheet metal pressing.

Fig. 8.23 Seam and stitch welding.

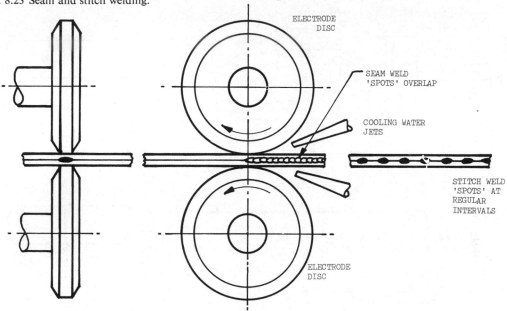

ELECTRODE
DISC

SEAM WELD
'SPOTS' OVERLAP

COOLING WATER
JETS

STITCH WELD
'SPOTS' AT
REGULAR
INTERVALS

ELECTRODE
DISC

Fig. 8.24 Butt seam welding of tube from strip.

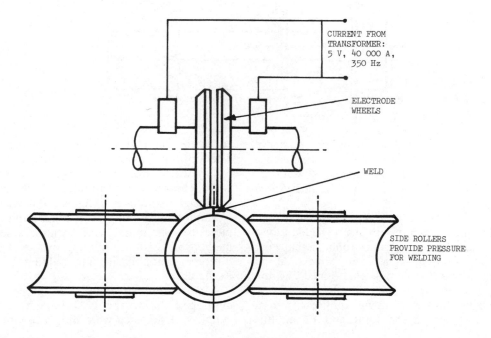

CURRENT FROM
TRANSFORMER:
5 V, 40 000 A,
350 Hz

ELECTRODE
WHEELS

WELD

SIDE ROLLERS
PROVIDE PRESSURE
FOR WELDING

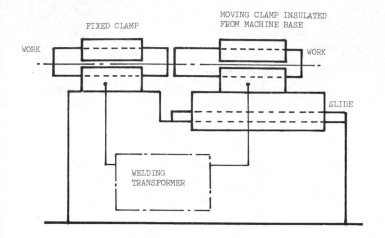

FIXED CLAMP

MOVING CLAMP INSULATED
FROM MACHINE BASE

WORK

WORK

SLIDE

WELDING
TRANSFORMER

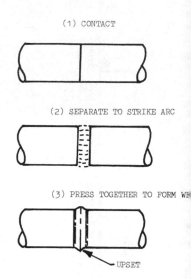

(1) CONTACT

(2) SEPARATE TO STRIKE ARC

(3) PRESS TOGETHER TO FORM WE

UPSET

Fig. 8.25 Diagram of flash butt weld in machine and
stages in formation of weld.

Fig. 8.26 Example of fabricated assembly using both
projection and flash butt welding.

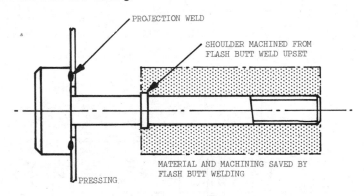

PROJECTION WELD

SHOULDER MACHINED FROM
FLASH BUTT WELD UPSET

PRESSING

MATERIAL AND MACHINING SAVED BY
FLASH BUTT WELDING

can be increased so that the pulses, and hence the welds, are more widely spaced. In this case a series of non-overlapping spot welds is produced and the process is called *Stitch welding*.

A specialised form of seam welding is used in the production of butt-seam welded tubes. Flat strip is formed into tubular shape by passing it through rollers and formers. At the stage where it is completely formed and the edges touch, it passes under a pair of disc electrodes as shown in fig. 8.24, the current passing through the joint and raising the

edges to the required welding temperature. The tube now passes through a further pair of rollers which exert the pressure to form the weld. The process is continuous and tube is produced at speeds in excess of 20 m/min.

Methods of joining sheet metal, and solid pieces to sheet metal, have been discussed. A method of resistance-welding two solid parts together called flash butt welding is also available.

4. *Flash Butt Welding*. This process was developed during the 1939–1945 war when supplies of tungsten were short. To conserve

this material, short lengths of high-speed steel, which contains tungsten, were welded to carbon-steel shanks for cutting tools. Since then the process has become used for other purposes.

It is not, strictly speaking, a resistance-welding process in that the heating is produced by a form of arc. The parts to be welded are gripped in carefully aligned clamps, one fixed and one moving, as shown in fig. 8.25. The moving clamp is brought up until the parts touch and is then immediately moved back a short distance so that an arc is struck. This rapidly raises the temperature of the ends of the parts and when they are hot enough for welding they are brought together again and pressure is exerted to form a weld.

The process is used today to save machining costs where a long rod with a head is required which it is not practicable to produce by cold-heading. An assembly with which the author was concerned is shown in fig. 8.26, the finished rod being afterwards projection-welded into a container. A feature of this component was that the upset produced by the flash butt weld was itself subsequently machined to form a shoulder on the part.

FRICTION WELDING

This is a recent development of pressure welding in which the required heat is generated by rubbing the two parts together. One component is held stationary while the other is rotated rapidly against it. When they are pressed together they quickly attain welding temperature, after which the rotating part is rapidly stopped and pressure applied to form the weld.

An interesting feature of the process is that it is self-cleansing and no oxidation of the surfaces can occur. This enables incompatible materials to be welded and the author has seen tubes of aluminium alloy and stainless steel welded together by this process. It can also be applied to thermo-plastic materials, in which industry it is known as *spin welding*.

The process is currently finding application

Fig. 8.27 Specification of bend test rig (BS 1295).

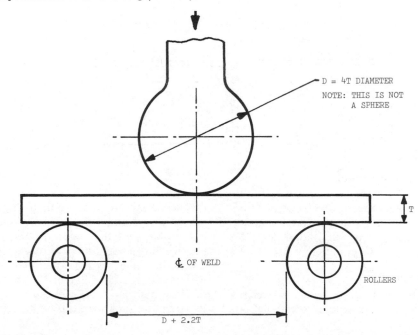

D = 4T DIAMETER
NOTE: THIS IS NOT
A SPHERE

T

℄ OF WELD

ROLLERS

D + 2.2T

Fig. 8.28 Diagram of a good spot weld after test.

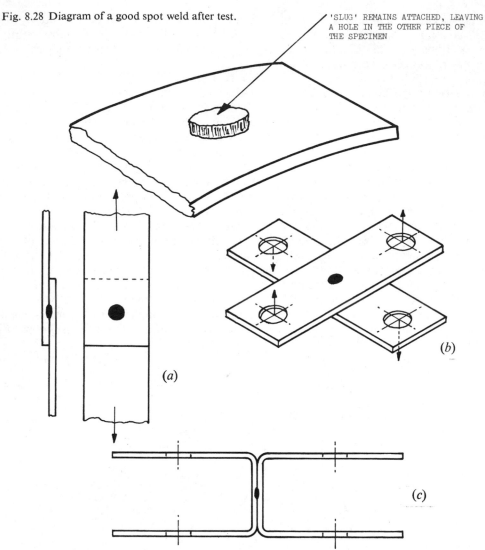

'SLUG' REMAINS ATTACHED, LEAVING A HOLE IN THE OTHER PIECE OF THE SPECIMEN

(a)

(b)

(c)

Fig. 8.29. Test pieces for testing spot welds. (a) Shear test. (b) Cross-tension test. (c) 'U' tension test.

in the automobile industry in the production of parts for rear axles, e.g., welding flanges to half shafts. Control is very good and the process lends itself to complete automation.

WELD TESTING

The only real way to determine the strength of a weld is to test it under load to destruction. By such destructive tests only a small sample can be tested and what is really being tested is the ability of the welder or the setting of the welding machine. Various methods of non-destructive testing are available which will be discussed in Chapter 11. These serve to disclose defects in the weld, which do affect its strength. Such methods of non-destructive

214

testing apply equally to other work, as well as welded joints, and will be discussed generally in Chapter 11. Here we shall consider only the destructive tests of welds.

TESTING OF FUSION WELDS For simple butt joints, the welder is required to produce a test piece. This is cut into sections across the weld and the different strips can then be submitted to different tests. These include tensile and impact tests, and a bend test using a rig whose basic dimensions are shown in fig. 8.27, in which, with the aid of a standard compression-testing machine, the test piece is bent through 180° into a 'U' shape, the surfaces of the weld having been machined level with the metal surface.

Such tests are covered by British Standards as follows:

BS 709: *Methods for testing fusion welds, welded joints and weld metal*
BS 1295: *Tests for use in the training of welders*
BS 2645: *Tests for use in the approval of welders.*

TESTING OF ELECTRICAL-RESISTANCE WELDS Although attempts are being made to find non-destructive methods for spot welds, at present the only reliable test is to pull the welded joint apart. If the welds themselves separate at the joint, usually with a light load and a metallic 'ping', the weld is defective. If, however, the parent metal fails and leaves a 'slug' of the welded part as shown in fig. 8.28, the weld is considered good and the machine setting correct.

Such tests are usually carried out on a test specimen of similar material to that used for the components. A simple test is to hold one part in a vice and 'peel' the other part back with a pair of pliers until the weld fails. More reliable results are obtained by using a tensile testing machine and standard test pieces as shown in fig. 8.29.

Fig. 8.29(*a*), showing the shear-test specimen, is self-explanatory. Fig. 8.29(*b*) shows a cross-tension test piece, the two parts of which are bolted to suitable 'T' pieces held in the jaws of a tensile testing machine. A similar test may also be made on a 'U' tension test piece as shown in fig. 8.29(*c*).

Apart from these tests, impact and fatigue tests are also made on spot welds.

SUMMARY
Welding in its earliest form was carried out by a combination of heat and pressure. It was used for artistic work, such as the great iron pillar at Delhi, and for the manufacture and repair of tools and implements. Later, fusion welding was developed when flame temperatures produced by the combustion of fuel gases with oxygen gave an intense source of heat suitable for the local melting of metals. These methods were, and still are, largely used in the repair and jobbing shop fields. The application of electricity to produce the heat required by an electric arc gave faster welding speeds and welding moved into the field of production, particularly in the areas of heavy engineering such as shipbuilding, bridge building and other structural work. At the same time the wheel turned full circle with the introduction of pressure welding as a volume-production process, using electrical resistance to give the required source of heat.

In all these fields there has been a continuous development, particularly in automatic methods, which have been facilitated largely by developments in electronics. Flame-cutting is carried out on numerically-controlled machines using identical control methods to those used on computer-controlled milling machines.

Thus the technician engineer working in the field of welding also requires a considerable knowledge of electricity and electronics. Although specialist knowledge in this field will largely come from his electrical technician colleague it behoves him to familiarise himself with the processes available if not their electrical details.

9

Precision Casting

INTRODUCTION

In Book 1 of this work the casting process was discussed as a primary production process, sand casting being considered at some length and mention being made of other methods of manufacturing castings which included die-casting, shell moulding and investment casting.

A detailed study of sand casting is more properly the province of the foundry technician and here we shall consider it no further. The mechanical engineering technician is likely to require more knowledge of the other casting processes, which lend themselves to high-volume production of very accurate castings and these methods will now be considered further. Die-casting is essentially a process for casting alloys of low melting temperature. It follows that no costly melting equipment is necessary and indeed the melting equipment is an integral part of the machine in many cases. For this reason the process is often used in firms which do no other form of casting, a bay of one of the production areas being given over to a few die-casting machines. Of course, the bulk of die-castings is made by specialist firms but the mechanical engineering technician is quite likely to come into direct contact with the process. The treatment here of die-casting will therefore be rather more detailed.

DIE-CASTING

Many components are required whose shape is such that they can most easily be produced by casting but whose strength requirements are so low that they can be made of a relatively weak, low melting-point alloy. Where such parts are required in quantity it is economical to make a permanent metal mould in which the metal is cast. The fact that the mould is permanent enables a high production rate to be achieved, for as soon as one casting is removed the mould is ready for the next.

The mould used in this process is made from a mating pair of *dies* and the process is therefore known as *die-casting*. Die-castings are made by three methods:

1. Gravity Die-Casting
2. Cold-Chamber Die-Casting ⎫ *Pressure*
3. Hot-Chamber Die-Casting ⎬ *Die-Casting*
                                   ⎭

In all cases the high finish of the die gives a high surface finish to the casting. The accuracy of the die is similarly repeated in the casting, so that little final machining is normally required.

GRAVITY DIE-CASTING This process is known in the U.S.A. as permanent-mould casting, which is possibly a better name since it tends to prevent the process from being considered as the poor relation of pressure die-casting. In the gravity process a permanent mould and core are used, usually made of cast iron, and the metal to be cast is poured into the mould as it is for a sand casting. The only pressure involved is the hydrostatic pressure due to the head of molten metal.

Except for one-piece dies for very simple parts, gravity dies are usually made from a number of blocks which can be separated to remove the part. This also permits the die blocks to be removed in a set sequence so that the component is allowed to contract freely instead of being constrained by the die. For this reason, gravity die-casting is not so sensitive to changes in section as pressure die-casting. The thin sections, contracting naturally, do not fail as they would if restrained during cooling. Further, the process is flexible and allows design changes to be made by changing one or two die blocks.

As gravity dies are freestanding, neither the product designer nor the die designer is restricted by having to design dies for a particular machine of given platen size, stroke and metal capacity.

Thus gravity die-casting is an extremely useful process in its own right, advantages being summarised as follows:

(i) Wide size-range of castings possible, from as small as 50 g mass up to 100 kg.

(ii) Less sensitive to changes in section than other methods of die-casting.

(iii) Readily adaptable to design changes.

(iv) Design of work not restricted by machine considerations.

(v) Low capital cost of equipment compared with pressure die-casting.

PRESSURE DIE-CASTING Unlike gravity die-casting, in pressure die-casting the metal is forced into the mould under a positive pressure which is maintained until solidification has taken place. The essentials of the equipment required are as follows:

1. Split dies containing a negative cavity of the form to be produced.
2. A positive method of closing the dies, holding them closed under pressure and opening them when solidification has occurred.
3. A means of forcing the molten metal into the dies under pressure and maintaining the pressure until solidification has taken place.
4. A means of ejecting the cast component

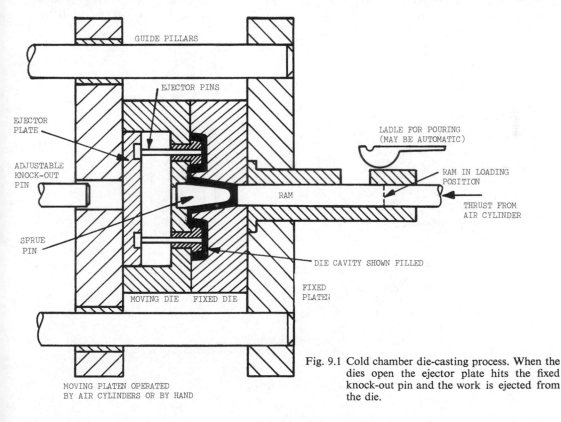

Fig. 9.1 Cold chamber die-casting process. When the dies open the ejector plate hits the fixed knock-out pin and the work is ejected from the die.

217

when solidified.

Apart from the actual process of casting, some specialised finishing and machining operations are necessary before the casting can be used, and must be considered.

A fundamental difference between pressure die-casting and gravity die-casting is that the dies are made of hardened steel and of as few parts as possible.

(*a*) *The Cold Chamber Process.* The basic principle of the cold chamber process is shown in fig. 9.1. A measured quantity of molten metal is ladled into the pouring hole and the ram is moved forward under pressure to force the metal into the dies. After solidification the dies are opened and since they are usually designed so that the work tends to remain in the moving die, the work is ejected by the ejector pins.

Use of the cold-chamber process is largely restricted to the casting of those alloys which have higher melting temperatures, such as aluminium alloys which melt at approximately 660°C, compared with 420°C for the zinc-based die-casting alloys. In the cold-chamber process the dies, sprue and cylinder have time to cool between shots and do not attain the same temperature as the alloy. This prevents 'iron pick-up', a transfer of iron from the machine and die steels to the alloy, which can occur if steel is in continuous contact with aluminium, magnesium and copper-based alloys for long periods at high temperatures.

Generally, the higher the melting point of the alloy the shorter the die life, even in the cold-chamber process. For this reason the metal temperature should be controlled carefully to the lowest temperature at which it can be successfully cast. In the case of copper-based alloys, such as brass, with a melting temperature of the order of 900°C, die life was found to be extremely low. For this reason much of the die-casting of brass is now

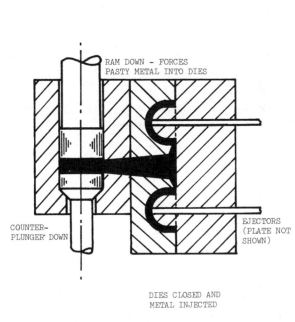

RAM DOWN - FORCES
PASTY METAL INTO DIES

COUNTER-
PLUNGER DOWN

EJECTORS
(PLATE NOT
SHOWN)

DIES CLOSED AND
METAL INJECTED

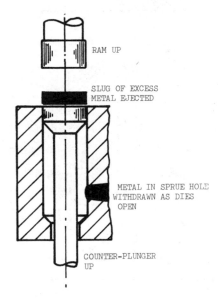

RAM UP

SLUG OF EXCESS
METAL EJECTED

METAL IN SPRUE HOLE
WITHDRAWN AS DIES
OPEN

COUNTER-PLUNGER
UP

BEFORE DIES OPEN, RAM RISES.
COUNTER-PLUNGER RISES AND EJECTS
SLUG OF EXCESS METAL

Fig. 9.2 Polak cold chamber process for die-casting semi-molten metals.

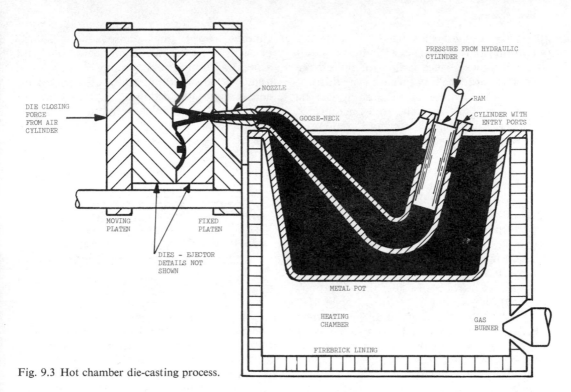

Fig. 9.3 Hot chamber die-casting process.

carried out with the metal in a pasty, or semi-liquid, condition at a much lower temperature.

The Polak machine used for die-casting brass in this manner has a vertical sleeve into which the semi-molten metal is placed. The ram now comes down and forces the metal into the die as shown in fig. 9.2. This inevitably leaves a residue of metal in the sleeve in the form of a slug which would prevent removal of the work from the dies, so the counter-plunger is forced up to shear off and eject this slug before the dies are opened and the part is ejected.

Generally, brass die-castings are cheaper than hot brass stampings but tend to be porous and cannot be made to the same density as hot stampings. Brass die-castings should therefore not be used to carry fluids under pressure.

(b) *The Hot-Chamber Process.* Unlike the cold-chamber process, the hot-chamber process incorporates the metal-melting equipment in the machine itself. As with the cold-

chamber process, the moving die is mounted on a moving platen as shown in fig. 9.3. The fixed die and platen are attached to the melting pot, the connection to the sprue or die inlet being by a 'goose-neck', as shown. When the injection plunger is withdrawn molten metal flows into the goose-neck via a filling port. The dies are closed and the injection plunger is depressed, forcing the molten metal into the die cavity.

Usually the injection pressure of up to 140 MN/m^2 is created by hydraulic pressure. On large machines the die closure is performed by the ram of an air cylinder, the ram operating a toggle linkage so that the dies cannot open even if there is a failure in the pneumatic circuit. On smaller machines the die closure is performed by a hand-operated lever with a toggle action to ensure that the dies remain closed against the injection pressure.

The hot-chamber process is generally used for the lower melting temperature zinc-based alloys. Its design lends itself to automatic operation and it is faster than the cold-chamber process since ladling of the charge from a separate melting furnace is avoided.

The wall thickness of the casting can be from 1·5 mm to 5 mm and to a tolerance of about ±0·08 mm. Cored holes require a draft taper of 1° for holes over 25 mm, falling to $\frac{1}{2}$° on holes of 10 mm diameter or less. The tolerances on hole centres are of the order of ±0·05 mm up to 40 mm, and ±0·025 mm for each additional 25 mm above that if the cores are located in the same die block. If cores are located in different die blocks a greater tolerance is necessary.

Studs and bushes can be cast into the work, the inserts usually being made of brass. They must of course be inserted into locations provided in the die while it is open and designed so that they remain anchored when the casting has solidified. Coarse knurling is often sufficient for this but other methods include the use of slotted-head screws, deliberately deformed components and slotted inserts, while bushes may be anchored by knurling or by milling flats on the outside diameter.

Screw threads and gears can readily be cast. If possible the die is designed with a split line on the diameter of the thread so that when the dies are opened the thread can be removed from the cavity without unscrewing. This method leaves a slight flash on the thread which has to be cleared by a machining operation. An alternative is to cast the part on a removable plate from which it is unscrewed while another is being cast.

FINISHING DIE-CASTINGS When the die casting is ejected from the machine it is still attached to the sprue, runner and possibly a rim, used to avoid ejector pins operating on the cast surface. These attachments are generally broken off but there is also a thin 'flash' around the joint line. This is removed by a flash-clipping operation in a simple press tool. An alternative method, where the profile is complex and a flash-clipping tool would consequently be expensive, is to run the components by hand around a routing tool running at a speed of about 30 000 rev/min. If the joint line runs across a flat face such as a flange, an abrasive belt with a backing plate is frequently used, as shown in fig. 9.4. In both cases, only a light contact pressure is required.

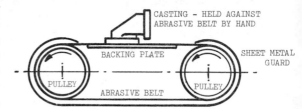

Fig. 9.4 Simple belt sanding machine for removing split line flash from die-castings.

Die-cast alloys are readily machineable and, although a feature of the die-casting process is that its accuracy obviates most machining, all the usual processes such as drilling, reaming, tapping etc. can be carried out. An interesting technique is the finishing of round holes for bearings by a push broach of the type shown in fig. 9.5. In this example, the cutting teeth gradually increase in diameter from 12·25 mm to 12·50 mm, there being ten such teeth. The last four cutting teeth are all of 12·50 mm diameter to allow for regrinding, and the final four 'teeth' do not have cutting edges but are rounded, polished and made oversize by 0·005 mm as shown. These finish the hole by 'swaging' and in so doing impart a very good surface finish with fine surface cracks due to the work hardening which is caused. These cracks help to retain lubricant and help to provide an excellent bearing surface. The operation is very simple and is carried out by hand in a mandrel press, the broach dropping straight through the fixture into a suitable container under the press.

Many die-cast components are used for decorative brightware, particularly in the motor industry. Zinc-based die-castings lend themselves readily to nickel and chromium

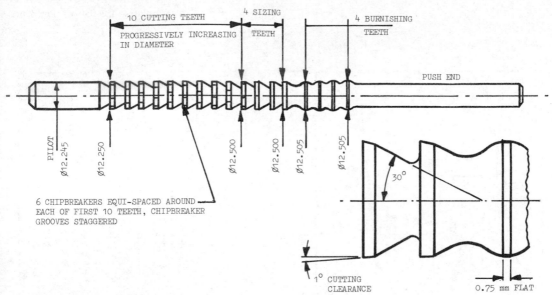

10 CUTTING TEETH

PROGRESSIVELY INCREASING
IN DIAMETER

4 SIZING
TEETH

4 BURNISHING
TEETH

PUSH END

PILOT
Ø12.245

Ø12.250

Ø12.500

Ø12.500

Ø12.505

Ø12.505

6 CHIPBREAKERS EQUI-SPACED AROUND
EACH OF FIRST 10 TEETH, CHIPBREAKER
GROOVES STAGGERED

30°

1° CUTTING
CLEARANCE

0.75 mm FLAT

ENLARGED VIEW OF TEETH

Fig. 9.5 Push broach for finishing round holes in die-
castings.

plating. The part is first polished, cleaned and then copper plated. This enables a coat of nickel plate to be deposited on the copper, after which the thin final layer of chromium plating is added and the final polishing is carried out.

Aluminium alloys do not lend themselves to finishing by electro-deposition but are more readily finished by anodising. Unlike plating, where the work is made the cathode in an electrolytic bath and the current flow is *towards* it, the aluminium alloy is made the anode and the current flows away from it. This produces a hard oxide surface which can be dyed to a required colour and polished. The anodised surface will not tarnish and is used for various purposes, from finishing item of domestic equipment to badges and buttons for the armed forces.

A cautionary note on the die casting process should be added here. If for some reason the dies do not close properly the molten metal will be shot out with great force and can cause bad burns if it hits a person even some distance from the machine. To ensure

that the dies close properly they should be cleaned with an air blast between each shot so that any foreign matter is removed. The machine should be guarded from floor to ceiling—hardboard on a light wooden frame is adequate—and the guards should extend for some distance on either side of the split line of the dies. The operator may have to move around inside the barriers but he should wear safety glasses and suitable protective clothing and boots.

Die-casting is a precision casting process limited to the production of castings in low-melting point alloys. Obviously processes are required which will produce castings of equal precision in materials whose strength is greater and whose melting point is higher than the zinc-based and aluminium alloys discussed up to now.

SHELL MOULDING

The author understands that this process was developed in Germany during the 1939–1945 war. It enables a precision sandmould to be made from a metal pattern in a few minutes

Fig. 9.6 Pair of pattern plates for a flanged pipe bend.

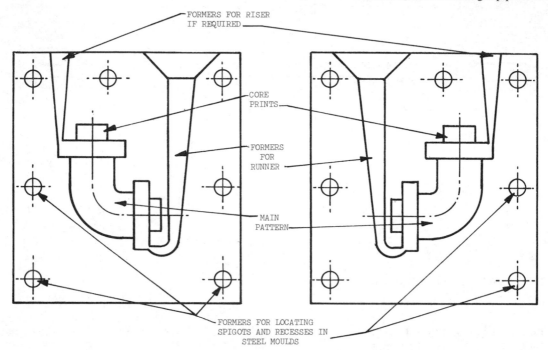

FORMERS FOR RISER
IF REQUIRED

CORE
PRINTS

FORMERS
FOR
RUNNER

MAIN
PATTERN

FORMERS FOR LOCATING
SPIGOTS AND RECESSES IN
STEEL MOULDS

and in such a way that, apart from good accuracy ($\pm 0\cdot1$ mm in 100 mm), a reasonable surface finish is produced.

Briefly the process consists of the following stages:

(a) Making the metal pattern
(b) Making the shell moulds
(c) Pouring the casting.

The pattern plates are made in pairs, corresponding to the two halves of a split pattern used for sand casting, and are made from metal, usually mild steel, as shown in fig. 9.6. Note that one plate has depressions to produce location bosses on the mould and the other plate has bosses to produce the mating depressions on the other half of the mould. Draft is required on the pattern plates to enable the finished moulds to be stripped from them and core prints are also necessary in this case. Patterns to form the runners are included but risers may not be necessary, depending upon the casting. This is because the finished moulds are porous (it is possible to blow cigarette smoke through them) and entrapped air can escape through the sides of the moulds.

Contraction must be allowed for in two ways. The pattern will be heated to about 450°C and will therefore expand, giving a larger mould than would be obtained from a cold pattern, and the molten metal, when cast, will shrink on cooling.

The mould is made from a mixture of sand and uncured synthetic resin. It is contained in a dump box as shown in fig. 9.7, and the heated pattern is clamped to the open end of the box, which is then inverted. This dumps the sand/resin mixture on the pattern, the heat from which cures the resin evenly to a depth depending on the pattern temperature and the curing time. The box is turned upright and the uncured resin and sand fall off the pattern which can then be removed. The shell mould thus formed is removed from the pattern.

The moulds are usually made in pairs and can be easily stored until required. They are light in weight and small in volume, so they occupy a minimum of floor space.

Before pouring, the moulds are clamped together as shown in fig. 9.8 by simple 'G' clamps. In practice, the shape of the component is not outlined as clearly on the outside of the mould as appears in fig. 9.8. The cured sand/resin mixture tends to have a blurred outline as indicated in fig. 9.7. Accurate mould alignment is ensured by the registers provided on the patterns and reproduced on the mould shells. If necessary, the mould can be reinforced by a backing of dry moulding sand but the metal is often poured directly into the clamped shells. No special arrangements are necessary for venting because the shells are naturally porous. The castings produced are of good finish and high accuracy, are remarkably sound and are free from scabs, porosity or blowholes.

Shell moulding can be used for high melting-point materials and, due to their accuracy and finish, the castings produced require no machining on non-critical working surfaces. A typical component is a domestic water tap, whose hexagonal section on which a spanner is fitted is accurate enough not to require machining. Another and more complex casting is the finned cylinder for a two-stroke motor cycle engine, often made by the shell-moulding process.

INVESTMENT CASTING (LOST WAX PROCESS)

When the gas turbine engine was developed it was found necessary to produce alloys for the turbine blades which were heat resistant and also resistant to the phenomenon known as 'creep', i.e., a gradual increase in length under a steady load at high temperatures. It is unfortunate that alloys with these properties are extremely difficult to machine and casting techniques had to be found to produce blades of such precision that an absolute minimum of machining was necessary. Ironically, one of the oldest casting processes known was

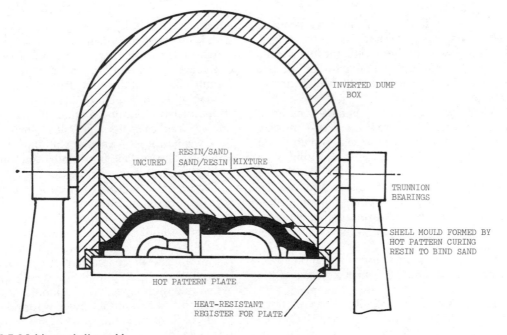

Fig. 9.7 Making a shell mould.

223

Fig. 9.8 Shell mould after pouring.

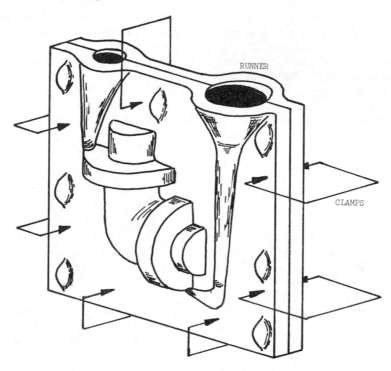

RUNNER

CLAMPS

adopted—the lost wax process—which has been used for centuries to cast statues, emblems, religious figures etc. throughout the East. It is particularly suitable for an intricate casting whose pattern would be difficult to remove from the mould.

A replica of the casting is made or carved in wax, which is covered in layers of fireclay and allowed to dry. The fireclay is then baked and the wax pattern melts and runs out, leaving an internal hollow space which is a replica of the pattern inside the fireclay mould. Molten metal is poured in and solidifies on cooling to produce the casting required. The casting is removed by breaking off the surrounding fireclay.

Modern techniques use an accurate permanent metal mould in which a replica of the component is cast in wax, complete with runner sections. The resulting wax patterns are fixed to a central wax sprue by a hot soldering iron to form a 'Christmas Tree' of patterns. The whole assembly is then sprayed with a fine refractory material which dries to form a coating adhering to the wax. Successive coats are given until a sufficient body of ceramic has built up and dried. The whole assembly is now baked to harden and strengthen the ceramic mould, during which the wax replica melts and is lost—hence the 'lost wax' process—leaving a mould of high accuracy and surface finish into which metal of high melting-point can be cast.

The mould produced by the above method is rather fragile and a more robust mould is made by the *flask method*. The process is similar to that described above but before the mould is baked it is placed in a flask as shown in fig. 9.9 and a coarse refractory slurry is poured and vibrated around the assembly. When the assembly is baked a mould of great precision and fine surface finish is formed in a solid block of ceramic, with the wax melting out as before.

The metal is poured and allowed to solidify, and the mould is then broken up to free the castings, which are accurate in size and have good surface finish. The method lends itself to the production of castings which would normally present difficulties through the high melting-point of the metal used. Fig. 9.10 shows such a component cast in stainless steel. The limits on the casting are ±0·10 mm and, if produced from solid bar stock, the finished component would weigh only 20% of the original bar. To machine away so much material would be uneconomic and, in stainless steel, would be extremely difficult.

Fig. 9.10 Typical investment casting in stainless steel.

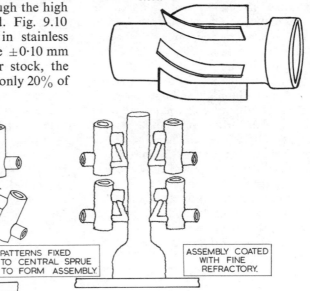

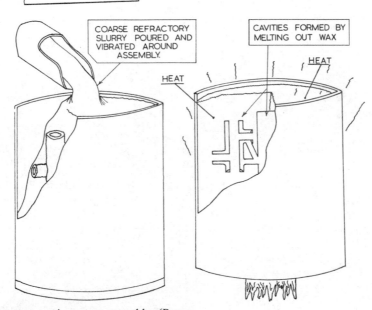

PATTERNS FIXED TO CENTRAL SPRUE TO FORM ASSEMBLY.

ASSEMBLY COATED WITH FINE REFRACTORY.

COARSE REFRACTORY SLURRY POURED AND VIBRATED AROUND ASSEMBLY.

CAVITIES FORMED BY MELTING OUT WAX

HEAT

HEAT

Fig. 9.9 Investment casting sprue assembly. (Reproduced by courtesy of British Investment Casting Manufacturers' Association.)

SUMMARY

Precision castings are required in a variety of materials ranging from the low melting-point zinc-based alloys to the sophisticated Nimonic alloys and stainless steels. The low melting-point materials are produced in permanent metal moulds and dies, and can be cast in gravity dies or under pressure. Pressure die-castings in zinc-based alloys are produced in hot-chamber machines which have the melting equipment incorporated in the machine itself. Aluminium and magnesium alloys, if cast in this type of equipment, tend to pick up iron from the mould should the dies get too hot. They are therefore cast in cold-chamber machines where the hot metal is in contact with the equipment only while a shot is being made.

Die-castings are frequently used where the applied loads are small and appearance is important, e.g., decorative brightware.

Shell moulding uses expendable moulds which can be made very quickly by semi-skilled labour, and which produce accurate well-finished castings in a wide range of materials. The accuracy and finish are not quite as high as in die-casting and the process is slower but, compared with conventional sand-casting methods, output is very high.

Investment casting produces precise well-finished castings from expendable moulds in very high melting-point materials. The castings produced require very little machining. and are often of heat and creep-resistant alloys whose melting temperature is so high that a mould of refractory material is required.

A comparison of casting methods must consider such factors as cost of pattern, cost of mould, speed of process, dimensional accuracy, surface finish and any limitations. These factors are compared in the table below.

MOULDING METHOD

Factor	Sand casting	Shell moulding	Die casting	Investment casting
Cost of pattern	Low	High	—	High
Cost of mould	High	Low	High	High
Speed of process	Slow	High	Very high	Slow
Surface finish and accuracy	Poor ± 0.40 mm up to 100 mm	Good ± 0.10 mm up to 100 mm	Very good ± 0.03 mm up to 100 mm	Very good ± 0.03 mm up to 100 mm
Comments	Medium and low production of ferrous and non-ferrous castings	High production of ferrous and non-ferrous castings	High production of castings in low melting-point alloys	Production of precision castings in high melting-point alloys

10

Powder Metallurgy, Sintering and Heat-Treatment Furnaces

INTRODUCTION

The manufacture of solid objects by compressing and heating finely-divided powders of suitable materials and grain size is thought by many to be a relatively recent process. In fact, W. H. Wollaston showed in 1829 that he could produce a malleable form of the metal platinum by compressing finely-divided platinum powder in simple dies in a hand-operated press to produce a briquette or compact. When this was heated in a furnace to *below the melting point of platinum* it formed a solid block of the metal which could then be forged. This is essentially the process employed today to manufacture components from metallic, and indeed non-metallic, powders. Little further work was done, and the process was considered a metallurgical oddity, until 1909, when W. H. Coolidge patented a method of manufacture of tungsten wire for the production of filaments of electric lamps. The process was similar in that tungsten powder was compressed and heated to below its melting point to produce blocks of tungsten which could be drawn out into wire of only 0·02 mm diameter and with a tensile strength of 4×10^6 kN/m². Since then, the process has been developed to produce a variety of materials and components for all sorts of applications.

The bonding of the compacted powder is called *sintering* and is done by heating the briquettes in a controlled atmosphere. Since the furnaces used are essentially similar to those used in other heat-treatment processes a discussion of conveyor-hearth processes is included below and at the same time the surface-hardening process of *nitriding* is considered. Nitriding has nothing to do with powder metallurgy but the type of furnace used is similar to that of some furnaces used for sintering and this is a convenient place to include the process.

POWDER METALLURGY

Too many people seem to think that the only parts made by powder metallurgy are the tips for cemented-carbide cutting tools. That this is not so can be shown by considering some of the components and materials made from powders.

Electrical relay contact-points have dual requirements. They must stand up to the electrical erosion which occurs through sparking when they open and close, and at the same time they must be good conductors of electricity. Copper is a good conductor but will not withstand the arcing, and tungsten, which has a long life under these conditions, is not a good conductor. By making the points from a *mixture* of powdered copper and tungsten, both properties are achieved in a material which could not be produced as a cast alloy.

After the first world war, the porous bearing was first made by compacting a mass of metal powder in such a way that it remained porous. The pores were filled with oil under pressure and the oil was drawn to the surface by capillary attraction when the bearing was in use. Later the bearings were made to incorporate graphite. Controlled porosity has also enabled fine filters to be made by these methods.

Heavy metals can be made by sintering. A material made by compacting a powder of 90% tungsten, 5% cobalt and 5% nickel has a relative density of 17, compared with lead, which has a relative density of 11·3. Such a material is used for storing radio-active isotopes in relatively thin-walled containers.

General Motors used the technique for manufacturing involute gears for gear-type oil pumps and an interesting comparison has been made[1] between the processes of manufacture by conventional methods and by powder metallurgy which shows that 30 man-hours were required per 1000 gears by conventional methods while powder metallurgy required only 15 man-hours per 1000 gears and gave a stronger gear.

Other parts made by powder metallurgy include diamond-impregnated grinding wheels and drill heads, magnets etc.

The author has deliberately laboured the diversity of parts made by this process in order to break down the idea that only cemented-carbide tool bits are made by sintering. These tools are of course an important development in metal cutting and would not have been possible without powder metallurgy but they are by no means the only parts made in this way.

The applications of powder metallurgy can be generally stated as follows:

1. To produce solid pieces from material which cannot be melted in commercially-available furnaces, e.g., sparking-plug insulators.

2. To produce components incorporating the properties of different materials which, because of their physical characteristics, cannot readily be combined.

3. To make precision parts which are so hard that they cannot readily be shaped by conventional processes, e.g., cemented-carbide tool tips.

4. To produce parts with characteristics which cannot be obtained by conventional methods, e.g., porous and graphite-impregnated bearings, and fine filters.

5. To produce precision parts and virtually eliminate machining.

In all cases, the method of manufacture of

[1] Baeza: *A Course in Powder Metallurgy* (Rheinhold, New York, 1943).

parts by powder metallurgy is as follows:

1. Production of powder.
2. Compacting into a briquette.
3. Sintering, the application of heat to produce the required bonding and hardening.

1. PRODUCTION OF POWDER The powder required may be produced by mechanical, physical or chemical methods.

Mechanical methods of manufacturing powder are usually modifications of the old apothecary's pestle and mortar in which the powder is crushed by impact pressure to the size required. The modern version of this technique is the *ball mill*, which consists of a drum about one-third full of hardened steel balls. The material to be milled is poured into the mill which is rotated at 80–100 rev/min. After the required time, the entire contents of the mill are transferred to a coarse sieve to separate the balls from the powder, which is then graded by passing through a tower of sieves.

Another mechanical method of powder production is *shotting*. This is frequently used for making powders from alloys of low melting-point such as aluminium and zinc. The materials are melted and allowed to fall, through a screen, the height of a shot tower; the metal may be collected under water. Finer particles are produced by atomising, in which, instead of falling freely, the molten metal is dropped in front of a stream of air which blows it along a tunnel in the form of fine particles. This process gives much closer control over particle size than shotting does.

The distinction between physical and chemical methods of powder production is slight. Probably the only purely *physical method* is that of electro-deposition. Unlike in electro-plating, the deposit is deliberately made of a spongy nature so that it can be removed from the anode upon which it is deposited, and then ground to a powder.

A number of metals, particularly iron, nickel, magnesium and zinc, form organic compounds called *carbonyls* which can be broken down to give off a gas containing the carbon and leaving the metal in powder form. These powders are extremely fine and almost perfectly spherical, rarely exceeding 10 μm in diameter. At high temperature and pressure, iron and nickel combine with carbon monoxide gas to form the carbonyl liquid which, at a reduced pressure but still a high temperature, decomposes to give the metal powder and the carbon monoxide, which is retained to produce more carbonyl liquid.

The greatest quantity of metal powder is produced by the *chemical reduction* process. Most metals are used in the form of oxides which are reduced by heating in the presence of carbon monoxide, which combines with the oxygen to form carbon dioxide. Alternatively, hydrogen can be used to combine with the oxygen to form water. Thus the reduction of iron by carbon monoxide may be:

$$Fe_3O_4 + 4CO = 3Fe + 4CO_2$$

(as in a blast furnace) or, by hydrogen:

$$Fe_3O_4 + 4H_2 = 3Fe + 4H_2O$$

The hydrogen reduction is preferred since it tends to leave a purer iron uncontaminated by iron carbide or flake graphite.

To prepare the powder for the next stage of the process, pressing, it must be mixed so that correct quantities of each constituent are present. Further milling may be necessary to give the correct grain-size distribution and during the final mixing a small amount of wax is added to act as a lubricant during pressing. When pressure is exerted in the dies, the powder must 'flow' smoothly, that is, it must move to give complete and even filling of the die, to produce a briquette of even

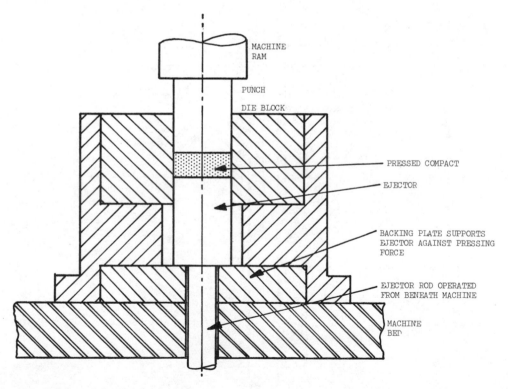

MACHINE RAM

PUNCH

DIE BLOCK

PRESSED COMPACT

EJECTOR

BACKING PLATE SUPPORTS EJECTOR AGAINST PRESSING FORCE

EJECTOR ROD OPERATED FROM BENEATH MACHINE

MACHINE BED

Fig. 10.1 Simple tool for powder pressing.

density. The wax assists this flow and is removed by the first heating stage of the sintering process.

The above by no means exhaust the methods of powder production but they are the most common methods and produce the bulk of the powders used today.

2. PRESSING After the powder has been prepared it is placed in a suitably-shaped die and pressure is applied. Due to this pressure, the final volume of the briquette is about one-third of that of the original powder. In the simplest case the tool consists of a die to form the shape of the part, a lower punch which acts as an ejector, and an upper punch through which the pressure is applied. These details are shown in fig. 10.1.

Fig. 10.2 shows a tool for the production of a plain bearing bush. The die is let into the machine table, with the core pin passing through the lower punch and finishing flush with the top of the die. The upper punch is let into the machine ram and applies the pressure to form the briquette. Operation is automatic. As the top punch is withdrawn, the lower punch rises to eject the briquette, which is then moved aside by the loading shoe as it

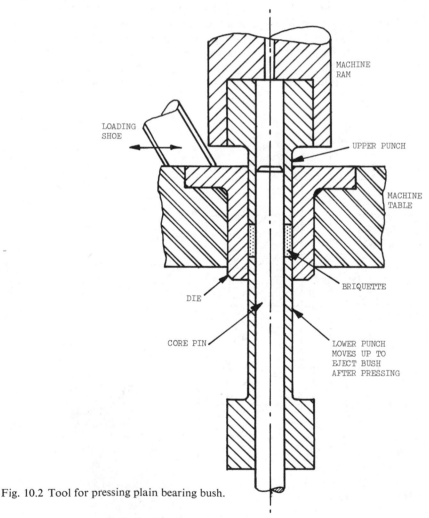

Fig. 10.2 Tool for pressing plain bearing bush.

moves across to load a predetermined amount of powder into the die, and the cycle repeats itself.

It may be of interest that the author once had occasion to replace the bearing bush on the water pump of a 1934 motor car. The bush was a self-lubricating graphited bronze component probably made with tooling of this type—nearly forty years ago.

The pressure used in briquetting is expressed in meganewtons per unit cross-sectional area of the part being pressed, i.e.:

If F = applied force in meganewtons
A = cross-sectional area in square metres,

then pressure $= \dfrac{F}{A}$ meganewtons per square metre.

Magnitudes of pressure range from 140 MN/m² for large parts up to 150 mm diameter, to 350 MN/m² for small parts. Generally, the higher the pressure the stronger the finished part.

Work has been done on hot pressing, that is, applying the required heat at the same time as the pressure. This has shown beneficial results but most work is done at room temperature, due, the author suspects, to the simplicity of the equipment and the manner in which it lends itself to automation. The machine cycle of *load/press/eject/move clear* is fully automatic and the operator simply has to stack the finished parts on a tray ready for the sintering process. For very high speed operation, mechanical presses are used but more often the hydraulic press is favoured. Although it is slower, a more uniform density of compact is produced by it and greater control of the pressure is possible.

3. SINTERING The final stage in the manufacture of parts by powder metallurgy is that of heating the briquettes to bond the particles together so that the finished part becomes a solid piece of material. This bonding process is the actual sintering process but the word *sintering* has, by common usage, become the name by which the whole manufacturing process is known, and the parts produced are often called *sintered products*. The heating or sintering process must avoid any contamination of the product by harmful gas. Various atmospheres are used and the gas adopted has two functions:

(*a*) it must prevent the formation of an oxide film on the work and

(*b*) it must reduce any oxide film which may already be present.

Nitrogen gives protection against the formation of an oxide film but does not reduce any oxides present. Hydrogen both protects against oxide film and reduces any which may be present, but is expensive. A mixture of hydrogen and nitrogen can be used, produced by 'cracking' ammonia into its constituents by passing it over a heated catalyst.

Modern techniques include the use of a vacuum for sintering materials where contamination by any gas would be harmful. The parts are sealed in containers, which are evacuated, and heating is provided either by high-frequency induction or by heating elements. During sintering a small amount of argon gas may be admitted to the chamber to prevent evaporation of the lower melting point material.

Sintering can, in certain circumstances, be a *liquid-phase* process. If the briquette consists of two or more materials which have widely different melting points, the temperature required for the sintering of the material of high melting point will generally cause melting of the material of low melting point, i.e., the latter will be in the liquid phase during the sintering process. This can be of advantage in removing porosity in or increasing the density of a product. It is usually limited to applications where:

(*a*) There is a great difference in the melting points of the constituents and (*b*) the constituent with the lower melting point is present in the smaller proportion.

Typical examples of work produced by liquid-phase sintering are hard metals (cemented carbides), heavy metals, magnets and electrical contacts.

PRODUCTION OF CEMENTED-CARBIDE[1] CUTTING TOOLS

The point has been made that a great many articles other than cutting tools are produced by powder metallurgy but it is still true that the sintered part with which the mechanical engineering technician is most likely to be acquainted is the cemented-carbide tool tip, the manufacturing process of which is as follows:

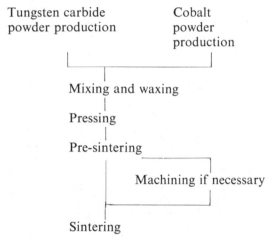

Tungsten is produced by heating tungsten oxide in a reducing atmosphere, the pure metal then being powdered, mixed with powdered carbon and heated to 1 600°C, again in a reducing atmosphere, to form a lump of tungsten carbide. This is crushed and milled to a powder in a ball mill, using tungsten carbide balls, and then mixed in the correct proportions with cobalt powder. Wax is added and the mixture is milled for several days to give thorough mixing and ensure that

[1] The author prefers the name 'cemented-carbide' to 'tungsten-carbide'. Other carbides than tungsten carbide are used, e.g., boron carbide and titanium carbide. Nor is the material ever wholly of tungsten carbide since cobalt is used to 'cement' the particles into a solid block—hence cemented-carbide.

each particle of powder is coated with wax. The material, now ready for pressing, is stored in stainless steel containers in a temperature-controlled room until required.

The tips are pressed in automatic hydraulic machines, the tools being similar to those shown in figs. 10.1 and 10.2. The compact thus produced can be handled but is friable and easily broken. It now passes into a furnace for *pre-sintering*, a low-temperature process which volatizes and removes the wax and renders the material strong enough to be machined but not yet fully hard. The tip is now machined, if necessary, using diamond grinding wheels to produce any features which cannot readily be produced by pressing.

The final sintering is carried out by heating the tips for one hour at 1 500°C in a vacuum. This temperature is just above the melting point of cobalt and the sintering is thus a liquid-phase process, characterised by the large degree of shrinkage which occurs. About 20% reduction in volume takes place and must be allowed for in the design of the die at the pressing stage. The final result is a hard, dense piece of cemented-carbide which can be machined only with great difficulty, a diamond wheel being required, and which cannot be affected by further heat-treatment.

Until a few years ago cemented-carbide tips were normally brazed on to carbon steel shanks but improvements in production methods have enabled solid tips to be made (see Chapter 3) and the author has seen paper cutters consisting of discs about 3 mm thick by 100 mm diameter made from solid blocks of cemented-carbide.

CONTROLLED-ATMOSPHERE FURNACES

This section deals with furnaces used in the sintering process but similar furnaces can be used for other heat-treatment processes. Thus a conveyor type of furnace as shown in fig. 10.4 can, with a different atmosphere, be used for gas carburizing; a bell type of furnace used for vacuum sintering can, if a suitable atmosphere is maintained, be used for nitriding, and so on.

The furnaces dealt with should thus be considered not only as sintering furnaces but also as furnaces usable for general heat-treatment, on a batch or continuous-production basis, where a controlled atmosphere is required.

The basic principle of the controlled-atmosphere furnace is best shown by reference to fig. 10.3 which shows a small tube type of furnace used for experimental and laboratory work. It has a tube of refractory material around which is wound the heating coil. Into a plug at one end are inserted the gas inlet and the thermocouple; at the other end is the port through which workpieces are put into the tube furnace. This port is kept closed but has a small hole from which the gas can escape and, since it is usually inflammable, burn off in air. Note that the furnace must be completely cleared of air before hydrogen is allowed to enter, or an explosion may result. It is therefore first purged with nitrogen, which is then joined by hydrogen to give the controlled atmosphere required. As the gas

mixture leaves the exit port, the hydrogen burns off.

MOVING–HEARTH FURNACES

When a furnace is used for continuous production, either for sintering or heat treatment, it is usually provided with a moving hearth on which the workpieces travel steadily through the furance. They are loaded at one end, pass through a tunnel which is the heated zone and are removed at the other end. Various types of furnace are available, the type of hearth used depending largely upon the temperature required. The types discussed below are:

1. conveyor-hearth furnaces
2. pusher-type furnaces
3. shaker-hearth furnaces.

1. *Conveyor-Hearth Furnaces.* These consist essentially of a tunnel of refractory material with suitable heating arrangements. A short tunnel at each end is provided for entry and exit and the gas inlet is at the work-outlet end. A simple flap is provided at entry and exit to help contain the gas, which burns

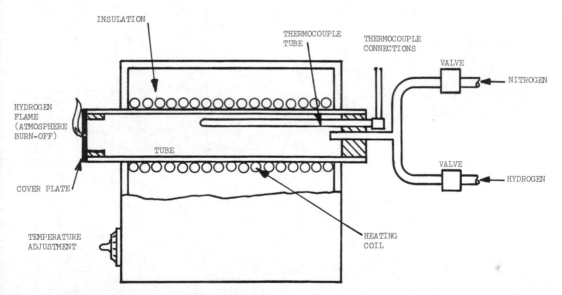

Fig. 10.3 Simple tube-type controlled atmosphere furnace.

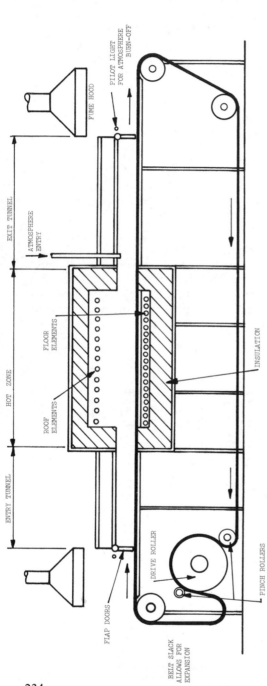

Fig. 10.4 Conveyor hearth-type furnace. (Based on a diagram supplied by Wild-Barfield Ltd.)

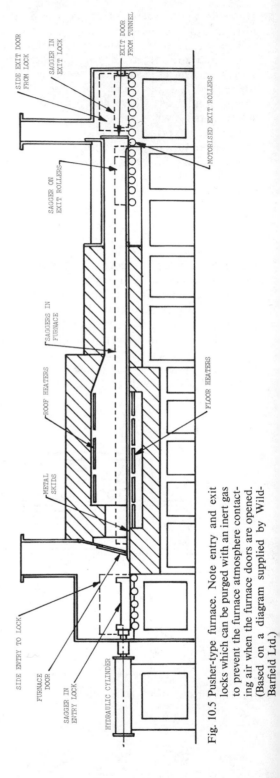

Fig. 10.5 Pusher-type furnace. Note entry and exit locks which can be purged with an inert gas to prevent the furnace atmosphere contacting air when the furnace doors are opened. (Based on a diagram supplied by Wild-Barfield Ltd.)

away when it combines with atmospheric oxygen. Gas extractor hoods are provided at each end as shown in fig. 10.4. The conveyor belt is usually made of expanded metal or woven mesh to provide the required flexibility for its circuit over the drive and other rollers at the ends of the furnace.

Although this type of furnace, with a suitable mesh belt, can operate up to 1 200–1 300°C, it is generally used for lower-temperature work such as pre-sintering tungsten carbide and sintering copper and iron, operations which take place at about 800°C.

2. *Pusher-Hearth Furnaces.* Where much higher temperatures are called for, as in the sintering of cemented oxides and ceramics, the pusher type of furnace is preferred. This again is a tunnel-type furnace but the parts to be heated are placed on refractory boats or saggers which themselves form the hearth of the furnace. These boats or saggers travel on rollers or skids which form the floor of the furnace, and the rollers, being outside the heated zone, can be water-cooled if necessary. The pusher mechanism, which is usually a hydraulic ram, is of course placed well outside the furnace area, as shown in fig. 10.5. The saggers are inserted one at a time, already loaded, and as a new one enters at the entry end a sagger of completed parts emerges at the exit. With suitable heating arrangements these furnaces can operate up to 2 000°C, for firing ceramics, although they can be operated equally well at much lower temperatures.

3. *Shaker-Hearth Furnaces.* The hearths of both the previous furnaces move through the furnace and, in the case of the pusher type the boats or 'saggers' must be returned to the entry end for replacing and reloading. The shaker hearth is permanently in the furnace and simply reciprocates along the line of the furnace, the oscillation being arranged with a slow-speed forward stroke and a rapid return stroke. The parts on the hearth move forward with it but on the rapid return stroke the hearth slides back under the parts. The work therefore progresses slowly through the furnace on a hearth which, apart from its

oscillations, remains in the same place. Note the shape of the serrations in the hearth which help to push the workpieces along.

Shaker-hearth furnaces also lend themselves very well to gas-carburising, since the parts tend to roll about a little and thus present all surfaces to the gas which, in this case, is used not as a protective atmosphere but to create the high-carbon steel surface on the parts.

A diagram of a shaker hearth furnace is shown in fig. 10.6.

SURFACE HARDENING PROCESSES

Many components must have a hard surface to resist wear and a tough core to withstand shock loads. In Book 1 we saw how this condition was produced in plain low-carbon steel by the lengthy carburising and hardening process. Processes are now available whereby the same condition can be produced in a medium-carbon steel, in which all the necessary heat treatment and conditioning of the core is completed before the final hardening. The two processes considered here are *nitriding*, where the surface treatment is carried out at a temperature which has little effect on the core, and *high-frequency induction heating*, where the surface is heated so rapidly that quenching is carried out before the heat can be conducted from the skin into the core.

The type of furnace used for nitriding can also be used for low-temperature sintering processes to give a controlled atmosphere while the high-frequency induction-heating process is used for sintering blocks of material inside a vacuum chamber.

NITRIDING When ammonia is heated to above 520°C, no change occurs, that is, if ammonia is passed through a tube with a zone at this temperature, the same ammonia comes out at the other end. If, however, the tube contains alloy steel parts whose alloying elements include small proportions of chromium and aluminium, the ammonia at the

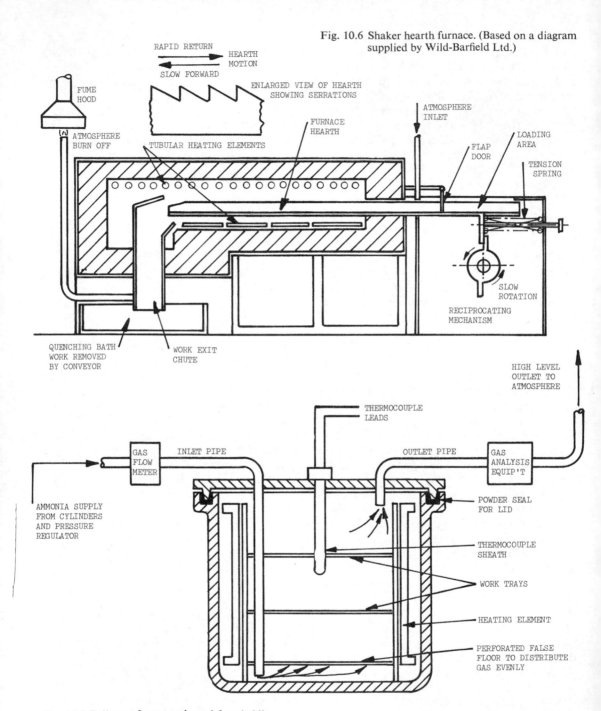

Fig. 10.6 Shaker hearth furnace. (Based on a diagram supplied by Wild-Barfield Ltd.)

RAPID RETURN

HEARTH MOTION

SLOW FORWARD

ENLARGED VIEW OF HEARTH SHOWING SERRATIONS

FUME HOOD

ATMOSPHERE BURN OFF

TUBULAR HEATING ELEMENTS

FURNACE HEARTH

ATMOSPHERE INLET

FLAP DOOR

LOADING AREA

TENSION SPRING

SLOW ROTATION

RECIPROCATING MECHANISM

QUENCHING BATH WORK REMOVED BY CONVEYOR

WORK EXIT CHUTE

HIGH LEVEL OUTLET TO ATMOSPHERE

THERMOCOUPLE LEADS

GAS FLOW METER

INLET PIPE

OUTLET PIPE

GAS ANALYSIS EQUIP'T

AMMONIA SUPPLY FROM CYLINDERS AND PRESSURE REGULATOR

POWDER SEAL FOR LID

THERMOCOUPLE SHEATH

WORK TRAYS

HEATING ELEMENT

PERFORATED FALSE FLOOR TO DISTRIBUTE GAS EVENLY

Fig. 10.7 Bell-type furnace adapted for nitriding.

236

surface of the material dissociates into its constituents, nitrogen and hydrogen, thus:

$$2NH_3 = N_2 + 3H_2$$

However, although nitrogen molecules contain *two* atoms of nitrogen, when the ammonia dissociates the nitrogen is present in its monatomic or nascent form, i.e., as single atoms. In this form the nitrogen atoms can penetrate the space lattice of the atoms of the metal and form extremely hard metallic nitrides. At the same time the hydrogen tends to form a protective atmosphere, so the work surface is only dulled and mottled but not scaled.

The following points should be noted about the process:

1. It takes place *below* the toughening temperature of steel so that all previous heat-treatment can be completed before nitriding.

2. An increase in size of the work occurs of approximately 0·2% or 2 μm/mm. This must be allowed for in manufacture.

3. The hardness decreases with the depth of 'case' and the surface is glass-hard and extremely brittle. This outer layer is usually removed by skimming with a green-grit wheel, removing about 0·01 mm, since it is liable to break up under load and form an extremely abrasive powder. This is par-

ticularly true under conditions of line-contact loads such as occur between a cam and its follower.

4. The depth of penetration of 'useful hardness' is approximately:

> 0·15 to 0·18 mm in 20 hours
> 0·25 to 0·30 mm in 40 hours
> 0·40 to 0·50 mm in 90 hours

It is thus obvious that nitriding is a very lengthy process.

5. The process is not effective with plain-carbon steel. 'Nitralloy' alloy steels are used, a typical material containing 0·4% C, 1·25% Cr and 1% Al.

The rate of flow of the ammonia gas is fairly critical; too high a rate of flow does not allow dissociation of the ammonia and too low a rate allows the nascent ammonia to form into normal molecules of nitrogen before nitriding has occurred. The rate of flow of gas is therefore monitored and a gas analysis apparatus is usually incorporated into the system to check that the ammonia has broken down into its constituents.

A simple nitriding furnace is shown in fig. 10.7. It is of the bell type, ammonia being led down from the cylinder, via a pressure regulator and flow meter to the bottom of the furnace below a perforated false floor which

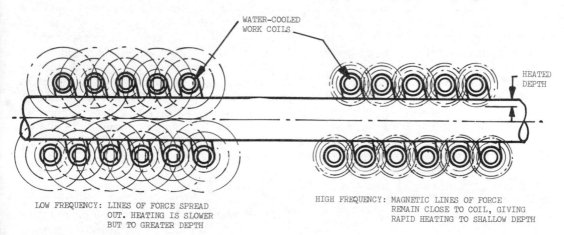

LOW FREQUENCY: LINES OF FORCE SPREAD OUT. HEATING IS SLOWER BUT TO GREATER DEPTH

HIGH FREQUENCY: MAGNETIC LINES OF FORCE REMAIN CLOSE TO COIL, GIVING RAPID HEATING TO SHALLOW DEPTH

Fig. 10.8 Effect of frequency on depth of heating.

Fig. 10.9 Essentials of high frequency induction heating equipment.

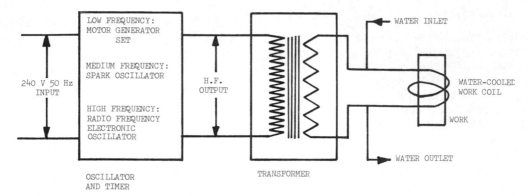

distributes it evenly over the work. The work is supported on mesh trays and the gas flows out through the furnace cover to a simple gas analysis apparatus and away to the atmosphere.

HIGH-FREQUENCY INDUCTION HEATING In Chapter 8 we saw that when an electric current is passed through a conductor the heating effect is given by $H = I^2RT$.

If then a very high current can be produced in a block of metal, such as a compact to be sintered or a piece of work to be heat treated, the desired temperature can be attained. It is in fact possible to do this without touching the component. Consider a coil surrounding a cylindrical piece of metal, the coil carrying an alternating current of high amperage. A magnetic field is set up around the coil, as shown in fig. 10.8, whose lines of force cut the metal core, in this case the workpiece. These magnetic lines of force induce an alternating current of high amperage in the workpiece which has an extremely powerful heating effect. Thus a part to be sintered could be placed in a tube of refractory material with the coil on the outside and rapidly raised to sintering temperature. The essentials of the equipment are shown in fig. 10.9.

This process has applications in heat treatment, and also in soldering and brazing operations. The heating process is so rapid

that it can be used to harden selected parts of a workpiece or alternatively, if alternating current of a radio frequency is used, to harden the surface only of a piece of high-carbon steel. If the a.c. frequency is high, the lines of force are held very close to the coil and do not penetrate far into the work. Thus only the surface layers of the workpiece are heated and hardened on quenching, the core remaining tough. This effect is shown in fig. 10.8.

The author has demonstrated the speed of heating obtainable by holding a piece of steel rod about 10 mm diameter and 300 mm long in his bare hand, with the other end in a powerful heating coil. The hot end dripped molten steel before the other end became warm. It can thus be readily appreciated how only the surface layers reach hardening temperature and can be quenched off before the core of the material is affected by the high temperature. This is another example of carbon steel with a tough core being given a hard surface or case without the lengthy process of carburising.

SUMMARY
Sintered parts, produced by compressing powder to form a briquette and then heating it to make a solid or, if necessary, porous block of material, are used far more widely than is generally assumed for other applica-

tions than the now commonplace cemented-carbide cutting tool. The furnaces used for sintering can be used for other heat-treatment processes which require a controlled atmosphere.

Surface-hardening processes are now available in which only the skin of the material is hardened, the core already being toughened and unaffected by the surface-hardening treatment. Thus the complete heat-treatment can be performed without the lengthy carburising and hardening process used to produce this condition in plain low-carbon steels.

11

Non-Destructive Testing

INTRODUCTION

Many components can be inspected and checked, to ensure that they will perform the function for which they were designed, by simple tests which do not affect the component or its subsequent functioning. A visual inspection or a measurement of the part is an example of such tests. A visual inspection will not, however, reveal microscopic surface defects, or voids and blowholes below the surface of the component which might cause failure under load. Obviously, every part cannot be loaded to destruction to find the load it can carry, nor can every casting be cut open to disclose blowholes, for such tests of necessity destroy the workpiece and render it valueless. Such tests can therefore only be applied to a small sample of the work as a check, the inference being that if the samples are of good quality the rest of the work is similar.

Situations arise where such assumptions are not practicable and it is necessary to test all the workpieces, or maybe a given part is too valuable for even a small sample to be tested to destruction. For such cases, *non-destructive tests* have been devised to reveal both surface and sub-surface defects without in any way damaging the part. It must be realised that such tests give no indication of the strength of the part; they simply reveal defects which, by their presence, reduce the strength and soundness of the part.

Non-destructive tests fall into four categories:

1. Penetrant flaw detection for surface defects
2. Magnetic and electrical methods for surface and sub-surface defects
3. Radiography for deep-seated defects

4. Sonic and ultra-sonic methods.

1. PENETRANT FLAW DETECTION

This method can only be used to disclose flaws such as cracks and porosity which are open to the surface of the specimen. Essentially the method consists of immersing the component to be tested in a liquid of low surface tension which will be absorbed into surface defects by capillary attraction. The excess liquid is then removed and the flaws 'developed' and made visible by drawing out the penetrant liquid by a 'blotting paper' effect.

The penetrant method can be used on both metallic and non-metallic materials, the author having used it to reveal surface defects in electrical insulators. However, care must be taken to ensure that the penetrant does not react chemically with the material being examined.

HOT OIL AND CHALK METHOD

This is the pattern for all penetrant methods of testing. The workpiece is thoroughly cleaned by degreasing and immersed in a bath of hot oil for 5–10 minutes, the oil being absorbed into any surface defects which may be present. The part is removed and placed in a bath of emulsifying liquid to enable the excess oil to be removed by a water rinse, after which the part is dipped in a bath of a suspension of chalk in water or a more volatile liquid.

As the chalk wash dries out, penetrant is drawn out of the voids and discolours the even white film. Large cracks show up as distinct lines on the chalk while a hair-line crack or an area of porosity is revealed as a series of fine dots.

DYE PENETRANT METHOD The lack of contrast obtained with hot oil as a penetrant led to the use of a crimson dye in place of the oil. In other respects the process is similar but the manufacturers' instructions must be followed closely, since different dyes require different solvents.

FLUORESCENT PENETRANT PROCESS The penetrant in this case is an oil-based compound containing a fluorescent dye which glows a vivid green under an ultra-violet lamp. A developer is still normally required and although direct examination will reveal defects a magnifying glass is required if no developer is used. Care must be taken to avoid damage to the eyes through prolonged exposure to ultra-violet rays.

All penetrant methods use fundamentally the same procedure:

(a) Immerse in penetrant
(b) Wash off excess penetrant
(c) Develop with a chalk wash
(d) Scan for defects.

Considerations which are common to all methods of penetrant examination are as follows:

(a) The process is generally static, requiring tanks for immersion, washing and developing. Portable techniques have been developed for large parts, using penetrants and developers which are brushed on or sprayed from aerosol cans.
(b) Many of the penetrants used are toxic or inflammable. Strict safety precautions must be observed and spray techniques must not be carried out in a confined space.

(c) Final cleaning is essential as some penetrants can be extremely corrosive under certain conditions.

Against these limitations, the equipment is very simple and can be applied to both metallic and non-metallic workpieces.

2. MAGNETIC AND ELECTRICAL METHODS

Magnetic flaw detection can only be applied to ferro-magnetic materials. The test is carried out in four stages:

(a) Magnetisation of the workpiece
(b) Application of finely-divided particles of a suitable ferro-magnetic material
(c) Visual examination for defects
(d) De-magnetisation.

If a bar of steel is magnetised the lines of magnetic flux, or force, normally pass straight along the specimen and lie entirely within the

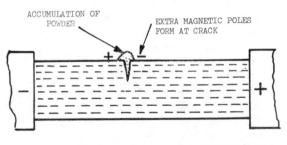

(a) SURFACE DEFECT

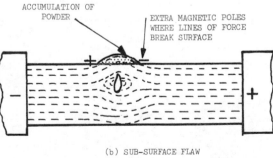

(b) SUB-SURFACE FLAW

Fig. 11.2 Effect of flaws on magnetic lines of force: (a) Surface crack; (b) Sub-surface defect.

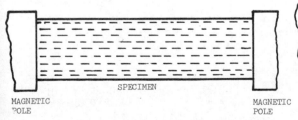

Fig. 11.1 Magnetic lines of force in a sound specimen.

241

metal as shown in fig. 11.1. If, however, there is a flaw in the workpiece a leakage of magnetic flux occurs and free magnetic poles are formed on either side of the crack or discontinuity, as shown in fig. 11.2. Any magnetic material is attracted strongly to the flux-leakage field and accumulates to indicate a crack as a firm line and a larger subsurface crack or discontinuity as a more diffuse band of black magnetic powder.

To have maximum effect, the flaw should lie at right angles to the lines of magnetic flux. The test should therefore be carried out in different planes if magnetisation is induced by an electromagnet. When an electric current is passed along the bar a magnetic field is set up at right angles to the current flow. And since most cracks, discontinuities and inclusions are rolled out along the length of the bar this method is most useful for checking bar stock. It may also be used for testing welds, as shown in fig. 11.3.

Other methods of magnetisation include threading hollow workpieces on a bar carrying the electric current as shown in fig. 11.4 or placing them inside an encircling coil as in fig. 11.5. The method chosen should be such that the lines of magnetic force, which are at right angles to the direction of current flow, are at right angles to any likely flaws. Both methods are, however, often used since flaws in welds can occur in either direction.

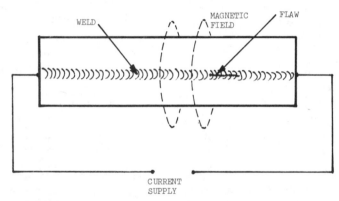

Fig. 11.3 Electric current flow method of magnetic flaw detection.

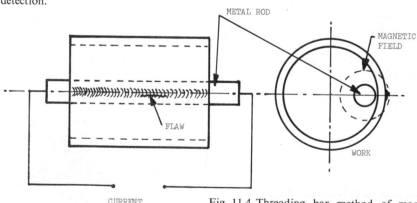

Fig. 11.4 Threading bar method of magnetisation applied to longitudinal seam weld in a tube. Note the position of the bar so that lines of force cut the weld.

242

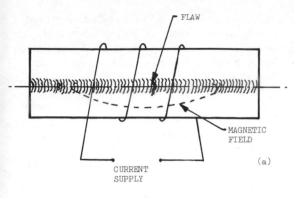

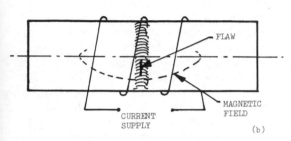

Fig. 11.5 Encircling coil method of magnetisation applied to: (*a*) Seam weld in tube; (*b*) Butt weld.

Direct current or half-wave rectified alternating current is normally used. Alternating current can be used but tends to concentrate the lines of magnetic force near the surface and may not detect deep sub-surface defects.

The finely-divided particles used in magnetic flaw detection can be applied in the dry state but it is more usual to apply them in the form of 'magnetic ink', a suspension of ferro-magnetic powder in paraffin. This may be applied by dip, spray or simply by pouring it over the specimen. The ink used may be red, black or fluorescent, the latter requiring an ultra-violet light source for observing the results.

The workpiece should always be demagnetised after being tested, to prevent the magnetic pick-up of ferrous particles which might cause damage when the workpiece is put to use.

The method is suitable for detecting grinding and fatigue cracks and for the examination of heavy castings, forgings and welds but it is, of course, limited to ferro-magnetic material.

D.C. SEARCH-COIL METHOD This method employs the normal magnetisation methods using direct current as a magnetising current. Instead of powder to detect magnetic flux leakages, a search coil is used in which a voltage is generated by the magnetic flux. Any variation in the flux appears on instruments as a change in voltage. This has the advantages of being a faster and cleaner method, and an autographic recording can be made. It lends itself to the testing of wire ropes and bars, and railway lines can be tested by it from a truck moving above them.

ELECTRICAL-RESISTANCE METHODS Any metal component of uniform dimensions carrying an electric current should exhibit a fixed voltage drop between any two points the same distance apart. The presence of a discontinuity or inclusion affects the potential difference and can thus be detected.

Both alternating current and direct current are used in these tests, alternating current mainly for surface defects and direct current more for sub-surface defects. Materials which lend themselves to such methods of testing are bars of constant cross-section such as bar stock, tubes, railway lines etc.

3. RADIOGRAPHIC FLAW DETECTION

Radiography can be used to detect deep-seated flaws in a variety of materials and employs the use of either X-rays, generated in a suitable tube, or gamma-rays obtained from a radioactive source. The rays are similar in that they both have the following characteristics:

(*a*) They can pass through optically dense material.

(*b*) They travel in straight lines and are not affected by electric or magnetic fields.

(*c*) They affect photographic emulsion.

(d) *They are harmful to the living cells of which our bodies are composed.*

X-RAY RADIOGRAPHY

X-rays are produced by halting the progress of a high-speed stream of electrons, the energy being changed to heat and X-rays. The electrons are directed at a target in a vacuum tube and the resulting X-rays are reflected through a window in the tube on to the component under test.

The part is placed between the X-ray tube and the film. If the part is of the same density throughout, the film will receive a uniform exposure but if there is a void, such as a blow-hole in a casting or a slag inclusion in a weld. the exposure under that area will differ and, when the film is developed, will appear as a sharply-defined dark or light area, depending upon the nature of the defect.

Fig. 11.6 shows the set-up in diagrammatic form.

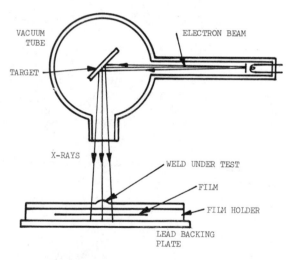

Fig. 11.6 Diagram of set-up for X-ray testing of weld.

GAMMA-RADIOGRAPHY

This method is fundamentally similar to the X-ray method but the source of radiation is a radio-active isotope produced in a nuclear reactor. Sources generally used are cobalt-60, iridium-192 and caesium-137. Small pieces of these materials are supplied in an aluminium capsule held on a telescopic rod which, when not in use, folds down into a lead-lined container. When not in use the container is stored in a lead-lined bunker.

Unlike X-rays, which travel in the direction planned, the source of gamma-rays emits radiation in all directions. It is thus possible to arrange a number of castings around the radioactive material, as shown in fig. 11.7, with the film cassettes behind the castings. The process is much slower than X-ray radiography and, by setting the castings at a suitable distance from the source, overnight exposures can be arranged. As the source is portable and needs no power supplies, it is an extremely useful method for site work, checking welds in pipes, girders and large structures.

The exposure required varies with the age of the source since the radiation intensity falls off with age. The working life of the source is generally taken as its 'half-life', when the radiation intensity has decayed to half its original value, after which the source is returned to the manufacturer for reactivation.

HEALTH HAZARDS

Any prolonged or indiscriminate exposure of human tissue to X- or gamma-rays (and indeed other similar radiations) can give rise to serious burns, blood conditions and genetic problems. It is therefore imperative to ensure adequate protection against these rays.

The Factories Act sets out stringent safety measures, such as lead-lined walls, barium plaster and concrete, lead-glass windows etc. for the construction of X-ray rooms. All control panels must be outside the exposure room and the room should be monitored frequently for stray radiation.

With site work, the area in which work is to be carried out should be clearly marked and roped off, operators in the affected area staying behind lead screens.

Finally, all personnel working in the vicinity of radiographic testing should be

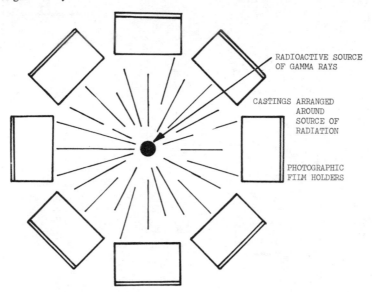

Fig. 11.7 Arrangement for radiographic testing of castings using a radioactive isotope as a source of gamma rays.

RADIOACTIVE SOURCE
OF GAMMA RAYS

CASTINGS ARRANGED
AROUND
SOURCE OF
RADIATION

PHOTOGRAPHIC
FILM HOLDERS

equipped with monitoring devices such as film badges and dosimeters. Regular medical examinations are also recommended.

4. SONIC AND ULTRA-SONIC METHODS OF TESTING

RINGING TESTS The ringing test has become so common in so many walks of life that the phrase 'sound as a bell' has become part of our language. Grinding wheels are tapped to see if they 'ring true' before being mounted, the wagon examiner rings wheels with his hammer on the railways and the shop assistant in the china shop taps cups with a pencil to ensure they are not cracked.

Generally, a sound piece of material will emit a clear ringing sound when struck while a defective piece will not. The test is simple but qualitative and can only be applied in certain instances, although the examples quoted show that the test is not confined to metallic materials.

ULTRA-SONIC TESTING Ultra-sonic

waves are sound waves with frequencies beyond the range audible to the human ear. The waves are produced by a quartz crystal held between the plates of a condenser connected to an a.c. supply. The supply is adjusted until its frequency is the same as the natural frequency of oscillation of the crystal, and the resonance set up produces an oscillation of maximum 'noise' but at too high a frequency to be heard.

These ultra-sonic waves pass readily through metal but not through air. When an ultra-sonic wave is transmitted through a block of metal it is reflected back off the underside and produces an echo which can be detected by a suitable probe. If the transmitted signal and the echo are then compared, the time lag between them is a measure of the thickness of the part. This can be displayed on an oscilloscope screen as shown in fig. 11.8. Note that in order to get the signal into and out of the work a film of thin oil is necessary under the transmitter and receiver probes.

245

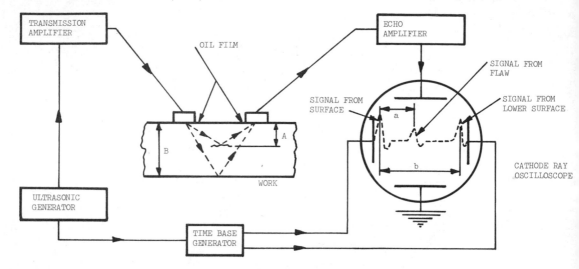

Fig. 11.8 Block diagram of ultra-sonic flaw detection. The depth of the flaw below the surface can be estimated from $A/B = a/b$.

A flaw in the component will also give rise to an echo but, because the distance travelled by this echo is less, the echo signal will appear on the screen between the two signals from the top and bottom surfaces of the work as shown in fig. 11.8.

SUMMARY

Non-destructive testing employs various techniques, ranging from those requiring simple equipment and low capital outlay to the sophisticated X-ray and ultra-sonic machines. Whichever method is used, the interpretation of results is a skilled job and any doubt should err on the side of rejection rather than acceptance, particularly if people's lives depend upon the soundness of the part.

The British Standards Institution has issued certain standards for guidance in the use of these techniques, listed below for reference.

BS 3683: 1963:
Part I: *Penetrant flaw detection methods*
Part II: *Magnetic-particle flaw detection*
Part III: *Radiological flaw detection*
Part IV: *Ultrasonic flaw detection*
Part V: *Eddy-current flaw detection*.

BS 3889 deals with similar techniques specifically applied to pipes and tubes, and BS 3513 with the use of gamma-radiography sealed sources, while BS 4397 deals with methods for magnetic-particle testing of welds.

Like other devices used in engineering, it is particularly true of X-rays and gamma-rays that, handled properly, they are perfectly safe, but if handled foolishly or irresponsibly they can be deadly. The safety regulations must be studied and adhered to.

Appendix 1

Selected ISO Fits—Hole Basis

EXTRACTED FROM BS 4500[1]

Reproduced on pages 248-9

The ISO system provides a great many hole and shaft tolerances so as to cater for a very wide range of conditions. However, experience shows that the majority of fit conditions required for normal engineering products can be provided by a quite limited selection of tolerances.

The following selected hole and shaft tolerances have been found to be commonly applied:

Selected hole tolerances: **H7**; **H8**; **H9**; **H11**
Selected shaft tolerances: **c11**; **d10**; **e9**; **f7**; **g6**; **h6**; **k6**; **n6**; **p6**; **s6**

The table in this data sheet shows a range of fits derived from these selected hole and shaft tolerances. As will be seen, it covers fits from loose clearance to heavy interference and it may therefore be found to be suitable for most normal requirements. Many users may in fact find that their needs are met by a further selection within this selected range.

It should be noted, however, that this table is offered only as an example of how a restricted selection of fits can be made. It is clearly impossible to recommend selections of fits which are appropriate to all sections of industry, but it must be emphasised that a user who decides upon a selected range will always enjoy the economic advantages this conveys. Once he has installed the necessary tooling and gauging facilities, he can combine his selected hole and shaft tolerances in different ways without any additional investment in tools and equipment.

For example, if it is assumed that the range of fits shown in the table has been adopted but that, for a particular application the fit **H8–f7** is appropriate but provides rather too much variation, the hole tolerance **H7** could equally well be associated with the shaft **f7** and may provide exactly what is required without necessitating any additional tooling.

For most general applications it is usual to recommend hole basis fits as, except in the realm of very large sizes where the effects of temperature play a large part, it is usually considered easier to manufacture and measure the male member of a fit and it is thus desirable to be able to allocate the larger part of the tolerance available to the hole and adjust the shaft to suit.

In some circumstances, however, it may in fact be preferable to employ a shaft-basis. For example, in the case of driving shafts where a single shaft may have to accommodate a variety of accessories such as couplings, bearings, collars etc., it is preferable to maintain a constant diameter for the permanent member, which is the shaft, and vary the bore of the accessories. For use in applications of this kind, a selection of shaft basis fits is provided in Data Sheet 4500B.

[1] This extract from BS 4500: 1969: *Limits and Fits for Engineering* is reproduced by permission of the British Standards Institution, 2 Park Street, London W1A 2BS, from whom copies of the complete standard may be obtained.

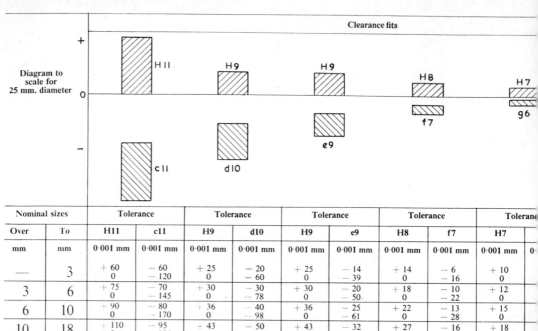

Diagram to scale for 25 mm. diameter

Clearance fits

Nominal sizes		Tolerance		Tolerance		Tolerance		Tolerance		Tolerance	
Over	To	H11	c11	H9	d10	H9	e9	H8	f7	H7	
mm	mm	0·001 mm	0·001 mm	0·001 mm	0·001 mm	0·001 mm	0·001 mm	0·001 mm	0·001 mm	0·001 mm	0·
—	3	+ 60 0	− 60 − 120	+ 25 0	− 20 − 60	+ 25 0	− 14 − 39	+ 14 0	− 6 − 16	+ 10 0	
3	6	+ 75 0	− 70 − 145	+ 30 0	− 30 − 78	+ 30 0	− 20 − 50	+ 18 0	− 10 − 22	+ 12 0	
6	10	+ 90 0	− 80 − 170	+ 36 0	− 40 − 98	+ 36 0	− 25 − 61	+ 22 0	− 13 − 28	+ 15 0	
10	18	+ 110 0	− 95 − 205	+ 43 0	− 50 − 120	+ 43 0	− 32 − 75	+ 27 0	− 16 − 34	+ 18 0	
18	30	+ 130 0	− 110 − 240	+ 52 0	− 65 − 149	+ 52 0	− 40 − 92	+ 33 0	− 20 − 41	+ 21 0	
30	40	+ 160 0	− 120 − 280	+ 62 0	− 80 − 180	+ 62 0	− 50 − 112	+ 39 0	− 25 − 50	+ 25 0	
40	50	+ 160 0	− 130 − 290								
50	65	+ 190 0	− 140 − 330	+ 74 0	− 100 − 220	+ 74 0	− 60 − 134	+ 46 0	− 30 − 60	+ 30 0	
65	80	+ 190 0	− 150 − 340								
80	100	+ 220 0	− 170 − 390	+ 87 0	− 120 − 260	+ 87 0	− 72 − 159	+ 54 0	− 36 − 71	+ 35 0	
100	120	+ 220 0	− 180 − 400								
120	140	+ 250 0	− 200 − 450								
140	160	+ 250 0	− 210 − 460	+ 100 0	− 145 − 305	+ 100 0	− 84 − 185	+ 63 0	− 43 − 83	+ 40 0	
160	180	+ 250 0	− 230 − 480								
180	200	+ 290 0	− 240 − 530								
200	225	+ 290 0	− 260 − 550	+ 115 0	− 170 − 355	+ 115 0	− 100 − 215	+ 72 0	− 50 − 96	+ 46 0	
225	250	+ 290 0	− 280 − 570								
250	280	+ 320 0	− 300 − 620	+ 130 0	− 190 − 400	+ 130 0	− 110 − 240	+ 81 0	− 56 − 108	+ 52 0	
280	315	+ 320 0	− 330 − 650								
315	355	+ 360 0	− 360 − 720	+ 140 0	− 210 − 440	+ 140 0	− 125 − 265	+ 89 0	− 62 − 119	+ 57 0	
355	400	+ 360 0	− 400 − 760								
400	450	+ 400 0	− 440 − 840	+ 155 0	− 230 − 480	+ 155 0	− 135 − 290	+ 97 0	68 − 131	+ 63 0	
450	500	+ 400 0	− 480 − 880								

DATA SHEET

	Transition fits				Interference fits			
H7/h6	H7	k6	H7	n6	H7	p6	H7	s6	Holes / Shafts

Tolerance h6	Tolerance H7	k6	Tolerance H7	n6	Tolerance H7	p6	Tolerance H7	s6	Over	To
0·001 mm	0·001 mm	0·001 mm	0·001 mm	0·001 mm	0·001 mm	0·001 mm	0·001 mm	0·001 mm	mm	mm
−6 / 0	+10 / 0	+6 / +0	+10 / 0	+10 / +4	+10 / 0	+12 / +6	+10 / 0	+20 / +14	—	3
−8 / 0	+12 / 0	+9 / +1	+12 / 0	+16 / +8	+12 / 0	+20 / +12	+12 / 0	+27 / +19	3	6
−9 / 0	+15 / 0	+10 / +1	+15 / 0	+19 / +10	+15 / 0	+24 / +15	+15 / 0	+32 / +23	6	10
−11 / 0	+18 / 0	+12 / +1	+18 / 0	+23 / +12	+18 / 0	+29 / +18	+18 / 0	+39 / +28	10	18
−13 / 0	+21 / 0	+15 / +2	+21 / 0	+28 / +15	+21 / 0	+35 / +22	+21 / 0	+48 / +35	18	30
−16 / 0	+25 / 0	+18 / +2	+25 / 0	+33 / +17	+25 / 0	+42 / +26	+25 / 0	+59 / +43	30	40
−16 / 0	+25 / 0	+18 / +2	+25 / 0	+33 / +17	+25 / 0	+42 / +26	+25 / 0	+59 / +43	40	50
−19 / 0	+30 / 0	+21 / +2	+30 / 0	+39 / +20	+30 / 0	+51 / +32	+30 / 0	+72 / +53	50	65
−19 / 0	+30 / 0	+21 / +2	+30 / 0	+39 / +20	+30 / 0	+51 / +32	+30 / 0	+78 / +59	65	80
−22 / 0	+35 / 0	+25 / +3	+35 / 0	+45 / +23	+35 / 0	+59 / +37	+35 / 0	+93 / +71	80	100
−22 / 0	+35 / 0	+25 / +3	+35 / 0	+45 / +23	+35 / 0	+59 / +37	+35 / 0	+101 / +79	100	120
−25 / 0	+40 / 0	+28 / +3	+40 / 0	+52 / +27	+40 / 0	+68 / +43	+40 / 0	+117 / +92	120	140
−25 / 0	+40 / 0	+28 / +3	+40 / 0	+52 / +27	+40 / 0	+68 / +43	+40 / 0	+125 / +100	140	160
−25 / 0	+40 / 0	+28 / +3	+40 / 0	+52 / +27	+40 / 0	+68 / +43	+40 / 0	+133 / +108	160	180
−29 / 0	+46 / 0	+33 / +4	+46 / 0	+60 / +31	+46 / 0	+79 / +50	+46 / 0	+151 / +122	180	200
−29 / 0	+46 / 0	+33 / +4	+46 / 0	+60 / +31	+46 / 0	+79 / +50	+46 / 0	+159 / +130	200	225
−29 / 0	+46 / 0	+33 / +4	+46 / 0	+60 / +31	+46 / 0	+79 / +50	+46 / 0	+169 / +140	225	250
−32 / 0	+52 / 0	+36 / +4	+52 / 0	+66 / +34	+52 / 0	+88 / +56	+52 / 0	+190 / +158	250	280
−32 / 0	+52 / 0	+36 / +4	+52 / 0	+66 / +34	+52 / 0	+88 / +56	+52 / 0	+202 / +170	280	315
−36 / 0	+57 / 0	+40 / +4	+57 / 0	+73 / +37	+57 / 0	+98 / +62	+57 / 0	+226 / +190	315	355
−36 / 0	+57 / 0	+40 / +4	+57 / 0	+73 / +37	+57 / 0	+98 / +62	+57 / 0	+244 / +208	355	400
−40 / 0	+63 / 0	+45 / +5	+63 / 0	+80 / +40	+63 / 0	+108 / +68	+63 / 0	+272 / +232	400	450
−40 / 0	+63 / 0	+45 / +5	+63 / 0	+80 / +40	+63 / 0	+108 / +68	+63 / 0	+292 / +252	450	500

B.S. 4500 A

Appendix 2

Selected ISO Fits—Shaft Basis

EXTRACTED FROM BS 4500[1]

Reproduced on pages 252–3

The ISO System provides a great many hole and shaft tolerances so as to cater for a very wide range of conditions. However, experience shows that the majority of fit conditions required for normal engineering products can be provided by a quite limited selection of tolerances.

The following selected hole and shaft tolerances have been found to be commonly applied:

Selected hole tolerances: **H7; H8; H9; H11**

Selected shaft tolerances: **c11; d10; e9; f7; g6; h6; k6; n6; p6; s6**

For most general applications it is usual to recommend hole basis fits, i.e., fits in which the design size for the hole is the basic size and variations in the grade of fit for any particular hole are obtained by varying the clearance and the tolerance on the shaft. Data Sheet 4500A gives a range of hole basis fits derived from the selected hole and shaft tolerances above.

In some circumstances, however, it may in fact be preferable to employ a shaft basis. For example, in the case of driving shafts where a single shaft may have to accommodate a variety of accessories such as couplings, bearings, collars etc., it is preferable to maintain a constant diameter for the permanent member, which is the shaft, and vary the bore of the accessories. Shaft basis fits also provide

[1] This extract from BS 4500: 1969: *Limits and Fits for Engineering* is reproduced by permission of the British Standards Institution, 2 Park Street, London W1A 2BS from whom copies of the complete standard may be obtained.

a useful economy where bar stock material is available to standard shaft tolerances of the ISO System.

For the benefit of those wishing to use shaft basis fits, this Data Sheet shows the shaft basis equivalents of the hole basis fits in Data Sheet 4500A. They are all direct conversions except that the fit **H9–d10**, instead of being converted to **D9–h10**, is adjusted to **D10–h9** to avoid introducing the additional shaft tolerance **h10**.

As will be seen, the table covers fits from loose clearance to heavy interference and may therefore be found suitable for most normal requirements. Many users may in fact find that their needs are met by a further selection within this selected range.

It should be noted, however, that this Table is offered only as an example of how a restricted selection of fits can be made. It is clearly impossible to recommend selections of fits which are appropriate to all sections of industry, but it must be emphasised that a user who decides upon a selected range will always enjoy the economic advantages this conveys. Once he has installed the necessary tooling and gauging facilities, he can combine his selected hole and shaft tolerances in different ways without any additional investment in tools and equipment.

For example, if it is assumed that the range of fits shown in the table has been adopted but that, for a particular application the fit **h7–F8** is appropriate but provides rather too much variation, the shaft tolerance **h6** could equally well be associated with the hole **F8** and may provide exactly what is required without necessitating any additional tooling.

Clearance fits

Diagram to scale for 25 mm diameter

Nominal sizes		Tolerance		Tolerance		Tolerance		Tolerance		Tolerance	
Over	To	h11	C11	h9	D10	h9	E9	h7	F8	h6	C
mm	mm	0·001 mm	0·001 mm	0·001 mm	0·001 mm	0·001 mm	0·001 mm	0·001 mm	0·001 mm	0·001 mm	0·00
—	3	0 / − 60	+ 120 / + 60	0 / − 25	+ 60 / + 20	0 / − 25	+ 39 / + 14	0 / − 10	+ 20 / + 6	0 / − 6	+
3	6	0 / − 75	+ 145 / + 70	0 / − 30	+ 78 / + 30	0 / − 30	+ 50 / + 20	0 / − 12	+ 28 / + 10	0 / − 8	+
6	10	0 / − 90	+ 170 / + 80	0 / − 36	+ 98 / + 40	0 / − 36	+ 61 / + 25	0 / − 15	+ 35 / + 13	0 / − 9	+
10	18	0 / − 110	+ 205 / + 95	0 / − 43	+ 120 / + 50	0 / − 43	+ 75 / + 32	0 / − 18	+ 43 / + 16	0 / − 11	+
18	30	0 / − 130	+ 240 / + 110	0 / − 52	+ 149 / + 65	0 / − 52	+ 92 / + 40	0 / − 21	+ 53 / + 20	0 / − 13	+
30	40	0 / − 160	+ 280 / + 120	0 / − 62	+ 180 / + 80	0 / − 62	+ 112 / + 50	0 / − 25	+ 64 / + 25	0 / − 16	+
40	50	0 / − 160	+ 290 / + 130								+
50	65	0 / − 190	+ 330 / + 140	0 / − 74	+ 220 / + 100	0 / − 74	+ 134 / + 60	0 / − 30	+ 76 / + 30	0 / − 19	+
65	80	0 / − 190	+ 340 / + 150								
80	100	0 / − 220	+ 390 / + 170	0 / − 87	+ 260 / + 120	0 / − 87	+ 159 / + 72	0 / − 35	+ 90 / + 36	0 / − 22	+
100	120	0 / − 220	+ 400 / + 180								+
120	140	0 / − 250	+ 450 / + 200	0 / − 100	+ 305 / + 145	0 / − 100	+ 185 / + 85	0 / − 40	+ 106 / + 43	0 / − 25	+
140	160	0 / − 250	+ 460 / + 210								+
160	180	0 / − 250	+ 480 / + 230								
180	200	0 / − 290	+ 530 / + 240	0 / − 115	+ 355 / + 170	0 / − 115	+ 215 / + 100	0 / − 46	+ 122 / + 50	0 / − 29	+
200	225	0 / − 290	+ 550 / + 260								
225	250	0 / − 290	+ 570 / + 280								
250	280	0 / − 320	+ 620 / + 300	0 / − 130	+ 400 / + 190	0 / − 130	+ 240 / + 110	0 / − 52	+ 137 / + 56	0 / − 32	+
280	315	0 / − 320	+ 650 / + 330								+
315	355	0 / − 360	+ 720 / + 360	0 / − 140	+ 440 / + 210	0 / − 140	+ 265 / + 125	0 / − 57	+ 151 / + 62	0 / − 36	+
355	400	0 / − 360	+ 760 / + 400								+
400	450	0 / − 400	+ 840 / + 440	0 / − 155	+ 480 / + 230	0 / − 155	+ 290 / + 135	0 / − 63	+ 165 / + 68	0 / − 40	+
450	500	0 / − 400	+ 880 / + 480								+

DATA SHEET

Diagram legend: Transition fits (H7/h6, K7/h6, N7/h6) and Interference fits (P7/h6, S7/h6). Holes and Shafts.

Tolerance H7	Tolerance		Tolerance		Tolerance		Tolerance		Nominal sizes	
H7	h6	K7	h6	N7	h6	P7	h6	S7	Over	To
0·001 mm	0·001 mm	0·001 mm	0·001 mm	0·001 mm	0·001 mm	0·001 mm	0·001 mm	0·001 mm	mm	mm
+ 10 / 0	0 / − 6	0 / − 10	0 / − 6	− 4 / − 14	0 / − 6	− 6 / − 16	0 / − 6	− 14 / − 24	—	3
+ 12 / 0	0 / − 8	+ 3 / − 9	0 / − 8	− 4 / − 16	0 / − 8	− 8 / − 20	0 / − 8	− 15 / − 27	3	6
+ 15 / 0	0 / − 9	+ 5 / − 10	0 / − 9	− 4 / − 19	0 / − 9	− 9 / − 24	0 / − 9	− 17 / − 32	6	10
+ 18 / 0	0 / − 11	+ 6 / − 12	0 / − 11	− 5 / − 23	0 / − 11	− 11 / − 29	0 / − 11	− 21 / − 39	10	18
+ 21 / 0	0 / − 13	+ 6 / − 15	0 / − 13	− 7 / − 28	0 / − 13	− 14 / − 35	0 / − 13	− 27 / − 48	18	30
+ 25 / 0	0 / − 16	+ 7 / − 18	0 / − 16	− 8 / − 33	0 / − 16	− 17 / − 42	0 / − 16	− 34 / − 59	30	40
									40	50
+ 30 / 0	0 / − 19	+ 9 / − 21	0 / − 19	− 9 / − 39	0 / − 19	− 21 / − 51	0 / − 19	− 42 / − 72	50	65
							0 / − 19	− 48 / − 78	65	80
+ 35 / 0	0 / − 22	+ 10 / − 25	0 / − 22	− 10 / − 45	0 / − 22	− 24 / − 59	0 / − 22	− 58 / − 93	80	100
							0 / − 22	− 66 / − 101	100	120
+ 40 / 0	0 / − 25	+ 12 / − 28	0 / − 25	− 12 / − 52	0 / − 25	− 28 / − 68	0 / − 25	− 77 / − 117	120	140
							0 / − 25	− 85 / − 125	140	160
							0 / − 25	− 93 / − 133	160	180
+ 46 / 0	0 / − 29	+ 13 / − 33	0 / − 29	− 14 / − 60	0 / − 29	− 33 / − 79	0 / − 29	− 105 / − 151	180	200
							0 / − 29	− 113 / − 159	200	225
							0 / − 29	− 123 / − 169	225	250
+ 52 / 0	0 / − 32	+ 16 / − 36	0 / − 32	− 14 / − 66	0 / − 32	− 36 / − 88	0 / − 32	− 138 / − 190	250	280
							0 / − 32	− 150 / − 202	280	315
+ 57 / 0	0 / − 36	+ 17 / − 40	0 / − 36	− 16 / − 73	0 / − 36	− 41 / − 98	0 / − 36	− 169 / − 226	315	355
							0 / − 36	− 187 / − 244	355	400
+ 63 / 0	0 / − 40	+ 18 / − 45	0 / − 40	− 17 / − 80	0 / − 40	− 45 / − 108	0 / − 40	− 209 / − 272	400	450
							0 / − 40	− 229 / − 292	450	500

B.S. 4500 B

253

Appendix 3

Past Examination Papers

The following examination papers from the Mechanical Engineering Technicians' Course (no. 293), Part II, in the subject Workshop Technology (General), are reproduced by kind permission of the City & Guilds of London Institute. They have been converted to approximate SI equivalents by the author; the C.G.L.I. is not responsible for this conversion.

In each case:

1. Three hours are allowed to complete the paper.
2. All questions carry equal marks.
3. *Five* out of the nine questions should be answered.
4. Answers should be illustrated with pencil sketches wherever possible.
5. Candidates should have:
   an answer book which includes squared paper
   mathematical tables
   drawing instruments
   Data Sheet of limits and fits, extracted from BS 4500 (where appropriate).

JUNE 1967

1. (*a*) Explain briefly *each* of the following terms showing its importance in the measurement of surface texture:
   (i) lay,
   (ii) centre-line average (CLA),
   (iii) sampling length,
   (iv) primary texture.
   (*b*) Explain how an assessment of surface finish to British Standard numerals can be made using simple *comparison* standards. Give details of typical standards and their method of use.

2. (*a*) Using simple line diagrams, show the sequence of operations involved in investment moulding.
   (*b*) Investment moulding is said to have made possible the production in quantity of components otherwise impossible to manufacture. Give an example to justify and explain this claim.
   (*c*) Name *three* important limitations of investment moulding compared with alternative methods of casting.

3. (*a*) Using a diagram representing a twist drill in action, show which forces must be measured in order to investigate its performance.
   (*b*) Explain the principle of operation of any typical drill force dynamometer.
   (*c*) If a correctly sharpened twist drill were tested on a dynamometer at intervals between being new and reaching its scrap length, what changes will be found in the cutting forces and why?

4. (*a*) Explain briefly the method of use for each of the *two* main radiation sources available for radiographic testing.
   (*b*) Show that the *two* sources lend themselves to quite different types of application.
   (*c*) What is the main safety hazard arising from radiographic testing and how is it minimised?
   (*d*) Explain why the interpretation of radiographs requires great care in order to be dependable.

5. (*a*) Explain the main differences in construction, operation and application between the electrode type and the

heated pot type salt bath furnaces.

(b) Briefly describe the type of temperature measuring device and method of temperature control usually adopted for each of the above types of furnaces and explain why they are chosen.

6. (a) Make a neat sketch of the main casting only of a typical lathe tailstock, giving the centre-height dimension and indicating the machining required.

(b) Lay out an operation sequence for the complete machining of the casting indicating the type and capacity of each machine used

(c) Explain briefly what further fitting and checking would be required after complete machining in order to obtain satisfactory operation.

7. (a) Explain the 'fiducial' principle employed in the measuring system of certain measuring instruments and jig borers and say why this principle is adopted.

(b) Give details, diagrammatically, of the measuring system of any measuring machine or jig borer which incorporates a fiducial indicator. Explain the type of

ALL DIMENSIONS IN mm UNLESS OTHERWISE STATED

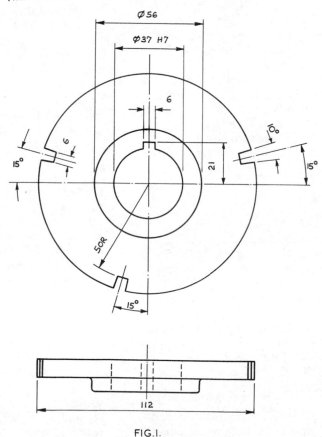

FIG.I.

This diagram refers to Question 9.

instrument used for the indicator and outline a typical measuring operation.

8. (a) Explain what is meant by 'area of contact' between grinding wheel and work by reference to *two* different types of surface grinding machine. What effect do the conditions of contact have upon the selection of grinding wheels?
(b) Show by simple line diagrams the general arrangement of a typical vertical spindle grinding machine explaining:
  (i) what is a segmental wheel,
  (ii) a typical type of work and work-holding arrangement,
  (iii) *two* main safety hazards and the precautions to be taken.

9. *Fig. 1* shows details of a flange. Slots are to be cut in its periphery in accurate relationship to the existing keyway.
Explain how the slots could be machined on a milling machine equipped with a dividing head, indicating:
  (i) the indexing operation required,
  (ii) the type of cutter to be used,
  (iii) how the initial setting of the cutter in relation to the work is obtained.

JUNE 1968

1. (a) Make a simple line diagram showing the light path and essential elements of the optical system of any typical optical projector suitable for inspecting profiles. Indicate the plane of the object and of the image.
(b) Explain why it is not possible to project thick profile gauges satisfactorily.
(c) Explain the conditions for projecting the profile of a standard vee thread satisfactorily.

2. (a) Explain the difference between spot-welding and projection welding referring to:
  (i) the basic principles of each process

  (ii) the workpiece preparation
  (iii) a typical application in each case.
(b) What general effect does increasing carbon content have on the weldability of plain carbon steels?
(c) Briefly explain the action of an ordinary oxy-acetylene cutting flame and show why it is normally limited to cutting plain steels.

3. Six holes, each 25 mm diameter, are to be accurately positioned and bored on a 200 mm pitch circle diameter in a circular plate 250 mm diameter and 25 mm thick.
(a) Select one of the following positioning methods for this job:
  (i) a precision rotary table
  (ii) the rectilinear settings of a compound table.
Give *three* reasons for your choice.
(b) For the method selected, and using sketches, explain briefly:
  (i) how to set, clamp and position the plate for the first hole,
  (ii) how the plate should be dimensioned to suit the process being used.

4. Explain briefly, with the aid of diagrams, the equipment, technique and principle of operation involved in the detection by non-destructive methods of:
(a) surface cracks due to grinding in a ferrous component
(b) internal flaws in a steel forging
(c) cracks reaching the surface in a small cast iron component.

5. Give details of any workshop experiment or investigation carried out during the course in connection with *one* of the following:
(a) grinding machine performance
(b) milling cutter grinding
(c) lathe work.
The account should set out:
  (i) the object of the investigation

(ii) the setting and operating procedure
(iii) the observations made
(iv) the interpretation of the results.

SELECTOR RING

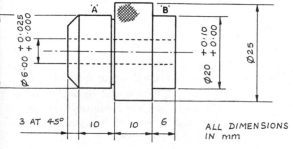

3 AT 45° | 10 | 10 | 6

ALL DIMENSIONS IN mm

CONCENTRICITY OF DIAMETERS A AND B IS ESSENTIAL

MATERIAL EN IA 25 DIAMETER STOCK SIZE

6. The component shown above is to be produced on a capstan lathe and about 800 are required.
(a) Give a suitable sequence of operations.
(b) Show diagrammatically a suitable tooling layout.
(c) Explain what is meant by the synthetic production time and why it is obtained.

7. (a) Explain the basic principle of a typical pneumatic measuring instrument. Use for illustration an enclosed box having an inlet, a variable outlet, and a pressure measuring device as the elements involved.
(b) By referring to typical instruments show briefly how a pneumatic instrument can be used:
(i) as a comparator
(ii) for either internal or external limit gauging.

8. (a) List (i) the equipment and (ii) the instruments required for carrying out a normal range of alignment tests on a centre lathe.

Give an indication of the order of accuracy required for (i) and the accuracy of reading to be expected in (ii) in *each* case.
(b) Show, diagrammatically, the arrangements for *two* major alignment tests on a centre lathe indicating clearly:
(i) which element of geometry is being checked
(ii) what movements are involved
(iii) what readings are taken
(iv) the normally acceptable error
(v) the effect of the error on the performance of the machine.

9. (a) Explain briefly the difference in chip formation in negative rake milling as compared with conventional positive rake cutting and say how this affects cutting speed, power consumption, and finish.
(b) With the aid of a diagram, give details of a typical negative rake milling cutter and a common application.

DECEMBER 1968

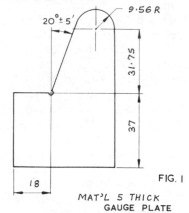

20° ± 5′   9·56 R

31·75

37

18

FIG. I

MAT'L 5 THICK
GAUGE PLATE

ALL DIMENSIONS ARE IN mm EXCEPT WHERE OTHERWISE STATED

GENERAL TOLERANCES :
DECIMAL DIMENSIONS ± 0·01 mm
OTHER DIMENSIONS ± 0·5 mm

257

1. *Fig. 1* shows the leading dimensions of a plate gauge which has been finished all over by precision grinding.

By means of sketches and brief notes, outline a procedure for carrying out an inspection of the gauge.

Assume that a well-equipped standards room is at your disposal.

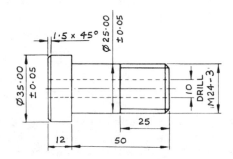

2. The component shown above is to be produced in batches of 100 from bright mild steel bar of 40 mm diameter.

Draw up an operation layout, make a simple tooling diagram and estimate the cycle time per component.

Assume that high-speed steel cutting tools are to be used and allow 20% for all contingencies.

The available speeds and feeds are:
Speeds:
rev/min 1 531 834 453 241 131 71 46
Feeds:
mm/rev 0·15 0·22 0·30

3. (*a*) Name THREE essential qualities required in instruments used to measure small linear displacements.
   (*b*) By means of a simple line diagram and brief notes, explain the principles of a pneumatic comparator.
   (*c*) What type of comparator would you recommend to measure:
   (i) the bore
   (ii) the outside diameter of hardened steel bushes 40 mm ±0·005 outside diameter, 22 mm ±0·005 inside diameter and 40 mm long?

Give reasons for your answer.

4. (*a*) Explain the relative advantages and disadvantages of oxy-acetylene and electric arc welding for joining mild steel plates ranging in thickness from 1 mm to 6 mm.
   (*b*) Describe the procedure and sketch the equipment required for making a U-bend test on a single-vee butt-welded joint in 25 mm by 6 mm bar.

5. (*a*) Describe, with the aid of sketches or line diagrams, how the following alignment tests should be performed:
   (i) for parallelism between the centre Tee-slot and the longitudinal traverse on a horizontal milling machine table
   (ii) for squareness of the feed movement with the table surface of a vertical spindle drill.
   (*b*) If each of the above tests indicated that the machine required adjustment, show by means of sketches and brief notes the effect of the alignment error on the workpieces produced.

6. A milling cutter 100 mm outside diameter, 6 mm wide, and 30 mm diameter bore has 20 teeth.
   (*a*) Make a sketch of the cutter and an enlarged sketch to show the shape of one tooth.
   (*b*) List the operational sequence for the production of one cutter, stating clearly the type of machine upon which each operation is performed.
   (The raw material is normalised high speed steel 105 mm diameter and 9 mm thick.)

7. (*a*) Describe briefly the structure of a grinding wheel and state the functions of each element.
   (*b*) On what basis are grinding wheels classified as hard or soft?
   (*c*) Describe the operations of truing and

258

balancing a grinding wheel. Why are both operations necessary for the production of well finished workpieces?

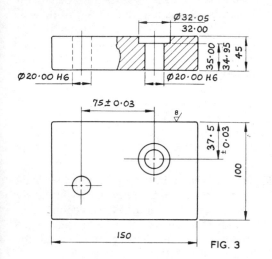

FIG. 3

8. Describe how the component shown in *Fig. 3* can be set up and the counterbored hole produced on a jig boring machine.

Assume that the component is fully machined except for the counterbored hole and that the jig boring machine has a full range of accessories.

9. *Fig. 4* shows part of one face of a cast iron gearbox. The casting is received with a cored hole of 120 mm diameter.
(*a*) Explain how the hole of 150 mm diameter may be machined.
(*b*) Sketch a tool and toolholder suitable

for producing the chamfer of 10 mm × 45°.
(*c*) Explain the procedure for drilling and tapping the six holes of 20 mm diameter, giving details of any special equipment required.

JUNE 1969

1. (*a*) Explain what is meant by shielded arc welding, referring to any typical modern equipment. Give an example of the kind of work on which it can be most usefully employed.
(*b*) The welding of steel over about 6 mm in thickness is now more commonly carried out by electric arc welding than by gas welding. Give **three** significant reasons for this preference.

2. (*a*) What are the main features of the BS system for the marking of grinding wheels and why is such a marking system necessary?
(*b*) For any **two** of the following types of work outline the main factors affecting the grade of grinding wheel and indicate a suitable choice.
(i) Sharpening of milling cutters
(ii) rough facing of cast iron articles
(iii) cutting-off operations on steel bar
(iv) cylindrical grinding of plug gauges.

3. (*a*) Give an example of any form of chip breaker commonly used on single point

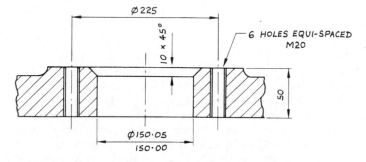

FIG. 4

cemented carbide tools. Explain the action of the chip breaker and how it helps to reduce machining problems.

(b) Explain why it is necessary to maintain a very high quality cutting edge on cemented carbide tools and the method by which such edges are maintained.

4. (a) Explain how Grade II slip gauges may be checked for accuracy using a Grade 00 set, a precision comparator and an optical flat.

(b) Indicate
  (i) the comparative accuracy of Grade II and Grade 00 slip gauges
  (ii) the order of accuracy to which the comparator should indicate
  (iii) the precautions necessary during checking in order to secure dependable results
  (iv) the kind of errors to be expected in Grade II slip gauges after considerable use.

5. Using a sketch of the set-up required, explain the procedure for resharpening one of the following types of milling cutter, showing clearly how the correct cutting angles are obtained
(a) a helical slab mill
(b) a face-milling cutter.

6. (a) Explain the significance of the term 'black body conditions' as applied to the use of optical pyrometers.

(b) Explain why thermo-electric pyrometers generally require re-calibrating after a period of service and outline any procedure by which either checking or re-calibration may be carried out.

7. Assuming you have been appointed to be in charge of a machine shop, give a list of **eight** measures in relation to layout, services, equipment and/or general shop conditions which you would insist upon in the interests of safety. Reasons should be

added where necessary to make the measures clear.

8. Using sketches or diagrams, indicate the general arrangement and set-up of **three** of the following items of capstan tooling equipment. Show the kind of work feature each would produce and what settings are required.
  (i) Knee tools
  (ii) roller steady box
  (iii) recessing tool
  (iv) a floating holder
  (v) a knurling head.

9. Outline the conduct of any experiment designed to investigate properties of a welded article or joint. The account must include the purpose of the experiment, the set-up used, the readings taken and the information obtained from them.

JUNE 1970

1. (a) Explain briefly the principle of the optical lever as applied to a comparator, or to any other measuring instrument.

(b) Give an outline diagram showing the essential features of any practical optical comparator.

(c) Outline the procedure for setting the comparator to make a given measurement.

(d) Give **two** of the main sources of temperature error in the use of the comparator for production purposes. How serious are such errors and how can they be minimised?

2. (a) One of the limitations of the use of powder metallurgy for metal forming is that a powder will not flow as easily as a liquid. Explain **two** ways in which this factor may restrict the application of the process.

(b) Two developments made possible by

powdered-metal forming are maintenance-free and throw-away components. Give an example of a typical component in each case and explain the reasons for the use of the technique.

(c) Give and explain **two** of the main factors which determine the surface quality of a powdered-metal component.

3. (a) State **three** of the main causes of distortion in heat-treated parts. Explain briefly in each case how the difficulty can be minimised.

(b) Explain briefly what is meant by *stress-relieving* and how this can be accomplished by heat treatment.

(c) Explain clearly the difference between stress-relieving and tempering.

4. (a) Since the honing of holes is an additional operation following turning or boring, give **three** reasons justifying the additional cost involved.

(b) Sketch a typical surface profile for a turned surface. Explain what happens

to the profile as a result of honing.

(c) Using diagrams, show the main features of a hone suitable for a hole of diameter 40 mm.

(d) Explain briefly how the hone operates so as to produce straightness and roundness in the hole.

5. The chain link conveyor sprocket shown in *Fig. 1* is supplied as a good quality cast iron casting. In this form, the bore and the grooves G need to be machined. Outline any suitable method for machining the grooves G, indicating

(a) the type of machine and cutting tools to be used

(b) how the sprocket would be held and positioned

(c) how the correct size and position of the grooves would be ensured.

6. (a) *Fig. 1* shows a chain link conveyor sprocket, at present produced as a cast iron casting. Using diagrams, explain how this sprocket could be fabricated with the aid of welding and flame-

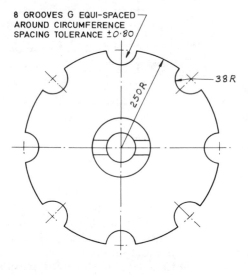

8 GROOVES G EQUI-SPACED
AROUND CIRCUMFERENCE
SPACING TOLERANCE ±0·80

250R

38R

FIG. 1   CONVEYOR SPROCKET

MATL. CAST IRON

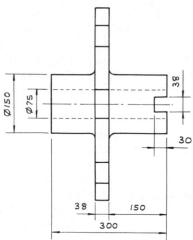

Ø150
Ø75
38
30
38
150
300

DIMENSIONS IN mm

cutting processes, indicating clearly
  (i) the processes that would be used
  (ii) the extent of the flame cutting
  (iii) where the welds would be placed.
(b) State which welding process should be used, giving reasons for the choice.
(c) What machining would be needed in order to complete the sprocket?

7. (a) Sketch the tooth form of a simple disc-type milling cutter such as a slitting saw. Indicate the tooth angles and the surface to be ground when re-sharpening.
(b) Explain, with the aid of diagrams, how a disc-type milling cutter would be re-sharpened, indicating clearly
  (i) the relative positions of the tooth and the grinding wheel.
  (ii) how the cutter would be mounted
  (iii) how the cut would be applied
  (iv) the type of grinding wheel which would be used.

8. A quantity of plain bearing bushes of internal diameter 40 mm, produced by turning, are found to give unreliable fits when assembled. A technician is asked to investigate the two standard **Go/Not-Go** plug gauges used to control the internal diameter. Both of the **Not-Go** ends are found to be satisfactory. The **Go** end of one gauge is worn by insertion so that the leading edge is 0·08 mm below size. The **Go** end of the other is parallel but 0·08 mm oval.
   Set out a brief report to the manager on this investigation under the following headings
(a) the steps taken to examine the gauges
(b) the measurements obtained, showing the errors in relation to the limits required by BS 4500 for an average running fit
(c) the effects of the gauge errors on the product.

9. (a) Make a line diagram showing in outline the main features of a typical horizontal boring machine.
(b) Indicate by means of arrows and notes the main movements obtainable on the head and on the table of the machine stating which are the traverses and which are for setting.
(c) Explain briefly what is meant by *in-line* boring using such a machine.

DECEMBER 1970

1. (a) By means of a line diagram and brief notes, explain 'the principles of any pneumatic comparator.
(b) Using further sketches and explanatory notes, show how pneumatic gauging may be used for
  (i) simultaneous inspection of several dimensions of one component
  (ii) gauging size and concentricity of a stepped bore (25 mm and 40 mm diameter).

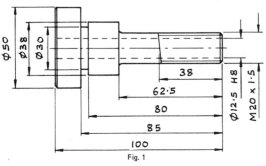

Fig. 1

ALL DIMENSIONS IN mm

2. (a) Make an operation layout for producing the bolt shown in *Fig. 1* from 50 mm diameter bright mild steel bar on a capstan lathe. Draw a line diagram of the tool set up.
(b) Calculate the time for machining the 20 mm diameter portion and the 12·5 mm diameter H8 hole. Use the cutting speeds and feeds shown on p. 263.

Operation	Surface speed m/min	Feed mm/rev
Turning	50	0·13
Drilling	50	0·10
Reaming	10	0·50

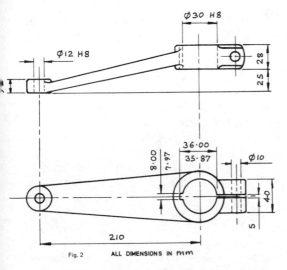

Fig. 2   ALL DIMENSIONS IN mm

3. The lever shown in *Fig. 2* has been finish machined except for the keyway, the 40 mm dimension and the 5 mm wide slot in the large end. Sketch the component set up for
   (i) machining the keyway
   (ii) machining the 40 mm dimension and the 5 mm wide slot.
   For each operation, show the method of setting the cutter/workpiece relationship; sketch the cutters used and specify their types and sizes clearly.

4. (*a*) Why are controlled atmospheres required for some heat treatment processes?
   (*b*) Suggest a suitable atmosphere and give reasons for your choice for each of the following
   (i) furnace brazing of tough pitch copper
   (ii) annealing aluminium.

5. (*a*) State two main advantages and two limitations of powder metallurgical processes.
   (*b*) List the main stages of manufacture of a part by powder metallurgy and outline the principles upon which the method depends.
   (*c*) Give examples of the types of components for which this method of fabrication is suitable.

6. (*a*) State the elements which must be measured in order to carry out a full inspection of a parallel vee-form screw ring gauge.
   (*b*) Explain carefully how measurement of two of the following may be performed
   (i) simple effective diameter
   (ii) root radius
   (iii) pitch.
   You may assume that a well equipped inspection room is at your disposal.

7. (*a*) Explain clearly two forms of tool wear which occur in metal cutting. With the aid of a diagram explain how wear develops during the life of the tool.
   (*b*) Give three reasons for the control of surface texture of a carbide cutting tool.

8. (*a*) List the sequence of operations for finish grinding the gauge shown in *Fig. 3*. You may assume that the gauge has been shaped to within 0·25 mm of its finished dimensions and that it has been fully treated.
   (*b*) Show by means of sketches the relationship of the wheel to the component when grinding the 9° 27′ inclined faces.

9. The last operation on the component shown in *Fig. 4* is the machining of the six 10 mm diameter spotfaced holes. Explain with the aid of diagrams how the holes may be produced on a jig boring machine, stating clearly,
   (i) the setting of the work-piece/machine–spindle relationship

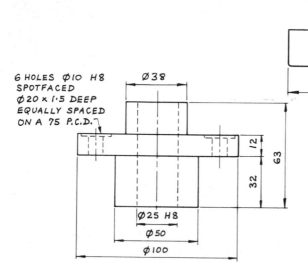

Ø12·5 ROLLERS

64·39

15·47

38

9°27' 9°27'

90

MATERIAL 5 THICK
GAUGE PLATE

Fig. 3
ALL DIMENSIONS IN mm

6 HOLES Ø10 H8
SPOTFACED
Ø20 x 1·5 DEEP
EQUALLY SPACED
ON A 75 P.C.D.

Ø38

12

63

32

Ø25 H8

Ø50

Ø100

Fig. 4
ALL DIMENSIONS IN mm

(ii) the tools required
(iii) the method used to control the spot face depth.

JUNE 1971

1. (a) Make a flow diagram, or outline the sequence of operations involved in any process for the production of metal powders suitable for sintered products.
   (b) Give TWO examples of sintered products which are cost-saving relative to alternative forms of production, and TWO examples where higher costs can be justified.
   (c) Some metals, such as brass, can be formed by die-casting or by powder metallurgy. Give an example of the application of each process for this metal and explain why it is used in preference to the other.

2. (a) Using simple line diagrams, explain the layout and geometry of a floating carriage screw thread diameter measur-

ing machine.
   (b) Show clearly, by diagrams, the contact conditions which apply when measuring the following features of a standard vee-form screw thread
      (i) the effective diameter
      (ii) the root diameter.
   (c) Explain how the root diameter of a standard M24 × 2 screw plug gauge would be determined from the readings obtained on a floating carriage diameter measuring machine.

3. (a) Explain, with the aid of a line diagram, the principle of operation of any type of three-component tool-force dynamometer.
   (b) For a given feed rate and depth of cut, what is the general effect of increasing cutting speed on the forces indicated by the dynamometer for a single point tool? Explain the effect also in terms of the changes occurring in chip formation.
   (c) Explain briefly the main relationship between cutting speed and tool performance.

4. (a) Make sketches or line diagrams of any type of inserted tooth face mill to show clearly
      (i) how the mill is held and driven
      (ii) how the tooth insert is held and given suitable cutting angles.
   (b) Give THREE examples of cutting conditions which can cause premature failure or poor performance with

inserted tooth face mills using tipped inserts.

(c) Large inserted tooth face mills are said to have a 'flywheel effect'. Explain the meaning and significance of this effect.

5. (a) Describe briefly, with the aid of diagrams, the main features of a typical precision-lapping machine, indicating clearly
    (i) the work holding or guidance provision
    (ii) the lapping surfaces
    (iii) the motions involved.
  (b) State a typical abrasive, abrasive grade and abrasive vehicle used in lapping and say what results could be expected from it in terms of
    (i) metal removal rate
    (ii) surface flatness
    (iii) surface finish.
  (c) Give brief details of any method which which can be used in conjunction with a lapping process to check the development of surface flatness and quality.

6. (a) Give an example to show the type of work for which each of the following machines is particularly suitable
    (i) a radial arm drilling machine
    (ii) a box column compound table drilling machine
    (iii) a multi-spindle or multi-unit drilling machine.
  (b) For any ONE of the above machines, make line diagrams and indicate
    (i) the principal motions available
    (ii) FOUR essential geometric relationships between parts and/or motions of the machine

(iii) how the capacity of the machine is usually specified.

7. Referring to the use of slip gauges and standard accessories, explain clearly
  (a) how one pile of slip gauges may be checked against another using the precision straight edge (state what order of accuracy is obtainable)
  (b) how a Go and Not Go limit gap gauge may be built up, taking a B.S. 1916 k6 shaft $3 \cdot 000^{+0 \cdot 8}_{+0 \cdot 1}$ inch dia (OR, a B.S. 4500A k6 shaft 75^{+21}_{+2} mm dia) as an example. How could the gauge making tolerance be accounted for?

8. (a) Give an outline of the procedure for testing welded joints using an isotope source. Explain
    (i) the type of weld for which such tests are justified
    (ii) the importance of interpretation
    (iii) what is done to minimise the hazards involved.
  (b) B.S. 1295 refers to 'Tests for use in the Training of Welders'. Explain why it is necessary to control the quality of welded joints by testing the ability of the welder.

9. Give a logical outline of the procedure followed, the readings taken, and the results obtained in any experiment, investigation, or test on ONE of the following topics
  (a) the hardenability of steel
  (b) control of furnace temperature
  (c) effect of furnace atmosphere on heat-treatment.

Index

Index